On the Feminist Philosophy
of Gillian Howie

Also available from Bloomsbury

The Subject of Rosi Braidotti, edited by Bolette Blaagaard and Iris van der Tuin
Breathing with Luce Irigaray, edited by Emily A. Holmes and Lenart Skof
In the Beginning, She Was, Luce Irigaray
Intimacy: A Dialectical Study, Christopher Lauer
Biopolitics and the Philosophy of Death, Paolo Palladino
The Politics and Pedagogy of Mourning, Timothy Secret

On the Feminist Philosophy of Gillian Howie

Materialism and Mortality

Edited by
Victoria Browne and Daniel Whistler

Bloomsbury Academic
An imprint of Bloomsbury Publishing Plc

B L O O M S B U R Y
LONDON · OXFORD · NEW YORK · NEW DELHI · SYDNEY

Bloomsbury Academic

An imprint of Bloomsbury Publishing Plc

50 Bedford Square	1385 Broadway
London	New York
WC1B 3DP	NY 10018
UK	USA

www.bloomsbury.com

BLOOMSBURY and the Diana logo are trademarks of Bloomsbury Publishing Plc

First published 2016

British Library Cataloguing-in-Publication Data
A catalogue record for this book is available from the British Library.

ISBN:	HB:	9781474254120
	ePDF:	9781474254137
	ePub:	9781474254144

Library of Congress Cataloging-in-Publication Data
Names: Browne, Victoria, editor.
Title: On the feminist philosophy of Gillian Howie : materialism and mortality / edited by Victoria Browne and Daniel Whistler.
Description: New York : Bloomsbury, 2016. | Includes bibliographical references.
Identifiers: LCCN 2016018059 (print) | LCCN 2016031711 (ebook) | ISBN 9781474254120 (hardback) | ISBN 9781474254137 (epdf) | ISBN 9781474254144 (epub)
Subjects: LCSH: Feminist theory. | Materialism. | Mortality. | Critical theory. | Death. | Howie, Gillian.
Classification: LCC HQ1190 .O625 2016 (print) | LCC HQ1190 (ebook) | DDC 305.4201–dc23
LC record available at https://lccn.loc.gov/2016018059

Typeset by Fakenham Prepress Solutions, Fakenham, Norfolk NR21 8NN
Printed and bound in Great Britain

Contents

Acknowledgements   vii

Notes on Contributors   ix

Editors' Introduction: Gillian Howie's Philosophies of Embodied
Practice *Victoria Browne and Daniel Whistler*   1

Part 1   Feminism, Materialism, Critical Theory

1   When Feminist Philosophy Met Critical Theory: Gillian Howie's
Historical Materialism *Stella Sandford*   21

2   Feminist Knowledge and Feminist Politics: Reflections on Howie
and Late Feminism *Kimberly Hutchings*   43

3   Between Negative Dialectics and Sexual Difference: Generative
Conjunctures in the Thinking of Gillian Howie *Joanna Hodge*   59

4   Scholarly Time and Feminist Time: Gillian Howie on Education and
Intellectual Inheritance *Victoria Browne*   81

5   The Cloistered Imaginary *Daniel Whistler*   103

Part 2   Living with Dying

6   How to Think about Death: Living with Dying *Gillian Howie*   131

7   Gillian Howie's Situated Philosophy: Theorizing Living and Dying
'In Situation' *Christine Battersby*   145

8   The Relationality of Death *Alison Stone*   165

9   Reflections on Living up to Death *Morny Joy*   181

10   Learning to Die, Finally *Claire Colebrook*   197

11   'What the Living Do': Poetry's Death and Dying *Deryn Rees-Jones*   215

12   *Cancer Sucks*: Photography and the Representation of Chronic
Illness *Nedim Hassan*   229

13 Movie-making as Palliative Care *Amy Hardie*   247

14 Experience and Performance whilst Living with Disability and
    Dying: Disability Art as a Pathway to Flourishing *Janet Price and
    Ruth Gould*   267

Index of Names   285

Acknowledgements

This book is inspired by and dedicated to the example of Gillian Howie, as friend, colleague, teacher, and feminist philosopher. It began to take shape in the wake of her untimely death in March 2013, and, for their support in helping us realize this volume, we wish to thank colleagues in the Department of Philosophy and School of the Arts at the University of Liverpool, Liverpool, UK, the members of the New Thinking on Living with Dying research network, delegates at the 'Feminism, Materialism, Critical Theory' symposium in December 2013, DaDaFest, Laura Green, J'annine Jobling, Susan Pickard, Pamela Sue Anderson, Margrit Shildrick, Liza Thompson, Frankie Mace, Mark Peel, Grace Whistler, Sam Bryant, and – most of all – the contributors.

Notes on Contributors

Christine Battersby is Reader Emerita in the Department of Philosophy and an Associate Fellow of the Centre for Research in Philosophy, Literature and the Arts at the University of Warwick, Warwick, UK. She is the author of *Gender and Genius: Towards a Feminist Aesthetics* (The Women's Press 1989, 1994), *The Phenomenal Woman: Feminist Metaphysics and the Patterns of Identity* (Polity 1998) and *The Sublime, Terror and Human Difference* (Routledge 2007), as well as numerous articles on feminist aesthetics, feminist metaphysics and the history of philosophy and culture.

Victoria Browne is Lecturer in Politics at Oxford Brookes University, Oxford, UK. She has published articles on feminist philosophy, temporality and memory, and is the author of *Feminism, Time and Nonlinear History* (Palgrave Macmillan 2014). Victoria is also a member of the Editorial Collective for the journal *Radical Philosophy*. Her current research is exploring the politics, ethics and temporalities of reproduction and pregnant embodiment.

Claire Colebrook is Edwin Erle Sparks Professor of English at Pennsylvania State University, USA. She is the author of *New Literary Histories* (Manchester University Press 1997), *Ethics and Representation* (Edinburgh University Press 1999), *Deleuze: A Guide for the Perplexed* (Continuum 1997), *Gilles Deleuze* (Routledge 2002), *Understanding Deleuze* (Allen and Unwin 2002), *Irony in the Work of Philosophy* (Nebraska University Press 2002), *Gender* (Palgrave 2003), *Irony* (Routledge 2004), *Milton, Evil and Literary History* (Continuum 2008), *Deleuze and the Meaning of Life* (Continuum 2010), *William Blake and Digital Aesthetics* (Continuum 2011), *Sex After Life* (OHP 2015), and *Death of the Postman* (Open Humanities Press 2015). She co-authored *Theory and the Disappearing Future* with Tom Cohen and J. Hillis Miller (Routledge 2011), and a follow-up volume, *Twilight of the Anthropocene Idols* (OHP 2016), and co-authored *Agamben* with Jason Maxwell (Polity 2015). She co-edited *Deleuze and Feminist Theory* with Ian Buchanan (Edinburgh University Press 2000), *Deleuze and History* with Jeff Bell (Edinburgh University Press 2008), *Deleuze and Gender* with Jami Weinstein (Edinburgh University Press 2009) and *Deleuze and Law* (Palgrave) with Rosi Braidotti and Patrick Hanafin.

Ruth Gould was born and raised in Liverpool. In her early twenties, she trained in performing arts covering all disciplines, leading to a specialism in physical theatre and devising her own performances and producing community productions in the UK, Australia and New Zealand. Since 2001, she has been working as creative director with DaDaFest, founding the festival model and growing it into one of the most consistent disability arts festivals in the UK. Within her work, Ruth seeks to bring to the fore issues that are often neglected and stigmatized, and her encounter with Gillian Howie raised questions surrounding the very real need to not feel like we are living with dying, but living until we are dead.

Amy Hardie is Head of Research at the Scottish Documentary Institute, University of Edinburgh, Edinburgh, UK. Her main research is in knowledge through practice, focusing on expanding cinematic storytelling. Publications include 'Rollercoasters and Reality: A Study of Big Screen Documentary Audiences' for *Participations: Journal of Audience and Reception Studies* (2008) and 'Symbolic Cinema and the Audience' for *Participations* (2010). Previous films include *Kafi's Story* (1990), several films for BBC and Channel 4 including *Inside the Wig* (1993), *Looking for Allah in England* (1994) and collaborations with scientists and healthcare professionals: *Stem Cell Revolutions* (2011), *Tuesdays* (2012) and *Seven Songs for a Long Life* (2015). *The Edge of Dreaming* (2010) is her first personal film. Awards include BP Expo, Joris Ivens, Basil Wright; Grand Jury Prize, Kiev International Film Festival and the Tam Dalyell medal for public engagement.

Nedim Hassan is Senior Lecturer in Media and Cultural Studies at Liverpool John Moores University, Liverpool, UK. He previously worked as the New Thinking on Living with Dying research network administrator at the University of Liverpool for which he co-organized several events with Gillian Howie. His published work has focused on popular music culture, history and audiences. In particular, this work has been based upon extensive ethnographic research and has explored the significance of musical activities in everyday lived culture. He remains interested in researching the socio-cultural roles of musical and other artistic activities from an ethnographic perspective.

Joanna Hodge is Professor of Philosophy at Manchester Metropolitan University, Manchester, UK. Her doctoral thesis was on the account of truth in Heidegger's *Being and Time* (Oxford 1983). Her two monographs, *Heidegger and Ethics* (1995) and *Derrida on Time* (2007), were published by Routledge/Taylor and

Francis, and a third, on the way, *The Return of the Thing: Reading Jean-Luc Nancy* (2017) will appear from Bloomsbury. She has recently published articles on 'Queering Hegel', and on '*Différance*: rewriting transcendental aesthetics'. She is currently working on a study of the transformation of transcendental aesthetics, in phenomenology, through the thematics of horizonality, touch, trace and writing at the limit of sense, which will focus on a relation between film and philosophy.

Kimberly Hutchings is Professor of Politics and International Relations at Queen Mary University of London, London, UK. Her research interests include feminist political and ethical philosophy. She is the author of several books, including *Kant, Critique and Politics* (Routledge 1996), *International Political Theory* (Sage 1999), *Hegel and Feminist Philosophy* (Polity 2003) and *Time and World Politics* (Manchester University Press 2008). Her current work is focused on theorizing political violence (in collaboration with Elizabeth Frazer) and on moral reasoning in the ethics of war.

Morny Joy is Professor of Religious Studies at the University of Calgary, Calgary, Canada. Her research has been published in the areas of philosophy and religion, postcolonialism and intercultural studies in South and South-East Asia, as well as in diverse aspects of women and religion. Recent publications include: *Women and the Gift: Beyond the Given and the All-giving* (Indiana University Press 2013), *Continental Philosophy and Philosophy of Religion* (Springer 2011) and *After Appropriation: Explorations in Intercultural Philosophy and Religion* (University of Calgary 2011). Morny was awarded an Honorary Doctorate by the University of Helsinki in 2011.

Janet Price is a disabled feminist who is based in Liverpool, UK, with links to Taranaki, New Zealand. She is active in queercrip politics and has a connection of over thirty years with friends, art and social justice activism in India. She is on the board of DaDaFest (www.dadafest.co.uk), a disability and deaf arts organization in Liverpool, which has a growing global reach. Her commitment to global social justice is further reflected through her long-term academic contribution to the gender groups at Liverpool University and the School of Tropical Medicine. She writes intermittently, through blogs, discussion papers and occasional papers, and she is committed to producing work with others, on the basis that, in Deleuze and Guattari's words, 'since each of us was several, there was already quite a crowd'.

Deryn Rees-Jones is Professor of Poetry at the University of Liverpool, Liverpool, UK, widely published as a poet as well as critic specializing in women's writing and poetry. Her most recent book of poems, *Burying the Wren*, was shortlisted for the T. S. Eliot Prize; *What It's Like to Be Alive: Selected Poems* was published by Seren in 2016. She is the editor of the newly launched Pavilion Poetry series (Liverpool University Press) and recently joined the editorial board of *Women: A Cultural Review*. She collaborates frequently with artists and is currently writing a book on the work of Paula Rego.

Stella Sandford is Professor at the Centre for Research in Modern European Philosophy at Kingston University, Kingston, UK. She is the author of *The Metaphysics of Love: Gender and Transcendence in Levinas* (Athlone 2000), *How to Read Beauvoir* (Granta 2006) and *Plato and Sex* (Cambridge University Press 2010). She is a long-standing member of the editorial collective for Radical Philosophy, and has also co-edited collections on *Further Adventures in the Dialectic of Sex: Critical Essays on Shulamith Firestone* (Palgrave 2010) and *Philosophies of Race and Ethnicity* (Continuum 2002).

Alison Stone is Professor of Philosophy at Lancaster University, Lancaster, UK. Her books are *Petrified Intelligence: Nature in Hegel's Philosophy* (SUNY 2004), *Luce Irigaray and the Philosophy of Sexual Difference* (Cambridge University Press 2006), *An Introduction to Feminist Philosophy* (Polity 2007) and *Feminism, Psychoanalysis and Maternal Subjectivity* (Routledge 2011). She has also edited *The Edinburgh Critical History of Philosophy Volume 5: The Nineteenth Century* (Edinburgh University Press 2011). She is currently co-editing the *Routledge Companion to Feminist Philosophy* (Routledge 2017) and finishing a book entitled *An Aesthetics of Popular Music*. She is an Associate Editor of *Hypatia: A Journal of Feminist Philosophy*.

Daniel Whistler is Senior Lecturer in Philosophy at the University of Liverpool, Liverpool, UK and Humboldt Research Fellow at the Westfälische-Wilhelms Universität, Münster, Germany. He is author of *Schelling's Theory of Symbolic Language: Forming the System of Identity* (Oxford University Press 2013) and co-editor of *After the Postsecular and the Postmodern: New Essays in Continental Philosophy of Religion* (Cambridge Scholars Publishing 2010).

Editors' Introduction: Gillian Howie's Philosophies of Embodied Practice

Victoria Browne and Daniel Whistler

If there is one lesson to be learned from the work of Gillian Howie, it is that philosophy and theory cannot transcend their material conditions. Accordingly, the theoretical has to incessantly undergo a process of contextualization, revealing those extra-theoretical conditions that make any act of theorizing possible. Philosophy always takes place in a world of economic forces, political structures, bodily relations and existential projects; 'political beliefs are unintelligible in isolation from claims about the real states of the world'.[1] Charting the embodied practices that underwrite intellectual abstraction and 'the social conditions that give rise to theory'[2] is thus one of the central continuities in Howie's thought stretching across her wide range of interests, from the early critiques of Deleuze and polemics against managerialism in higher education, to the development of her distinctive feminist materialism and late research on the phenomenon of living with non-curative illness. What connects these different projects is the need to critically describe the situatedness (corporeal, political and existential) of a body of thought – that is, to provide an account of how subjects are variously positioned within institutions such as the academy, hospitals and public spaces and, in particular, the role of philosophy in facing very real situations, like sexual oppression and abuse, illness and death.

This overarching critical practice is thematized most explicitly by Howie through 'the context principle' with which her defining monograph, *Between Feminism and Materialism: A Question of Method*, begins:

> To grasp what a thing is … we need to place it in context that is at once social, political, and historical. Any attempt to analyze what a thing is, if abstracted from context, will lead to erroneous and often ideological judgment. Historical

---

[1] Gillian Howie, *Between Feminism and Materialism: A Question of Method*, Basingstoke: Palgrave Macmillan, 2010, p. 3.
[2] Ibid., pp. 2–3.

materialism is thus a theory of relations such that individual identity can be seen to be a consequence of antecedent social processes.[3]

This is a mode of critique that is not merely intended to unmask the pernicious abstractions of thought, but, moreover, to appropriate what is powerful in thought in the name of living. As Howie remarks in *Between Feminism and Materialism* on this latter point, 'Every philosophy is practical, even when it seems at its most contemplative: its method a social and political weapon.'[4] Critique, according to Howie, has both negative and positive valences: it can puncture intellectual pretension but it can also orient an art of living.

In full accordance with her 'context principle', Howie's own work was resolutely both textual and extra-textual – intertwining the two throughout her career as a politically committed academic. Pursuing her DPhil at the University of Cambridge, she served on the executive committees of the Cambridge Labour Students and Cambridge University Students' Union, and later became an executive member of the Association of University Teachers, the British Philosophical Association and the Society for Women in Philosophy.[5] At the University of Liverpool, on the way to becoming its first female Professor of Philosophy, she directed the Institute for Feminist Theory and Research and founded the Centre for Health, Arts and Sciences. These centres not only allowed Howie to engage substantially in interdisciplinary work, but also with practitioners and organizations outside the university. This fed directly into the network New Thinking on Living with Dying, funded by the Arts and Humanities Research Council, on which her research was focused during the last years of her life, and which – as the contributions to this volume attest – took thinking outside of the academy, confronting academic speculation with the experiences of illness, disability and death as communicated by patients, clinicians, artists and support groups.

This book follows in the spirit of Howie's critical theory and practice. The essays that follow engage with her myriad interests to ensure a continuing critical conversation involving philosophers, social scientists and researchers in the humanities, as well as practitioners outside the academy. The contributions

---

[3] Ibid., pp. 5–6. On the role of contextualization in Howie's philosophy, see further Daniel Whistler, 'Howie's *Between Feminism and Materialism* and the Critical History of Religions', *Sophia* 53.1 (2014).

[4] Howie, *Between Feminism and Materialism*, p. 9.

[5] For further biographical details, see the obituaries written by J'annine Jobling ('"The Personal is the Political": Gillian Howie, 1965–2013', *Radical Philosophy* 180 [2013], https://www.radicalphilosophy.com/obituary/gillian-howie-1965-2013) and Jon Harris ('Gill Howie obituary', *Guardian*, 17 April 2013, http://www.theguardian.com/theguardian/2013/apr/17/gill-howie-obituary).

do not simply pay homage to Howie's achievements, or try to 'fix' what she left unfinished or half-thought; in what follows, Howie's writings are taken as provocations to thought, enabling an enrichment of current and emerging debates around the intersections of feminism, critical theory and philosophies of illness and death. Hence, the wide range of questions considered in this volume include: how can feminist politics be reconceived in the wake of postmodernism? What becomes of pedagogy and intellectual practice within changing conditions of higher education? What does it mean to 'live right up to death' and how can we communicate experiences and issues relating to life-limiting illness?

Feminism, materialism, critical theory

The majority of Howie's publications can be broadly grouped into four categories, which will be explored across the various chapters in this volume.[6]

Feminist theory

Most significant in Howie's output are her several interventions into feminist theory, particularly the critical examination of the significance and limits of third-wave or 'late' feminism, the long-standing engagement with Irigaray's thought and, above all, the renewed interest in the relationship between feminism, Marxism and critical theory. Common to all this work is an abiding scepticism regarding the capabilities of 'postmodern' or 'linguistic' theory to get at what really matters within the feminist project. Thus, in her own contribution to her co-edited volume *Third Wave Feminism: A Critical Exploration*, Howie analyses the 'problem of the linguistic turn' in feminism as follows: 'Post-1980s feminist strategy became constrained within an increasingly sophisticated demonstration of the ambivalence or ambiguity of conceptual discrimination ... Without wanting to collapse the third wave into the poststructuralist, and the poststructuralist into the postmodern, [the] problem of substantive goal remains a common feature.'[7] She continues in *Between Feminism and Materialism*, 'Now

---

[6]   One aspect of Howie's work we do not consider in this volume is her collaboration with J'annine Jobling on 'women and the divine' that resulted in a volume of the same title (discussed below). However, this has begun to be explored elsewhere – see the special issue of *Sophia*, ed. Pamela Sue Anderson, on feminist philosophy of religion (53.1 [2014]), particularly the Introduction and essays by Haynes and Whistler.

[7]   Gillian Howie and Ashley Tauchert, 'Feminist Dissonance: The Logic of Late Feminism', *Third Wave Feminism: A Critical Exploration* ed. Stacy Gills et al., Basingstoke: Macmillan, 2004, p. 43.

we have feminist theories that recognize the diversity of women but are unable to figure out any community or collective goal-oriented activity. We have feminist theories sensitive to the capillaries of power but unable to answer the question "what systematic changes would be required to create a just society?" And we have an entire "feminist theory" academic industry but are unable to communicate with the women's movement, such that it is.'[8]

To try and find ways out of this perceived impasse, Howie sought to strengthen links between feminists inside and outside of the academy. For instance, in 2011, she co-organized the 'Radical Women, Radical City' event at the Bluecoat Centre in Liverpool with colleagues from Liverpool University and Liverpool John Moores University, and members of the Merseyside Women's Movement, to celebrate and reflect on the centenary of International Women's Day in 2011. The day included public discussions and exhibitions showcasing the work of local women activists past and present, and culminated in a 'Reclaim the Night' march across the city. Another key project was Palgrave Macmillan's 'Breaking Feminist Waves' series that Howie established and co-edited with Linda Martín Alcoff, which, according to the Series Foreword, aims to 'reassess the established constructions of feminism' and unearth 'neglected contributions', thereby 'unlock[ing] conversations between feminists and feminisms' and 'open[ing] up feminist theory and practice to new audiences'.

In her own writings, Howie proposes that feminist politics can be 'unlocked' via 'a refreshed and revised engagement with Marxism',[9] a position she sets out most fully in *Between Feminism and Materialism* (published as part of the 'Breaking Feminist Waves' series). Here, she argues that feminist theory needs to rediscover its 'epistemological bite' – that is, to become politically engaged once more in a way that can ensure feminist theory contributes substantially to feminist scholarship and, indeed, the feminist movement more generally. To achieve this end, she regroups feminism around the grounding methodological tenets of dialectical materialism, thereby both recovering a neglected strain of radical feminist theory from the 1970s and also providing a way for feminism to traverse the terrain of 'new materialisms' and 'speculative ontologies' in a critically and politically conscious manner. As Howie succinctly outlines at the beginning of *Between Feminism and Materialism*, 'I attempt to demonstrate the usefulness of Marxist categories and thereby revive a dialectical method.'[10]

---

[8]   Howie, *Between Feminism and Materialism*, p. 2.
[9]   Ibid., p. 26.
[10] Ibid., p. 7.

A key part of the project in *Between Feminism and Materialism* is the defence of notions of realism, objectivity and identity from a broadly Marxist perspective, i.e. protecting such concepts against appropriation in naïve, non-political materialisms as well as against attack from subject-oriented, sceptical or idealist discourses. That is, she brackets 'Nietzsche, Bergson, Freud and Foucault'[11] in favour of 'a refreshed and revised engagement with Marxism'[12] which involves using dialectical materialism to illuminate the practical, economic and socially specific bases of concept-use, so as to distinguish a theoretically productive form of reason or universality from those forms that are politically problematic. The task is, as Howie puts it, 'to disaggregate objectivism from objectivity',[13] enabling a 'recovery of emancipatory critique' for feminism[14] by situating its critical project in terms of the legacy of the Enlightenment:

> Feminism is fundamentally an Enlightenment or modernist project; it concerns the emancipation of morally valuable individual subjects. Yet recent feminist theory rails against the principal tenets of Enlightenment thought: reason, autonomy, identity, universals, science and – in the end – freedom itself. As a consequence, unable to articulate common grounds of oppression, the rug seems whipped from under our feet – leaving feminism struggling to articulate its relevance and purpose.[15]

The opening contribution to this volume, Stella Sandford's 'When Feminist Philosophy Met Critical Theory: Gillian Howie's Historical Materialism', expounds and defends Howie's critical feminist materialism. Sandford argues that just as the tradition of critical theory is the outcome of the encounter between philosophy and historical materialism, Howie's critical feminist materialism is the outcome of the encounter between critical theory and feminist philosophy: a model of the necessarily transformed forms of philosophy, critical theory and feminist theory that emerge when these three meet. Moreover, whilst Sandford is critical of Howie's own conceptualization of 'sex' in *Between Feminism and Materialism* as a weak 'natural kind', she nevertheless suggests that the critical feminist method outlined in this book has much to recommend it as feminists seek to further develop a critical theory of sex and a critique of the 'gender industry'. Kimberly Hutchings provides further elaboration of Howie's materialist interventions in her chapter 'Feminist Knowledge and

---

[11] Ibid.
[12] Ibid., p. 26.
[13] Ibid., p. 37.
[14] Ibid., p. 3.
[15] Ibid., p. 12.

Feminist Politics: Reflections on Gillian Howie and Late Feminism'. Hutchings is not entirely persuaded by Howie's critique of 'late feminism', nor her proposed remedy of reinventing the link between knowledge and feminist politics. Progressive feminist politics, Hutchings suggests, might not necessarily require grounding in a theoretical approach drawn from dialectical materialism. Nevertheless, in Hutchings view, Howie's coalitional, multi-dimensional model of feminist politics, which moves beyond homogenous conceptions of the feminist revolutionary subject, offers a useful way forward for feminism.

Affirmation and negation

A corollary of Howie's attempted transformation of feminist theory is her critique of Deleuze, Spinoza and feminist appropriations of affirmation and 'becoming-woman'. As Howie puts it in *Between Feminism and Materialism*, 'Before affirmation there should be criticism'.[16] She first airs her unease with philosophies of affirmation in the doctoral work that resulted in her first monograph, *Deleuze and Spinoza: Aura of Expressionism*. Once again, her fundamental target is those elements of feminism and philosophy that she believes have failed to provide the tools and conditions for politically relevant theory. As she puts it on the very first page of the work (alluding to similar complaints made elsewhere by Alex Callinicos and Christopher Norris), large sections of 'left-liberal intelligentsia' had been

> won over to consensus-based doctrines of meaning and truth that left them unable to articulate any kind of reasoned or principled opposition ... Although the melancholic period of Thatcherism ... has since been superseded by Tony Blair's new times, and Anthony Giddens' third way, their language of change and modernisation might be considered a sanitised version of the familiar obfuscating pragmatism. As a prolegomena towards a critique of the discourse of globalisation, social exclusion and identity politics, this present work is a commentary on such obfuscation, the process of concealment common to both 'modernisers' and postmodernists. It is in effect a commentary on ideology.[17]

Deleuze is used here and elsewhere as the paradigm for philosophy gone awry.

Another key aspect of this critique is Howie's insistence on the embodied conditions of theory and practice. She regularly takes issue with the Cartesian image of philosophy as disembodied contemplation, and her criticisms of

[16] Ibid., p. 8.
[17] Gillian Howie, *Deleuze and Spinoza: Aura of Expressionism*, Basingstoke: Macmillan, 2002, p. 1.

Deleuze's 'body without organs' and conception of 'becoming-woman' as abstractions from lived embodiment are part of this project. Her key point here is that the abstract concept of 'becoming-woman' entirely lacks reference to 'the historical and epistemological specificity of the female feminist standpoint':[18]

> The idea of 'becoming-woman' is an attempt to transform embodied experience but, because it is unable to concern itself with mechanisms, structures and processes of sexual differentiations, fails in this task ... Working in the abstract, 'becoming-woman' stands with 'becoming-animal' and 'becoming-imperceptible' as a form of minoritarian becoming. But there seems little to say about the peculiarities of becoming-*woman* rather than, say, becoming-insect.[19]

In opposition to feminist philosophies of affirmation inspired by Deleuze, Howie explores the potential offered by the idea of non-identity in both critical theory and existentialism. Once again, such a move is premised on a dissatisfaction with the prevalent 'turn' to psychoanalytic and poststructuralist theory as politically debilitating. She counter-poses 'materialism' to 'postmodernism', putting poststructuralism, psychoanalytic theory and all subject-oriented theories on trial in the name of a re-engagement with Marxism and critical theory, particularly in the tradition of Adorno. And 'notwithstanding the uneasy conceptual and historical relationship between existentialism and critical theory',[20] Howie brings together a rigorous reading of the early pages of *Being and Nothingness* with post-Adornoan theory to provide an account of non-identity that is intended to do justice to lived experience as well as the critique of structures. That is, Howie follows Adorno in conceiving non-identity as a central concept for articulating the experience of social contradiction, an experience 'informed by contradiction, alienation and reification',[21] but she also follows Sartre (*pace* Adorno's own rejection of Sartre) in placing non-identity at the heart of a description of consciousness. The consequences of this attempt to 'supplement or enhance Adorno's critical theory' with Sartrean phenomenology[22] are articulated by Howie as follows,

> Negative experience is not dependent on the experience of social contradiction: a world without social conflict would still be subject to the principle of nonidentity, perhaps then to the thought of multiplicity ... Individual subjects

---

[18] Gillian Howie, 'Becoming-Woman: A Flight into Abstraction', *Deleuze Studies* 2 (2008), p. 85.
[19] Ibid., pp. 83–4.
[20] Gillian Howie, 'Nonidentity, Negative Experience and the Pre-Reflective Cogito', *European Journal of Philosophy* 23.3 (2012), p. 589.
[21] Ibid., p. 595.
[22] Ibid., p. 603.

continually question, interrogate and destabilize the appearance of identity, permanence and presence. However this does not lead to reconciled rational identity. Because consciousness is 'elsewhere' there can be no authentic recovery of the self or the Subject.[23]

Throughout her work Howie draws upon Adorno and Horkheimer's critique of instrumental reason and in particular the varieties of abstraction and reification such thinking gives rise to. Following Jameson, she insists that 'the loss of objects in the process of abstraction poses and disguises real threats to the subject',[24] and so is particularly interested in the ways in which such abstractions impact on the lived experience of subjects: 'Subjects are compelled to behave as detached observers rather than active participants in life and ... the demand to calculate oneself and others for profit leads to an attempt to regard the world from a purely rational and emotionless stance – a view-from-nowhere.'[25] What is more, this emphasis on the deficiencies of instrumental reason allows Howie to bolster, on the one hand, her insistence on the need for critique to be understood as a continual process of contextualization (counteracting the 'tendency to abstract – and try to make sense of – events, roles, human characteristics away from their social contexts')[26] and, on the other hand, a recovery of categories such as objectivity, reason and identity for feminist theory. As she argues at length in *Between Feminism and Materialism*, feminist problems with such categories are merely 'the problems of *instrumental* reason: a distinctively historical cognitive orientation to the world of experience'.[27]

It is this latter point that Joanna Hodge examines in her contribution to the volume, 'Between Negative Dialectics and Sexual Difference: Generative Conjunctures in the Thinking of Gillian Howie'. She subjects to scrutiny Howie's use of Adorno's writings as a useful tool for feminist theory, considering how Howie 'follows Adorno's lead' but 'under the guidance of [Luce] Irigaray's insight that in this modern epoch what is to be thought are the differences between human beings, both within, and between epochs'. Irigaray may seem an unlikely interlocutor for Howie, given that Irigaray is usually identified as a key figure in those poststructuralist and psychoanalytic feminisms that Howie positioned herself against. Yet, in fact, Irigaray is one of the thinkers that Howie most frequently returns to – an interest which led her to co-organize with J'annine

[23] Ibid., pp. 603–4.
[24] Howie, 'Becoming-Woman', p. 101.
[25] Howie, *Between Feminism and Materialism*, p. 47.
[26] Ibid., p.37.
[27] Ibid., p. 64.

Jobling the major five-day 'Women and the Divine' conference in Liverpool in 2005 at which Irigaray was in attendance, and out of which the volume *Touching Transcendence* (co-edited by Howie and Jobling) emerged.[28] In her chapter, Hodge argues that the tensions and lines of conflict between Adorno and Irigaray provide Howie with a 'productive space' for conceptualizing the connection between philosophy and politics, and developing a distinct, 'hybrid' theorization in which 'Irigaray's dogmatism may be corrected by appeal to a speculative logic derived from Adorno; and Adorno's limited vision may be corrected by Irigaray's account of such blind spots, and by her attention to the silent force of an accumulating historical derogation of women'.

The state of education

Such innovations in critical theory and feminist theory are already applied to non-theoretical problems in Howie's published work – in line with her conception of the critical project. Indeed, the need to connect social science research on concrete problems to theoretical speculation is a constant in her thought; thus she laments of 'a rich stream of critical social science [which has been] forgotten rather than repressed; the result of the overwhelming dominance of cultural theory, poststructuralism, psychoanalysis and – perhaps – the municipalisation of feminist theory'.[29] From her very earliest publications, the question of the changing historical conditions of knowledge production, particularly in the UK higher education sector, was a recurring topic in her writing – as it was in her own academic practice as well. Particularly pressing, she felt, was the need to hold up to scrutiny the dizzying array of changes that higher education was undergoing in the wake of the Bologna accord in the late 1990s: the Research Excellence Framework, the widening participation agenda and modularization are just some of the topics that Howie subjects to critique,

---

[28] Gillian Howie and J'annine Jobling (eds), *Women and the Divine: Touching Transcendence*, Basingstoke: Palgrave, 2009. As Jobling reflects in the obituary she wrote in *Radical Philosophy* for Howie, 'In a move typical of Gill's integrative view of academic pursuit, she suggested that the programme extend beyond the presentation of papers: ultimately it included a local, grassroots interfaith forum, yoga, Shiatsu, jazz and poetry recital' (p. 67).

[29] Gillian Howie, 'Feminist Histories: Conflict, Coalitions and the Maternal Order', *Studies in the Maternal* 2.1 (2010), p. 9. Howie elsewhere writes, 'Feminism will only move forward, reconnect theory and praxis, if we can find a way to bring together the somatic, living and experiencing body with critical social science. To reveal, to make explicit, to investigate, and to change the ways in which situations are organized, we must synthesize objectivist tendencies in social science with subjectivist tendencies within hermeneutics and phenomenology. A theoretical reorientation toward the condition and objects of experience will help to bridge feminist theory in the humanities and empirical research in social sciences' (Howie, *Between Feminism and Materialism*, pp. 2–3).

and here as elsewhere her strategy is the same – to uncover the real conditions of production underlying these phenomena through a rigorous process of contextualization and localization. Moreover, Howie then compares this picture of higher education as it is to an ideal of critical inquiry and the cultivation of a reflective art of living: 'I suggest that students are now educated within a system that promotes a form of thought antithetical to the recognition of "otherness": a prerequisite for any substantial thought about diversity.'[30] She continues,

> The style of thinking demanded from academics and transmitted to students frustrates the explicit end of social justice but it is ideally suited to a transformed education service within an internationally agreed 'global' market. Unless the rational kernel of truth, the aim of social justice, is prised away from the widening access shell of government policy, and the management discourse of quality that acts as its conduit, then the future of higher education looks bleak.[31]

In her chapter 'Scholarly Time and Feminist Time: Gillian Howie on Education and Intellectual Inheritance', Victoria Browne brings Howie's writings on the changing conditions of higher education together with her analyses of feminism in the academy, paying particular attention to the question of how feminism is shared and transmitted between different generations of theorists and practitioners. Examining not only Howie's critical dissection of the 'audit culture' in UK academic institutions, and the generational 'wave' model of feminist theory, Browne also considers her attempts to move towards more promising ways of transmitting knowledge and intellectual inheritance via alternative modalities of scholarly time and feminist time. In a similar vein to Browne, Daniel Whistler considers in his chapter 'The Cloistered Imaginary' the spatial, temporal and corporeal conditions of the university ideal at play in Howie's writings on higher education. He identifies an ambiguity in Howie's attitude towards the ideal of liberal education in the modern university: on the one hand, it instantiated discriminatory practices under the guise of disembodied neutrality, but on the other hand it fostered an ethos of critical enquiry and autonomous thinking that, Howie laments, has recently been lost from the university through bureaucratization. The 'cloistered ideal' is both negated and partially affirmed, and Whistler excavates the 'imaginary' conditions that result in such ambivalence.

---

[30] Gillian Howie, 'A Reflection on Quality: Instrumental Reason, Quality Audits and the Knowledge Economy', *Critical Quarterly* 44.4 (2002): 140.
[31] Ibid., p. 146.

Living with dying

Throughout her work, Howie attests to the transformative power of philosophical thought, whether directed towards gendered power relations, labour conditions, or educational practices and institutions. In her final research project, both the potentials and the limitations of philosophy are explored, as she considers experiences (including her own) of living with non-curable or life-limiting illness. 'Terry Eagleton once described the meaning of life as a subject fit for either the crazed or the comic', Howie wrote, and when faced with one's own mortality, one may well ask 'what is the point or value of philosophy after all'?[32] It might seem unlikely that any intellectual discipline could play a positive role in 'easing suffering', perhaps especially philosophy with its reputation for being 'unworldly' and unconcerned with matters of the body. Philosophers, she acknowledges, have often been 'caricatured as lofty, bearded and anachronistic beings … as strangers to the everyday and aspiring to be free from the demands of the particular and quotidian'.[33] Yet in a blog post written in 2012 – 'Death: you can't live with it, you can't live without it' – Howie is not willing to give up on philosophy quite so easily. She proposes here that 'philosophical reflection … ought to be able to relieve anxiety, to provide the conceptual clarification that could be placed as a series of stepping-stones through any dark night … help[ing] us navigate the contours of this complicated, morally ambiguous and frail life.' Indeed, for Epicurus, 'there is no point to philosophy if it does not expel the suffering of the soul'.[34]

In an article published posthumously in 2014, 'Alienation and Therapy in Existentialism: A Dual Model of Recognition', Howie explores the potential of philosophy to help 'settle the questions' that arise in the event of a poor prognosis in more detail. Here, she seeks to recover an alignment between philosophy and *therapeia*, between 'philosophical method, medical practice and cure'. She highlights Buddhist and non-Buddhist Indian philosophical traditions and ancient Greek philosophies, as well as Wittgensteinian and pragmatist philosophy, as schools of thought for whom 'philosophical practice can help to cure mental or spiritual disorder and restore psychological health … through the exercise of reason, which can iron out linguistic confusion, excise poorly

---

[32] Gillian Howie, 'Death; You can't live with it, you can't live without it', New Thinking on Living with Dying blog, 28 June 2012, https://newthinkingaboutlivingwithdying.wordpress.com/2012/06/28/death-you-cant-live-with-it-you-cant-live-without-it/

[33] Gillian Howie, 'Alienation and Therapy in Existentialism: A Dual Model of Recognition', *Ethical Theory and Moral Practice* 17.1 (2014): 56.

[34] Howie, 'Death; You can't live with it, you can't live without it'.

formulated or inadequately justified beliefs and identify the cause of unpleasant emotional affect'.[35] But Howie's key focus in the article is the tradition of existentialist phenomenology, which she claims is able to

> engage with prejudicial structures that not only shape our thinking but also our somatic and affective being-in-the-world. Therapeutically, it is thus able to offer insight into the conditions of experience that allow for the critical dissolution of illusion and alter habitual harmful behaviours which, with practice, could prompt a radical conversion. In the process, it shows how to live a life always in question.[36]

This positive view of the contribution that philosophy can make to the project of 'living well right up to death', however, is not repeated with such confidence in the public lecture 'How to Think about Death: Living with Dying'[37] that Howie gave in 2012 (suggesting, as Christine Battersby argues in her contribution to this volume, that her position was not settled during this period). Howie presents her project here as an investigation into the 'phenomenology of living with dying', and considers different philosophical perspectives on the relationship between death and life. A common view, elaborated by Heidegger, is that 'death illuminates the meaning of life', that 'anxiety in the face of death liberates us from possibilities that count for nothing, and lets us free for those that do count for something'. Yet, Howie argues in the lecture that those who have a poor prognosis of non-curative illness often experience 'depression … anxiety … dislocation and an evacuation of meaning' which seems to contradict the Heideggerian thesis. 'When a patient receives a prognosis', she claims, 'then the future itself is disturbed and the problem of meaningfulness in time emerges. When projects are truncated, the present – the folds of the past and the future – seems exhausted and evacuated of meaning.'

Thus, whilst Heidegger was right to claim that 'humans are the only animals that confront their own situation as a question', Howie claims, dying does not 'enable authentic existence'. Rather, it 'clogs the mind with terror and evacuates meaning from the world, from my world'. Moreover, in the face of such fear, anxiety, and the 'evacuation of meaning', Howie argues that we confront the limitations of philosophy as an intellectual practice that can enable us to 'live right up to death with hope'. She affirms that philosophy can do useful 'conceptual work', pointing out, for instance, 'where our hopefulness is hope for an object

---

[35] Howie, 'Alienation and Therapy in Existentialism', p. 56.
[36] Ibid., p. 57.
[37] Transcribed in Chapter 6 of the present volume.

that can't be realised', but contends that what philosophy cannot do is help us cultivate 'a state of mind of hopefulness even in the face of a shortened future'. Her conclusion is that other fields, such as art, music, literature or horticulture, hold more promise than philosophy in providing answers to her fundamental research question: 'How can we live right up to death, even that period during life-limiting illness when we know we only have a few years to live?'

The full transcript of Howie's 'How to Think About Death' lecture is included as Chapter 6 of this volume, and in her subsequent chapter, 'Gillian Howie's Situated Philosophy: Theorizing Living and Dying "In Situation"', Christine Battersby provides a rich engagement with Howie's evolving philosophy of living with dying. The chapter outlines in close detail the development of Howie's thinking, locating her position alongside other phenomenological accounts of being 'situated', especially those of Sartre and Heidegger. Battersby concludes by suggesting that Howie ascribes 'an exactly similar function to free-floating hope that Heidegger attributes to anxiety ... For Howie it is *hope* in the face of death that makes *Dasein* authentic, not Heideggerian *Angst*.' Moreover, she argues that despite the scepticism that Howie expresses in her lecture towards philosophy's capacity to cultivate hopefulness in the face of death, in fact this lecture itself demonstrates that 'engaging in philosophy can ... be a part of the transformative journey and therapeutic practice'.

Alison Stone also engages in depth with the arguments proposed by Howie in her 'How to Think about Death' lecture; though in her chapter 'The Relationality of Death' she seeks to defend the relational model of death that Howie appears to reject. For Howie, the non-individualistic view of death as the cessation of a 'web of relations' is counter-intuitive 'because there is a radical asymmetry: I might mourn losing relationships with others, but actually I'm the one that's going to die'. As such, she states in her lecture that 'This death is my death, and the life in question is mine. It has an irrefutable first-person quality ...' Stone's argument is that the relational view of death can accommodate this intuition because 'the world whose end I anticipate and fear is a shared world ... and it is by virtue of its being shared that I am attached to it and do not want it to end'. Accordingly, she suggests *pace* Heidegger that 'Confronting the prospect of my death will not individuate but "relationalize" me, revealing to me the ultimate value or the fundamental impact upon me of the relationships with which I have been living.'

In Morny Joy's chapter, 'Reflections on Living up to Death', the focus shifts from Heidegger to Paul Ricoeur, as Joy explores Ricoeur's reflections on finite existence, affirmation and hope. In fact, though Howie claimed *Living up to*

Death by Ricoeur to be one of the key inspirations for her Living with Dying project, her own work on the topic includes no detailed engagement with this text, or indeed with Ricoeur's work more generally. However, Joy suggests that Ricoeur's philosophical conception of 'consent to life, with its appeal to hope', and his 'refusal to be governed by necessity', may have given Howie substantial material to draw upon if she had been able to continue developing her own philosophy of living right up to death.

The subsequent chapter by Claire Colebrook, 'Learning to Die, Finally', similarly takes Howie's lecture as a provocation to further consideration of the 'conundrums' and questions posed by living with dying. Yet, Colebrook pushes the 'living with dying' analytic beyond the subject-centred framework of phenomenology, arguing that whilst 'the prognosis appears to be exceptional, out of time, and destructive of the meaning we ought to have', 'this seemingly "non-natural death" should in fact be the way we think about *all* death, and indeed, about nature itself. Just as "the man" of European memory and "being-towards-death" has reached his limit', she claims, so too has the notion of a 'harmonious, stable, bounded, landscape-like nature that is in accord with a moral vision of time'. Accordingly, not only as individuals but moreover, *as a species*, 'we will have to learn how to die'.

The chapters outlined above attest to the considerable contribution that philosophy can make to the project of cultivating hope, meaning and critical understanding in the face of death. Yet, as discussed above, Howie herself was adamant that other fields of practice and intellectual enquiry have just as much (if not more) to contribute, and this conviction informed the interdisciplinary approach Howie took in her role as Principal Investigator of the AHRC-funded network, New Thinking on Living with Dying. A central aim of the project was to involve organizations and individuals from outside the academy, and hence the network brought together not only academics but also practitioners interested in 'the psychology and phenomenology of living with dying', including clinical practitioners, artists, community workers and 'anyone else who is interested'.[38] Three workshops were planned: *Thinking about Dying, Chronic Illness and Wellbeing*, and finally *The Clinical Model of Care*.[39] In addition to these research workshops, the network planned three public events. The first, *Changing Capacities, Changing Identities*, which took place on 1 September 2012, was co-organized with the Disability and Deaf Arts Festival – an organization that

---

[38] Quotations from the next two paragraphs are all taken from Howie's lecture, 'How to Think about Death', Chapter 6 of the present volume.

[39] This final workshop did not take place due to Howie's death in 2013.

promotes deaf and disability arts in north-west England and beyond – as Howie believed it is disability practitioners and critical disability theorists 'who have the most to teach us about how to live a changing body without living that as a loss with norms that you are continually trying to recover'. The second public event, in collaboration with the Reader Group, was to explore 'reading as therapy' and the idea that 'sometimes the unsayable can be expressed otherwise', and the third was to have been co-organized with Ness Gardens and Sefton Allotment Groups in Liverpool in order to put into practice the idea of cultivating nature, 'without, for example, having to take on the responsibility for a garden at a point when you're tired and not very fit, but just the experience of tending, being attentive to, enables the patients themselves to care for themselves'.[40]

The workshops and events planned by the network spanned a huge range of areas and involved a wide range of people and practices. It would be impossible to reproduce this range within the scope of this volume; however, the final four essays give a flavour of the rich plethora of ideas, methods and practices that were engaged and experimented with. Deryn Rees-Jones' chapter, 'What the Living Do: Poetry's Death and Dying', considers the role of writing and reading at the end of life, suggesting that the complexities of the lyric poem as 'a complex structure built around space and silences, might be a useful model for thinking about the experience of death'. Illustrating this through a close analysis of Jorie Graham's 'San Sepolcro', Rees-Jones argues that lyric poetry has the potential to reinvent and deconstruct the realities of life and death, 'in a way which might allow us also to continually encounter the "not-being" which creates meaning as well as the language which evokes or represents the being that is lost'.

Taking us from poetry to photography, Nedim Hassan's chapter 'Cancer Sucks: Photography and the Representation of Chronic Illness' focuses upon an exhibition of digital photography entitled *Cancer Sucks* that was displayed at the *Changing Capacities, Changing Identities* event co-organized by the New Thinking on Living with Dying research network and DaDaFest. Drawing upon research into the photographic project, which was put together by the late performer/model Tutu and the photographer Ashley Savage, the chapter argues that, in spite of existing concerns about the photograph's ability to objectify the human subject, a project like *Cancer Sucks* can enable the viewer to gain insights into the embodied experiences of breast cancer in ways that challenge common representations of the illness.

---

[40] Again, these public events ultimately did not take place owing to Howie's death, but the thinking behind them perfectly encapsulates Howie's approach to the project.

Amy Hardie's chapter, 'Movie-Making as Palliative Care', similarly asks what artistic practice can bring to the palliative care environment, focusing on the contribution of film-making. She outlines an approach that uses the camera as 'an actual and metaphorical mirror', referring to three documentary films she made which were screened as works in progress during the activities of the New Thinking on Living with Dying network: *The Edge of Dreaming, Tuesdays* and *Seven Songs for a Long Life*. Through discussing the process of making the films and the subsequent impact they have had on their audiences, Hardie traces the development of an innovative use of the tools of cinema – camera, sound, projection – that engages with what gives meaning to people's lives in their last months and years.

Finally, Janet Price and Ruth Gould scrutinize Howie's aims in the New Thinking on Living with Dying network from the point of view of disability theory. Drawing on their work with Howie for the *Changing Capacities, Changing Identities* event in 2012, they argue for a convergence of research on disability and illness, since both fields reconceive the body such that the category of normality is put into question. Price and Gould further consider the role of the arts in providing a means for all bodies to be expressed in their singularity, free from and across social, political and embodied norms.

*

Taken together, the chapters in this volume open up several pathways into the feminist philosophy of Gillian Howie and her engagements with materialism and mortality; however, the richness of her work and its potential for further exploration could never be fully captured in just one collection. As such, we intend this volume to serve as a springboard to further engagements with Howie's work, initiating new critical conversations across different topics and fields of thought and practice. In her writings, Howie never tried to claim absolute novelty; instead, she saw herself as part of a historical trajectory and collaborative effort, beginning her conclusion to *Between Feminism and Materialism* with the claim that 'we all stand on the shoulders of giants'.[41] That is true, but at the same time Howie was a highly original thinker and a highly original person, with a finely tuned understanding of the political stakes of philosophical enquiry. Her insistence that philosophy must be adequate to the political challenges of the times results occasionally in a polemical style,

---

[41] Howie, *Between Feminism and Materialism*, p. 201.

and she consistently refused to acquiesce to academic fashions. Not only was she prepared to 'call out that this particular emperor is naked'[42]; she was also unafraid to return to theoretical frameworks such as dialectical materialism, or figures such as Shulamith Firestone,[43] that have seemingly been discarded in the clamour for the next new trend in the academic marketplace. Though she insists that philosophy should always remain reflexively aware of its own investments and contextual embeddedness, in Howie's hands this does not result in a 'touchy-feely' approach to philosophical engagement. Rather, if philosophy is to do its work, it must be bold, unflinching and provocative, as well as illuminating and precise. As Howie herself puts it so characteristically:

> My guiding principle is that the work of philosophy should be concerned with the intelligibility of the world. This is not because everything can be explained, grasped, or even communicated, but because if, as feminists, we wish to change the world, then we need to know what we are dealing with. Identity, representation, and objectivity may be implicated in an oppressive social real but are actually politically neutral concepts. Without them we are unable to investigate and change relations of oppression, and the point, after all, is to change the world.[44]

References

Harris, Jon, 'Gill Howie obituary', *Guardian*, 17 April 2013, http://www.theguardian.com/theguardian/2013/apr/17/gill-howie-obituary [accessed 30 January 2016].

Howie, Gillian, *Deleuze and Spinoza: Aura of Expressionism*, Basingstoke: Macmillan, 2002.

Howie, Gillian, 'A Reflection on Quality: Instrumental Reason, Quality Audits and the Knowledge Economy', *Critical Quarterly* 44.4 (2002): 140–7.

Howie, Gillian, 'Becoming-Woman: A Flight into Abstraction', *Deleuze Studies* 2 (2008): 83–106.

Howie, Gillian, 'Feminist Histories: Conflict, Coalitions and the Maternal Order', *Studies in the Maternal* 2.1 (2010): 1–12.

Howie, Gillian, 'Sexing the State of Nature: Firestone's Materialist Manifesto', *Further Adventures of The Dialectic of Sex*, edited by Mandy Merck and Stella Sandford, New York: Palgrave Macmillan, 2010, pp. 215–35.

---

[42] Howie, *Deleuze and Spinoza*, p. 2.
[43] Gillian Howie, 'Sexing the State of Nature: Firestone's Materialist Manifesto', *Further Adventures of The Dialectic of Sex*, ed. Mandy Merck and Stella Sandford, New York: Palgrave Macmillan, 2010.
[44] Howie, *Between Feminism and Materialism*, p. 9.

Howie, Gillian, *Between Feminism and Materialism: A Question of Method*, Basingstoke: Palgrave Macmillan, 2010.

Howie, Gillian, 'Nonidentity, Negative Experience and the Pre-Reflective Cogito', *European Journal of Philosophy* 23.3 (2012): 589–607.

Howie, Gillian, 'Death: You can't live with it, you can't live without it', New Thinking on Living with Dying blog, 28 June 2012, https://newthinkingaboutlivingwithdying. wordpress.com/2012/06/28/death-you-cant-live-with-it-you-cant-live-without-it/ [accessed 30 January 2016].

Howie, Gillian, 'Alienation and Therapy in Existentialism: A Dual Model of Recognition', *Ethical Theory and Moral Practice* 17.1 (2014): 55–69.

Howie, Gillian and J'annine Jobling (eds), *Women and the Divine: Touching Transcendence*, Basingstoke: Palgrave, 2009.

Howie, Gillian and Ashley Tauchert, 'Feminist Dissonance: The Logic of Late Feminism', *Third Wave Feminism: A Critical Exploration*, edited by Stacy Gills et al., Basingstoke: Macmillan, 2004, pp. 37–48.

Jobling, J'annine, '"The Personal is the Political": Gillian Howie, 1965–2013', *Radical Philosophy* 180 (2013): 66–8, https://www.radicalphilosophy.com/obituary/gillian-howie-1965-2013 [accessed 30 January 2016].

Whistler, Daniel, 'Howie's *Between Feminism and Materialism* and the Critical History of Religions', *Sophia* 53.1 (2014): 183–92.

Part 1

Feminism, Materialism, Critical Theory

When Feminist Philosophy Met Critical Theory: Gillian Howie's Historical Materialism

Stella Sandford

What is, or has been, the relationship between feminist theory and critical theory? What should it be? These are the central questions in Gillian Howie's *Between Feminism and Materialism*,[1] together with their implied corollary: what is the relation of both to philosophy? This chapter will suggest, via a discussion of *Between Feminism and Materialism*, that the relation between feminist theory and critical theory is a contradictory one in which the partners are at the same time close and yet estranged. It will examine how Howie characterizes this state of affairs and how she 'put[s] Critical Theory to work for feminist theory' (p. 115). It will also suggest how Howie's specific attempt to bring a certain aspect of critical theory to bear on the understanding of sex and gender is limited by its relation to feminist philosophy, and will criticize that part of *Between Feminism and Materialism*. However, it will then suggest that the work undertaken in *Between Feminism and Materialism* can be extended in another direction to begin the project of a critical theory of sex and a critique of the gender industry.

Feminism and critical theory

What does it mean to say that the relation between feminism and critical theory is a contradictory one in which the partners are at the same time close and yet estranged? How are they close? How are they estranged? The answer depends, in part, on what we mean by 'critical theory', whether we take it in its narrow sense

---

[1] Gillian Howie, *Between Feminism and Materialism: A Question of Method*, New York: Palgrave Macmillan, 2010. All page references in the chapter refer to this book.

to refer to a twentieth-century 'school' of German thinkers and their successors, or in its broad sense to mean any theory with an emancipatory aim.

It is in relation to the narrower definition of critical theory that feminism and critical theory can seem somewhat estranged, when – for reasons to be discussed below – we might have expected it to be exceptionally close. Histories and classificatory overviews of feminist theory (which identify radical, Marxist, socialist, liberal, difference and so on, as variants of feminist theory and feminism) never include a specific 'critical theory' variant. Why is this? It goes without saying that Theodor Adorno et al. were little interested in feminist issues,[2] but the feminist appropriation of intellectual work has never required that from its sources. There is a relatively small feminist literature on Adorno and feminism and on the theme of femininity in Walter Benjamin's work. We can also see the influence of Benjamin, in particular, on feminist thinkers in a range of disciplines, especially in comparative literature and cultural history, and the influence of Herbert Marcuse in some recent feminist literature.[3] But so-called 'first generation' critical theory did not seem to give rise to a specific mode of feminist theory even when, in retrospect, it seems so perfectly adapted to certain forms of feminist analysis and critique. High profile exceptions like Nancy Fraser, Seyla Benhabib and Drucilla Cornell, more associated with so-called 'second generation' critical theory, do not contradict this general point.[4] (A search for the name 'Adorno' in the electronic editions of the journal

---

[2]   Adorno's student Regina Becker-Schmidt notes, for example, that 'Adorno's image of femininity is more conformist than progressive'. Becker-Schmidt, 'Critical Theory as Critique of Society: Theodor W. Adorno's Significance for a Feminist Sociology', in Maggie O'Neill (ed.), *Adorno, Culture and Feminism*, New York: Sage, 1999, p. 104. Herbert Marcuse did appreciate the importance of the Women's Liberation Movement: see Marcuse, 'Marxism and Feminism', *Women's Studies* 2 (1974): 279–88.

[3]   See, for example, Carrie L. Hull, 'The Need in Thinking: Materiality in Theodor W. Adorno and Judith Butler', *Radical Philosophy* 84 (July/August 1997): 22–35; Maggie O'Neill (ed.), *Adorno, Culture and Feminism*, New York: Sage, 1999; Renée Heberle (ed.), *Feminist Interpretations of Theodor Adorno*, State College, PA: Pennsylvania State University Press, 2006; Judith Butler, 'Can One Lead a Good Life in a Bad Life?', *Radical Philosophy* 176 (November/December 2012): 9–18; Christine Buci-Glucksmann, 'Catastrophic Utopia: The Feminine as Allegory of the Modern', *Representations* 14 (Spring 1986): 220–9; Susan Buck-Morss, *The Dialectics of Seeing: Walter Benjamin and the Arcades Project*, Cambridge, MA: MIT Press, 1989; Janet Wolff, 'Memoirs and Micrologies: Walter Benjamin, Feminism and Cultural Analysis', *New Formations* 20 (1993): 113–22; Helga Geyer-Ryan, *Fables of Desire: Studies in the Ethics of Art and Gender*, Cambridge: Polity, 1994; Eva Geulen, 'Toward a Genealogy of Gender in Walter Benjamin's Writing', *The German Quarterly* 69.2 (Spring 1996): 161–80; Nina Power, *One Dimensional Woman*, Ropley: Zero Books, 2009.

[4]   As Barbara Umrath has pointed out, the work of German-language feminist theorists is more often inspired by so-called first-generation Critical Theory, while the second generation, Habermas especially, has been more influential in English-language feminist theorists. See Barbara Umrath, 'Feminist Critical Theory in the Tradition of the Early Frankfurt School: The Significance of Regina Becker-Schmidt', http://canononline.org/archives/spring-2010/feminist-critical-theory/ [accessed 20 December 2015]. See Umrath's article for a German bibliography.

Feminist Review yielded the reply: 'Sorry, no results were found.' A search in the journal *Women's Studies International Forum* elicited in response the question: 'did you mean "adorned"?' Surprisingly, even a search in *Hypatia* only threw up three references.) Work that 'maps points of convergence'[5] between, for example, Adorno and feminist theory is interesting but limited, as is all 'points of convergence' work. The question of the relation between feminist theory and critical theory concerns the extent to which feminist theory more generally has *metabolized* critical theory and the extent to which mainstream critical theory – if there is such a thing – has undergone a metabolic change in response to feminist critique; in relation to the latter it is probably correct to say that it has not.[6]

On the other hand, it could equally be said that feminist theory was always already critical theory, and not just in the broadest sense of the night of 'critical theory' in which all cows are black. Why is this? The concept of 'critique' that animates critical theory is derived from Marx. 'Critique' is a name for the transformed practice of philosophy that has become political. When the goal of knowing and understanding the world is no longer an end in itself but one of the necessary means through which we seek to change the world, philosophy becomes critique.[7] This concept of critique is also, of course, a criticism of the old idea of philosophy, or perhaps we should say of the traditional idea of philosophy, since it is still with us. It is critical of the traditional idea of philosophy to the extent that this philosophy conceives itself to be driven by the exercise of reason independently of the historical, social and political conditions of its appearance. Unable to acknowledge the real conditions of its existence, such philosophy can be called putatively 'self-sufficient' or idealist. Disavowing these conditions, such philosophy is unable to see how it reflects them. Unable to see how it reflects them it will tend to reproduce them uncritically. On the other hand, critical philosophy, or critical theory, not only acknowledges the 'real' social and historical conditions of possibility for its conceptual abstractions, but also uses its conceptual abstractions to criticize social reality.

As Kate Soper pointed out in 1989, when 'critique' in Marx's sense applies itself to the criticism of other theoretical accounts of the world, it identifies the source of the shortcomings of those theories in the reality that gives rise

---

[5] Alison Stone, 'Review of *Feminist Interpretations of Adorno*', *British Journal of Aesthetics* 47.3 (2007): 322–4.

[6] Thus, David Held, *An Introduction to Critical Theory: Horkheimer to Habermas* (London: Hutcheson, 1980) includes no mention of feminist theory at all.

[7] See Peter Osborne, *How to Read Marx*, London: Granta, 2005, esp. Ch. 5, 'The Carnival of Philosophy'.

to them. Criticism of these theories is thus simultaneously criticism of reality. And although, as I have noted, the narration of the history of feminist theory identifies no such thing as a specifically critical theory-inspired variant, it is easy to see that this description of critical theory applies equally to feminist theory.[8] This is perhaps most obvious when we remember that all feminist theory, as practical criticism, is explicitly tied to an emancipatory political agenda for social change – that is what makes it *feminist*. As critique, in the specific sense recalled here, feminist theory must also be critique of philosophy, traditionally understood. This means that philosophy cannot just absorb feminist theory or add feminist theory on or in to itself and remain the same. When feminist theory truly confronts philosophy, philosophy can only come out of the encounter critically transformed and not just contentfully enhanced. Or, if it does just come out of it only contentfully enhanced, traditional philosophy has merely recruited feminist theory to its own ideological agenda.

Howie's *Between Feminism and Materialism* exemplifies feminist critical theory as just described, and particularly because the relation to philosophy is still explicit in Howie's work. The range of reference in *Between Feminism and Materialism* is unusually wide, covering analytical philosophy, continental philosophy, political theory, feminist and queer theory, as well as Marxist analyses. But, while the book demonstrates a willingness and rare ability to range across disciplines, to employ the analytical methods of the social sciences quite as much as those of the humanities, it is still very clearly the work of someone saturated in the history of philosophy. Nevertheless, Howie does not describe or present the book as a work of philosophy; if any one description or presentation dominates it is *critical theory*. According to Howie: 'A theoretical reorientation toward the condition of objects of experience will help to bridge feminist theory in the humanities and empirical research in social sciences'; this is 'the recovery of emancipatory critique' (p. 3). In this endeavour philosophy – particularly in its hermeneutical and phenomenological aspects – is just one of the various theoretical sources to which, according to Howie, we should turn.

In fact, the theoretical kernel of *Between Feminism and Materialism* comes not from philosophy traditionally understood, but from the critique of political economy. In Chapter 3, 'Reason', Howie writes that 'We are looking for a critical method [i.e. not a philosophy or set of philosophical positions] that can

---

[8] Kate Soper, 'Feminism as Critique' [review of Seyla Benhabaib and Drucilla Cornell eds, *Feminism as Critique*], *New Left Review* 176 (July/August 1989), 93. See also Toril Moi, 'Appropriating Bourdieu: Feminist Theory and Pierre Bourdieu's Sociology of Culture', *New Literary History* 22.4 (Autumn 1991): 1017–49.

denaturalize appearances and provide an analysis of purported generality, disinterestedness, and universality' (p. 69). She claims that we can find this in Adorno and Horkheimer's *Dialectic of Enlightenment*, an emblematically transdisciplinary text.[9] Paradoxically, perhaps, Howie only identifies *Between Feminism and Materialism* as a work of philosophy at the end of the Introduction where she also evokes Marx's famous eleventh thesis on Feuerbach: 'Philosophers have only interpreted the world in various ways, the point is to change it';[10] that is, she identifies it as a work of philosophy whilst invoking the most famous *criticism* of philosophy in the Western canon. This is not to dismiss philosophy *per se*, although it is to criticize its historical disengagement from politics. Howie is clear that a certain kind of philosophy remains crucial for feminists:

> My guiding principle is that the work of philosophy should be concerned with the intelligibility of the world. This is not because everything can be explained, grasped, or even communicated, but because if, as feminists, we wish to change the world, then we need to know what we are dealing with. (p. 9)

Between Feminism and Materialism then stages and enacts the encounter between feminist theory, feminist philosophy and critical theory in such a way as to embody the practice of critique.

Torn halves

But if the kinship between feminist and critical theory described above is right, what accounts for their apparent estrangement? If feminist theory is critical theory but critical theory is much less often feminist, this might suggest that any estrangement between them is, as it were, all critical theory's fault, a result of its tendency to ignore feminist theory except insofar as it represents a kind of specialized off-shoot. Howie, however, saw things somewhat differently.

According to Howie, the estrangement is mutual, not one-sided. For if contemporary 'mainstream' critical theory pays little attention to feminist theory, feminist theory for its part fails to engage with critical theory because of its own issues, we might say. Howie points out that second-wave feminist

---

[9]   On this concept of transdisciplinarity see Stella Sandford, 'Contradiction of Terms: Feminist Theory, Philosophy and Transdisciplinarity', *Theory, Culture & Society* (Special Issue 'Transdisciplinary Problematics', ed. Peter Osborne, Stella Sandford and Eric Alliez) 32.5–6 (September–November 2015): 159–82.

[10]   Karl Marx, 'Concerning Feuerbach', in *Early Writings*, trans. Rodney Livingstone and Gregor Benton, London: Penguin/New Left Review, 1992, p. 423.

theory was no sooner born than it turned critically upon itself. As a case history of responsive self-criticism in a theoretical discourse, there has never been anything to match this. The theoretical response to 'the experience of conflict within the feminist movement' recognized that 'there are multiple locations from which to speak [and] that there is not one but polyvalent causes of oppression' (p. 2). The implicit presumption of the model of the white, Western, heterosexual and often middle-class woman was quite quickly unmasked. (It may not have seemed quick to black and lesbian feminists in the 1970s and 1980s, and of course feminist theory is not now free of all this; even so, in the longer view the speed of transformation is remarkable.) But now, Howie writes

> we have feminist theories that recognise the diversity of women but are unable to figure out any community or collective goal-oriented activity. We have feminist theories sensitive to the capillaries of power but unable to answer the question 'what systematic changes would be required to create a just society?' And we have an entire 'feminist theory' academic industry but are unable to communicate with the women's movement, such that it is. (p. 2)

Given the relationship between 'the social conditions that give rise to a theory and the theory itself', Howie suggests that the fragmentation of feminist theory was born of the fragmentation of the times themselves. Specifically: 'The fragmentation of the labour market, appropriated and diversified by capital, an aggravated individualism of the 1980s, and a splintered labour movement rather suits utopic – idealist – cognition of differences in terms of philosophies of subjectivities and desires' (p. 2). What is to be done? According to Howie,

> In need of a [feminist] theory with adequate epistemological bite, we should recuperate the rich stream of critical social theory ... Feminism will only move forward, reconnect theory and praxis, if we can find a way to bring together the somatic, living and experiencing body [implicitly, the subject of diversified feminist theory] with critical social science [implicitly, 'critical theory'].
> (pp. 2–3)

Howie sees this as the need to synthesize the subject-oriented tendencies within feminist theories with the object-oriented tendencies of critical and empirical social science. Thus, the torn halves are not just theory and practice but feminist theory and critical theory (although *Between Feminism and Materialism* devotes much more space to recommending critical theory to feminism than vice versa). Howie diagnoses the problem as an apparent contradiction between the objectivity of a certain realism – with its commitment to mind-independent realities about which we can make truth claims (p. 3) – and the 'subjectivism' of social constructionism. The suggested prescription, however, may be surprising. 'If the problem before us', she writes, 'is the relationship between "the subject", however construed, and the "object", however construed, then I suggest we should regroup around the idea of *dialectical materialism*' (p. 3). Howie could not have been unaware of the eyebrow raising that this would cause, and even more so on the side of feminism than on the side of critical theory. Because, my goodness, who talks about *dialectical materialism* these days?

Actually, Howie identifies dialectical materialism with historical materialism (p. 3), but nevertheless chooses to introduce the idea with the more surprising Engelsian term, perhaps because Adorno's negative dialectics plays such an important part in her methodological considerations. The Introduction and the first couple of chapters repeatedly invoke the reader's scepticism with regard to this and other classical Marxist terms while still insisting on their contemporary relevance. In the Introduction we read that: 'Dialectical materialism is a rather rusty, and some might say worn out, set of theoretical commitments' (p. 3). Further: 'Over the past couple of decades, historical materialism has received bad press' (p. 6). In Chapter 1, 'Production', we find the frank admission that 'the idea that political economy may be relevant to feminist theory – let alone its characterization in terms of the labour theory of value – may seem antiquated' (p. 13). But Howie argues that the labour theory of value, while it 'has something archaic and even tedious about it' (p. 12) 'can actually help to make explicit the relationship between the context and content of problems concerning feminist theorists, between exploitation, reification, commodification and problems of objectivity, essentialism, and difference' (p. 13). In Chapter 2, 'Objectivity', she writes, 'I have to admit that if Marxist political economy seems otiose, "ideology" fares little better – perhaps even worse' (p. 37). Nevertheless, she argues that 'the notion of ideology can assist in articulating a link between sensation-affect and meaning-making within local and global contexts' (p. 37). This is very characteristic of Howie's work, the integrity of which was never swayed by fashion.

Even so, it is only by acknowledging the historical cul-de-sacs of reductive or crude Marxisms and recognizing the limits of even its most sophisticated forms that Howie is able, in *Between Feminism and Materialism*, to revivify Marxist critical analysis for feminist theory. Her 'dialectical materialism', she explains, is *not* naturalism or physicalism, the reduction of the real world to the physical world (p. 4), just as, of course, materialism was not this for Marx. The dialectical or historical materialism at the core of Howie's book, and which for her is a development of realism, is distilled into three principles. First, the world is mind-independent. Howie sees this as a commonsensical point, but also elaborates it, distinguishing between the materialist claim that 'the world is shaped by human activity' and the idealist claim that 'the world is given shape through human ideas and concepts'. Thus, the ontological independence of the world from mind does not preclude the practical interdependence of humans and world, and indeed 'consciousness, ideas, and concepts emerge from the social experience of productive and active engagement with the world' (p. 5).

The second principle of Howie's historical materialism, the 'context principle', is that the things in this mind-independent world can only be understood in their social, political and historical contexts, which means that the relations between things are not conceptual but social, political and historical. Any attempt to analyze things in abstraction from their context of relations will of necessity 'lead to erroneous and often ideological judgement' (pp. 5–6). Historical materialism, Howie writes, is a theory of such relations, 'such that individual identity can be seen to be a consequence of antecedent social processes' (p. 6) The third principle, the 'principle of scientific enquiry', is that the only method capable of examining the economic, social and psychological processes that give rise to such abstract but real entities as the family, the state and culture, the only method that is adequate to their processual reality (encompassing change, difference, contradiction and so on) is a *dialectical* method. In fact, this 'is not a method as such', that is, it cannot be reduced to a set of principles or laws that apply in all instances (p. 7), but rather means, primarily, the negative dialectical presupposition which 'permit[s] the thought that some integrity is demonstrated at an ontological level and that this integrity may never be fully expressed conceptually' (p. 111).

We may now recall and understand the earlier claim: 'If the problem before us is the relationship between "the subject", however construed, and the "object", however construed, then I suggest we should regroup around the idea of *dialectical materialism*' (p. 3). The ontological integrity of the object (nature) can only be understood in a dialectical relation with the situated subject of knowledge (consciousness), mediated by 'human productive activity' (p. 16). The great originality and achievement of *Between Feminism and Materialism* is to have articulated this so precisely, and to have brought this essentially Adornian approach to bear on specific issues in contemporary feminist theory.

Objectivity vs objectivism

In *Between Feminism and Materialism*, Howie sees the main obstacle to the regrouping of feminism in what appears to her to be the effective hegemony in feminist theory of an overarching suspicion of the idea of objectivity, when what it should really be attacking is 'objectivism', which is an 'ideology' distinguished from objectivity. In objectivism the object-world and claims about it are abstracted from social contexts in such a way as to mask interests, a process that can only work by emphasizing the similarities in the object-world, reducing these to sameness and treating everything as fundamentally equivalent for the purposes of explanation (reductive naturalism, for example) (pp. 36–7). Objectivism is a theory, or a theoretical presupposition. But Howie's aim is not just to try to show why it is wrong: 'Critical reflection on the conditions of objectivity should reveal what is required to maintain the illusion of Cartesian objectivity and neutrality [that is, objectivism]' (p. 36). In a move familiar to critical theorists, Howie's claim is that, to some extent, it is the form and conditions of commodity exchange and its structural consequences that lie behind the ideology of objectivism in philosophy and elsewhere. This explains her otherwise unlikely claim that Marx's 'theory of value can actually help to make explicit the relationship between the context and content of problems concerning feminist theorists, between exploitation, reification, commodification and problems of objectivity, essentialism, and difference' (p. 13). How is this the case?

The labour theory of value concerns the exchange value of commodities. Marx claims that the value of a commodity lies in its 'congealed quantities of homogenous human labour, i.e. of labour power expended without regard to the form of its expenditure.'[11] The idea of 'homogenous human labour' is an abstract concept of labour – abstracted, that is, from the multitude of different forms of labour, or abstracted from what people actually do and the context in which they do it. The 'quantity' of labour congealed in any given commodity, determining the exchange value of the commodity, is measured in terms of average or 'socially necessary' labour time – the time required to produce the commodity. But this idea of 'labour time' is itself another abstraction: being not the time that any given person actually takes to perform a particular task but

> equal human labour, the expenditure of identical human labour-power. The
> total labour-power of society, which is manifested in the values of the world of

[11] Karl Marx, *Capital*, Vol. 1, trans. Ben Fowkes, London: Penguin, 1990, p. 128.

> commodities, counts here as one homogenous mass of human labour-power, although composed of innumerable individual units of labour-power. Each of these units is the same as any other, to the extent that it has the power of a socially average unit of labour power, and acts as such, i.e. only needs, in order to produce a commodity, the labour time which is necessary on average, or in other words is socially necessary. Socially necessary labour-time is the labour-time required to produce any use-value under the conditions of production normal for a given society and with the average degree of skill and intensity of labour prevalent in that society. (p. 129)

The idea of abstract labour as a common quality in commodities makes them commensurable and thus exchangeable, but it also renders the specific conditions of their production opaque and hides, under these abstractions, the real relations between the labourer and the product of labour, between labourers and between the labourer and owner of the means of production. Marx famously wrote that, these relations having become invisible, the commodity confronts the labourer not as the product of her own labour but as a hostile thing that appears to carry its value within itself as an objective property of its own – this is the 'fetish' character of the commodity (pp. 163ff.).

Chapter 1 of *Between Feminism and Materialism*, 'Production', gives a more detailed account of the labour theory of value than this, further specifying its constituent abstractions. Some readers, no doubt, are surprised to find a book of contemporary feminist theory opening like this. But in *Between Feminism and Materialism* this follows, perfectly consistently, from Howie's commitment to historical materialism and from the philosophical aim of rendering the world intelligible ('we need to know what we are dealing with' (p. 9)) in order to think about how to change it. If we assume, Howie writes, 'that the logic of capitalism is still the logic of Marx's *Capital*, then – through an analysis of underlying systematic economic processes – we will be able to address a number of key problems within feminist theory' (p. 13). In particular, the labour theory of value explains how the form and conditions of commodity exchange are reflected in the theory of knowledge that Howie calls 'objectivism'. The weaker version of this claim is that 'the labour theory of value identifies ways in which the heteronomous is transformed through a process of abstraction into the homogenous ... help[s] us to explain the cognitive inclinations to work in abstraction and to reduce dissimilar things to examples of the same' (p. 43), that is, it explains 'reified cognition' (p. 41) by analogy. But Howie aligns herself with the stronger claim that we can *demonstrate* a link between 'this cognitive orientation and the political economy' (p. 59), that a political economy based on the sale and purchase of labour power is the historical, social and political condition for the theory of objectivism, and the critique of objectivism is the critique of those social and political conditions.

In my view, Howie makes good on this claim: 'Objectivation [which, recall, is 'good' objectivity] is appropriated,' Howie claims, 'and we "forget" that the world in which we live is produced by us. Reification is the moment in this process of alienation in which the characteristics of independent and self-regulating "thing-hood" become the standard of objective reality' (p. 41). But once we have the labour theory of value as background, we can see that reified cognition is not merely a mistaken theory about the way that the world is; it is a theory that reflects the way that the world actually reveals itself to us under certain conditions, that is, the conditions of societies whose economic form is based on the exchange of commodities. Relating this to the fetish character of commodities, Howie reminds us that this 'appearance of the world as constituted by hostile and independent objects is not a mere illusion but a lived reality' (p. 60).

But what does all this have to do with feminist theory? Howie suggests that what she calls 'postmodern' and 'poststructuralist' feminist theory, which she takes to be dominant in the field, has tended to conflate objectivism with objectivity. The perfectly justified feminist critique of objectivism thus slides into an unjustified critique of objectivity itself. Thinking that the critique of objectivism requires scepticism about objectivity, feminist theorists give up too much, unwittingly lapsing into a reactive and politically eviscerated subjectivism. The anti-essentialist denial of any 'objectivity' to the category of women – which category Howie, like many others, sees as foundational for feminism – is emblematic of this theoretical-political cul-de-sac.

It is on this point that, for Howie, the estrangement between objective social theory or critical theory and 'subjectivist' feminist theory is most evident. Against the idea that the category of woman is merely discursively constructed and thus has no ontological reality, Howie argues that we need to understand it with what she calls 'a weak doctrine of natural kinds' (p. 94). According to this doctrine (in which Howie follows John Dupré), classifications of natural phenomena, including human beings, are both 'constrained by the things themselves' (p. 98) and dependent on the context of classification – especially the aims and interests that drive classification – rather than any 'real essence' in sets of given objects. According to this view, the classification of things into groups or kinds rests on the selection of shared relevant properties of the things classified, properties that those things really do have: 'physical phenomena provide the boundaries for legitimately admissible interpretations' (p. 98). Thus, for Howie, natural kinds are indeed 'real', but the selection of relevant properties, which ones are taken to be relevant, 'takes place according to criteria related to our *interests*' (p. 98). On the basis of this theory of natural kinds, Howie then argues that it is possible (contra certain 'postmodern' claims) 'to develop a realist explanation for resemblances that make sense of the classification of an individual as an individual "woman"' (p. 98). That is, the term 'woman' is not just a discursive construction, but is the name for a weak natural kind (bearing in mind that for Howie there are *only* 'weak' natural kinds).

Without attempting a definitive list of the relevant shared features and regularities that warrant the application of the concept 'woman', Howie includes biological sex, social role, self-attribution and a range of phenomenological features (p. 98). In any such list, she says, the only *necessary* component is 'the biological body' (p. 99), but 'sex' (effectively equated with the relevant aspect of 'the biological body') is merely '*one* feature amongst many others used to explain observed regularities and may be rather low in explanatory value' (p. 101). Sex is necessary but not sufficient, Howie argues, to determine membership of the category 'woman'; 'sex' is not determining and not necessarily linked with any of the other relevant features and regularities (it 'does not take a primary explanatory role for the entire cluster' (p. 102)).

But this is where Howie's argument falters, both philosophically and, more importantly, *as critique*. Biological sex – being female, being male – is treated in the argument as one feature among many in the identification of the kinds of 'women' and 'men', but its status as unquestioned in fact concedes the existence of natural sexed kinds which are not themselves the cluster-concepts that, she claims, constitute weak natural kinds. Howie says that the number of sex-based categories is conventional, and that the clusters of features that are identified as kinds will change as social conditions change (p. 99), but then it could not be claimed – as Howie does claim – that sex is the only necessary feature in the classificatory category 'woman'.

This specific problem in Howie's argument is actually symptomatic of the more general tendency in *Between Feminism and Materialism* to prioritize the criticism of feminist theory, at the expense of the criticism of the reality that feminist theory criticizes. Howie proceeds as if feminism is stymied by the 'postmodern' and 'poststructuralist' scepticism of feminist theory with regard to the category of women, but is it really the case that these feminist theories have hobbled feminism so much? What, today, are the major obstacles to the achievement of the demands of feminism? Anti-feminist arguments do not hinge on turning these sophisticated feminist theories against feminism. And, even if it were granted that academic feminist theory has disappeared down a rabbit hole of relativism, the world outside of academic feminist theory has not taken much – if any – notice of this. These observations do not imply that we are faced with a choice between feminist theory and social criticism because, as has been argued here, feminist theory *is* social criticism. They also do not imply that feminist criticism will not proceed by criticizing existing feminist theories in its efforts to produce one more adequate to the realities to be criticized. Indeed, Howie's criticism of the conflation of objectivity and objectivism in feminist theory is emblematic of this procedure and demonstrates its value. But, still, we may ask: what, today, calls for criticism most urgently? Is it so-called 'postmodern' feminist theory and its scepticism with regard to the category of woman? Or is it, rather, the everyday ideology of sex? Where are our critical energies best directed at this moment in time?

A critical theory of sex

Howie treats the question of 'woman' as an epistemological and an ontological issue. But it may be that it needs to be confronted as a primarily *ideological* problem. For while Howie's sophisticated feminist theory of the classification of weak natural kinds says that sex is merely '*one* feature amongst many others used to explain observed regularities', that the number of sex-based categories is conventional, and that the clusters of features that are identified as kinds will change as social conditions change, the reigning ideology of sex says quite otherwise.

'Sex' is a complicated social phenomenon, and part of its complexity is precisely its guise of simplicity. While apparently referring to a value-neutral, merely biological natural division in kind, it always in fact means more than this. The presumption that biological sex determines what it is to be a girl or a boy, or a woman or a man, is fully part of the meaning of the popular natural-biological category of sex – by which is meant, *not* a category that belongs to or originates in the field of biology, but one which is thought to so belong, which signifies as 'biological', with all that that entails. The problem is that the presumed fact of 'sex' does not function in explanations of the everyday lives of boys and girls and men and women as '*one* feature amongst many others used to explain observed regularities', but as *the* feature that supposedly explains all others.

Judith Butler, as is well known, incorporated a critique of the category of 'sex' into gender theory by arguing that the metaphysical category of sex is the discursive effect of gender. Butler argued that sex is the metaphysical efflorescence of the material practices of gender, but has paraded itself as their substantial basis. Sex 'postures' as a foundation for gender, but *Gender Trouble* deflates this pretension theoretically. For Butler the very being of sex is illusory; sex *is not*.[12] But sex is not so easily dethroned in practice as it is in theory. For granted that the substantialist idea of sex that Butler rightly criticizes is indeed a metaphysical 'illusion', there are other ways in which sex is 'real'. If feminist critical theory wants to understand how in fact little girls and little boys are socialized in gendered ways, if it wants to understand how in fact the everyday gendered lives of men and women are ideologically underpinned and justified, feminist theory needs also to acknowledge the *social reality* of the idea of sex. What does this mean?

One of the major achievements of twentieth-century feminist theory was the politicization of the sex-gender distinction. In the 1960s sociologists and psychologists had begun to distinguish, conceptually and terminologically, between the biological givenness of 'sex' (the distinction between male and female) and the social constructions of 'gender' (the social roles assigned to men and women and expectations concerning 'masculine' and 'feminine' behaviour, capacities, etc.). Feminists saw the sense and usefulness of the sex/gender distinction, as it enabled them to say that while sex could not be changed (or so they thought then …), the social forms of gender could; the compelling evidence for the historical and cultural diversity of gender norms seems to back this up.[13]

Even though the sex/gender distinction has been subject to criticism within feminist theory, the category of gender, in its specifically political, feminist sense, continues to be widely used across a range of disciplines. But, even today, outside of feminist theory, or outside of the relatively small circle of influence of feminist theory, the sex/gender distinction has never – or extremely rarely – even been made, let alone criticized. In English, the tendency of the popular cultural use of the word 'gender' gives a false impression, as if we are all gender theorists now. This is false because, on the whole, when people speak of gender what they mean is 'sex', and not the sex of feminist theory's sex/gender distinction – a sex that could be considered to be in important contexts irrelevant – but what Toril Moi calls 'the pervasive picture of sex', 'sex' in the sense

---

[12] Judith Butler, *Gender Trouble: Feminism and the Subversion of Identity*, London: Routledge, 1990, p. 34.

[13] On the feminist appropriation of the sex/gender distinction see Sandford, 'Contradiction of Terms', pp. 166–9.

in which it was employed *before* the sex/gender distinction, where sex is thought as relevant in all contexts.[14]

This is what we may call the 'popular', 'natural-biological' concept of sex. The two presumptions that constitute this category are (i) that there simply *is* sex duality (the exclusive division between male and female) and (ii) that that duality is both naturally determined and – more importantly – naturally determining. This concept has no purely descriptive function in relation to human being because the constitutive and exclusive duality of its terms is empirically inadequate. It is empirically false, for example, that every human being is possessed of either an XX or XY chromosonal configuration – there are plenty of other variants, including XX men and XY women. This exclusively binary concept of sex is thus *normative* and *prescriptive*. In *allegedly* describing a natural foundation for human existence, the popular concept of sex *stipulates* a duality, the nature of which is taken to be more or less determining of human psycho-social existence and behaviour. This is, of course, the concept of sex that Butler subjects to the criticism that it so richly deserves. But the criticism of the concept cannot be the end of the story. The presumption of this concept of sex, which, for example, is so commonly heard in the everyday discourse of many parents of young children, may be able to be demonstrated to be wrong, but the effects of its presumption continue to have material consequences, and it is the *persistence* of this presumption and the *social reality* of its affects that still need to be understood. This is what a critical theory of sex would take as the object of analysis and critique: the enemy's concept of sex, which is neither the sex of the sex/gender distinction, not the 'sexual difference' or 'sexuate' difference of the positive, psycho-philosophical feminisms of difference, nor the metaphysical pretension of the sex of *Gender Trouble*. All of these views of sex have a place in feminist theory; but they are not the object of analysis in a critical feminist theory of sex. And if this critical theory of sex is absent from Howie's *Between Feminism and Materialism* it is not just the consequence of the place given to 'sex' in her account of the category of 'woman' as the name for a weak natural kind. It is also because the place of a potential critical theory of sex is supplanted there by a philosophy of the lived body.

Between Feminism and Materialism includes a discussion of the sex/gender distinction which acknowledges both its outstandingly important historical role in feminist theory and the problems with it. Arguing that the concept of gender is too vague and generalized to be of any use, Howie suggests that it would be

---

[14] Toril Moi, *What is a Woman? And Other Essays*, Oxford: Oxford University Press, 2001, p. 6.

much simpler to be able to drop both terms, sex and gender (p. 175), but knows that this is not on the cards. She turns, instead, to the category of the 'lived body' as situation (p. 165). An appreciation of the body-as-lived 'offers more refined tools for theorizing sexed subjectivity and the experience of differently sexed men and women than the blunt category of gender' (p. 165), she writes. But can it be deployed in a critical theory? Or is it a rather part of a more purely philosophical phenomenology?

The object of a critical theory of sex is the actualized presumption of sex in gender practice and ideology, a presumption with material consequences. Sex in this sense needs to be acknowledged as a *socially effective presumption*; which is not to say that sex does not exist, but rather than it exists precisely *as* the *actualized presumption* of sex in gender practice and ideology. A critical theory of sex would have to include a consideration of *all* of the factors – including the re-iterative performance of gender – that make what Butler describes as the 'metaphysical' illusion of sex a *social* reality, that constitute what might be thought of as the *historical* transcendental illusion of sex.[15] These factors include the purported relation between sex-based explanations of purported gender differences and the perpetuation of some gender differences by those explanations. They include the popular cultural reception and consumption of those sex-based explanations of gender differences, and the deployment of the cultural authority of the signifier 'science' in their dissemination and reception. An example will hopefully make this clear.

In 2007 the Western media widely reported a study, published in the journal *Current Biology*, that purported to show that, as the BBC News Channel put it, 'A little girl's love of all things pink may not be entirely due to marketing by clothes and toy firms.'[16] A University of Newcastle study asked 208 people in their twenties 'to choose their favourite colours between two options, repeatedly, and then graphed their overall preferences. It found overlapping curves, with a significant tendency for men to prefer blue, and female subjects showing a preference for redder, pinker tones.'[17] The BBC reports that 'experts say it may have helped women gather ripe fruit, or pick healthy mates. Most earlier studies into colour suggest a universal liking for blue, regardless of sex. This is one of the few studies that have tried to spot differences between the likes of males

---

[15] For an explanation of this, see Stella Sandford, 'Sex: A Transdisciplinary Concept', *Radical Philosophy* 165 (January/February 2011): 23–30.

[16] 'Why girls "really do prefer pink"', BBC News Channel, Tuesday, 21 August 2007. http://news.bbc. co.uk/1/hi/health/6956467.stm [accessed 3 December 2015].

[17] Ben Goldacre, 'Out of the Pink and Blue', 25 August 2007. http://www.theguardian.com/ science/2007/aug/25/genderissues [accessed 3 December 2015].

and females.' *Time* magazine quotes one of the authors of the study: "'This is the first study to pinpoint a robust sex difference in the red-green axis of human color vision ... And this preference has an evolutionary advantage behind it.'" The author 'speculates' (the journalist's word) 'that the color preference and women's ability to better discriminate red from green could have evolved due to sex-specific divisions of labor: while men hunted, women gathered, and they had to be able to spot ripe berries and fruits. Another theory suggests that women, as caregivers who need to be particularly sensitive to, say, a child flushed with fever, have developed a sensitivity to reddish changes in skin color, a skill that enhances their abilities as the "emphathizer".'[18]

It does not take a genius to spot why this is, in Ben Goldacre's words, 'bad science'.[19] It tests preference, but makes claims about discriminative ability. It speculates about the sexual division of labour in the Pleistocene period through which humans evolved, although almost nothing is actually known about this. The results for those test subjects who happened to be Chinese produced overlapping curves that were less extreme than their non-Chinese counterparts; both male and female Chinese participants showed a preference for red overall. This may be explained by the fact that red is a lucky colour in contemporary Chinese culture. But the possibility that there may also have been cultural factors influencing the different colour preferences between men and women is not considered as a significant factor by the 'scientists'.[20]

But what is symptomatic in this example is not just the details of the study itself. The researchers clearly began with a robust *presumption* of sex difference, and *looked for* sex differences. Even more telling is the fact that this small and frankly overblown study, which was not only based on but also shored up the ideology of sex, was reported around the world, in a series of highly respected news outlets, gaining the kind of exposure of which most academic researchers can only dream. The hundreds of other studies that find, on balance, no significant differences between boys and girls and men and women, across a whole range of phenomena but especially concerning *ability*, tend not to be reported at all, let alone to this extent.[21] The news outlets

[18] 'Time Science and Space', 20 August 2007. http://www.time.com/time/health/article/0,8599, 1654371,00.html [accessed 3 December 2015].

[19] Goldacre, 'Out of the Pink and Blue'. See also http://www.badscience.net/2007/08/pink-pink-pink-pink-pink-moan/ [accessed 28 December 2015].

[20] Anya C. Hubert and Yazhu Ling, 'Biological Components of Sex Differences in Color Preferences', *Current Biology* 17.16 (2007). At the end of this short, three-page article the authors say that 'while these differences may be innate, they may also be modulated by cultural context or individual experience.' No news outlets were interested in that bit.

[21] For a detailed study of purported sex-based explanations for purported gender differences see

produce but also service what appears to be an enormous public appetite for stories of this kind about sex differences. A critical theory of sex would need to understand how and why we appear to be so desperate to have our prejudices about sex difference affirmed. What is it in contemporary social reality that leads people to *want* to explain themselves and others according to the most reductive form of the distinction of sex? And, as Howie would no doubt ask: whose interests does this serve?

A critical theory of sex with any hope of answering these questions would need to understand the most general social and cultural conditions and the form of society within which gender differences appear. Such a theory would have to take into account the relation between the presumption of sex and the production of commodities – that is, the creation of gendered markets – in relation both to adults and also, and perhaps more importantly, in relation to children and their production as gendered consumer-subjects. Any critical theory of sex thus has to deal with the complex ensemble of gender identity (requiring both psychological and sociological analysis), capitalist forms of production, scientism and its popular consumption and various modes of communication, and the reflection and perpetuation of this in public policy.

On this last point another example is instructive. In 2011 the Bailey Report of an Independent Review of the Commercialisation and Sexualisation of Childhood was published in the UK, responding to parents' expressions of concern over gender stereotyping in children's clothing and toys. In one of the recommendations of the report the authors state that gender preferences are biologically driven and part of 'a normal, healthy development of gender identity'. As Meg Barker noted in a response to the Report, it accepts that the 'reinforcement' of gender stereotyping by 'the commercial world' will continue so long as there is consumer demand; that is, it makes no recommendations in that area, seeing nothing wrong.[22] Here the complicity between public policy, commodities and sex is particularly clear. It also shows that popular morality (concerning the 'normal, healthy development of gender identity') and its modes of enforcement are part of the complex social reality of sex. It also

---

Cordelia Fine, *Delusions of Gender: The Real Science Behind Sex Differences*, London: Icon Books, 2011.

[22] Reg Bailey, 'Let Children Be Children: Report of an Independent Review of the Commercialisation and Sexualisation of Childhood', commissioned by the UK Department for Education, June 2011. https://www.gov.uk/government/publications/letting-children-be-children-report-of-an-independent-review-of-the-commercialisation-and-sexualisation-of-childhood#downloadableparts [accessed 28 December 2015]; Meg Barker, 'Sexualisation and Gender Stereotyping? One response to the Bailey Review'. http://learn1.open.ac.uk/mod/oublog/view.php?user=35001&tag=sexualisation [accessed 28 December 2015].

demonstrates the ways in which the gender industry concentrates itself most intensely around childhood. In this the gender industry is, as it were, cleverer than either critical theory or feminist theory, which tend to neglect a consideration of children as subjects. A critical theory of sex and of the gender industry would probably need to focus primarily on the world of children if it wants to have any practical effect.

I do not think that Gillian Howie, who I was lucky enough to have known, would disagree with what I have said here; I am very sure that she would have strongly encouraged a critique of the gender industry. Howie lines up with those who claim that the logic of advanced capitalism is such that it is perfectly indifferent to the gender of the worker; the abstract labour power that makes up the value of a commodity abstracts from race, sex, age and so on (although it produces class in the classic Marxist sense), thus tending to level those differences in one respect (p. 32).[23] But it is also the case, she held, that women do still tend to play particular roles in production and reproduction, such that they are disproportionately exploited or disadvantaged. Howie was also well aware that the logic of capitalism is to maintain this exploitation and to pursue differentiated markets that maximize profits by exacerbating cultural and sexual difference (p. 34), most obvious, of course, in the hyper-gendering of children's clothes, toys, furniture, bed linen, nappies, crayons, toothbrushes, cutlery: everything. This is just one of the ways that capitalist reality is contradictory, both levelling and producing gender differences at the same time. It thus seems to me that Howie would be fully on board with a critical theory of sex as outlined above, not least because it relies on precisely that commitment to historical materialism that forms the core of *Between Feminism and Materialism*.

Howie's claim that an appreciation of the body-as-lived 'offers more refined tools for theorizing sexed subjectivity and the experience of differently sexed men and women than the blunt category of gender' (p. 165) may be true if the aim is for a philosophical phenomenology. Further, a philosophical phenomenology can also be put to work as criticism, to the extent that it would contradict the objectivist ideology of bodies and sex. If, however, such a theory becomes an end in itself, the old philosophy, in the new guise of feminist philosophy, has

---

[23] This is not to deny that there is discrimination in employment practices, for example. It merely means that, *from the standpoint of capital*, what Howie calls 'extra-economic identities' (p. 32) are irrelevant. However, the pursuance of profit will mean that some people will as a matter of fact be super-exploited because they belong to certain gendered or racialized groups, because of global inequalities and because of more local efforts to drive down wages. Even with this caveat, however, Howie's claim is not uncontentious.

won out over critique. It is possible that at one point *Between Feminism and Materialism* teeters on the edge of this. But if it does, every reader knows which way Howie would push it: hard towards critique.

References

Becker-Schmidt, R., 'Critical Theory as Critique of Society: Theodor W. Adorno's Significance for a Feminist Sociology', in M. O'Neill (ed.), *Adorno, Culture and Feminism*, New York: Sage, 1999.

Buci-Glucksmann, C., 'Catastrophic Utopia: The Feminine as Allegory of the Modern', *Representations* 14 (Spring 1986): 220–9.

Buck-Morss, S., *The Dialectics of Seeing: Walter Benjamin and the Arcades Project*, Cambridge, MA: MIT Press, 1989.

Butler, J., *Gender Trouble: Feminism and the Subversion of Identity*, London: Routledge, 1990.

Butler, J., 'Can One Lead a Good Life in a Bad Life?', *Radical Philosophy* 176 (November/December 2012): 9–18.

Fine, C., *Delusions of Gender: The Real Science Behind Sex Differences*, London: Icon Books, 2011.

Geulen, E., 'Toward a Genealogy of Gender in Walter Benjamin's Writing', *The German Quarterly* 69.2 (Spring 1996): 161–80.

Geyer-Ryan, H., *Fables of Desire: Studies in the Ethics of Art and Gender*, Cambridge: Polity, 1994.

Heberle, R. (ed.), *Feminist Interpretations of Theodor Adorno*, Pennsylvania: Pennsylvania State University Press, 2006.

Held, D., *An Introduction to Critical Theory: Horkheimer to Habermas*, London: Hutchinson, 1980.

Howie, G., *Between Feminism and Materialism: A Question of Method*, New York: Palgrave Macmillan, 2010.

Hull, C. L., 'The Need in Thinking: Materiality in Theodor W. Adorno and Judith Butler', *Radical Philosophy* 84 (July/August 1997): 22–35.

Marcuse, H., 'Marxism and Feminism', *Women's Studies* 2 (1974): 279–88.

Marx, K., *Capital*, Vol. 1, trans. Ben Fowkes, London: Penguin, 1990.

Marx, K., 'Concerning Feuerbach', in *Early Writings*, trans. Rodney Livingstone and Gregor Benton, London: Penguin/New Left Review, 1992.

Moi, T., 'Appropriating Bourdieu: Feminist Theory and Pierre Bourdieu's Sociology of Culture', *New Literary History* 22.4 (Autumn 1991): 1017–49.

Moi, T., *What is a Woman? And Other Essays*, Oxford: Oxford University Press, 2001.

O'Neill, M. (ed.), *Adorno, Culture and Feminism*, New York: Sage, 1999.

Osborne, P., *How to Read Marx*, London: Granta, 2005.

Power, N., *One Dimensional Woman*, Ropley: Zero Books, 2009.

Sandford, S., 'Sex: A Transdisciplinary Concept', *Radical Philosophy* 165 (January/February 2011): 23–30.

Sandford, S., 'Contradiction of Terms: Feminist Theory, Philosophy and Transdisciplinarity', *Theory, Culture & Society* (Special Issue 'Transdisciplinary Problematics', ed. Peter Osborne, Stella Sandford and Eric Alliez) 32.5–6 (September–November 2015): 159–82.

Soper, K., 'Feminism as Critique' [review of Seyla Benhabaib and Drucilla Cornell, eds, *Feminism as Critique*], *New Left Review* 176 (July/August 1989).

Stone, A., 'Review of *Feminist Interpretations of Adorno*', *British Journal of Aesthetics* 47.3 (2007): 322–4.

Umrath, B., 'Feminist Critical Theory in the Tradition of the Early Frankfurt School: The Significance of Regina Becker-Schmidt'. http://canononline.org/archives/spring-2010/feminist-critical-theory/ [accessed 29 December 2015].

Wolff, J., 'Memoirs and Micrologies: Walter Benjamin, Feminism and Cultural Analysis', *New Formations* 20 (1993): 113–22.

2

Feminist Knowledge and Feminist Politics: Reflections on Howie and Late Feminism

Kimberly Hutchings

But now we have feminist theories that recognize the diversity of women but are unable to figure out any community or collective goal-oriented activity. We have feminist theories sensitive to the capillaries of power but unable to answer the question 'what systemic changes would be required to create a just society?' And we have an entire 'feminist theory' academic industry but are unable to communicate with the women's movement, such that it is.[1]

Howie begins her major work on feminism and materialism with the above trenchant summary of the ills of 'late' feminism. This chapter focuses on Howie's critique of what she termed late feminism, made in *Between Feminism and Materialism* and elsewhere.[2] It will focus particularly on the ways in which her argument depends on forging a link between feminist politics and the capacity through critical, empirical research, to identify relations of systematic oppression and the existence of real interests. This was a link that Howie argued had been lost in the turn towards difference, pluralism and postmodernism in late feminism. It will be proposed that although Howie was mistaken in insisting on the reinvention of this link between knowledge and politics within feminism, her attempt to do so offers a useful way forwards for contemporary feminist debates on how feminist politics can be conceived in a context in which homogenous concepts of the feminist revolutionary subject have been abandoned. The argument proceeds in three sections. In the first section we consider Howie's diagnosis of the problems of late feminism, in the second her account of how

---

[1] Gillian Howie, *Between Feminism and Materialism: A Question of Method*, Basingstoke: Palgrave, 2010, p. 2.

[2] Gillian Howie and Ashley Tauchert, 'Feminist Dissonance: The Logic of Late Feminism', *Third Wave Feminism: A Critical Exploration* (2nd edn), ed. Gillian Howie, Stacey Gillis and Rebecca Munford, Basingstoke: Palgrave Macmillan, 2007; Howie, *Between Feminism and Materialism*.

they need to be addressed; we will then move on, in the third section, to reflect on the strengths and weaknesses of Howie's diagnosis and prescription for contemporary feminism.

Late feminism: Problems

Howie is always careful to problematize any straightforward generational account of feminism as theory or as politics. In her joint work with Tauchert, she unpacks the dangers of 'wave' metaphors and the ways in which they oversimplify the history of feminism.[3] However, her particular concern is that in Kristeva's account in 'Women's Time', it is suggested that each phase of feminist thinking is distinct and marks some kind of progress in relation to previous phases. So that the latest phase, associated for Howie primarily with poststructuralist and postmodernist thought, is understood as responding to and transcending problems in the previous phase. For Howie, Kristeva's account not only oversimplifies the complexity of earlier stages of feminist theory and practice but also suggests, mistakenly, that late or 'third wave' feminism is something which you cannot or should not go 'back' from. For Howie, this prevents a proper critical engagement with contemporary feminism and the problems that it poses. These problems are simultaneously, and relatedly, political, historical and theoretical.

Although she is self-conscious about the potentially misleading temporal language of 'late' and 'third wave', Howie uses these terms as a shorthand to refer to the fracturing of the feminist movement in Western contexts (largely the UK and US) in the wake of black and lesbian critiques of dominant white and heterosexist identification of the meaning of women's oppression in the 1980s. Theoretically, she associates this fracturing with the growth in importance of postmodernist and poststructuralist feminisms, which argued against the alleged essentialism and universalism of earlier forms of feminist thought. At the level of both practice and theory, late feminism endorses the importance of diversity across the category of women and the dangers of attributing common-ality of identity or interest across women as a category. Politically, one of the key points that Howie makes repeatedly about late feminism is that it sits in an uneasy relation with post-feminism. Post-feminism is the position which came to prominence in populist literature in the 1990s in Western capitalist states,

---

[3]　Howie and Tauchert, 'Feminist Dissonance', pp. 46–7.

in which it was argued that feminism as a political movement had achieved its aims and women were now in a situation in which they could play with feminine and masculine identities, and abandon concerns about patriarchal interests in binary constructions of those identities. Howie argues that the emphasis on play and desire in post-feminism is echoed in aspects of third wave feminism, with its stress on plurality and difference, its refusal to draw clear lines between categories, its critique of universalism, its focus on representation, its reliance on psychoanalytic categories, and its reluctance to generalize about women's positions or women's interests. Although Howie acknowledges activist strands within third wave feminism, for her it marks a retreat from the political: 'the goals of feminism as a political movement become harder to identify with any confidence' and feminism declines as a political force.[4] Howie argues that this loss of political ground is rooted in the way that feminism has been shaped by and responded to broader historical conditions in the present, in contrast to earlier eras.

In Howie's view, late feminism and post-feminism are both structured by the cultural logic of late capitalism. This is a neo-liberal logic, in which a pluralization of identities and affiliations is necessary for the proliferation of markets: 'for the reproduction of capitalism to take place it is economically rational to exacerbate cultural, racial and sexual differences and differentiate markets'.[5] Post-feminism is explicitly celebratory of neo-liberal individualism and consumerism. Third wave feminism, in contrast, is *unconsciously* complicit in the differentiation of identities central to neoliberalism. Although wary of using the term, Howie presents late feminism as a kind of feminist false consciousness, analogous to the way that, on Marx's account, consciousness is tricked into a misunderstanding of the source of surplus value under capitalism.[6] Without realizing it, the well-meant respect for difference in late feminism serves the ends of the patriarchal capitalist system to which it is opposed. Howie also sees the co-option of the academy as distinctive of the neo-liberal era and its neo-conservative political agenda:

> this is endemic to all forms of academic inquiry but was exacerbated, specifi-
> cally in relation to feminist research, by the impact of vicious budget cuts and
> related casualisation dating from the 1980s just as Women's Studies courses had
> been gaining ground. This coincidence offers a case for claiming that the type

[4] Ibid., p. 52.
[5] Howie, *Between Feminism and Materialism*, p. 34.
[6] Howie and Tauchert, 'Feminist Dissonance', p. 47; Howie, *Between Feminism and Materialism*, pp. 38–45, 85.

of academic work sustainable under these conditions is of a form and content that could be safely funded and published.[7]

The context of neoliberalism operating through audit cultures and austerity programmes encourages academic research not to challenge the status quo. By implication, this is strongly compatible with the production of theory and analysis characteristic of late feminism which is self-reflective, hard to understand, and has no direct connection to political practice outside of the academy. Howie argues that this helps to explain the way in which feminist theory becomes increasingly autogenetic in the 1990s and beyond in Western universities.

Key to the failure of third wave feminism on Howie's account is its inability to understand itself as structured in and through late capitalism. Not only is feminism the product of particular historical conjunctures, but it is also unable to distance itself from its own conditions of possibility in order to mount a critique of those conditions. This is because it has abandoned the critical tools of earlier generations of Marxist and Socialist, materialist feminist thought. Specifically, feminism has embraced an anti-realism that deprives it of the possibility of making claims about the world that can form the basis for prescription.[8] It denies the possibility of discriminating between appearance and reality and lapses into scepticism and relativism:

> Owing to its rejection of the values of modernity and its anti-realism in ethics, post 1980s feminist strategy became constrained within an increasingly sophisticated demonstration of the ambivalence or ambiguity of conceptual discrimination. The only aim left was to experience, or perhaps to desire, outside the parameters of 'Western logic'.[9]

It is clear from the above that Howie diagnosed late feminism as being in a parlous state. In this respect she shared ground with other feminists concerned about the apparent loss of political direction and critical purchase in contemporary feminist practice and theory in the context of Western late capitalism. Loosely speaking, advocates of liberal and radical feminism have frequently expressed disquiet about the political implications of late feminism with regard to macro-level concerns about economic and political freedom and equality for women. Howie's position, however, is different from that of theorists such

---

[7]   Ibid., p. 52.
[8]   Howie, *Between Feminism and Materialism*, p. 3.
[9]   Howie and Tauchert, 'Feminist Dissonance', p. 53.

as Okin or MacKinnon.[10] Okin, in ways that echo aspects of Howie's analysis, identifies postmodern feminisms as complicit in patriarchal power insofar as they give priority to the importance of cultural differences between women. Famously, she argued that multiculturalism was 'bad for women' and that it was perfectly legitimate to deploy the universal category 'women' as a class of beings, and to call upon universalist accounts of the meaning of justice, in order to challenge patriarchal cultural practices. MacKinnnon also argues that the ways in which women are oppressed *as women* in different parts of the world has to remain central to feminist analysis. In doing so she reasserts the homogeneity of the category 'women', effectively denying efficacy or validity to the ways in which this homogeneity has been challenged repeatedly by third wave movements and arguments. Although she shares aspects of their disquiet, Howie's response to her diagnosis of late feminism is different. In *Between Feminism and Materialism*, she articulates an argument in which macro-level, anti-patriarchal feminist politics is rendered compatible with the rejection of the homogeneity argument.

Late feminism: Solutions

Howie's answer to late feminism works through a combination of insights drawn from Marxism, critical realism and phenomenology. At its heart is a bringing together of an idea of critical social science, premised on philosophical assumptions about the existence of a mind-independent world and theoretical arguments about the nature of capitalist social reality and ideology, with a phenomenological account of the body as situation (subject and object). Howie spends a lot of time in the book elaborating a critical realist interpretation of Marxism and critical theory, which seeks to disrupt the apparent choices between reality and representation, objectivism and subjectivism, universalism and relativism, essentialism and anti-essentialism that have structured feminist (and more broadly leftist) theoretical debate since the 1980s. These are, on her account, *false* choices. They are premised on idealizations of the above categories as mutually exclusive. When these categories are understood dialectically, it is possible to marry a realist and objective, though always fallible, understanding of the logics of natural and social reality to an appreciation of difference,

[10] Catherine Mackinnon, *Are Women Human? And Other International Dialogues*, Cambridge, MA: Belknap Press, 2006; Susan Moller Okin et al., *Is Multiculturalism Bad for Women?*, Princeton, NJ: Princeton University Press, 1999.

fragmentation and dissonance as fundamental to subjective experience in a late capitalist era.

We can see this at work in Howie's critical engagement with the concepts of sex and gender in the book. As she states it, her aim is to 'develop a conceptual approach to women's oppression that does not assume women constitute a coherent group with identical interests and desires'.[11] In order to do this, Howie rejects what she terms the 'homogeneity error', which rests, she argues, on three analytic assumptions: first that 'women' can be objectively defined through their common institutional conditions of oppression; second that it is plausible to understand women's oppression in terms of a single global narrative of relations of dependency and resource distribution; and third that all women are oppressed. Howie is uneasy about the usefulness of the categories of 'sex' and 'gender' as she sees them both as tending to reinforce the homogeneity error. Of the two, she is happier with the category of 'sex', which she argues can be shown to lack explanatory value in accounting for gender difference, and understood as a relatively neutral biological classification. Gender, in contrast, is typical of other ideological categories in the ways in which it seems both to reflect and reinforce the binary differentiation of men and women: 'The term "gender" presumes dimorphism which it then discovers everywhere';[12] it is 'a broad concept signifying the implicit and general processes of enculturation, sexual differentiation and patterns of conduct, as well as more narrowly depicting obvious stereotypes and representation'.[13] Howie is therefore very wary of using 'gender' as a central analytical category, and casts doubt on its critical purchase more especially as it becomes divorced from any relation to 'sex' or materiality.

In contrast to the language of sex/gender, Howie argues for a phenomeno-logical understanding of the 'body-as-lived', which allows for theorizing sexed subjectivity in ways that are open to the relevance of a whole range of factors, including biology, contributing to the meaning of any specific sexed identity. Although conscious of the ways in which conceptions of sex are socially constructed, Howie denies that social construction goes all the way down when it comes to the lived body, and argues that female biological sex characteristics are one of the factors through which women experience their body as sexed. In the light of this, Howie claims: 'A woman is someone with a female body lived as her situation, demonstrating relevant resemblances to other members of the

---

[11] Howie, *Between Feminism and Materialism*, p. 155.
[12] Ibid., p. 160.
[13] Ibid., p. 174.

same kind'.[14] This makes it possible to understand how and why the non-binary, complex and always distinct experience of the lived body often clashes with reified stereotypes of gender. But it also explains why gender cannot be understood as a choice or a performance. There are constraints on what can count as meaningful gendered identity inherent in the body-as-lived, which will vary and create internal dissonances as well as connections and differentiations in relation to other lived bodies. The category of dissonance is important to Howie's project to rescue feminist politics without repeating the homogeneity error:

> It is the dissonance of ordinary lived experience that reveals, more profoundly than social science, discourse analysis, or psychoanalytic therapies ever could, the awkwardness and inappropriateness of many body-images.[15]

The experience of dissonance in the body-as-lived is important for Howie because it alerts us to experiences of oppression and coercion, and the lack of fit between appearance and reality. In itself, however, the dissonance of lived experience is only a starting point, a necessary but not sufficient condition for grounding specifically feminist political struggles. Two further steps are necessary to link the phenomenological level of lived existence to its broader conditions: first critical empirical research that can identify not just where specific asymmetries of power occur but where oppression is systematically linked to sexed subjectivity; second the development of a political strategy to address systematic oppression.

> Dissonance, for Rosi Braidotti in *Patterns of Dissonance* is the effect of lack of symmetry between the discourses of the crisis of modernity and the impossible elaboration of theories of subjectivity. Rather than conceiving the crisis in this way, it seems more effective to define the *true* crisis in terms of the fragile attempts of the subject to express her conflicting and dissonant experiences of modernity as a struggle against the very forces that incorporate her (constituted) subjectivity. The notion of dissonance itself presents this uncomfortable and almost unintelligible experience of contradiction and gestures towards the social antinomies structuring it.[16]

Behind the experience of dissonance are 'the social antinomies structuring it'. Investigating the nature and significance of those social antinomies requires that

---

[14] Ibid., p. 173.
[15] Ibid., p. 171.
[16] Howie and Tauchert, 'Feminist Dissonance', p. 56.

we are able to identify the operation of power as domination and subjection and the mechanisms underlying that operation.[17] This means that we have to go beyond experience as a foundation for knowledge and develop adequate accounts of power. Here Howie is once more critical of late feminism for its embrace of Foucauldian conceptions of power, in which, she argues, it becomes impossible to tell the difference between systematic, hierarchical and exploitative relations of power and patterns of socialization in general. In order to rescue the possibility of this discrimination, she returns to Marxist critical theory and the idea of objective interests.

Howie is highly aware of the well-established critique of Marxist notions of objective interests and false consciousness. And she endorses aspects of that critique, both in relation to its reliance on homogeneity errors in relation to class, and in the ways it appears to sidestep questions of agency and responsibility. Nevertheless, she argues that the idea that some interests may be more or less partial or comprehensive in relation to aspects of lived experience remains persuasive. This requires the capacity to elicit generalizations about interests and to make ethical claims about social relations in which fulfilment of more comprehensive interests is systematically blocked in ways that advantage some and disadvantage others. One of the examples she uses to illustrate how this might be done without making crass assumptions about the interests that lived bodies *ought* to have is that of female genital mutilation (FGM).[18]

The practice of FGM has been the subject of long-term campaigning by feminist groups from all parts of the world. In many cases it causes ongoing pain and discomfort and is known to have a range of effects on women's health, including premature deaths from infections caused by the procedure. For thinkers such as Okin, it provides a clear example of how multiculturalism is 'bad for women'. Like Okin, Howie argues that even though most feminists remain opposed to FGM, late feminism does not have the tools to explain why it should be opposed, especially since it appears that the practice continues to have widespread support from women within the contexts in which it takes place. For third wave feminists, to ignore the active participation of women in the practice is to reinforce the notion of third world women as passive victims without agency in need of rescue from white feminists. Consent to FGM as a practice is linked to the endorsement of social norms of feminine modesty and

---

[17] Ibid., p. 199.
[18] The use of the term 'female genital mutilation' is contentious as it implies a critique of the practice by definition; some would favour the more neutral terms 'female genital cutting' or 'female circumcision'.

marriageability. To the extent that options in many of the contexts in which it is practised are virtually non-existent for an unmarriageable woman, there appears to be a clash of interests between social and physical flourishing. Howie argues that the problem for postmodernist feminists is that they cannot demonstrate why one set of interests should be subordinated to another *because* their analysis has to respect difference and women's agency and therefore has no reason not to give equal weight to expressed interests. Politically, therefore, late feminists end up being caught in a bind in which, regardless of their condemnation of a practice, they cannot take political action without reproducing a colonizing move that undermines their expressed commitment to difference.

In contrast, Howie claims that her own critical theoretical position allows her to delve deeper into the factors underlying the choice made by older women on behalf of female children, potentially between social and natural death in this situation. Where do these competing interests originate? For Howie, as soon as one asks this question, one can see that the interest in FGM is parasitic on a socially constructed world in which female sexuality is produced so as to confirm and perpetuate men's control over women as sexual beings. By contrast, the interest in health is a prerequisite for the flourishing of any lived body in any kind of social arrangement.[19] Neither of these interests is straightforwardly true or false, both are rooted in experienced reality, but Howie is in no doubt as to which is more comprehensive and compatible with just social relations. In order to see this, one has to consider interests not as simply either phenomenological (experienced) or functional (based on hypothetical imperatives) but also as *positional*, that is to say benefits or costs linked to a particular social role: 'Patriarchy is where *men* have the positional capacity to further their own interest in a way that is to the detriment of, or harms, women *even in cases of compliance.*'[20] This applies to direct or indirect benefits/harms of particular practices or actions, but also to the conditions under which choices are made. So that if the background conditions that make sense of women complying with FGM are background conditions that systematically favour men and disadvantage women, then this is a reason for condemning the practice regardless of that compliance. Howie uses a language of partiality to capture the *reality* of the two sets of interests, arguing that women's interest in participating in the practice should be seen as *partial*, and of resisting the practice as more *comprehensive*.

[19] Ibid., p. 195.
[20] Ibid.

For Howie, feminism is a commitment to identifying and challenging patterns where there are consistent 'dissonances' between women's partial and more comprehensive interests, where a relation of domination is exercised *unjustly*, that is to say in ways that systematically advantage men at the expense of women: 'When we say that there is *systematic oppression*, we mean that across fields of social activity and practices we can detect patterns of resemblances that may be explained through underlying mechanisms.'[21] Within this account, women's experience as lived bodies and their situated knowledge are important, but the feminist critical theorist must also work beyond this to find patterns of oppression and the mechanisms that underlie them across time and space.[22] This is necessary in order to enable the identification of the basis for political alliances across different lived bodies. Such knowledge is essential for the translation of feminist theory and social science into feminist politics: 'to form political alliances we need to account for located situated knowledge and to map the systematic nature of interests: we need both a respect for differences and to know which differences are relevant.'[23]

At the end of the fifth chapter of *Between Feminism and Materialism*, Howie refers to the idea of Marxism as involving a particular kind of triangulation that brings together: a historical social science of capitalism; a philosophy of contradiction with epistemological and ethical ambition; and a mode of politics that provides a compass or road map.[24] And she suggests that a revitalized feminism would involve a similar triangulation of elements: 'a reinvigorated notion of dialectical materialism will help us to grasp the dynamics of the historical processes of capitalism and this will, in turn, inform, be informed by, and support a radical feminist politics.'[25] At the end of the book, the three elements needed for a reinvigorated feminism are perhaps more modest: 'a way to think women in similar contexts across the world in different local geographical spaces rather than all women across the world; an analysis of differential relationships rather than natural characteristics; and a way to make sense of "international" that foregrounds economics, politics, and ideological processes.'[26] However, what remains constant across the argument of the book is the need to rescue the possibility of feminist politics through dialectical materialism without reliance on homogenizing the subject

[21] Ibid., p. 199.
[22] Ibid., p. 202.
[23] Ibid., p. 204.
[24] Ibid., p. 129.
[25] Ibid.
[26] Ibid., p. 202.

of feminist politics. This is analogous to Marxism without the revolutionary subject.

Reflections on Howie's diagnosis and prescription

As already noted, Howie's identification of the problems with late feminism reflects concerns shared by many feminist theorists since the 1990s, perhaps particularly within the British context where the tradition of socialist feminism has been particularly well established. We have seen these concerns registered philosophically in debates over women and culture, the meanings of sex/ gender, the issue of autonomy for the feminist subject, and many others. We have seen them registered politically in campaigns over issues from veil-wearing to pacifism, to whether UNSCR 1325 is a co-optation of feminist goals or a major victory for the international feminist movement.[27] What makes Howie's position distinctive is that she does not want to reassert previous claims about women and patriarchy found within liberal, radical, Marxist and socialist feminisms. Rather, she wants to dig deeper in order to understand the meaning and significance of lived, situated subjectivity in a world that is simultaneously radically plural and cross-cut by common conditions, notably the globalization of capitalism. What follows from her analysis is not a singular feminist struggle but complex, coalitional feminist politics, which she refers to as 'problem-based' and 'micro-political' in origin, but which may aspire to global resonance and bring struggles over patriarchy together with struggles over economic and racialized forms of oppression.

In terms of her critique of late feminism there are questions about its empirical accuracy. For one thing, there is a tendency for her account of the ills of late feminism to generalize from the experience of Britain and the US. Her diagnosis neglects the importance of national and transnational feminist politics since the end of the Cold War. Her account of feminism as being in retreat does not line up with the success of feminist coalitions campaigning in relation to mainstreaming the concerns of women in international peace and security, or with the flourishing of ongoing campaigns in relation to care

---

[27] This refers to the UN Security Council Resolution supporting the inclusion of women in all aspects of conflict resolution, peacemaking and peacebuilding (2000). Within the resolution gender is largely equated with 'women' and women are presented primarily as victims or peacemakers. For some feminists the resolution represents a major victory for feminist campaigning at the transnational level; others argue that it perpetuates essentialist views about women and gender.

chains, sex-trafficking and sexual violence in contemporary world politics. In underplaying the continued presence of feminist activism across national and international contexts, Howie perhaps risks making the same mistake of which she accuses late feminism, of being out of touch with or denigrating activists for not having the right kind of sophisticated theoretical framework for thinking about women's oppression. In addition, when discussing feminism within the academy, Howie focuses almost entirely upon theoretical work and neglects the enormous amount of feminist social science which is precisely dedicated to mapping and understanding the roots of systematic gender inequalities. Much contemporary feminist scholarship in the Western academy is focused on empirical research oriented towards political change in relation to the unequal gendered distribution of wealth, labour, opportunities and power.

Howie's critique of late feminism is not only that it has ceased to ground feminist politics but also that it incorporates deep philosophical and theoretical weaknesses. To put it crudely, at the heart of these weaknesses is an inability to discriminate, which follows from the rejection of notions of objectivity and realism. This inability to discriminate manifests itself in subjectivism, relativism and scepticism at the level of theory, and in an incapacity to judge and prescribe in relating theory to practice. There are two responses one might make to Howie about this characterization. One relates to her prior commitment to interested knowledge. Even supposing that her analysis is correct, it only becomes a problem if one requires knowledge to work in a particular way. Debates over subjectivism, relativism and scepticism have not been philosophically settled, and late feminists might respond to Howie by pointing out that even if her view about the necessity of knowledge for action is correct, to shift their account of knowledge to suit their political ends would be to render philosophical debate about knowledge redundant. More importantly, Howie's presentation of the philosophical and theoretical commitments of late feminism often falls into the either/or trap that she seeks to avoid in her own theorizing. Much work carried out under the broad labels of poststructuralism and postmodernism resembles Howie's in seeking to refuse the choice between binary oppositions. When Howie argues that in rejecting objectivity late feminists are necessarily committed to subjectivism, she is undermining her own dialectical understanding of these terms and failing to do justice to those she is criticizing. Similarly, in her critique of postmodern accounts of power, she neglects how readings of Foucault can provide tools for distinguishing between power as an ever-present relation on the one hand, and power as domination on the other.

The above objections may seem somewhat trivial in comparison to Howie's positive construction of materialist feminism. However, Howie's claims about feminist activism and the feminist academy are fundamental to her argument. She implies that it is *because* things have gone wrong at the level of feminist knowledge that things are also going wrong at the level of feminist politics. In contrast to this, I would argue that politics produces, as opposed to being grounded in, critical empirical research. Coalitions are forged politically around shared visions, they do not require a truth to be established in advance to provide a ground for the fight, and more often than not will actually disagree about what such a truth would be, presuming one was needed. This is not to say that feminist critical knowledge is not valuable for feminist struggle, but it is to claim that it is not a necessary prerequisite of that struggle. Clearly, this is not an argument that can be settled in principle. It would require empirical research to trace the relations between feminism in the academy and feminist politics. But although Howie identifies correlations between second and third wave feminism and different degrees and kinds of feminist politics, her conviction as to the importance of a particular kind of feminist theorizing has its roots in Marxism. Within this tradition, the role of the theoretician in providing the 'compass' or 'road map' for political practice is well-established. And it is regarded as necessary in part because of the *hidden* nature of the mechanisms governing the oppression and exploitation of the proletariat. Ideology is what makes science necessary. Whilst I would agree with Howie that the reality is almost always more complex than it appears, I am less convinced that specialist academic knowledge is needed in order to bring contradictions to the surface. As Howie herself points out: 'It is the dissonance of ordinary lived experience that reveals, more profoundly than social science, discourse analysis, or psycho-analytic therapies ever could, the awkwardness and inappropriateness of many body-images.'[28]

For some feminist philosophers, the failure of late feminism has been its abandonment of the autonomous subject of the nineteenth-century revolutionary tradition. This might be the individual autonomous subject, central to liberal feminist projects, who, with the defeat of patriarchy, becomes free from material and ideological constraints. Or it might be the collective revolutionary subject of women as a class, who act together to emancipate themselves from patriarchal relations on analogy with Marx's proletariat. The latter is clearly a tradition to which Howie is deeply attached, but she avoids the traps inherent

---

[28] Ibid., p. 171.

in making autonomy the ground and goal of feminist politics. Her sensitivity to the ways in which subjectivity and thought are structured by broader social, economic and political relations leads her to reject the fantasy of autonomy at both individual and collective levels. Lived bodies are always situated in ways that constrain as well as enable them. And the complexity of sexed subjectivity precludes identifying women as a homogenous category or class.

Rather than focusing on freedom, Howie insists on a focus on substantive inequality for feminist politics. This foregrounding of equality issues makes Howie's feminism less vulnerable to standard feminist critiques of the idea of a feminist standpoint. It allows her to acknowledge the multiplicity of women's standpoints and of ways in which they are differently positioned within patterns of distribution, whilst at the same time identifying grounds for women's solidarity and for arguments about when and how that solidarity trumps or accords with other solidarities. Moreover, it re-orients feminist politics towards the ends of feminist activism as opposed to its grounds. Although Howie spends a lot of time demonstrating how feminism should understand itself in terms of its material conditions, her argument also pushes us to think about visions of the future, counterfactual worlds in which one's interests would not be structured in such a way as to make the experience of embodied living so much harder for some than for others.

Conclusion

There is a dissonance running throughout Howie's argument in *Between Feminism and Materialism* between a more thoroughly phenomenological and a more realist 'scientific' account of feminist critical theory. This is a tension that Howie acknowledges but has difficulty reconciling, so that in the end we are left with a juxtaposition of the Marxist triangulation of elements outlined in the middle of the book, and the three elements of a reinvigorated feminism outlined at the end of the book. There is much to be said for her view that centrality in feminist analysis should be accorded to issues of justice as opposed to issues of freedom. This focus allowed her to attend to complexities related to patterns of distribution of goods, power and status, and to open up questions about patriarchy in relation to those patterns, without claiming a commonality of gendered oppression across all women. It also fits well with her model of coalitional and multi-dimensional feminist politics – a model which, ironically, also accords with the prescriptive implications of what Howie calls late feminism. Ultimately it may be that Howie's negotiation of feminism and materialism, however theoretically persuasive, is unnecessary for the possibility of progressive feminist politics. But one can only respect the passionate commitment to fighting injustice that underpinned Howie's aspiration to ground feminist politics in emancipatory science.

References

Howie, Gillian, *Between Feminism and Materialism: A Question of Method*, New York and Basingstoke: Palgrave Macmillan, 2010.

Howie, Gillian and Ashley Tauchert, 'Feminist Dissonance: The Logic of Late Feminism', *Third Third Wave Feminism: A Critical Exploration* (2nd edn), ed. Stacey Gillis, Gillian Howie, and Rebecca Munford, New York and Basingstoke: Palgrave Macmillan, 2007: 46–58.

Mackinnon, Catherine A., *Are Women Human? And Other International Dialogues*, Cambridge, MA: Belknap Press, 2006.

Okin, Susan M. (ed.), *Is Multiculturalism Bad for Women?*, Princeton, NJ: Princeton University Press, 1999.

3

Between Negative Dialectics and Sexual Difference: Generative Conjunctures in the Thinking of Gillian Howie

Joanna Hodge

Introduction

Gillian Howie's first monograph, *Deleuze and Spinoza: Aura of Expressionism* (2002), is controversial and contestatory.[1] She is unconvinced by recent materialist re-readings of Spinoza, and challenges the reading of Spinoza, inspired by Deleuze, as pursued variously by Rosi Braidotti and Moira Gatens, Paul Patton and John Protevi.[2] Howie disagrees with those forms of feminist critique, which suppose that some combination of Spinozan, Nietzschean, or Deleuzian affirmations is a good route for feminist theorizing to follow today. Here is not the place to assess the detail of these disagreements, but they provide important points of reference for setting out the trajectory of her thinking. They also provide a context for the central intent of this chapter, which is to assess Howie's surprising proposal instead to combine an enthusiasm for Adorno's version of dialectics and for Irigaray's interrogations of gender as an alternative route into recasting the connection between philosophy, feminist critique and political engagement. Irigaray's interrogation of gender, in the form of a sexual difference, arrives in her claim: 'Sexual difference is one of the questions, if not the question which is to be thought in our epoch.' This claim arrives as the opening for her text, *The Ethics of Sexual Difference*, and it begs the questions: what is our epoch?

---

[1] Gillian Howie, *Deleuze and Spinoza: Aura of Expressionism*, London: Palgrave Macmillan, 2002.
[2] See Rosi Braidotti, *Nomadic Theory: The Portable Rosi Braidotti*, New York: Columbia University Press, 2012; Moira Gatens and Genevieve Lloyd, *Collective Imaginings: Spinoza Past and Present*, London and New York: Routledge, 1999; Paul Patton, *Deleuze and the Political*, London: Routledge, 1998; and John Protevi, *Political Physics: Deleuze, Derrida and the Body Politics*, London: Athlone, 2001.

and what might the other questions be?[3] It makes a connection back to Martin Heidegger, for whom the question of thinking the defining issue for an epoch remains a signature theme.

The proposed conjunction of Irigaray, on sexual difference, and Adorno, on dialectics, would thus seem to come immediately into difficulties, granted the oppositional stance of Adorno towards Martin Heidegger and all his works, and the oppositional stance of the feminist movement, at least in Germany, to Adorno's mandarin masculinism. In this chapter, I propose to explore how these lines of conflict both provide Howie with a productive space for a wide-ranging thinking, and reveal the nature of Howie's ambitions for a contribution from philosophy, to contest how philosophy can engage with, and contribute to, discussion of social and political process today. Howie's view is that the combination of Adorno's thoroughgoing challenge to Heidegger's fundamental ontology, with Irigaray's identification of sexual difference as the defining issue for this epoch, can provide a philosophical conceptuality more adequate for analysis of current conditions and the connection between philosophy and politics, than that proposed in the names of Deleuze and Spinoza.

Deleuzian neo-materialism has itself over the past twenty years been exposed to, and challenged by, Graham Harman's object-oriented ontologies, and by various versions of speculative realism, in the name of which yet another revival of political critique is surmised to be on the way.[4] Howie develops her version of a connection between philosophy and political commitment in opposition to all these accounts. Her account draws rather on a critically inflected inheritance of the feminist and Marxist critiques of the 1980s, affirming a continuity with the projects of the Enlightenment, and of a universal emancipation, proposing a defence and elaboration of the ideals of reason and rights. In this context, theories of desire, associated with Freud and Lacan, have been conjoined to critiques of power in various combinations. These theories of desire have in turn been targeted by feminist critique, in general, in terms of a certain masculinist, or phallogocentric bias, and, more specifically, in terms of a Spinozan critique of the founding role in them of negation and disavowal, positing a primordial lack and experience of castration. Desire is thus to be emancipated from negation, and recast using components from the thinking of Marx, Foucault and Deleuze, in a general theory of energetics, forces and nerve systems. Howie resists such a line of argument, insisting with Adorno on a continuing

---

[3] Luce Irigaray, *An Ethics of Sexual Difference*, trans. Carolyn Burke, London: Athlone, 1993, p. 5.
[4] See Graham Harman, *Tool Being: Heidegger and the Metaphysics of Objects*, New York: Open Court, 2002; and Peter Gratton, *Speculative Realism: Problems and Prospects*, London: Bloomsbury, 2014.

potential, and indeed necessity for thinking in terms of conceptions of negation and negativity, and affirming the powers of resistance contained within them. Critiques of power, associated with Marx and Engels, have also been put in question, both internally, with respect to Stalinist autocracy, and then externally, with respect to the failure of Soviet Communism. Louis Althusser, in his account of ideological state apparatuses, and Michel Foucault, on the enabling forces at work in power knowledge, provided analyses of the specific locations of discrete empowerments, ensuring some limited scope for effective interventions, and thus permitting a work of analysis to proceed, if always in opposition to powerful contravening forces. The development of a bio-politics of resistance in the writings of Antonio Negri and Michael Hardt does not come into Howie's overview, but she is sceptical about the limitations imposed on critique and on the power of negation, under the rubric of bio-politics. For Howie, the analyses of Althusser continue to show how academic philosophy provides one such relatively protected stance from which the task of critique is the less obstructed by forces above and beyond the control of individual citizens. While receptive to the claims of disaggregated emancipatory critique, in the names variously of the subaltern, the postcolonial and of disability studies, Howie remains committed to a strong version of philosophical universality, both with respect to rights and with respect to conceptual scope.

In the closing page of this first monograph, *Deleuze and Spinoza: Aura of Expressionism*, Howie briefly invokes Adorno's thinking as a resource for setting out an alternative route into materialism through a revival of his negative dialectics and of classical Marxist critique of ideology:

> The task of criticising ideology, Adorno maintains, is to judge the subjective and the objective moments, and their dynamics. This returns to thought its three moments, the thought or judgement, the intentional object and the materiality of the object as well as returning to substance its content.[5]

This is no more than a gesture, and it is regrettable that extended treatment of Adorno's thinking, to demonstrate access to a materiality of its objects, remains lacking. In her second book, *Between Feminism and Materialism: A Question of Method* from 2010, Howie traces out how versions of feminist critique have sought to combine components from Freud and Marx, from Lacan and Althusser, and from Foucault and Barthes, to advance the cause of emancipation. In this context, the proposal to read Irigaray with Adorno, and

---

[5]　Howie, *Deleuze and Spinoza*, p. 205.

Adorno with Irigaray, is perhaps the less startling. These various conjunctures of a post-Freudian theory of desire, and of post-Stalinist critiques of power, proffer accounts of subjectivity, as subjectivation, and subjectification; and of matter, as consisting in productive potentialities rather than as a set of positive givens. These latter are shown by Adorno, and, with his assistance, by Howie, as constantly at risk of reification into a naturalized *potestas* (power as possession), commodity fetishism, and a reification of economic process, in finance capital. Reification and subjectivation are the danger; genealogies of concepts and critiques of patriarchal power the cure. But, for Howie, these always remain subordinated to the imperatives of reason, and to analysis in terms of rationally grounded principles of identity, as pre-conditions for the very possibility for thought and critique. She thus inserts her analyses into the cumulative reception of these conjunctures, opening herself up to all the problems arising from the attempt to survey a truly vast range of material.[6]

Howie's two monographs, and the lines of enquiry subtended by them, thus arrive into a complicated, highly contested context, and they make a distinctive and unusual intervention. For while she insists on the claim of reason and argues for a priority of identity over difference, she is all the same focused on the processes whereby some are at ease, and some are set apart by current ways of thinking and of conceiving reason and identity. The title of her second monograph, *Between Feminism and Materialism: A Question of Method*, itself makes clearer her angle of entry into this context of accumulating differentiations, between ways of reading Spinoza, and between ways of reworking a relation between philosophical and political commitments. The task in the second monograph is framed as that of pursuing the accounts of their lived experience offered variously by Kate Millett and Virginia Woolf. They, like Howie, are alert to concerns and experiences which fail to register within a dominant delimitation of the tasks of philosophy, even when a commitment to politics, as an awareness of the continuing work of extracting surplus value, is to the fore. The citation from Virginia Woolf's *A Room of One's Own*, placed at the head of the Acknowledgements to this second monograph, is instructive:

> And I thought of all the women's novels that lie scattered, like small pock-marked apples in the orchard, about the second-hand book shops of London.

---

6   There is some confirmation of her sense of a risk of losing something valuable in this work, in the current celebration of a new materialism, in the analysis offered in the Introduction to a recent collection, *New Materialisms*. See Diana Coole and Samantha Frost (eds), *New Materialisms: Ontology, Agency, and Politics*, Durham, NC: Duke University Press, 2010.

It was the flaw at the centre that had rotted them. She had altered her values in deference to the opinion of others.[7]

The longer citation runs:

One has only to skim those old forgotten novels and listen to the tone of voice in which they are written to divine that the writer was meeting criticism; she was saying this by way of aggression, or that by way of conciliation. She was admitting that she was 'only a woman', or protesting that she was 'as good as a man'. She met that criticism as her temperament dictated, with docility and diffidence, or with anger and emphasis. It does not matter which it was; she was thinking of something other than the thing itself. Down comes her book upon our heads. There was a flaw in the centre of it. And I thought of all the women's novels that lie scattered, like small pock-marked apples in an orchard, about the second-hand book shops of London. It was the flaw in the centre that had rotted them. She had altered her values in deference to the opinion of others.

Remarkable here is Woolf's easy command of the move from the 'I' of experience, and authorial activity, to the 'she' of the condition of the writer, condemned to obscurity by neglect and marginalization, to loss of confidence and failure of nerve. I am put in mind of all the volumes entitled 'Feminism and Philosophy' which similarly adorn the shelves of second-hand book shops, and fail to feature on lists of introductions to philosophy.

The charge made by feminists who are not philosophers is just that: feminist philosophers have altered their values in deference to the opinions of their male colleagues and become both compromised and silenced. The groups addressed by Howie are then feminists within philosophy, and feminists outwith philosophy; philosophers with feminist commitments, and philosophers without feminist commitments; and a whole range of writers on philosophy, politics and the logics of exclusion who may not wish to align themselves with either philosophy, or feminism, at all. For there are critiques of notions of being, and of becoming woman, of concepts of the subject and of identity, and of concepts of gender as non-binary, which appear to preclude commitments to feminist theory and critique. This is where Gayatri Spivak's concept of a strategic essentialism might come in: adopting a theoretical stance for the purposes of political solidarity, a limited conception of subject positions may thus be taken to provide a basis for forming alliances, and taking up forms of

---

[7] Gillian Howie, *Between Feminism and Materialism: A Question of Method*, London: Palgrave Macmillan, 2010, p. xi.

political activism.[8] The range of reference in both of Howie's monographs is vast, and what follows must of necessity be selective and schematic in its account of her discussions. It is the fate of philosophical feminists to read both the women and the men, both inside and outside the discipline, whereas those with a less hospitable notion of the scope of the discipline have shorter reading lists. The following discussion falls into two sections: first, reading Adorno taking some instruction from Irigaray; and, second, reading Irigaray taking some instruction from Adorno, and they are designed to bring out the trajectory and distinctive tone of Howie's thinking.

Reading Adorno with Irigaray

As remarked, it is only towards the end of the first book, on Deleuze and Spinoza, that Howie introduces a suggestion, which remains important for her second monograph: an affirmation of Adorno's critique of ideological thinking. Objects of analysis adequate for giving an account of what there is are not available: the concepts are lacking, and these objects present themselves, if at all, only in distorted guise. This is the result both of the malign effects of historically dissociating contexts and, specifically, of processes associated with the commodity fetishism and a division of labour of late capitalism. Social relations appear as natural givens, and relations which should be thought as systems are taken as isolated parts, and subjected to cultural analysis rather than made part of a political critique. The forces and relations of late capitalist production restrict and distort processes of economic and cultural reproduction, imposing constraints on the stances and capacities available for those supposed to do the thinking. Thinking is obstructed and distorted by the noise and complicities generated in everyday transactions, and at best takes flight into relatively protected domains, shielded from the full force of a cultural appropriation. What appears valuable is made to appear so by interests concealed by the mechanics of a series of accommodations to what is.

Thus far, curiously, Adorno and his arch-enemy, Heidegger, find themselves in agreement. For Adorno, in his *Minima Moralia: Reflections on a Damaged Life*,[9]

---

[8]   In an interview, 'Criticism, Feminism and the Institution', with Elizabeth Grosz from 1984, Spivak and Grosz rehearse the theoretical considerations which give rise to this notion of 'strategic essentialism', widely attributed to Spivak, but which Spivak herself has disputed. 'I think we have to choose again strategically, not universal discourse, but essentialist discourse' (p. 11), from Gayatri Chakravorty Spivak, *The Post-Colonial Critic: Interviews, Strategies, Dialogues*, ed. Sarah Harasym, London: Routledge, 1990.

[9]   See T. W. Adorno, *Minima Moralia: Reflections on a Damaged Life*, trans. E. F. N. Jephcott, London: New Left Books, 1974.

regrets the passing of an overview from which what there is might be viewed in its entirety. Heidegger, by contrast, develops a critique of the total mobilization of cultural forces under Nazism, while remaining a supporter of the regime and the party until its demise in 1945. According to Heidegger's analysis, technology is not a question of technicity, politics is not a question of political forces: both must be relocated in terms of a far-reaching return to a founding philosophical question, why is there meaning rather than nothingness; and how has human inhabitation of the world resulted rather in a deepening nihilism rather than in a deepening sense for meaning and being?[10] Adorno has biting critiques of the abstract nature of Heidegger's language and concepts of history and technology in *Jargon of Authenticity* (1964) and *Negative Dialectics* (1966), but they share an analysis of a break in any supposed continuous history, with Adorno attempting to construct a connection back to a time before Nazism, and Heidegger vainly trying to peer into a future, after a completion of nihilism. They are marooned in a between time of history, for which Howie seeks remedy.

In the concluding pages of the *Deleuze and Spinoza* book, Howie writes of the constraints on thinking imposed by the material and social conditions of thought, as obstructing or at least delaying the formation, or stabilization, of conditions for forming judgements about what there is; and for what there is to arrive in stable, identifiable form.[11] When 'all that is solid melts into air', it is all the more difficult to establish an order of priorities and a logical sequence of thought. She continues the thought a few pages later, providing context for the previously given citation:

> A break with idealism from the system of Hegel as well as Deleuze occurs when we pass to the object's preponderance and thereby to a material critique of the nature of the universal. The task of criticising ideology, Adorno maintains, is to judge the subjective and objective moments and their dynamics. This returns to thought its three moments, the thought or judgement, the intentional object and the materiality of the object, as well as returning to substance its content.[12]

The driving force here is, implicitly, the materiality of the object, or of the objectively given material conditions, however they may be socially manufactured, reproduced and re-enforced. The conception of substance is here inflected by the supposition that it acquires content by virtue of its modes of materialization,

---

[10] This analysis begins in *Being and Time* (1927) and is continued in *Of the Event: Contributions to Philosophy* (1936–44), first published in 1989, and in the, 'Letter on Humanism', written in 1946 and published in 1950, and the essay 'The Question of Technology' (1954).

[11] Howie, *Deleuze and Spinoza*, p. 191.

[12] Ibid., p. 205.

which may be rendered incomplete, or partially obscured because of conflict with dominant accounts of the processes in question.

Theory is here construed as a practice conducted not by isolated individuals, but in groups of socially and culturally enabled people, whose modes of access to and ease of functioning within the forces and relations of cultural production are highly differentiated and charged up by inherited privileges and acquired disenfranchisements of all kinds. In this context, to acquire the status of a 'subject' is, like that of citizenship, a long and hazardous process consisting in a combination of good and bad luck, good and bad health, self-formation, and a sometimes distinctly uncomfortable set of conformisms and assimilations. The struggle to emerge out of these conditions is under interrogation in Adorno's most Nietzschean book, *Minima Moralia*. Not least among the lines of conflict between Adorno and Heidegger is a struggle for the inheritance of the thought of Nietzsche. Adorno emphasizes the elements of cultural critique and a multiplication of modes of Germanness (Luther and Hölderlin, Bismarck and Benjamin). For Heidegger, what comes to the fore are the analyses of the devaluation of all values in the decline, marked up by a supposed European tendency to nihilism. The effects of social uprooting and disenfranchisement, as experienced by Adorno, when moving first from Germany to England, and then to the US, are both under analysis and made plain to see in that notion of a damaged life.

There are two surprises in Howie's account. Deleuze and Deleuze's Spinoza are more usually understood to break with the various idealisms of their day, with Deleuze's transcendental empiricism proposed as a radical corrective to the idealistic versions of transcendentalism advanced in the names variously of Kant and of Husserl; and Spinoza is usually understood as the thinker of nature *par excellence*. For Howie, Deleuze is still locked into a mystificatory account of a univocity of being, affirming a metaphysical tradition which Howie reads as antipathetical to the production of a conceptuality adequate for an analysis of a current conjuncture. Deleuze himself does not of course endorse a materialism, rather preferring the term 'vitalism', but his writings have been deployed in support of a new thinking of matter, sometimes phrased as a commitment to a materiality without matter, and he certainly puts in question commitments to nineteenth-century notions of matter, as defined by permanence and continuity. Against this reading, Howie ingeniously argues that for both Spinoza and Deleuze, there is still a role for a creator, or divine originator which guarantees what otherwise may remain in doubt: the unity and thinkability of what there is. While Howie is committed to such a thought of unity and thinkability, hence the importance to her of a reading of Deleuze and of Spinoza, she supposes their arguments and demonstrations to be insufficient. Howie supposes that, for all his attention to new modes of materialization, for Deleuze, as for Spinoza, the univocity of being is a metaphysical commitment, not a materially demonstrable truth. Thus, Howie mobilizes a notion of materialism against Deleuze, and against that form of feminist critique, sometimes called the Australian tendency, which has adopted a Deleuzian version of a double affirmation, as a move to unite ethical and metaphysical imperatives: yes to life, and yes to a necessary role for that affirmation in putting life in some kind of order, such that it might be thought. For Howie, this is yet another version of the Munchhausen attempt to extract oneself from the swamp of indeterminacy by one's own pigtail, as critiqued by Nietzsche.[13]

In the second book, *Between Feminism and Materialism*, the implications of such an appeal to ideology critique and, more specifically, to the resources provided by Adorno's inquiries lead to a proposal to reinvent dialectical materialism. She states in the Acknowledgements, which is headed by the citation from Virginia Woolf, given above:

> I also write to show that something politically relevant follows from the way we think about the relationship between subjects, objects, and their mediation.[14]

This of course is an echo of the remark in Virginia's Woolf's *To the Lighthouse*, in which philosophical research is described, I suggest satirically, in the following terms:

> Whenever she 'thought of his work' she always saw clearly before her a large kitchen table. It was Andrew's doing. She asked him what his father's books were about. 'Subject and object and the nature of reality', Andrew had said, and when she said Heavens, she had no notion what that meant. 'Think of a kitchen table then', he told her, 'when you're not there.'

The alteration is significant with the plurals, subjects and objects, and the substitution of the notion of mediation for that of an objectively given 'nature

---

[13] The reference is to Nietzsche, *Beyond Good and Evil*: 'On the Prejudices of the Philosophers', Section 21 (trans. R. J. Hollingdale, Harmondsworth: Penguin, 1990, p. 51), where he analyses the dangers of deriving philosophical concepts from the terms and concepts made available by the mechanics of the day. It would of course be necessary to interrogate the use made by Nietzsche of the image at the start of that text: 'Supposing truth to be a woman – what? Is the suspicion not well founded that philosophers, when they have been dogmatists, have had little understanding of women'. The marvellous, but clearly false, implication of this remark is that women philosophers either do not understand women or are not dogmatists. Nietzsche's commitment is more likely existential: to the view that women are not philosophers, one which Howie, of course, sees it is necessary to dispute.

[14] Howie, *Between Feminism and Materialism*, p. xi.

of reality'.[15] For Woolf's imagined philosopher, reality is one and indivisible, whereas for Woolf and Howie, Adorno and Marx, it is essentially contested. Howie writes, on the third page of her introduction:

> If the problem before us is the relationship between 'the subject', however construed, and 'the object', however construed, then I suggest we should regroup around the idea of dialectical materialism.[16]

In that book she thus develops an account of a version of dialectical materialism, affirming a role for negation, and for a concept of negativity, which, for example, the analyses of Rosi Braidotti put into dispute in her critique of the version of them proposed and endlessly performed by Slavoj Žižek. The negation opposed by Braidotti, however, is not the negativity affirmed by Howie. For Howie, and indeed for Adorno, negativity provides a potency for disengaging from a dominant, disempowering discursivity, enabling the taking up of a stance elsewhere, in critical awareness of the limitations imposed by any domestication within an existing order. For Adorno, this negativity is to be thought in opposition both to conceptions of positivity, which for him have always been appropriated by the twin forces of the positivisms of nineteenth-century science and liberal democracy, and to actually existing socialism, in which citizen spies on citizen, analyses proposed respectively by Karl Popper, and by the apologists for Stalin.[17] These kinds of positivity, for both Adorno and Howie, form the greatest single barrier to critical emancipatory thinking and action, and, for them, any philosophy worthy of the name must start with a critique of them.

In a later section, in which she analyses concepts of identity, Howie adds some helpful footnotes on Adorno, and on this commitment to dialectics,

---

[15] Howie is by implication sympathetic to the Nietzschean regret, as expressed in *Twilight of the Idols* Section 5: 'Reason, Philosophy' (trans. R. J. Hollingdale, Harmondsworth: Penguin, 1968, p. 38): 'Nothing, in fact, has hitherto had a more direct power of persuasion than the error of being as it was formulated by, for example the Eleatics: for every word, every sentence we utter speaks in its favour! – Even the opponents of the Eleatics were still subject to the seductive influence of their concept of being: Democritus, among others, when he invented his *atom*. "Reason" in language: oh what a deceitful old woman! I fear we are not dispensing with God, while we still believe in grammar.' She would of course question why 'reason' is figured as an old woman, in a pejorative sense. There would, however, be room here for an affirmative reclamation. As Adorno remarks: 'No-one, who writes in German and who knows how much his thoughts are saturated with the German language, should forget Nietzsche's critique of this sphere.' In 'On the question "what is German?"', from *Stichworten*, trans. Henry W. Pickford in *Critical Models: Interventions and Catchwords*, New York: Columbia University Press, 1998, p. 213.

[16] Howie, *Between Feminism and Materialism*, p. 3.

[17] For details of this in relation to sociology, see *The Positivist Dispute in German Sociology* with contributions from Adorno, Albert, Dahrendorf et al., ed. and trans. Glyn Adey and David Frisby, London: Heinemann, 1976.

providing a clue to the trajectory of her thinking. She writes in one footnote of the relation back to the previous book on Deleuze and Spinoza:

> Adorno continues by writing that positivity runs counter to thought and that it takes friendly persuasion by social authority to accustom thought to positivity. This idea was the impetus behind my Deleuze and Spinoza book.[18]

This notion of 'friendly persuasion by social authority' has strong resonances with György Lukács' notion of 'imposed reconciliation', and, for Howie, Lukács is another twentieth-century Marxist thinker important for her notion of developing philosophy as political critique. Relevant here are Lukács' notions of reification, and his analyses of the amphibolies of attributing human agency to commodities, and to the technical relations through which they are produced, while rendering human beings inert functionaries within these processes. These concerns come to attention in this second book, in which Howie explicitly invokes *History and Class Consciousness*, and remarks on Juliet Mitchell's intervention, in 1971 in a proposal for a transformed Marxism, as follows,

> That said, as early as 1971, Juliet Mitchell made an incontrovertible case against traditional Marxism: it would have to be a transformed Marxism. A workable account of women's oppression could not merely attach concepts of oppression to traditional Marxist theories.[19]

In another footnote, to the section on questions of identity, human and metaphysical, she marks a possible future development for a dialectical conceptuality, one which she takes up in her subsequent thinking of the disenablements, disempowerments and disenfranchisements specific to disabilities of various kinds, and attaching specifically to mortal illnesses. This conceptuality may provide resources for a preparation for death in life:

> In this way dialectics could help to make sense of the self as a composite site and host for various life-forms or help find content for claims to intersectionality.[20]

She indicates how Adorno's thinking provides a selective version of a Nietzschean affirmation of life: and she is not going to allow life, and indeed the reading of Nietzsche, to be simply handed over to the vitalists and new materialists.[21] Her

---

[18] Howie, *Between Feminism and Materialism*, pp. 232–3, fn. 51.
[19] Ibid., p. 28.
[20] Ibid., p. 232, fn. 39.
[21] Here attention is due to Nietzsche's observation in *Gay Science*, Book III, Section 109: 'Let us beware saying that death is opposed to life: the living is merely a species of the dead, and a very rare species at that', which might be read as a critique of Hegelian dialectical construals of life and death. He goes

discussion thus develops an account of concept formation informed by, but not continuous with, Adorno's analyses of how conceptions of a subject and an object are not as readily available as grammar might suggest.

Howie affirms a return to some version of a dialectical materialism within a certain history of philosophy, with a three-part account of materialism: reductionist, realist and dialectical. The first is shown to be hampered by a denial of the distinctiveness of conscious activity; and the second disenabled by the strangeness of what is to be encountered as states of affairs in the world. Dialectical materialism has for Howie the virtue of revealing how what there is in the world is in part produced by human activity, which is then denied by groups of human agents, seeking to evade responsibility for making it that way. Gaining access to what there is is part of the problem to be thought through, and Howie makes use of Hannah Arendt's distinctions between labour, work and action to mark up important differences between labouring within a given order, work to produce specific items within that given order and action to transform it. Howie writes:

> First, drawing some inspiration from Arendt, we can designate three human activities: work, labor, and action. ... To labor and to work, to produce independent objects for exchange, are historically and conceptually distinct and, although the distinction is masked, it reappears in Marx's categories of productive and unproductive labor.[22]

Thus, for example, primogeniture, patriarchy and Protestantism can be shown to be human artefacts, within a given order, confirmed in place by human action, not given as part of a natural order of things. However, they may be treated as the result of work and not of action, and thus responsibility for their maintenance and discriminatory effects may be denied.

In conclusion to her section on identity, she reveals that she is also proposing a reinvention of a radical feminism, revived by but not handed over to some of Irigaray's analyses. She invokes a triangulation of aims in theory informed by Marxist critique: a focus on the historical operations and processes of capitalist development; a deployment of a logic of contradiction to capture the conflictual and contestatory nature of relations in the world, as formed by capital; and a mode of political activism, designed to reveal and moderate the exploitative aspects of those two first features. She then remarks:

on to say: 'Let us beware thinking that the world eternally creates newness. There are no eternally enduring substances; matter is just such an error, like the God of the Eleatics.'

[22] Howie, *Between Feminism and Materialism*, p. 27.

It has been my contention in this chapter that if we can see feminism as a similar triangulation, a reinvigorated notion of dialectical materialism will help us to grasp the dynamics of the historical processes of capitalism and this will, in turn, be informed by, and support a radical feminist politics.[23]

The grand surprise, then, is the way in which Howie thus supplements and subverts Adorno's known insensitivity to the claims of gender and race by this complex endorsement of a radical feminism informed by a reception of Marx and by Irigaray's disputes with Lacanian orthodoxy.

Reading Irigaray with Adorno

In *Speculum of the Other Woman*, Irigaray challenges the rewriting of psycho-analysis by Jacques Lacan, which deepens the subordination in Freud's thinking of female desire and identity formation to the requirements of a logic of male desire and identity formation.[24] Irigaray appeals to a critique of a certain Engels in *The Origin of the Family, of Private Property and the State* (1884) of a naturali-zation of family relations in which human labour is laid open to exploitation. The implication is that Freudian and Lacanian theory serves to support the disenfranchisement of women with respect to these processes of appropriation. Those kinds of radical feminist critique which analysed the expropriation of value from women in the processes of human reproduction, and linked this to critiques of systems of enslavement worldwide, are not far away. Calling the child by the father's name and handing down property only to male heirs are merely the surface effects of a system of appropriation and control which finds its truth in the begetting of slave children on enslaved women, as enhance-ments of property rights. It is not just minerals and raw materials which are expropriated world-wide in the name of free trade, but populations sold into servitude and children born into slavery. These wider connections to a process of global exploitation, the middle class status of Freud's patients, and the relative privileges of those suffering from Lacanian and Žižekian angst, unfortunately drop out of view in Irigaray's subsequent work, but for Howie they remain to the forefront.

---

[23] Howie, *Between Feminism and Materialism*, p. 129.
[24] See Luce Irigaray, *Speculum of the Other Woman*, trans. Gillian C. Gill, Ithaca, NY: Cornell University Press, 1985.

Howie reads in an important supplement to Irigaray's well-known observation, used as the title to a section of the pivotal insert in Irigaray's: *Speculum:*

Any theory of the subject is always appropriated to the masculine.[25]

The transposed version of Irigaray's claim focuses on the parallel Marxist claim: 'any theory of the object has always been appropriated to market value'. Howie comments:

> In the previous chapter we saw that the plane of feminist theory already includes models of complex and variegated social, political, and economic mechanisms that create hierarchies and asymmetries as well as the differential distributions of primary goods. With this in mind, I suggest starting with, and then departing from Irigaray's notion of the symbolic: a modified if not entirely new line of flight.[26]

It might here be necessary to modify this appropriation of the language of Deleuze and Guattari, and insert a series of plurals, lines of flight and planes of immanence, as construed in the name of a feminist thinking. Certainly, there are a number of planes in Irigaray's writings, but no direct contact to the Deleuzo–Guattarian notions of planes of immanence and lines of flight. In *Speculum* Irigaray opens her discussion, 'A blind spot in an old dream of symmetry', by citing Freud's famous observation concerning femininity in the *New Introductory Lectures on Psychoanalysis,*

> The problem of femininity preoccupies you, if you are men. For the women, who find themselves among you, the question does not pose itself, since you are yourselves the enigma of which we talk.[27]

In Strachey's translation this is smoothed over, making less obvious the contrast between 'we men', who make up the group, talking amongst themselves, and 'you, the curious interloper'.[28] Reading Woolf makes for a greater sensitivity to the importance of such apparently minor shifts of register. This figure works for Irigaray, in this study, as an emblem for the manner in which from Plato to Hegel, from Socrates to Lacan, and beyond, men have talked and, from time to time, women have been talked about, as partially present, arriving somehow on the edge of the matter in hand, for brief consideration and attention. Here, the

---

[25] Irigaray, *Speculum*, p. 165.
[26] Howie, *Between Feminism and Materialism*, p. 58.
[27] Quoted in Irigaray, *Speculum*, p. 9.
[28] Sigmund Freud, *New Introductory Lectures on Psychoanalysis*, Penguin Freud Library Vol. 2, trans. James Strachey, Harmondsworth: Penguin 1973, p. 146.

power of a dominant hegemonic discourse posits the male as the norm, and the female as the exceptional aberrant case: in Hegel's words, the eternal irony of the tribe.

Summing up her discussion in that first section of her book of the blatant and more subtle expressions of sexism in Freudian theory, Irigaray draws on a Marxist account of value and of exploitation posing the well put question: 'what kind of economic infrastructure demands the conception of women provided by Freud?'[29] She goes on to quote Friedrich Engels' observation from the *Origin of the Family, of Private Property and of the State*:

> The first antagonism based on class which arrives in history coincides with the antagonism between men and women in monogamy and the first class oppression that of the female sex by the male sex.

Thus, Irigaray herself has motivated the thought that a critique of Freudian masculinism can go by way of an elaboration of Marxist theory. Her study of the derogation and exclusion of women in the history of philosophy, and in the practices of psychoanalysis, suggests how these practices replicate and reproduce the practices of an exclusion, transmitted through the two thousand-year history and practice of philosophy. These practices are still in evidence in an inherited conceptuality, in which differential entitlements remain to this day a difficult topic to locate and address. The surface effect is the derogation of women and of femininity in psychoanalytical theory; the source of such derogation is the actual functioning of social and political relations of production and reproduction. Critique of these exclusions forms part of a more general critique of ideology, and it is thus something of a surprise, and indeed disappointment, when Irigaray subsequently renaturalizes a distinction between the female and the male, which Engels and Marx have thus put in focus as precisely historically produced in specific exploitative contexts, and as precisely not an organically, universally natural given. Thus any affirmation of Irigaray's insights requires a careful modulation through the questions posed to Eurocentric, and heterosexist, as well as to masculinist prejudice and distortion.

Howie thus works through her encounter with Irigaray, protected by her Marxist account of the various disenfranchisements of human beings, at various stages of their development, and the resulting exclusions from cultural production. Howie is sensitive to the radical feminist view that differences in relation to roles and tasks in reproduction are so great as to give credence

---

[29] Irigaray, *Speculum*, p. 150.

to this notion, proposed by Irigaray, but not unquestioningly accepted by Howie, that sexual difference is the issue of our epoch. This claim arrives in the opening declaration of Irigaray's *The Ethics of Sexual Difference*, where Irigaray inserts her discussion of an exclusion of women and a repression of femininity within philosophy and psychoanalysis into her reception of Martin Heidegger's account of a series of epochs in the history of metaphysics. The inheritance from Adorno of rational critique, as critical immanentism, thus undergoes a startling transformation in Howie's hands, when she conjoins Adorno's critique to this reception of Irigaray's appropriation of the ontology of the arch-enemy, Heidegger, and of his thought concerning a word for being, which determines the fate of an epoch:

> Each epoch, according to Heidegger, has one matter to think. Only one. Sexual
> difference is probably that of our time. The matter of our time which, once
> thought, will provide '*salut*': rescue, health, welcome.[30]

The citation modifies Heidegger's claim, since the French '*salut*' goes well beyond the ambiguity of Heidegger's own phrase, concerning the need for a rescue, *Rettung*, in a time of need.

Adorno identifies as key the duplicity of Heidegger's commitment to ontology, and to a conception of being, as empty signifier, permitting both persecutory and emancipatory investment. Adorno therefore declines to engage in such ontological speculation, preferring the registers of Kantian antinomy and of a Hegelian speculative proposition, left open-ended by a failure of the moment of its actualization in history. Howie, in her discussion of identity, thus invokes Adorno's arguments in *Negative Dialectics* (1966) to propose a rethinking of identity, in all its registers, through an affirmation of concepts of speculative identity, articulated as three distinct counterpoised registers of being, not as a single unified monolithic set of processes of approaching and withdrawal. In her discussion of 'Identity and Non-identity',[31] Howie emphasizes differences between the 'is' of formal identity (an apple is an apple); the 'is' of a judgement with ontological commitment (here is an apple); and the evaluative 'is': this is a health-giving apple. Matters get lively when this is transposed onto the social and historical sphere. The apparently tautological claim, 'a people is a people', should be contested, since the compositions of populations are historical accidents not historical necessities; the claim 'here is a people' must be approached with caution, since it is likely to have been appropriated by some

---

[30] Irigaray, *Ethics of Sexual Difference*, p. 13.
[31] Howie, *Between Feminism and Materialism*, p. 115.

self-absorbed leader, or racially motivated clique, seeking to promote their own cause, preservation, promotion or *conatus*. The next step is the politically lazy and dangerous claim: this people embodies a world historical destiny, to which other peoples must give way.

Adorno in his *Jargon of Authenticity* does not focus on the oddity of Heidegger's notion of history, which fails to address the specific conditions of historical processes in Germany in the 1930s and 1940s. Adorno there is intent on a more general critique of the insistence on ontology, and its claim to provide a critique of the inadequate commitments of everyday, taken-for-granted identities, while actually still holding on to them. For Heidegger, 'Germany' is some mythical entity, flowing from the mouth of the Danube in the Black Sea back into a heartland constituted by the Black Forest, through which a Roman inheritance is transformed back into an affirmation of autochthonous existing. The loss of foundations [*Bodenlosigkeit*] of metaphysical enquiry is to be restored by an affirmation of an ethnically specific grounding [*Bodenständigkeit*] in a locality. In *Negative Dialectics*, the inadequacies of Heidegger's account of history is in focus, drawing on the critique of Karl Löwith, and Heidegger's history can be shown to be not the critical history of Nietzschean invention, nor yet the antiquarian history in which Nietzsche allows for an insight into how the present differs from the past, and different pasts differ from each other. This is monumental history, claiming supremacy and exclusive access to both past and future, thus blocking all routes to growth, transformation, differentiation.

Howie thus follows Adorno's lead, but she does so under the guidance of Irigaray's insight that in this modern epoch what is to be thought are the differences between human beings, both within and between epochs. Irigaray's mobilization of the Heideggerian word for being may thus be informed, indeed enveloped by Irigaray's attention to a Spinozan counter-discourse, for a critique of the use of a concept of a neutral 'man' in accounts of undifferentiated human rights. In her discussion of Spinoza, Irigaray makes the following remark:

> That 'man' wishes to be both man and woman is not news: the attempt always to return to an enveloping, to an interiority. But, in this willing to master every-thing, the master becomes the slave both of discourse and of a 'mother nature'.[32]

Howie borrows from these movements of a return to Spinoza, and from Irigaray's immanent critique of a conception of a threatening 'mother-nature', while distancing herself from the restrictions consequent on both the Deleuzian and the

---

[32] Irigaray, *Ethics of Sexual Difference*, p. 94.

Irigarayan re-deployments of ontology. Howie proposes a retrieval of ontology, within the terms of the logic of suspicion, as inscribed by Adorno under the rubric 'the jargon of authenticity'; and this retrieval is inflected by her proposed modification of Irigaray's word for being in this new epoch. The word is still 'sexual difference', but now no longer focused on sexuate being, and a givenness of two mutually delimiting essences, but on a sexual difference, conceived as generative of differential, multiple, intersectional identities, in accordance with a Spinozan logic of multiple affective potentialities. These affective potentialities are to be accessed by affirming rather than seeking to transcend the positionality of thinking, as variously and transformatively embodied: between the various births and rebirths, and between imaginary, symbolic and actual deaths, to which human nature, as first and as second nature, is prone.

In her last five years, Howie was exposed with a new urgency to the imperatives of thematizing this, without traducing the impact of the various forms of physical infirmity, and of all the indignities of medicalization to which human beings are susceptible. This gave her a new appreciation for the work of Foucault on the *Birth of the Clinic*, and for Deleuze on the workings of principles of originary difference, and differentiation. The model for philosophical method remains one of subjective thought, material conditions, and the mediations provided by the concept, but there is here also in play a series of supplementations, whereby the masculinism of Adorno's thinking, however pessimistic and piecemeal, is moderated by the insistence on a radical feminism, and on the thinking of Irigaray, on the difference it makes to be female, and the experience of an exclusion which has its origin somewhere other than its immediately expressed forms . Thereby the implicit and not so implicit heteronormativity of Irigaray's views may also be moderated by inserting them into real-world contexts of lived differences, and the failures of abstract identifications to provide people with the means to access an understanding of their own conditions. It becomes possible to analyse how naively accepted or maliciously imposed notions of naturally given gender distinctions ensnare all human beings, but cut down with differential force and differential degrees of damage, with respect to empowerments and disempowerments, to gender dysmorphia and intersex conditions of all kinds. From medical interventions to impose gender distinctiveness on intersexed bodies, to cultural normalizations of who may claim to be respectively female or male, the politics of embodied differences have never been more pressing.

In her study, *Luce Irigaray and the Philosophy of Sexual Difference*, cited by Howie, Alison Stone puts the point with customary incisiveness:

Intersexed bodies refute Irigaray's claims that all individuals are naturally either male or female: 'The whole human kind (*genre humain*) is composed of women and men and it is composed of nothing else.'[33]

Following that up with:

The most compelling conclusion from intersex, then, is that it implies that there is no natural sex difference at all. This challenges Irigaray more radically, not merely affirming more natural sexes than she countenances, but holding her entire belief in natural duality to be misguided.[34]

Howie sets up a context for analysis in which Irigaray's dogmatism may be corrected by appeal to a speculative logic derived from Adorno; and Adorno's limited vision may be corrected by Irigaray's account of such blind spots, and by her attention to the silent force of an accumulating historical derogation of women. Irigaray's analyses may thus be exposed as succumbing to the temptation to take for natural what is only a feature of class interest, dividing up against each other the various sources of resistance to oligarchical appropriations of power and property. For Irigaray's gesture of naturalizing sexual difference, and rendering it a matter of 'to be two', reifies the very structure which she supposes herself to be putting in question. Instead of examining a mediatized and medicalized preoccupation with sexual difference, as a relation between two sexes, and then revealing such preoccupation as providing access to a disruption of such a mechanical, outdated conception, Irigaray oddly re-imposes a dogmatic account of an immobilized bipolarity.

What Howie takes away from her encounter with Irigaray is a sensitivity to how – if, as a condition of entry into discussion, some irreducible aspect, necessary to one's own existence, may have to be disavowed – there will be crucially disenabling effects on any capacity to participate effectively. The arrival of Adorno on the scene suggests that in some way or other all individual human beings are excluded by the criteria of entry into philosophical analysis, simply because the idealized subject addressed by regimes of meaning formation is simply that: idealized. At this point, the master who refused Irigaray her licence to practise, Jacques Lacan, also arrives on the scene, with his analysis of how the master's discourse is no discourse, for the master has nothing to prove, and it is

---

[33] Alison Stone, *Luce Irigaray and the Philosophy of Sexual Difference*, Cambridge: Cambridge University Press, 2006, p. 114. Stone is quoting Luce Irigaray, *I Love to You: Sketch for a Possible Felicity in History*, trans. Alison Martin, London: Routledge, 1996, p. 84.

[34] Stone, *Irigaray*, p. 115.

only the one who aspires to mastery, who engages in the contradictory task of trying to demonstrate mastery, which must always lie out of reach.[35]

Conclusion

In these two monographs, a hybrid theorization is in process, with a crossflow of enquiry and conceptuality between three significant if unlikely sets of resources, within which Howie's thinking is to be situated: the writings of Adorno, the thinking of sexual difference proposed by Luce Irigaray, and a politics of a minoritarian resistance, released from the constraining artifice of anti-Oedipalism, and from the restricting ontology of a body without organs, to which the Deleuzo–Guattarian reception is prone. For even anti-Oedipalism is still by derivation Oedipal, and fails to reveal the full force of the exclusions, whereby those marked as other, and, amongst them, women, can never enter into a symbolic order whether governed by Oedipal or by anti-Oedipal conceptual regimes. In contrast to a notion of 'Maxima Moralia', implying a universal status for moral maxims, Adorno adopts the phrase *Minima Moralia*, moral thinking in a minor key, recognizing the unavailability of universalizing, teleological fulfilments as charted by Kant and Marx, in terms of a categorical imperative and a worldwide revolution. When he encounters non-thematizable horror, he abandons macro-analysis in favour of micro-logical interrogations of cultural formations, constructed through prismatic refraction, in the modes of *Eingriffe* (1963) and *Stichworten* (1969), translated as 'Interventions' and 'Catchwords'. In her second book, Howie begins to adopt and adapt something like that serial, paratactic mode of construction of analysis and argument, whereby the whole may be intimated, even while it remains beyond the compass of an available conceptuality. She risks the unlikely conjunctures of Adorno's negative dialectics with radical feminism, of Irigaray's thinking with an emancipatory programme, affirming hybrid resources for a new conceptuality. For Adorno, and for Howie, philosophy continues in an afterlife scarred by its encounters with various totalizations, and totalitarianisms, and their attendant harms and destructions. Howie accepts the diagnosis of a drastically changed milieu for philosophizing, with rationality, as closed system, no longer a viable model of philosophical

---

[35] See Jacques Lacan, 'The Production of the Four Discourses', *The Other Side of Psychoanalysis*, The Seminars of Jacques Lacan Book XVII (1969–70), trans. Russell Grigg, New York: Norton, 2007.

practice; but she also affirms the non-negotiable inheritance of the ideals of rational enquiry.

References

Adey, Glyn and David Frisby (eds), *The Positivist Dispute in German Sociology*, London: Heinemann, 1976.

Adorno, T. W., *Jargon of Authenticity*, trans. K. Tarnowski and F. Will, London: Routledge, 1973.

Adorno, T. W., *Minima Moralia: Reflections on a Damaged Life*, trans. E. F. N. Jephcott, London: New Left Books, 1974.

Adorno, T. W., *Critical Models: Interventions and Catchwords*, trans. Henry W. Pickford, New York: Columbia University Press, 1998.

Braidotti, Rosie, *Nomadic Theory: The Portable Rosi Braidotti*, New York: Columbia University Press, 2012.

Coole, Diana and Samantha Frost (eds), *New Materialisms: Ontology, Agency, and Politics*, Durham, NC: Duke University Press, 2010.

Freud, Sigmund, *New Introductory Lectures on Psychoanalysis*, Penguin Freud Library Vol. 2, trans. James Strachey, Harmondsworth: Penguin 1973.

Gatens, Moira and Genevieve Lloyd, *Collective Imaginings: Spinoza Past and Present*, London and New York: Routledge, 1999.

Gratton, Peter, *Speculative Realism: Problems and Prospects*, London: Bloomsbury, 2014.

Harman, Graham, *Tool Being: Heidegger and the Metaphysics of Objects*, New York: Open Court, 2002.

Howie, Gillian, *Deleuze and Spinoza: Aura of Expressionism*, London: Palgrave Macmillan, 2002.

Howie, Gillian, *Between Feminism and Materialism: A Question of Method*, London: Palgrave Macmillan, 2010.

Irigaray, Luce, *Speculum of the Other Woman*, trans. Gillian C. Gill, Ithaca, NY: Cornell University Press, 1985.

Irigaray, Luce, *An Ethics of Sexual Difference*, trans. Carolyn Burke, London: Athlone, 1993.

Irigaray, Luce, *I Love to You: Sketch for a Possible Felicity in History*, trans. Alison Martin, London: Routledge, 1996.

Lacan, Jacques, *The Other Side of Psychoanalysis*, The Seminars of Jacques Lacan Book XVII (1969–1970), trans. Russell Grigg, New York: Norton, 2007.

Nietzsche, Friedrich, *Twilight of the Idols*, trans. R. J. Hollingdale, Harmondsworth: Penguin, 1968.

Nietzsche, Friedrich, *Beyond Good and Evil*, trans. R. J. Hollingdale, Harmondsworth: Penguin, 1990.

Patton, Paul, *Deleuze and the Political*, London: Routledge, 1998.

Protevi, John, *Political Physics: Deleuze, Derrida and the Body Politics*, London: Athlone, 2001.

Spivak, Gayatri Chakravorty, *The Post-Colonial Critic: Interviews, Strategies, Dialogues*, ed. Sarah Harasym, London: Routledge, 1990.

Stone, Alison, *Luce Irigaray and the Philosophy of Sexual Difference*, Cambridge: Cambridge University Press 2006.

4

Scholarly Time and Feminist Time: Gillian Howie on Education and Intellectual Inheritance

Victoria Browne

Between 2008 and 2012, Gillian Howie was my PhD supervisor at the University of Liverpool. I arrived at our first supervisory meeting full of ambitious plans for researching my thesis on feminist conceptions of history and time, but was surprised when Gillian's first piece of advice was for me to go and read Kant's *Critique of Pure Reason* from cover to cover. After several weeks I triumphantly returned, only to be sent away again – this time with Hegel's *Phenomenology of Spirit*. I had not expected I would spend the first year of my doctoral research reading dense philosophical texts by long-dead white men: wasn't the whole point of feminism to overturn patriarchal, masculinist traditions of thought, to cultivate new ideas, methods and paradigms? Over time, however, I came to appreciate the time that philosophical enquiry takes, and the value of the historically embedded, temporally layered methodology that Gillian sought to instil as an educator, and consistently demonstrated within her own work. In this chapter, I will examine her critical reflections on education and the transmission of knowledge, drawing particularly upon a series of essays she wrote in the early to mid-2000s that discuss changing institutional practices and the culture of higher education in the UK. She also devoted considerable attention in her work to gendered power relations and feminism in the academy, and the question of how feminism is shared and transmitted between different generations of theorists and practitioners. My aim in the chapter is to bring together these strands of Howie's work, ultimately suggesting that one way of understanding her contributions to feminist philosophy and theory is through the lens of time and temporality: specifically, as interventions into the operations of *scholarly time* and *feminist time*.

Instrumental reason in higher education

The condition of higher education, and in particular its commercialization, was an enduring concern for Howie throughout her academic career. Her enquiries focus especially upon the rise of the 'audit culture' that was initiated in the 1980s and has become 'over-determined with surveillance procedures', including the Research Assessment Exercise (now the Research Excellence Framework), subject benchmarking, institutional reviews and teaching accreditation. Such procedures, she argues, should not be regarded as purely formal apparatuses for measuring and framing the processes of teaching and research in higher education; rather, they work to *determine* the transmission of knowledge, in terms of both method and content.[1] Howie's analysis is closely informed by her critical materialist approach and she refers consistently to the work of Adorno and Horkheimer to reappraise the political role and function of higher education in contemporary society, drawing a parallel between the culture industry and the transformed higher education sector, between mass culture and mass education. For Adorno, culture is not an autonomous, untouchable realm that escapes the reach of the market economy; cultural articles become commodities as the profit motive is transferred onto the cultural form. For Howie, as the quasi-autonomy of the education sector becomes eroded, and as we move from a liberal humanist model (where education is accorded an intrinsic value) to a market-based model (where its value is instrumental), we must ask ourselves 'whether education has, itself, become a commodity through and through'.[2]

It is important to stress that Howie's approach to such changing conditions is not conservative; indeed, she affirms that 'the transformation of the university, itself a site of critical and cultural struggle, is not self-evidently a bad thing'.[3] Her concerns, rather, pertain to the particular *kinds* of changes we are witnessing and participating in, namely, the 'conversion of education from process to product'[4] via the expansion and commercialization of the sector, the growth of commodifying logics, and the audit culture that accompanies them. With typical clarity and insight, she explores not only the fragmentation of the academic community, but further, what is happening to *thinking itself* as a

---

[1] Gillian Howie and Ashley Tauchert, 'Introduction', *Gender, Teaching and Research in Higher Education: Challenges for the 21st Century,* Aldershot: Ashgate, 2002, p. 1.
[2] Gillian Howie, 'Universities in the UK: Drowning by Numbers', *Critical Quarterly* 47.1–2 (2005): 5.
[3] Ibid., p. 2.
[4] Ibid., p. 1.

result of these institutional transformations, and the implications in terms of struggles for social justice. Her argument is that the conversion of teaching and learning into competency-based learning outcomes and assessable skills has significantly altered the education process and 'inculcates a particular cognitive orientation that is not compatible with social justice'. In the audit culture, she contends, there is 'a fraudulent, yet insistent, logical positivism at work', characterized by 'an obsession with collecting evidence to satisfy predetermined performance criteria'.[5] As learning outcomes need to be pre-specified, courses must be delivered according to an easily digestible and simplified template, presented in a straightforward, linear fashion. The world under investigation is therefore broken up into 'bite-sized chunks' of information or knowledge, which become mere steps on the way to a destination known and marked out in advance.

This fragmented, linear approach to learning, Howie argues, encourages the student to 'select and abstract the part from the whole, simplify the objects or ideas under consideration and decontextualise both the objects and the selection process':[6] features which are identified by Adorno and Horkheimer as marking the transition from practical to instrumental reason. To be regarded as reasonable or rational in the current climate of higher education, she explains, a competent, successful learner must first and foremost be able to demonstrate an awareness and capacity for effective means–ends reasoning, and will be 'one who is able to forget or repress anything extraneous and perform according to pre-formed criteria'.[7] The identification of learning with successful performance thus brings the individual's critical thought processes in line with the external demands of a market-driven economy: i.e. the demands of 'isolated, atomistic self-preservation'.[8] This is exacerbated by the emphasis on self-reflection as itself a learning outcome, which means the student will 'approach the self as an object to be known in the same way as he or she is shown how to apprehend all objects of thought'. Accordingly, Howie claims, the concept of the self is simplified, abstracted and atomized, and 'the power of thought perverted into a vehicle for delivering success at the stipulated tasks'.[9] Moreover, as the thinking and learning process becomes transformed in this way, the principle of social justice will necessarily be frustrated. First, this is because 'when

---

[5] Ibid., p. 3.
[6] Ibid., p. 4.
[7] Ibid., p. 5.
[8] Ibid.
[9] Ibid.

thought is unconcerned with an object's contextual embeddedness or sensuous particularity there is little or no chance that difference or diversity will be recognized'. Second, the historical contingency of these conditions of the self, relations and context becomes lost to 'an overpowering sense of necessity – this is the way things are – and freedom is identified with the potential success of individual performance'.[10] Howie relates this to Adorno's warnings that within the culture industry, techniques of mass distribution have introduced an interpretative framework of rigidly conservative categories, so that cultural products eventually come to express easily reproducible and simple formulas that foreclose any kind of critical, questioning engagement and have the effect of reconciling us to the status quo.

Howie's analyses of higher education also consider the rise of instrumental reason at the level of research, as well as teaching and learning, focusing particularly on the introduction of the Research Assessment Exercise, as it was then known, and the impact this has had upon the culture of professional philosophy in the UK. Triggered by the politics of selective funding, she explains, judgements and measures for quality and competency determine who has access to funds and status, and introduce a culture of constant self-assessment, promotion and performativity, which leads to increasingly instrumentalized research, and has 'a menacing psychological impact on those who are managed, or are ciphers for such judgments'.[11] Howie also draws attention to the circularity of the submission process, pointing out that if an academic is considered unlikely to satisfy the criteria, she will not be submitted to the assessment, and therefore will find it more difficult to secure appointments, promotions, research leave and research funding, with the result that the original judgement will seem to be confirmed. It is also circular in that those with status constitute the peer group who decides what is quality research and what is not, and also selects the next generation of gatekeepers and reviewers. In this sense, the audit culture exacerbates discriminatory practices within higher education, and cements the hierarchies and cliques which it claims to be breaking down.

Yet, though it is true that some stand to gain from (and indeed some have actively welcomed) increased audits and managerial processes, whilst others on insecure contracts have fewer options and are in more precarious positions, it is not simply a case of perpetrators versus victims. What we find, Howie claims, is a general level of complicity, because whilst we may have freedom to reason critically

---

[10] Gillian Howie, 'A Reflection of Quality: Instrumental Reason, Quality Audits and the Knowledge Economy', *Critical Quarterly* 44.4 (2002): 145.
[11] Howie, 'Drowning by Numbers', p. 1.

and voice resistance in papers or letters, this is not an option when acting within role. 'When at the pulpit' she writes, 'we must sing from the same management song sheet ... [which] means that academics inhabit an alien position where we have to pretend that we do not know what we know ... and above all, we must never bring to bear our learning on those very norms used to assess us. The effect of this contortion is that we discipline ourselves and alter our teaching; form and content.'[12] Accordingly, she concludes (in a rather Foucauldian vein) there has been a shift in the self-governance of the academic community: a substitution of a former 'collegial, if rather oligarchic, form of self-management', a 'fraternal Athenian contract', by a form of disciplinary self-regulation.[13] However, whilst suggesting here that the Athenian fraternal contract has largely been superseded by a new disciplinary structure, elsewhere Howie attests to the enduring power of the Athenian ideal, as she considers in further detail how gender is entangled in these changing conditions and in the reproduction of discriminatory practices.

Gender and feminism in the academy

In 2002, Howie co-edited a book with Ashley Tauchert on *Gender, Teaching and Research in Higher Education*, in which the authors probe the structural and cultural barriers to women's full participation as autonomous subjects and producers of knowledge, demonstrating how gender is a determining feature in a range of areas, ranging from research grant applications, undergraduate writing style, assessment outcomes, and curriculum design.[14] They discuss how women in higher education 'carry the burden of "gender" manifested as proportionately lower pay for equivalent work, poorer working conditions, greater instability of employment, institutional sexism, overt and covert discrimination, bullying and harrassment'.[15] Howie and Tauchert argue in their own contribution to the collection – 'Institutional Discrimination and the "Cloistered" Academic Ideal' – that whilst women may now be included in the academic community, it is as 'Athenic subjects' who have to '[fake] the masculine position' through feigning an impossible neutrality and disembodiment.[16] In the institutional context,

---

[12] Howie, 'A Reflection of Quality', p. 144.
[13] Ibid.
[14] Gillian Howie and Ashley Tauchert (eds), *Gender, Teaching and Research in Higher Education*, Basingstoke: Ashgate, 2002.
[15] Howie and Tauchert, 'Introduction', p. 3.
[16] Howie and Tauchert, 'Institutional Discrimination and the "Cloistered" Academic Ideal', *Gender, Teaching and Research in Higher Education: Challenges for the 21st Century*, Basingstoke: Ashgate, 2002, p. 61.

they contend, women academics must elide their corporeal specificity, and the institutional body as supposedly androgynous conceals a range of assumptions and discriminations. Academics both male and female all 'learn the language of neutrality', but a woman 'lives the dissonance between what any "neutral" observer claims to be the case and what she "knows" ... a successful female academic must repudiate this knowledge, must appear to have detachment yet be competitive, must agree that the public and the private are distinct spheres of endeavour and disavow her own knowledge that one supports and is the life-blood of the other'.[17] Moreover, as the ideal of quality remains staked on the image of the 'pure Cartesian mind', if women's work is judged to show signs of emotional engagement or to be openly partial, its quality is called into question.[18] This in turn has implications for how explicitly feminist work is received: to be included at all, Howie and Tauchert argue, feminism within the academy has to become de-politicized and mainstreamed, posing as disinterested enquiry, and purged of all traces of political agenda and engaged positioning.[19]

Such claims about the 'de-politicization' or 'de-radicalization' of feminist theory are expressed in several of Howie's other writings, including another co-authored chapter with Tauchert in 2004 that featured in the volume *Third Wave Feminism: A Critical Exploration*.[20] Here, they contend that 'the demise of feminism as a coherent political force occurred simultaneously with the consolidation of academic feminism', which they regard as part of a broader trend of the 'filtering women and feminist theory into public institutions', or 'municipal feminism'.[21] Reflecting on why growing numbers of women in higher education institutions seems to be linked to a 'de-radicalization' of feminist theory, Howie and Tauchert turn first to the influence exerted by the institutional body upon the type of work deemed worthy of production. 'A certain "norm" of academic practice', they write, and an 'image of an "ideal" academic practitioner filter through. The rules of academic practices produce normative principles in the material and questions appropriate to study and research. This is endemic to all forms of academic enquiry, but was exacerbated, specifically in relation to feminist research, by the impact of vicious budget cuts and related casualization dating from the 1980s just as Women's Studies courses had been gaining

---

[17] Ibid.
[18] Ibid., p. 66.
[19] Ibid.
[20] Gillian Howie and Ashley Tauchert, 'Feminist Dissonance: The Logic of Late Feminism', in Gillian Howie, Stacey Gillis and Rebecca Munford (eds), *Third Wave Feminism: A Critical Exploration* (2nd edn), Basingstoke: Palgrave, 2007.
[21] Ibid., p. 52.

ground. The coincidence offers a case for claiming that the type of academic work sustainable under these conditions is of a form and content that could be safely funded and published.'[22]

Another reason Howie and Tauchert identify for the 'de-radicalization' of feminist theory pertains to the nature of feminist theory itself, focusing especially upon 'feminist discourses of difference' which they claim have 'effectively pulled the rug from under feminism as a politics'.[23] The argument they make echoes the abiding concern within many feminist circles that 'once the *diversity* of women is recognised and privileged over *community*, any sort of collective and goal-directed action becomes harder to justify'. The target here, as so often in Howie's writings,[24] is a type of 'autogenetic feminist theory ... directly influenced by psychoanalytic literary theory and poststructuralist linguistics, which in effect amounts to a rejection of realism', and a reduction of feminist theory to a 'mode of reading'.[25] However, I would suggest that such characterizations of poststructuralist and psychoanalytic feminist theories are themselves rather reductive, and detract from Howie and Tauchert's more persuasive point about the value-coding of different research projects within a higher education context increasingly driven by instrumentalized conceptions of 'quality' research. Indeed, one might argue that the dismissal of feminist theories which prioritize issues of language, imagery and representation, rather than 'concrete' social practices and conditions, comes dangerously close to conservative 'common sense' claims about 'impact' and 'proper' objects of academic knowledge.

Nevertheless, this is not to say that feminists should refrain from critically investigating the 'internal' dynamics of feminist theory alongside the 'external' conditions within which it is produced and disseminated. As Diane Elam has argued, it is not enough to 'merely [institute] protective measures against threatening patriarchal intruders' and oppressive conditions. Rather, it is important to also ask 'some serious questions about what is happening *within* feminism'.[26] As indicated, I find Howie's treatment of poststructuralist and psychoanalytic feminist theories as partially responsible for 'de-politicizing' feminism somewhat problematic; however, this is not her only view on what ails

---

[22] Ibid.
[23] Ibid., p. 53.
[24] See, for example, Gillian Howie, 'Materialism, Feminism, and Postmodernism in British Universities', in Julian Wolfreys (ed.), *The Edinburgh Encyclopedia of Literary Criticism and Theory Since 1940*, Edinburgh: Edinburgh University Press, 2002.
[25] Ibid.
[26] Diane Elam, 'Sisters Are Doing it to Themselves', *Generations: Academic Feminists in Dialogue*, ed. Devoney Looser and Ann E. Kaplan, Minneapolis, MN: University of Minnesota Press, 1997, p. 55.

contemporary feminist theory. Her critical dissections of the widespread use of the generational 'wave' metaphor offer many fruitful insights into why feminism can at times feel stuck or undone by itself. From this angle, it is not necessarily that poststructuralist or psychoanalytic feminisms are responsible for robbing feminism of its vitality and political efficacy; it is rather that Western feminist theory in general has been stymied by the way it frames and constructs its own historical development.

Third Wave Feminism: A Critical Exploration, which Howie co-edited with Stacey Gillis and Rebecca Munford, has been a highly significant volume in terms of opening up a critical feminist debate concerning the notion of different 'waves' or 'generations' of feminism. The point of the volume is not simply to oppose the use of such metaphors, but rather to better understand why they have become so common and the political and relational effects of their usage. Howie's own perspective is deeply informed by her materialism which makes her acutely aware of the distinct context in which declarations of a new 'third wave' of feminism have been articulated: a context that is characterized by 'free-market' fiscal policy, new technologies, changing national demographics and economic decline.[27] In this sense, she acknowledges, one's age does affect one's relation to feminism, and the kind of feminism one practises, because 'the experiences that inspired individuals to become feminists in the era of Reagan and Bush are radically different from those of previous generations ... The political context of the third wave is thus "conservative modernisation" – a curious blend of neo-liberal commitments to the market, neo-conservative values, new managerial or bureaucratic processes and innovative information and communication technologies'.[28] As Leslie Heywood and Jennifer Drake similarly claim in the introduction to their edited collection *Third Wave Agenda*, 'transnational capital, downsizing, privatization, and a shift to a service economy have had a drastic impact on the world these generations have inherited'.[29]

Nonetheless, Howie is sharply critical of the ways in which these contextual changes are in fact consistently masked or belied by the generational account of feminist waves, which depicts 'second wave' feminism as somehow the 'mother' of 'third wave' feminism, and hence the relationship between 'second' and 'third wave' feminism in terms of an unconscious psychodynamic of identification

---

[27] Gillian Howie, 'Feminist Histories: Conflict, Coalitions and the Maternal Order', *Studies in the Maternal* 2.1 (2010): 2.

[28] Ibid.

[29] Leslie Heywood and Jennifer Drake, 'Introduction', *Third Wave Agenda: Being Feminist, Doing Feminism*, ed. Leslie Heywood and Jennifer Drake, Minneapolis, MN, London: University of Minnesota Press, 1997, p. 13.

and rejection between mother and daughter. Following Astrid Henry, Howie argues that this can be understood as a form of 'disidentification', when assertions of a new feminist identity by the 'third wave' are achieved through evoking a maternal figure – the 'bad mother' – to rebel and identify *against*.[30] 'The mother–daughter trope', she writes, thus 'accentuates inter-generational conflict between feminists and presents intellectual disagreement in terms of identification with, or breaking away from, symbolic, second-wave mothers. It is a trope within which Oedipal matricide, rather than patricide, renders identity and delivers just entitlement'.[31] From Howie's materialist perspective, 'if there is disappointment between generations, suggested by the wave metaphor, it does not indicate infantile conflict and its post-pubescent resolution, but instead gestures towards structural conditions of unfulfilled promise and aspiration'.[32] But these structural conditions, she argues, are covered over by the 'matraphor', which mystifies the causes and interests underlying conflict, and 'risks collapsing political resistance with resistance understood in a straightforward psychoanalytic sense'.[33] In other words, because of the over-use of the generational wave metaphor, tensions and conflicts between feminists are over-interpreted in terms of unavoidable or naturalized tension between 'overbearing mothers' and 'undutiful daughters'. And this, as Judith Roof outlines, can prevent feminists from exploring the more complex intellectual reasons for conflicts within fields of feminist praxis and discourse, and from examining larger institutional and cultural forces that 'perpetuate sexism, foster rivalry and undervalue women's work'.[34]

Another key concern of Howie's is the teleological structure of the generational wave model, whereby each 'wave' is associated with a particular theoretical perspective, and supersedes the former in a linear development. For instance, the 'first wave' is usually associated with liberal feminism, the 'second wave' with Marxist and radical feminisms, and the 'third wave' with poststructuralist feminism, and this is presented as a progressive journey as feminism supposedly becomes more sophisticated and aware of 'difference'. Howie's argument is that this progressive structure leads us to wrongly presume there is an easy correlation between the historical context and the type of theory that is required,

---

[30] Astrid Henry, *Not My Mother's Sister: Generational Conflict and Third Wave Feminism*, Bloomington and Indianapolis, IN: Indiana University Press, 2004, p. 14.
[31] Howie, 'Feminist Histories', p. 4.
[32] Ibid.
[33] Ibid., p. 3.
[34] Judith Roof, 'Generational Difficulties, or the Fear of a Barren History', in *Generations: Academic Feminists in Dialogue*, ed. Devoney Looser and Ann E. Kaplan, Minneapolis, MN: University of Minnesota Press, 1997, p. 85.

for instance, when 'postmodernism is mapped onto post-fordism as the next historical stage'.[35] For Howie, this is to confuse 'the logic of intellectual debate with the condition of the world'.[36] Moreover, it results in the presentation of 'certain strands of poststructuralism, postmodernism and psychoanalytic theory as the culmination of philosophical argument'.[37] That is, the temporal logic of the generational 'wave' model is doing the work which philosophical argumentation and political logic should be doing. This point is particularly pertinent, given that one of Howie's key aims throughout her work was to contest what she saw as the default hegemony of poststructuralism and psycho-analytic theory within feminist scholarship, and to insist upon the continuing relevance of theoretical perspectives influenced by Marxism that are usually associated with the 'second wave' and thus dismissed as outdated and obsolete. The deployment of generational and wave metaphors, then, is not simply a matter of terminology or 'window-dressing' for Howie. The political stakes of such representations are high.

Towards a different historical temporality

Howie's critical analyses of educational conditions and feminist academic communities are vigorous, and can at times make for rather depressing reading. However, her meticulousness, the depth of her research, and her ability to link the life of the institution with the life of thought and feeling, enable us to gain real insight into why the changes that are happening seem to be occurring so seamlessly, and why we may find ourselves to be participating in processes we know to be damaging to others and ourselves. Moreover, despite recognizing that there is no pure, heroic position from which to stand outside and oppose the situations that one is caught up in, Howie consistently affirms the possibility of resistance, and in several places across her writings she strives to articulate and develop alternatives to those pernicious trends and cultures she dissects and exposes.

One example is an essay she wrote for *Studies in the Maternal* in 2010, entitled 'Feminist Histories: Conflict, Coalitions and the Maternal Order', where she begins to set out alternative ways of imagining, conceptualizing and representing intergenerational relations between feminists. Without such

---

[35] Howie, 'Feminist Histories', p. 4.
[36] Ibid., p. 5.
[37] Ibid.

alternatives, she argues, it is all too likely that women will tend towards rivalry: 'a rivalry at the very least encouraged by the competitive aggression of the market'[38]. In this essay, therefore, Howie proposes a different model of collective organization and historical temporality, drawing primarily upon the work of Luce Irigaray. For Irigaray, if social relations between women are to become more fruitful and mutually enriching, we need to investigate psychic determinations of the social, rather than taking a purely socioeconomic perspective. Indeed at one point, Irigaray claims that feminism 'fails' precisely when it does not explore and unravel the symbolic structures, imaginary identifications, and psychic attachments that underpin social organization.[39] Howie's turn to Irigaray might seem surprising given the antipathy Howie expresses in some of her writings towards psychoanalytically-inflected feminist theory; yet, in her engagements with Irigaray, we see a more open attitude towards the kinds of insights and contributions such theory can make.

Irigaray strongly repudiates the patriarchal model of generational relations, whereby cultural and intellectual heritage is regarded as property that is not shared but rather *endowed* upon the next generation. Moreover, she claims that 'we live in accordance with exclusively male genealogical systems' which make the symbolization and cultivation of 'between-women' cultures, socialities, and genealogies extremely difficult, if not impossible.[40] To conduct themselves in social and cultural life, Irigaray contends, women are forced to mimic patriarchal kinship relationships modelled on patrilineal descent, Oedipal rivalry, and patrimonial debt. Women adopt these patterns and paradigms because 'we lack values of our own'.[41] Yet this does not mean Irigaray gives up on the possibility of what she terms a 'woman-to-woman' sociality. Rather, she incites us to *create* the values, imagery and language that we need. For 'how can we govern the world as women', she asks, 'if we have not defined our identity, the rules governing our genealogical relations, our social, linguistic, cultural order?'[42]

Following in this spirit, Howie claims in her *Studies in the Maternal* essay that 'a conversation between women, a woman-to-woman sociality, requires a new covenant; one that links the past, present and future'.[43] Yet in calling for a 'new covenant', Howie does not join those feminist critics who argue it is necessary

---

[38] Howie, 'Feminist Histories', p. 7.
[39] Luce Irigaray, *je, tu, nous: Toward a Culture of Difference*, trans. Alison Martin, New York and London: Routledge, 1993, pp. 4–5.
[40] Ibid., p. 16.
[41] Luce Irigaray, *Sexes and Genealogies*, trans. Gillian C. Gill, New York: Columbia University Press, 1993, p. 4.
[42] Irigaray, *je, tu, nous*, p. 51.
[43] Howie, 'Feminist Histories', p. 5.

for feminist theory to jettison generational and maternal metaphors altogether. Instead, she aligns herself with Irigaray's view that women's relation to the maternal is essential for developing strong, sustainable, female identities and relations.[44] Echoing Irigaray, Howie contends that 'if claims to know what is the case are actually subtended by an unacknowledged mother, and our historical narrative depends on such claims, then we need to find a place for maternal genealogy within the symbolic'.[45] Indeed, she argues, the 'image of maternity' could actually release feminists from Oedipal generational models, but 'only if we accept that temporal and maternal orders need not coincide'. This claim seems rather cryptic, but the argument is not that the maternal is somehow atemporal. It is rather that the image or thought of the maternal can reorient us towards 'mythical', relational, corporeal time, and away from the linear time of patriarchal models of inheritance. Her aim here is to explore maternity as the 'unhistoric' thought that is the 'condition for woman-to-woman sociality, which is itself a condition for conversation and historical narrative'.[46]

One way of reimagining the maternal relation considered by Howie is Irigaray's proposal in *je tu nous* of a 'maternal order' founded upon the 'placental economy'. Whilst in Lacanian psychoanalytic theory, the relation between mother and child *in utero* is envisaged as a fusion that needs to be interrupted and regulated by the paternal function, Irigaray suggests that if we paid attention to the mediating role played by the placenta, we might think instead that the mother and child are already separate, though conjoined.[47] In turn, this would enable us to cultivate a mode of sociality and exchange that does not depend upon paternal mediation as a necessary 'third term'. Irigaray refers here to the work of biologist Hélène Rouch, who likens pregnancy to a 'natural transplant'. As Rouch explains in an interview with Irigaray, the placenta stops the defence mechanism against the foetus, thereby facilitating 'regulating exchanges' between mother and foetus and modifying the maternal metabolism.[48] Following from this, Irigaray proposes that the 'placental economy' is an 'organized economy' which 'respects the one and the other'.[49] Although Lacan claims that genuine exchange depends upon the

[44] Luce Irigaray, *An Ethics of Sexual Difference*, trans. Carolyn Burke and Gillian C. Gill, Ithaca, NY: Cornell University Press (1993), p. 94.
[45] Howie, 'Feminist Histories', p. 7.
[46] Ibid., p. 5.
[47] Irigaray, *je tu, nous*, p. 38.
[48] Rouch, quoted in ibid., p. 39.
[49] Ibid., p. 41.

intervention of the paternal third term, the placental economy implies that the third term is already there.

On the face of it, the idea of a 'placental economy' may seem like biological essentialism, but it is important to stress that what interests Irigaray is the *figure* of the placenta, and the ways it might be interpreted at the level of culture and theory. 'Culture' she claims, is yet to give 'interpretation to the model of tolerance of the other within and with a self that this relationship manifests',[50] and as such we have failed to recognize or appreciate the 'almost ethical character' of the foetal relation and the placental economy.[51] Yet, as Elizabeth Weed explains it, 'were there a way for a child to symbolize its relations to the mother's body, and were that relationship imagined as always already separate and at the same time life sustaining, the whole fantasy of fusion, triangulation, law, loss, and refusal of loss would be interrupted ...'.[52] For Howie, moreover, Irigaray's 'maternal order' offers a way of reorienting and introducing a different ethical sensibility into intergenerational female relations, potentially initiating new 'pathways through feminisms and between feminists'. That is, by removing the necessity for daughters to become individuated through leaving the maternal relation behind, the notion of a maternal order opens up a promising relational model for feminists to draw upon. 'Side-stepping the truth claims of psychoanalysis', Howie writes, 'the thought of a different mythical origin provokes a different historical narrative and offers a way to hear the past in light of the new without anxious displacement'.[53]

Howie also reflects in this essay on Irigaray's remark that the metaphor of *waves* of feminism directs us 'back to the sea' and thus to the material, corporeal level of experience. For Irigaray, it must be acknowledged, a metaphor or an image always occurs within the context of a phallogocentric system of representation; yet she nevertheless attests to the power of metaphor to ignite the imagination. A metaphor, as Howie explains, establishes 'a relationship and yet leaves something to the imagination. If we conceive mental activity in its relation to bodily activity, then we could say that conceptual metaphors, such as that of the wave, could be motivated by underlying pre-linguistic schemas concerning space, time, and movement'.[54] In this sense, the wave metaphor can return us to embodied, sexed existence: where a subject is a fleshy being in a

[50] Ibid., p. 45.
[51] Ibid., p. 41.
[52] Elizabeth Weed, 'The Question of Reading Irigaray', *Rewriting Difference: Luce Irigaray and 'The Greeks'*, ed. Elena Tzelepis and Athena Athanasiou, Albany, NY: SUNY Press, 2010, p. 27.
[53] Howie, 'Feminist Histories', pp. 8–10.
[54] Ibid., p. 6.

material world, 'already in tune with the otherness of the specific other, oriented towards qualitative difference'. The claim 'I am sexed', Howie writes, 'implies I am not everything'.[55] Acknowledging that we are embodied, sexed subjects who do not spring into existence out of nowhere but from the fleshy existence of another – a mother – can help us to recognize our material interdependence, and to combat the tendency to try and assert full control over situations and to regard ourselves in an atomistic way, or in antagonistic relations with others who came before or coexist with us. From engaging the maternal claim 'I am called to you: a you that is and yet is not present to me', Howie writes, we can find a different relational ethic: a way of supporting becoming, of enabling and listening to others without trying to overdetermine or control them, or imagining we know everything about them. And reciprocally, appreciating the being and subjectivity of mothers can encourage a sense of humility and respect for the other, to whom one is tied but does not own.[56] In the words of Irigaray, it means agreeing to register 'a reality that is foreign to me, that will never be mine but which determines me and with which I am in relation ... Such a change in the nature of the constitution of subjectivity and the recognition of the other as another, irreducible to me ... could be the opening up of a period of history yet to come'.[57]

In sum, although Howie is all too aware that maternal, generational and wave metaphors have been conscripted in the service of linear, teleological models of feminist history, she nevertheless proposes that they can also refer us to a 'mythical' maternal time that offers 'a new hermeneutic of difference and a more developed sensibility; an image of the recognition by the mother of the other and her sensed responsibility towards the other; where the self and the other are continually renegotiated ... From this we can build a "we": a being-with'.[58] Howie does acknowledge the danger of idealizing the maternal and turning to the mythic: 'Any association of the feminine with maternity or generation may strike some as free play within the masculine symbolic. We risk assimilating all forms of difference to an idealised version of the feminine.'[59] Moreover, even in her most Irigarayan of moments, she is keen not to betray her materialist commitments and abstract from the historical conditions under which historical narratives are constructed and metaphors

---

[55] Ibid., p. 8.
[56] Ibid.
[57] Luce Irigaray, *I Love to You: Sketch for a Felicity Within History*, trans. Alison Martin, New York: Routledge, 1996, pp. 56–7.
[58] Howie, 'Feminist Histories', p. 9.
[59] Ibid., p. 8.

deployed. Yet, what she is ultimately arguing for is a transformation of the linear, singular understandings of time and history that have so often been tied to historical materialism more traditionally conceived.[60] Her concluding proposal is that we rethink the history of feminist theory according to a new understanding of historical temporality, which would operate according to both a diachronic and a synchronic mode. The synchronic or conjunctive mode, she argues, can take into account the particular social, political and intellectual contexts within which theory is formulated, but through interlacing this with a diachronic analysis, we would also be able to grasp the differing ways in which the reception of the theory might reformulate and reinterpret the key problems in new or transformed contexts. Further, she claims, there should be enough conceptual capacity to consider the trans-historical and inter-contextual conversations that occur around certain recurring issues and questions – such as the 'problem of subjection' – thus initiating conversations back and forth between feminist theorists of earlier and more recent times.[61]

To enable this kind of temporal analytic, Howie suggests that as well as fusing or weaving together diachronic and synchronic perspectives, it might also be productive to consider the *un*historical perspective, and explore how historical time intersects with mythic time, bodily time or planetary time.[62] So whilst Adorno and others provided Howie with the critical tools she needed to unpick and diagnose historical injustice and material oppression, Irigaray allows her a utopic moment, where she affirms the power of imagination and the possibility of thinking and acting differently – of building alternative relational models that have a different logic and temporality:

> From within the mythic time of the maternal order which ... is not bound by linear temporality, is generated a discursive and ethical orientation that helps us articulate the historic ebbs and flows of the women's movement. The recognition of otherness, of alterity, whilst not the supreme goal of feminism, may well be the condition of historical narrative and woman-to-woman sociality, which is itself the condition for political intervention. It means being able to attend to the call of others and enter into conversation without the psychoanalytic psychodrama of anxious displacement, sororal conflict and repression.[63]

[60] In this, she might have found common cause in the work of Walter Benjamin.
[61] Ibid., p. 10.
[62] Ibid.
[63] Ibid.

Scholarly time and feminist time

To conclude now, I would like to reflect further on time and temporality as a way of drawing together Howie's contributions to the critical theory of education, and to feminist theory and historiography. In her analyses of the ways in which commercialization, commodification and the accompanying audit culture are changing the life of the university, Howie notes that one of the key transformations is the increasingly frenetic speed of academic activity, resulting in the experience of time-shortage, 'hurry-sickness' and burn-out.[64] This concern chimes with a growing number of articles and blogs devoted to the acceleration and compression of time within the 'counting cultures' of contemporary academia that lead to 'intense, insidious forms of institutional shaming, subject-making, and self-surveillance'.[65] As Judith Walker writes, academic capitalism is essentially 'premised on faculty and students both justifying their use of time and seeking to outsmart it'.[66]

In the midst of such a temporal regime, Howie's work stands out for its epistemology and ethic of *taking time*: it exemplifies the patience required for rigorous critical scholarship, even when faced with the demands of the quantifying audit culture taking hold within academic institutions, and academic trends that implore us to embrace novelty and leave unfashionable traditions of thought behind. For instance, though Howie acknowledges in *Between Feminism and Materialism* that there may be something 'archaic and even tedious' about Marx's labour theory of value, she nevertheless devotes the first chapter of the book to carefully re-articulating the theory and demonstrating its continuing relevance for feminism.[67] Moreover, her insistence upon taking time over theoretical analysis is indispensible when it comes to representing and engaging with feminist traditions in all their variations and multiplicity. Whilst it may be quicker and easier for us to rely upon and reproduce shorthand 'common sense' narratives of feminist history and politics, these can be highly distortive and exclusive – relegating certain forms of feminism to the margins or dustbins of history, whilst other forms come to represent quintessential or 'hegemonic feminism' in the

---

[64] Howie, 'Drowning by Numbers', p. 8.
[65] Alison Mountz et al., 'For Slow Scholarship: A Feminist Politics of Resistance through Collective Action in the Neoliberal University', *ACME, International E-journal for Critical Geographies*, 14.4 (2015): 7.
[66] Quoted in ibid., p. 6.
[67] Gillian Howie, *Between Feminism and Materialism: A Question of Method*, New York and Basingstoke: Palgrave Macmillan, 2010, p. 12.

mainstream feminist imagination.[68] And this has serious political and relational effects, leading to what Shumei Shih refers to as an 'asymmetry of ignorance', whereby 'the Other woman is frozen in absolute difference (too difficult and too *time-consuming* to understand fully)'.[69] Taking time to question received wisdoms, explore unfamiliar terrain, and listen to the voices of others, is thus essential to forging a mode of feminist practice and scholarship that does not simply replicate the usual hierarchies and structures of privilege.

It is important to stress, however, that a commitment to taking time and care, and hence to transforming academic time cultures, need not constitute a straightforward (and some might say nostalgic) endorsement of 'slow time' as an antidote to the 'fast time' of high capitalism and contemporary academic production. Nor need it correspond to a simple demand for *more* time for ourselves as individual academics, as this does nothing to address the unequal *distribution* of time within the university. This is a particularly important point from a feminist perspective, given the ways in which the time of women has so often been exclusively directed towards the care of others and the service of production: a relational form of time distinguished from the masculine time of 'true creativity, innovation, and invention'.[70] As Angela McRobbie has recently reflected (reminiscent of Howie), some academics have always had more time for 'quality' work because others have had less, with the 'new managerialism' and audit culture simply reproducing old hierarchies and gendered divisions of time and labour. The ideal timeline and career track in the academy, she writes, still seem to be 'tailored around the image of the brilliant young man untrammelled by any of the fine details of domestic life'.[71] Alison Mountz and colleagues similarly argue that the managerial regimes and audit cultures of the contemporary university 'remake and reinforce academic subjectivities to serve institutional productivity in a way that entrenches the hierarchical valuation' of 'feminine' and 'masculine' time.[72]

In the conclusion to *Between Feminism and Materialism*, Howie clearly and explicitly links feminist politics to the politics of time, writing that 'a

---

[68] See Clare Hemmings, *Why Stories Matter: The Political Grammar of Feminist Theory*, Durham, NC and London: Duke University Press, 2011, and Chela Sandoval, *Methodology of the Oppressed*, Minneapolis, MN: University of Minnesota Press, 2000.

[69] Shih, Shumei. 'Towards an Ethics of Transnational Encounter, or "When" Does a "Chinese" Woman Become a "Feminist"?', *Differences: A Journal of Feminist Cultural Studies* 13.2 (2002): 94.

[70] Mountz et al., 'For Slow Scholarship', p. 15.

[71] Angela McRobbie, 'Women's Working Lives in the "New" University', *Open Democracy*. https://www.opendemocracy.net/5050/angela-mcrobbie/womens-working-lives-in-new-university [accessed 10 August 2015].

[72] Ibid.

complex pattern of diverse priorities, rhythms, and time scales expresses ... the differential distribution of roles and expenditure associated with those roles'.[73] Inspired by Virginia Woolf as a thinker who 'brings to our attention the differential distribution of time', Howie quotes from *A Room of One's Own*: 'We have borne and bred and washed and taught, perhaps to the age of six or seven years, the one thousand six hundred and twenty-three million human beings who are, according to statistics, at present in existence, and that, allowing that some had help, takes time'.[74] Nevertheless, despite the tentacular reaches of patriarchy in all its forms, Howie consistently affirms that feminists must never lose sight of the possibility of thinking and living differently, enacting a different economy of time, labour and care. She returns us again and again to what she sees as the very point of feminism: its 'will and capacity to change the world'.[75] Indeed, with Tauchert she claims that the very 'antinomy' or 'dissonance' women academics often experience between their embodied knowledges on the one hand, and the 'cloistered academic ideal' on the other, accords them a critical vantage point from which to build cultures and practices of resistance. Referring yet again to Woolf and her exclusions from fraternal academic communities in the 1920s – 'I thought how unpleasant it is to be locked out; and I thought how it is worse perhaps to be locked in' – Howie and Tauchert write that the 'almost inevitable failure to meet the normative ideal of academic practice is a positive failure, since it gives an insight into our own position, and the latent processes which are the conditions for the educational experience'. In the process of 'opening the portals of power and privilege to scrutiny ... new sites of resistance' are developed, both in terms of institutional practice and theoretical engagement.[76]

Thus in several of her writings, including those explored in this chapter, Howie began to articulate alternative modalities of scholarly time and feminist time, and accordingly has made valuable contributions to these areas of research and practice. In the *Studies in the Maternal* article discussed above, for example, Howie is adamant that linear chronologies and market-driven time economies are not the only forms of time that exist, asserting the value of stepping 'outside' linear, progressive, productive time and dwelling in other modes of temporal being. And as she writes at the very end of her chapter on patriarchy in *Between Feminism and Materialism*:

---

[73] Howie, *Between Feminism and Materialism*, p. 201.
[74] Ibid.
[75] Howie and Tauchert, 'Introduction', p. 5.
[76] Howie and Tauchert, 'Institutional Discrimination', p. 70.

Nothing about the account of an unjust and oppressive distribution of roles, duties and responsibilities detracts from an ethical orientation that also, and at the same time, runs through many household relationships, or those of kinship, friendship, or (sexual) loving relationships. While instrumental goal-oriented competition threatens to overwhelm us and the throw-away "just-in-time" pop culture makes us feel, if not actually be, replaceable, there remains a form of exchange based on gift. If social relations can be formed and enervated through the gift of part of oneself to another, we can see how the gift of one's labor and time – as a part of oneself – provides embodied counter-hegemonic experiences.[77]

The implication of this passage is that such counter-hegemonic experiences give us something to build upon, and as such can offer hope for a different kind of temporal existence, in which time is not simply a commodified resource that must be expended as efficiently as possible, with a quantifiable outcome or 'return'. To postulate an improved future existence, unharnessed from present conditions, does not require feminists to outline a detailed 'blueprint' for a new mode of organizing time, labour and care – a perfect feminist future as opposed to the patriarchal past and present. This would be to deny the inevitability of uncertainty, and imply that feminism is a linear, predetermined project whereby one generation works out all the solutions, and then passes these on to obedient future generations until the original target is met. As Howie argues in her higher education essays, when knowledge or intellectual inheritance is transmitted in such a linear fashion, the aims of social justice are in fact frustrated, because the thought of historical contingency – that things can be otherwise – becomes 'lost to an overpowering sense of necessity – this is the way things are' or will be.[78] Hope for a better future, then, need not be hope for a particular future that is known and marked out in advance. Rather, we can draw here on what Howie describes in her lecture 'How to Think about Death: Living with Dying' as 'open-ended hope': an idea of hope as 'a creative process, a sense of journey, becoming or transformation', without a specific object or outcome in mind.[79] She is referring here specifically to the kind of hope that can be cultivated in the event of living with life-limiting illness, but her notion of open-ended hope arguably applies equally well to a political project such as feminism, which depends upon the idea that the future can be positively different to the present,

---

[77] Howie, *Between Feminism and Materialism*, p. 200.
[78] Howie, 'A Reflection of Quality', p. 145.
[79] Gillian Howie, 'How to Think about Death: Living with Dying', Ch. 6 of the present volume, p. 140.

yet cannot know in advance what a 'feminist future' would be like, or when and how it would come into being. Accordingly, and as Howie demonstrated so inspiringly, whilst investing our hope open-endedly in feminism as a world-changing project, we also need to concentrate on our heres-and-nows, bringing what change we can in the time we have. In this sense, feminists are tasked with thinking big and small at the same time, operating in the horizon of both short-term and long-term transformation, 'in more than one time zone' [80] at once.

References

Elam, Diane, 'Sisters Are Doing it to Themselves', in *Generations: Academic Feminists in Dialogue*, ed. Devoney Looser and Ann E. Kaplan, Minneapolis, MN: University of Minnesota Press, 1997, pp. 55–68.

Hemmings, Clare, *Why Stories Matter: The Political Grammar of Feminist Theory*, Durham, NC and London: Duke University Press, 2011.

Henry, Astrid, *Not My Mother's Sister: Generational Conflict and Third Wave Feminism*, Bloomington and Indianapolis, IN: Indiana University Press, 2004.

Hesford, Victoria, 'Securing a Future: Feminist Futures in a Time of War', *Feminist Time Against Nation Time: Gender, Politics and the Nation-State in an Age of Permanent War*, ed. Victoria Hesford and Lisa Diedrich, Lanham, MD: Lexington Books, 2008.

Heywood, Leslie and Jennifer Drake, 'Introduction', *Third Wave Agenda: Being Feminist, Doing Feminism*, ed. Heywood and Drake, Minneapolis, MN: University of Minnesota Press, 1997.

Howie, Gillian, 'A Reflection of Quality: Instrumental Reason, Quality Audits and the Knowledge Economy', *Critical Quarterly* 44.4 (2002): 44–7.

Howie, Gillian, 'Materialism, Feminism, and Postmodernism in British Universities', *The Edinburgh Encyclopedia of Literary Criticism and Theory Since 1940*, ed. Julian Wolfreys, Edinburgh, Edinburgh University Press, 2002.

Howie, Gillian, 'Universities in the UK: Drowning by Numbers', *Critical Quarterly* 47.1–2 (2005): 1–10.

Howie, Gillian, *Between Feminism and Materialism: A Question of Method*, New York and Basingstoke: Palgrave Macmillan, 2010.

Howie, Gillian, 'Feminist Histories: Conflict, Coalitions and the Maternal Order', *Studies in the Maternal* 2.1 (2010): 1–12.

Howie, Gillian, 'How to Think about Death: Living with Dying', *On the Feminist*

---

[80] Victoria Hesford, 'Securing a Future: Feminist Futures in a Time of War', *Feminist Time Against Nation Time: Gender, Politics and the Nation-State in an Age of Permanent War*, ed. Victoria Hesford and Lisa Diedrich, Lanham, MD and Plymouth: Lexington Books, 2008, p. 180.

Philosophy of Gillian Howie: Materialism and Mortality, ed. Victoria Browne and Daniel Whistler, London: Bloomsbury, 2016, pp. 131–44.

Howie, Gillian and Ashley Tauchert, 'Institutional Discrimination and the "Cloistered" Academic Ideal', *Gender, Teaching and Research in Higher Education: Challenges for the 21st Century*, ed. Gillian Howie and Ashley Tauchert, Basingstoke: Ashgate, 2002, pp. 59–72.

Howie, Gillian and Ashley Tauchert, 'Introduction', *Gender, Teaching and Research in Higher Education: Challenges for the 21st Century*, ed. Gillian Howie and Ashley Tauchert, Basingstoke: Ashgate, 2002, pp. 1–6.

Howie, Gillian and Ashley Tauchert, 'Feminist Dissonance: The Logic of Late Feminism', *Third Wave Feminism: A Critical Exploration* (2nd edn), ed. Gillian Howie, Stacey Gillis and Rebecca Munford, New York and Basingstoke: Palgrave Macmillan, 2007, pp. 37–49.

Irigaray, Luce, *An Ethics of Sexual Difference*, trans. Carolyn Burke and Gillian C. Gill, Ithaca, NY: Cornell University Press, 1993.

Irigaray, Luce, *je, tu, nous: Toward a Culture of Difference*, trans. Alison Martin, New York: Routledge, 1993.

Irigaray, Luce, *Sexes and Genealogies*, trans. Gillian C. Gill, New York: Columbia University Press, 1993.

Irigaray, Luce, *I Love to You: Sketch for a Felicity Within History*, trans. Alison Martin, New York: Routledge, 1996.

McRobbie, Angela, 'Women's Working Lives in the "New" University', *Open Democracy*. https://www.opendemocracy.net/5050/angela-mcrobbie/womens-working-lives-in-new-university [accessed 10 August 2015].

Mountz, Alison et al., 'For Slow Scholarship: A Feminist Politics of Resistance through Collective Action in the Neoliberal University', *ACME, International E-journal for Critical Geographies* 14.4 (2015).

Roof, Judith, 'Generational Difficulties, or the Fear of a Barren History', *Generations: Academic Feminists in Dialogue*, ed. Devoney Looser and Ann E. Kaplan, Minneapolis. MN: University of Minnesota Press, 1997, pp. 69–87.

Sandoval, Chela, *Methodology of the Oppressed*, Minneapolis MN: University of Minnesota Press, 2000.

Shih, Shumei, 'Towards an Ethics of Transnational Encounter, or "When" Does a "Chinese" Woman Become a "Feminist"?', *Differences: A Journal of Feminist Cultural Studies* 13.2 (2002): 90–126.

Weed, Elizabeth, 'The Question of Reading Irigaray', *Rewriting Difference: Luce Irigaray and 'The Greeks'*, ed. Elena Tzelepis and Athena Athanasiou, Albany, NY: SUNY Press, 2010, pp. 15–33.

5

The Cloistered Imaginary

Daniel Whistler

Fancy understanding all those books! If one merely sits among them, whether one reads them or not, one becomes at once quite another being.

G. E. Lessing[1]

Shakespeare's *Love's Labours Lost* opens with the announcement, 'Navarre shall be the wonder of the world. / Our court shall be a little academe, / Still and contemplative in living art.'[2] The King thereby founds an ill-fated university that is no sooner instituted than subject to attack, and both the university itself and the assault upon it by female bodies (and male desires) are made possible by the institutional 'strict observances' and 'barren tasks' that entry into academia requires.[3] The scholar's body is 'mortified': 'The mind shall banquet, though the body pine.'[4] As Le Doeuff puts it in her discussion of the passage, the would-be academics here revel in 'the pleasure of ascesis'.[5] And in pursuit of an exact determination of these initiatory practices, this chapter will consider the spaces, times and bodies of the university that make it possible to, in Lessing's words quoted above, 'become at once quite another being' through scholarship – to 'wall oneself in [in] spiritual pregnancy', as Nietzsche puts it.[6] That is, I read Gillian Howie's essays on higher education through the lens of her ambivalent relation to the traditional 'cloistered ideal' of the university so as to identify

---

[1] G. E. Lessing, *The Young Scholar*, in *The Dramatic Works of G. E. Lessing*, Vol. 2, ed. and trans. Ernest Bell, London: Bell and Sons, 1878, II.iv, p. 58.

[2] William Shakespeare, *Love's Labours Lost*, in *The Oxford Shakespeare*, ed. Stanley Wells et al., Oxford: Clarendon Press, 1986, I.i 9–11.

[3] Ibid., I.i 36, 47.

[4] Ibid., I.i 28, 25.

[5] Michèle Le Doeuff, *The Philosophical Imaginary*, trans. Colin Gordon, London: Continuum, 2004, p. 13.

[6] Friedrich Nietzsche, *Ecce Homo*, in *Basic Writings*, ed. and trans. Walter Kaufmann, New York: Random House, 2001, p. 698.

practices of abstraction, alienation and disembodiment, i.e. 'the working conditions of philosophical thinking in general'.[7] I look to literature in particular (a strategy I justify in the concluding coda to the essay) as a privileged site for the representation of becoming-cloistered, juxtaposing a sustained exposition of Thomas Mann's *The Magic Mountain*, as well as passing references to other literary works, with Howie's critical essays.

A space for thinking

'What has happened to higher education in the United Kingdom?'[8], Howie asks, and in her essays on pedagogy and the university, she notes with some apprehension (often writing in collaboration with Ashley Tauchert) the changes that have overrun UK higher education over the last twenty-five years. In particular, she draws attention to 'the birth of "the education industry"'[9] out of the 1988 and 1992 Education Acts, as well as the incorporation of the Bologna Accords after 1999. This new-born 'knowledge-economy' with its managerialism was consolidated, on Howie's account, under New Labour's drive towards 'a system geared towards mass provision',[10] and, if it were not for her untimely death, it is certain that she would also have voiced in print her growing distrust of many of the post-Browne modifications of the sector which have, by all accounts, merely accelerated what Howie previously described as 'the transformation of learning from a process into a product'.[11]

At any rate, her published opinions on all these changes are blunt: 'The future of higher education looks bleak.'[12] She points to the 'deft commercialisation of the sector',[13] the transformation of learning into 'an article of commerce',[14] and worries especially over the 'external and internal quality auditing procedures'

[7]   Michèle Le Doeuff, *Hipparchia's Choice: An Essay Concerning Women, Philosophy, etc.*, 2nd edn, trans. Trista Selous, New York: Columbia University Press, 2007, p. 317.
[8]   Gillian Howie, 'Universities in the UK: Drowning by Numbers', *Critical Quarterly* 47.1–2 (2005): 1.
[9]   Gillian Howie, 'Teaching Philosophy in Context: Or Knowledge Does Not Keep Any Better Than Fish', in Andrea Kenkmann (ed.), *Teaching Philosophy*, London: Continuum, 2009, p. 8.
[10] Ibid., p. 7.
[11] Ibid. The Browne Review or Independent Review of Higher Education Funding and Student Finance (2010) proposed radical changings to funding structures in UK universities, including the removal of the fees-cap for undergraduates.
[12] Gillian Howie, 'A Reflection of Quality: Instrumental Reason, Quality Audits and the Knowledge Economy', *Critical Quarterly* 44.4 (2002): 146.
[13] Howie, 'Drowning by Numbers', p. 1.
[14] Gillian Howie, 'From Process to Product: Quality Audits and Instrumental Reason', in D. Preston (ed.), *Contemporary Issues in Education*, New York: Rodopi, 2004, p. 22.

exemplified by the Research Excellence Framework, internal reviews of outputs and administrative structures, as well as a culture of learning outcomes and modularization in teaching (in which concepts are taught as 'delectable item[s] in an array of supermarket specials'[15]). These features, she continues, are symptomatic of the conversion of 'critical reason into instrumental reason, imagination into passive pedantry, practical-virtue into skills accumulation and credit transformation; in effect learning into mental dryrot'.[16]

*

And yet Howie's critique of the managerial university is not free from ambiguity; in fact, I will argue in what follows that ambivalence and ambiguity are major conceptual devices within Howie's oeuvre: the tendency of theory to simplify is continually rejected in favour of lived (and lifelike) complexity. Hence, the relation between the university before and after the reforms listed above is understood in terms of both a radical break and a fundamental continuity:

(a) *The break model*: On the one hand, the above picture of present-day higher education seems to imply a break with the liberal-humanist pedagogy of traditional university teaching. Howie speaks in this way of a kind of 'change' that has had and will have 'unimaginable implications'.[17] The fullest suggestion that there has recently been a radical and problematic break in the history of the university comes in the introduction to her co-edited volume, *Gender, Teaching and Research in Higher Education*:

> We suggest that the enlightened ideal of education has been transformed into the modern ideal of skills provision … This is not to eulogise the erstwhile ideal but merely to note that at least the concept of educating, teaching the future citizen the enlightened ideals of autonomous critical thinking and social obligation, held a moment of political resistance or utopia.[18]

Out of this loss, however minimal, is born a pervasive, if often implicit, cynicism in Howie's work on the contemporary academy. To take the

---

[15] Ibid., pp. 23–4.

[16] Howie, 'From Process to Product', p. 22; see also Howie, 'Drowning by Numbers', p. 5.

[17] Gillian Howie and Ashley Tauchert, 'Introduction', to Gillian Howie and Ashley Tauchert (eds), *Gender, Teaching and Research in Higher Education: Challenges for the 21st Century*, Aldershot: Ashgate, 2002, p. 2.

[18] Ibid., p. 1; see also Howie, 'A Reflection of Quality', p. 141.

above example, the managerial structures of research and teaching since
the early 1990s, she argues, are making redundant the very disciplinary
activity that they are meant to manage: it becomes increasingly difficult
to undertake philosophy, understood as an activity of 'autonomous
critical thinking', in the face of the quantification of research and teaching
impacts. Colleagues are more likely to assess the REF-potential of each
other's work than do philosophy together; as Howie laments, 'It seems
laughable that we may ever have had the experience of a living, courteous,
analytical community of collegial discourse.'[19]

(b) *The continuity model*: On the other hand, however, Howie is equally
insistent that emphasis on the above break between traditional and
contemporary higher education has a tendency to downplay the
long-standing, discriminatory power structures that continue to be
reproduced in the academy. Hence, in collaboration with Tauchert, Howie
asserts, 'The modern university is the result of a process of accretion'
grounded in 'an underlying continuity' from the Renaissance through to
the contemporary university.[20] Howie and Tauchert continue at length,

> The modern university is the university of liberal modernity, and its
> academic work is governed by various Enlightenment, humanistic beliefs.
> The project of Enlightenment then bequeathed us the concept of a
> subject who could (and should) use his or her understanding, be neutral
> to context, and who would be able to come to know and categorise the
> empirical world. The ideal of an academic, unhampered by his or her
> embodied state, is the organising motif that has remained through the
> process of accretion. We have adopted the concept of 'cloister' to suggest
> an historical patrilineage between the humanism of the Renaissance, the
> Enlightenment and Modernity: between the medieval, the liberal, and the
> modern university; the religious past and the secular present.[21]

It is this image of the cloister as an ideal for higher education that I
want to examine in what follows. It will become clear that it plays at
least a threefold role in Howie's work: as a description of the persistent
'organizing motif' for academia from the Renaissance to the present; as
a normative ideal that has been lost in recent managerial reorganizations

---

[19] Howie, 'Teaching Philosophy in Context', p. 17.
[20] Gillian Howie and Ashley Tauchert, 'Institutional Discrimination and the "Cloistered" Academic
Ideal', in Gillian Howie and Ashley Tauchert (eds), *Gender, Teaching and Research in Higher
Education: Challenges for the 21st Century*, Aldershot: Ashgate, 2002, p. 59.
[21] Ibid., p. 60.

of the higher education sector;[22] and finally as the expression of a problematic ethos that both fosters and disguises gender discrimination.

The above quotation conceives the cloistered university as a space for the production of subjects who possess understanding and classificatory skills, who are indifferent to context and who live 'unhampered by his or her embodied state', 'a space in which we can think about thought itself and develop an aptitude for critical reflection'.[23] It is modelled as 'a pure and clear atmosphere of thought'[24] – an autonomous place walled off from the rest of the world that is supposed to generate 'an intellectual elite who … stand aside from pedestrian occupations'.[25] Academics should 'be cut off from everything else and yet persist in living', in Newman's words.[26]

This idea of the university as 'cloister' is long-standing, but was popularized by Clark Kerr, in his paraphrase of Newman's position,[27] and Howie herself explicitly mentions in this context Humboldt's 1809 *Über die Innere und Äussere Organisation der höheren wissenschaftlichen Anstalten in Berlin*,[28] although she also speaks more generally of its roots in the Renaissance and early modern periods. Humboldt had 'cloistered' the university as protection against state interference, whereas for Newman it was a defence against the 'becoming-useful' of knowledge.[29] In fact, Newman very literally pursues the image of the cloister as structuring the 'material dwelling-place and appearance' of the university, reporting to this end the words of an anonymous travelling companion from his youth:

> [My companion] was evidently fond of urging … the material pomp and circumstance which should environ a great seat of learning. He considered it was worth the consideration of the government, whether Oxford should not stand in a domain of its own. An ample range, say four miles in diameter, should be turned into wood and meadow, and the University should be approached on all sides by a magnificent park, with fine trees in groups and groves and avenues, and with glimpses and views of the fair city, as the traveller drew near it.

---

[22] Howie is explicit on this point in 'Teaching Philosophy in Context', p. 13.

[23] Ibid., p. 13.

[24] J. H. Newman, 'The Idea of a University'. http://www.newmanreader.org/works/idea/, Discourse 5 [accessed: 30 January 2016].

[25] Howie and Tauchert, 'Institutional Discrimination', p. 61.

[26] Newman, 'Idea of a University', Discourse 5.

[27] Clark Kerr, *The Uses of the University*, 5th edn, Cambridge, MA: Harvard University Press, 2001, pp. 1–3.

[28] Howie, 'Teaching Philosophy in Context', pp. 19–20.

[29] On Humboldt, see Hans Ruin, 'Philosophy, Freedom and the Task of the University: Reflections on Humboldt's Legacy', in Peter Josephson et al. (eds), *The Humboldtian Tradition: Origins and Legacies*, Leiden: Brill, 2014, p. 164; on Newman, see *The Idea of a University*, Discourse 5.

Newman concludes, 'Such as he would have made it, a University ought to be.'[30]

*

For Howie and many others, the problem with this idea of a university (or, at least, one of them) concerns the intertwining of intellectual achievement with neutral, disembodied subjectivity. Depending on the specific interpretation offered, such disembodied neutrality either is historically possible solely for a select number of male subjects or acts as an ideological disguise for the fact that universities intentionally privilege male subjects – that is, disembodied neutrality either indirectly discriminates or is a covert form of direct discrimination. The white male is – and has long been – the 'consecrated somatic norm'[31] within the university, and so, for Howie and Tauchert, the 'cloistered geography' of the university becomes a prime example of the way in which 'neutrality has already been colonised by the male subject'.[32] Or as they put it more fully,

> We contend that criteria and mechanisms for distribution [of intellectual privilege] might appear to be rational and neutral [in line with Enlightenment ideals], but manage to incorporate select values and thereby constitute the conditions for the repetition of the same ... Appearances of a neutral ideal in almost all cases conceal bias in practice. The group benefiting from the status quo, from the bias, tends to be of a type: male and white. And it is this group that hangs most fervently onto the belief that neutrality is possible and more often than not achieved.[33]

The cloistered imaginary has real discriminatory effects. The idea of an abstract space for education and research attained through ascetic practices of disembodiment provides one means by which generations of academics are inculcated into – and in turn inculcate – a problematic form of neutrality that disregards bodies. To quote a passage from Howie that is crucial for what follows: universities establish in a very concrete way 'determination[s] of space (for example in the architecture, the physical accessibility to buildings, the structuring of the lecture theatre), and of time (for example with efficiency studies, teaching rotas, distribution of administrative tasks) ... [that] reproduce the cloistered model

[30] J. H. Newman, 'The Rise and Progress of Universities'. http://newmanreader.org/works/historical/ volume3/universities/index.html· Lecture 1 [accessed 30 January 16].
[31] Nirmal Purwar, *Space Invaders: Race, Gender and Bodies Out of Place*, Oxford: Berg, 2004, p. 3.
[32] Howie and Tauchert, 'Institutional Discrimination', pp. 59, 65.
[33] Ibid., p. 60.

and thereby privilege some kinds of bodies over others'.[34] The result, of course, is the exclusion of female bodies from the university. Harding is often quoted in this context: women 'are forced to deny that they are women in order to survive … They are prohibited from becoming (masculine) science knowers and also from admitting to being what they are primarily perceived as being: women.'[35] The cloister excludes.

According to Howie, therefore, there is something extremely pernicious about the cloistered ideal. However, we must also remember that the 'continuity-model' which interprets this unfortunate ideal as the basis of our understanding of the university throughout modernity is not the only one Howie deploys – and this is to return to the fundamental *ambiguity* in her attitude. As we have seen, she also laments the loss of the cloistered ideal through managerial changes to higher education since the early 1990s. The passing of the otherworldly cloister has (in part) damaged the university, for previously it precisely allowed for 'the opportunity to consider the future anew, in light of the past, according to values which may – or may not – accord with the values of the present'.[36] On this model, it is somewhat ironic (if by no means a coincidence) that just at the moment when explicit, if bureaucratic, policing of gender discrimination becomes more prevalent in the university, something of its traditional standard of 'critical' and 'living' thought is lost. The anthropologist Judith Okely expresses this sentiment more fully: 'It is unfortunate that just when UK universities have to be sensitive to gender, race, class, and disability, they are under overwhelming pressures to mimic the ideals of the market economy and state-dictated ideas of utility and bureaucratic priorities rather than intellectual creativity'.[37]

A time for thinking

As we have seen, Howie claims that the 'cloistered ideal' gives rise to distinctive forms of space and time. As well as the space of the lecture theatre, there is also the time of the workload allocation procedure. Howie's conception of the temporalities of the cloister is fleshed out and furthered in Browne's essay in the

---

[34] Ibid., pp. 61–2. This quickly turns, in Howie's work, into a critique of the Cartesian subject of the university; see ibid., pp. 66–7.

[35] Sonia Harding, *The Science Question in Feminism*, Milton Keynes: Open University, 1986, p. 143.

[36] Howie, 'Teaching Philosophy in Context', p. 20.

[37] Judith Okely, 'Gendered Lessons in Ivory Towers', in D. F. Bryceson et al. (eds), *Identity and Networks: Fashioning Gender across Cultures*, Oxford: Berg, 2007, p. 245.

present volume (Chapter 4) under the label of 'scholarly time', and it is worth returning to her conclusions here.

Browne brings out Howie's 'hope for a different kind of temporal existence', arguing that Howie deploys her own academic writing as 'a utopic moment' in which to formulate 'another relationship to space and time'.[38] This is true of her reinterpretation of feminist wave imagery in terms of an alternative model of woman-to-woman sociality as well as her 'epistemology and ethic of *taking time* [that] exemplifies the patience required for rigorous critical scholarship, even when faced with the demands of the quantifying audit culture taking hold within academic institutions'.[39] Howie is insistent, then, that the bureaucratization that results in managerial imperatives to speed up, produce more, and communicate quicker is thoroughly misguided; it plays into the ever-greater hegemony of instrumental reason and marketization outlined in the previous section. However, she also makes use of such widespread dissatisfaction with the unending acceleration of demands to conceive academic work according to another framework, one of taking one's time. In Browne's words, Howie here asserts, 'the value of stepping "outside" linear, progressive, productive time and dwelling in other modes of temporal being'.[40]

Again, there is ambiguity here depending on whether such acceleration is to be interpreted according to the continuity model or the break model. On the latter model, Howie's insistence on taking one's time seems conservative – a reactionary call to reinstate a lost ideal of the cloistered university in which, as Gaita puts it, 'one needs time to muse, to meditate ... enabling one sufficient space and time to step back and to examine assumptions one might not otherwise have noticed'.[41] The drawn-out days of the cloistered university were halcyon, but are now lost. On the continuity model, however, there is a structural flaw in the very idea of a university (from the Renaissance onwards) that has allowed it to be exploited by the logics of the market in this way, but there is also the memory that this form of the university has previously given rise to alternative models of temporality and so to the promise that it could do so again. The university, on this model, retains some utopic potential.

The university, then, is the site of a bureaucratic time (the REF cycle, funding

---

[38] Victoria Browne, 'Scholarly Time and Feminist Time: Gillian Howie on Education and Intellectual Inheritance', Ch. 4 of the present volume, p. 95; Gillian Howie, 'Feminist Histories: Conflicts, Coalitions and the Maternal Order', *Studies in the Maternal* 2.1 (2010): 5, 9.

[39] Ibid., p. 96.

[40] Ibid., p. 98. See further Victoria Browne, *Feminism, Time and Nonlinear History*, Basingstoke: Palgrave, 2015.

[41] Raimond Gaita, 'Callicles' Challenge', *Critical Quarterly* 47.1 (2005): 43. (This issue of the journal was edited by Howie.)

cycles, audit culture in general) and it has been (and/or could be) the site of a 'scholarly time' (the taking of one's time needed for critical thinking); moreover, it is the site of multiple other temporalities too: the life-cycle of the student (over undergraduate, MA and research degrees); the time of 'submissive waiting' for official validation that Bourdieu perceives as structuring the university;[42] as well as publication times, marking times, lecture times, conference times and promotion times. In general, the university is an institution that may well be determined by the 'worldly' time of markets, but also has a history of putting it into question in precisely the way Howie demands – that is, by experimenting with other modes of time. I want to take this thought further by abruptly shifting terrain to another institution which experiments with temporalities in the context of education and speculation: the sanatorium of Thomas Mann's *The Magic Mountain*.

*

The Magic Mountain makes no claim to be an allegory of the university; however, there is a tradition of reading the novel as an exercise in extrapolating university practices of pedagogy into 'the literally disembodied discourses' of an Alpine sanatorium for the tubercular, a cloistered space 'away from the world at large'.[43] Indeed, the novel itself explicitly draws attention to similarities between its own setting and the medieval cloister. In the words of the protagonist, Hans Castorp,

> I am still laughing at your calling our dining hall a refectory. That is what they are called in a cloister, isn't it? After all, there is some resemblance – not that I have been in a cloister, but I imagine they are something like this. And I have the 'Rule' at my fingers' ends, and observe it faithfully.[44]

Similarly, later in the novel, in response to a description of monkish life in the Middle Ages, Hans responds,

> Devotion, retirement – there is something in it, it sounds reasonable. We practise a pretty high degree of retirement from the world, we up here. No doubt about it. Five thousand feet up, we lie in these excellent chairs of ours, contemplating the world and all that therein is, and having our thoughts about it. The more I think of it, the surer I am that the bed of repose – by which I mean my

---

[42] Pierre Bourdieu, *Homo Academicus*, trans. Peter Collier, Oxford: Polity, 1988, pp. 89, 95, 105.

[43] See Sheldon Rothblatt, *The Modern University and its Discontents: The Fate of Newman's Legacies in Britain and America*, Cambridge: Cambridge University Press, 1997, p. 26.

[44] Thomas Mann, *The Magic Mountain*, trans. H. T. Lowe-Porter, London: Vintage, 1999, p. 192.

deck-chair, of course – has given me more food for thought in these ten months than the mill down in the flat-land in all the years before.[45]

Key here is the emphasis on the relation between the cloister and thought: as with the university, so too with 'the magic mountain', being shut away from the world in an institution facilitates a kind of other-worldly speculation that would not otherwise have been possible.

Such an ascent into 'the heights of the spirit'[46] is of course the very idea of a *Bildungsroman*: the formation of subjects who thereby discover new realms of thought. And it is noticeable that Mann conceives *The Magic Mountain* very literally as a novel of education, where Hans receives a series of formal and informal lectures, participates in seminar discussions on standard metaphysical topics and begins to undertake his own twilight reflections on the nature of life, matter and the universe. This is clearest in Hans' conversations with Settembrini and Naphta, two 'representatives' from opposing intellectual camps.[47] Settembrini, especially, is characterized as a 'schoolmaster' and 'pedagogue' giving 'private lecture[s]'[48], while Hans is often labelled his 'pupil', a 'schoolboy' and 'student'.[49] Hans describes Settembrini's teaching in a way that is reminiscent of a (successful) academic lecture:

> 'Oh, what a schoolmaster! ... He never leaves off setting you right – first by means of anecdotes, then by abstractions. And the things one gets to talk about with him, things you would never have thought you could talk about, or even understand! And if I had met him down below', he added, 'I never should have understood.'[50]

Settembrini is characterized as a proponent of Enlightenment values and democratic progress, and is contrasted with Naphta, 'a reactionary revolutionist',[51] who also lectures Hans extensively; the 'dialectical rivalry' and 'endless academic strife' between these two 'establish, as it were, a pedagogic equilibrium'.[52]

More formally, Hans – alongside the other patients – attends lectures by Dr Krokowski which imitate more precisely the material conditions of academic pedagogy. Krokowski is dressed, like many academics before and since, to make 'an impression profoundly otherworldly'; he is the 'learned master', able

45 Ibid., p. 376.
46 Ibid., p. 596.
47 Ibid., p. 327.
48 Ibid., pp. 98–9, 241.
49 Ibid., pp. 241, 249, 462, 276.
50 Ibid., p. 200.
51 Ibid., p. 460.
52 Ibid., pp. 506, 519, 394.

to name the most subtle of phenomena 'by a Greek word, very scientific and impressive'.[53] Moreover, he lectures on the subject of erotic desire in a manner reminiscent of the academic theorist:

> How did one go about to discuss a subject of this delicate and private nature, in broad daylight, before a mixed audience? Dr Krokowski did it by adopting a mingled terminology, partly poetic and partly erudite; ruthlessly scientific ... He supported his statements with a wealth of illustration and anecdote from the books and loose notes on the table before him.[54]

It also says much about *The Magic Mountain*'s gender politics – as well as the claims to neutrality made by the cloistered ideal in general – that all this is characterized in terms of 'the blithe and manly spirit of disinterested research'.[55]

Hans, then, is educated. He loses his 'profound acquiescence and sense of well-being' and gains an 'inquiring metaphysical gaze'.[56] He begins to talk like a professional philosopher ('It seems to me you are contradicting yourself; first you say our cases are different; then you say they are alike. That seems sheer twaddle to me') or a curious undergraduate ('"What is the body?" he rhapsodically burst forth, "What is the flesh? What is the physical being of man? What is he made of?"').[57] At the height of his *Bildung*, he undertakes a series of studies on 'such vast problems as form and freedom, body and spirit, honour and shame, time and eternity'.[58] And throughout, his guiding methodological tenet is expressed in Settembrini's phrase, *placet experiri* – that is, 'make experiments with a variety of points of view'.[59]

Crucially, this process of education, or 'heightening' in Mann's language,[60] is understood as a form of ever-increasing alienation. At the beginning of the novel Hans is described as 'strikingly at home in his environment', embedded in the values of bourgeois Germany; however, acclimatization to the sanatorium means 'getting used to not getting used to it' – that is, Hans increasingly feels estranged from all value-systems; he becomes 'critical'.[61] Ascent into the mountains transforms Hans from apprentice-engineer into a 'quaint philosopher'

---

53 Ibid., pp. 125, 668.
54 Ibid., pp. 124–5; see also ibid., p. 653.
55 Ibid., p. 671.
56 Ibid., pp. 30, 345.
57 Ibid., pp. 169, 264.
58 Ibid., p. 389.
59 Ibid., pp. 95–6.
60 See ibid., p. 651.
61 Ibid., pp. 253, 218.

through abstraction and withdrawal – becoming-cloistered engenders 'sleeveless speculation'.[62]

> Down in the plain he had never been aware of [these intellectual problems], nor probably ever would have been. It was up here that the thing came about, where one sat piously withdrawn, looking down from a height of five thousand feet or so upon the earth and all that therein was.[63]

Entry into 'this narrow, lofty, isolated world'[64] instantiates a new form of existence: Hans takes on the cloister's 'queer way of talking', its 'strange, dislocated attitude' and the whole 'regimen of the cure'.[65] He is, in short, initiated and pities those down below 'living in the darkness of that flat landish incomprehension'.[66] He gains 'the self-confident poise of institutional life', and this is articulated by Mann most fully as a form of disinterested indifference, 'the purest indifference, an uncanny invulnerability or complaisance as though he long ceased to notice or to feel surprise'.[67] Such indifference is, in the terms of the novel, Hans' 'freedom'[68] – his abstract elevation above the cares of everyday existence into an institutional realm that heightens reflection and permits thought-experiments.

Crucial for our purposes is that such freedom liberates time too: Hans' experiments with thought are paralleled by experiments in alternative temporalities. The novel explores variously the time of habitual monotony in which small units might drag but greater ones pass quickly;[69] time in which seasons 'don't keep to the calendar';[70] the careless, irresponsible time of a holiday;[71] the weakening of the sense of time that leads to a 'baleful traffic with eternity';[72] the linear march of progress;[73] the time of tradition which 'bear[s] witness to the perpetual continuity of things';[74] moments of ecstasy which 'concentrate all the past in a single moment of the present';[75] the time of 'faithful waiting';[76] even 'the hastening while' experienced by supernatural spirits.[77] As one patient puts it, 'You know we are free with

---

[62] Ibid., pp. 597, 344.
[63] Ibid., p. 389.
[64] Ibid., pp. 266–7.
[65] Ibid., pp. 10, 18, 93.
[66] Ibid., p. 420.
[67] Ibid., pp. 433, 431.
[68] See ibid., pp. 222, 439.
[69] Ibid., p. 102
[70] Ibid., p. 92
[71] Ibid., pp. 547–8.
[72] Ibid., p. 548.
[73] Ibid., pp. 150–5.
[74] Ibid., p. 25.
[75] Ibid., p. 331.
[76] Ibid., p. 549.
[77] Ibid., p. 662.

the time up here ... [It] is a privilege we shadows have': they are 'practised time-consumers'.[78] Hans encounters each temporality in turn, testing its usefulness for health and speculation.

According to *The Magic Mountain*, therefore, entry into an institution alienates one from previous modes of living and so gains one a disinterested, even otherworldly standpoint. It liberates and heightens reflection and, out of such intellectual ascesis, time is also set free, taking on new forms and structuring new experiences.

A context for thinking

In his reflections on *The Magic Mountain*, Lukács traces the way in which this cloistered life in the Alps is subject to critique within the novel. Mann, Lukács claims, writes in 'double time' – a device that 'strengthens the sense of social reality'.[79] That is, in contrast to the modernist affirmation of fragmentary temporal experiences, Mann ironically relativizes the experimental times of the cloistered sanatorium in terms of the overarching objective time of the realist tradition:

> On the one hand, the consciousness of his most important characters recedes ever more distantly from objective reality; on the other, reality asserts its supremacy over all kinds of false consciousness ever more vigorously. For this reason Mann's playfulness never dissolves objective reality, but on the contrary underlines its inevitable and natural triumph.[80]

The proliferation of times on the mountain is described only to then be negated: there is an evident, if often implicit, contrast between Hans' increasing isolation from reality and the onwards march of what Mann calls the 'socio-critical sidelights':[81] Hans becomes 'incapable of distinguishing between "now" and "then", and prone to mingle these together in a timeless eternity', whereas 'time, however weakened the subjective perception of it has become, has objective reality in that it brings things to pass'.[82] This dialectic reaches its climax at the outbreak of World War I:

> That historic thunder-peal, of which we speak with bated breath, made the

[78] Ibid., pp. 56–7, 424.
[79] Georg Lukács, *Essays on Thomas Mann*, trans. Stanley Mitchell, London: Merlin, 1995, p. 106.
[80] Ibid., p. 109.
[81] Thomas Mann, *The Letters, 1889–1955*, ed. and trans. Richard and Clara Winston, London: Penguin, 1975, p. 137.
[82] Mann, *The Magic Mountain*, pp. 544–5.

foundations of the earth to shake; but for us it was the shock that fired the mine beneath the magic mountain, and set our sleeper urgently outside the gates. Dazed he sits in the long grass and rubs his eyes.[83]

Objective reality takes the spoils and Hans is thrown back into the maelstrom of events, 'freed from enchantment.'[84] Lukács puts it thus:

> The experience and measurement of time differ considerably for the world above (the sanatorium) and the world below (everyday bourgeois reality) ... But Mann is quite conscious – and so, therefore, is the reader at every step of the leisurely narrative – that the magic mountain belongs in real time, that only its inhabitants (and then only in their imagination) regard it as a reality-in-itself, as an isolated self-subsisting world with a time-scheme of its own ... He treats what is subjective as subjective and can thereby let it take its place in an objective narrative world.[85]

Mann himself labels this practice irony: 'With me, the experience of the self-denial of the intellect in favour of life became irony.'[86] It names the means of revealing the material conditions of ideal experiences. In other words, ideas are forever being contextualized as domain-specific: the cloistered sanatorium is neither absolute nor autonomous; it is one small domain of objective reality.

*

Ambivalence and ambiguity are common in Howie's writings. Take, for example, her treatment of abstraction (which I have discussed at greater length elsewhere[87]): in an early discussion of feminist appropriations of Deleuze and Guattari's notion of becoming-woman, Howie writes,

> We are encouraged to abstract relations of movement and rest, speed and slowness and emission of particles from the body. Abstraction here is not supposed to be the work of reason but, instead, to indicate a material process. And this is the point of contention ... This move into abstraction could equally well be described as disembodiment ... It certainly seems a long way from feminist phenomenology.[88]

---

[83] Ibid., p. 709.
[84] Ibid., p. 711.
[85] Lukács, *Essays on Mann*, pp. 82–3.
[86] Thomas Mann, *Reflections of a Nonpolitical Man*, trans. Walter D. Morris, New York: Ungar, 1983, p. 13.
[87] Daniel Whistler, 'Howie's *Between Feminism and Materialism* and the Critical History of Religions', *Sophia* 53.1 (2014).
[88] Gillian Howie, 'Becoming-Woman: A Flight into Abstraction', *Deleuze Studies* 2 (2008): 85.

Howie continues: deployments of abstractions rarely serve a critical function, presumably because abstractions fail to locate and delimit the particular, situated bases of a concept, which is something all critique, according to Howie, must be capable of. As such, there is only ever critique of abstraction, never critique with abstraction.

Yet, a few years later, in *Between Feminism and Materialism*, Howie's position has become much more ambivalent: 'Despite the dangers of abstraction, it is only through a process of cognitive abstraction that the particular can be revealed within its relations.'[89] In other words, abstractions can be useful. Thus, in addition to a continual insistence on abstraction as 'erroneous', 'ideological' and a 'falsification', there is now a counter-emphasis on abstraction as a productive component of materialist methodology.[90] In this vein, in a surprising passage that qualifies somewhat her earlier critique of Deleuze, Howie invokes the plane of immanence positively as a conceptual abstraction that is in fact helpful for theory:

> I suggest that we think about feminist theory in terms of a plane, similar to that expressed by Deleuze and Guattari as a plane of immanence: an intellectual heuristic through which we can create critical distance to pursue and reflect upon the problems of sexual difference ... We approach this plane tentatively. As an abstraction it risks folding reification back in on itself ... [It is] only one explanatory model amongst many and it should be considered alongside other models. Different contexts may call upon different explanatory models.[91]

Abstractions are to be deployed strategically, according to local conditions and contexts. Howie here advocates a form of metaphilosophical pragmatism with respect to abstractions: they are to be legitimated on account of their *in situ* productivity. This is a model-pluralism according to which – to return to the idea of a university – two conclusions are confirmed: first, the practices of abstraction that constitute academia are in some contexts helpful, in others pernicious; second, the cloistered ideal can be understood on more than one model, sometimes as a problematic structure that continues to organize university space-time (the continuity model) and on other occasions as a lost exemplar of critical thinking destroyed by managerialism (the break model).

In Mann's terms, concepts and intellectual models are to be treated ironically – subjected to a critique that shows up their domain-specificity – a procedure

---

[89] Gillian Howie, *Between Feminism and Materialism: A Question of Method*, Basingstoke: Palgrave, 2010, p. 83.
[90] Ibid., pp. 6, 67.
[91] Ibid., pp. 58–9.

which is a constant in Howie's work (an assault on the theoretical 'tendency to confuse the logic of intellectual debate with the condition of the world'[92]). When it comes to the university, this is particularly evident in Howie's critique of the lack of critique in contemporary syllabi:

> [Through modularization] the concept of self is simplified, abstracted and atomised, and the power of thought perverted into a vehicle for delivering success at the stipulated tasks ... The conditions of self, relations and contexts, become mysterious. The historical contingency of these conditions is thus lost.[93]

Howie here puts into practice her critical method, at the very same time as she laments its passing from university teaching. She draws attention to the historical and material conditions of a kind of thinking neglectful of historical and material conditions. In other words, academic thinking is abstract – and the full ambiguity of that term for Howie should be borne in mind: it might make more 'heightened' forms of reflection possible, it might free up the academic or student to experiment with alternative temporalities, but it also stifles awareness of its own material conditions and so fails to be sufficiently critical.

A body for thinking

The university is supposed to be inhabited by disembodied minds; bodiless subjects who 'cut off from everything else ... yet persist in living ... [in] a pure and clear atmosphere of thought', to repeat Newman's claims. Thus, the female academic must, according to Howie and Tauchert, 'feign an impossible disembodiment'.[94]

Clark has traced much of this negative attitude to embodiment back to the educational reforms of early eighteenth-century Germany which came to be so influential on Humboldt's plans for the University of Berlin. It was during this period, Clark argues, that scholars began to 'find academic freedom as depoliticized thinking substance, as pure spirit'.[95] In particular, Clark identifies the disappearance of the 'juridical persona' of the scholar as the key moment: prior to this period, 'to be a student and to be able to advance to candidacy for exams, one needed a specific juridical persona: a candidate had to be

---

92 Howie, 'Feminist Histories', p. 5.
93 Howie, 'A Reflection of Quality', p. 145.
94 Howie and Tauchert, 'Institutional Discrimination', p. 61.
95 William Clark, *Academic Charisma and the Origins of the Research University*, Chicago, IL: University of Chicago Press, 2006, p. 182.

legitimately born, Christian, male, the proper age, essentially corporeally intact, present, alive, sane, and able to see and speak.[96] However, from the 1670s onwards, there emerges an emphasis on examining the mind unencumbered by corporeal, social and biographical specificities – 'a progressive disembodiment of the academic, ideally, into pure intellectual ability manifested in writing and speaking.'[97] Clark concludes, 'The academic was on the way to a rather complete disembodiment.'[98]

What is most interesting for our purposes is a phenomenon that takes place simultaneously with this institutional disembodiment: the academics' obsession with their own bodies. Those who are becoming bodiless begin to speak obsessively about bodies, particularly the bodies of scholars themselves. The titles of doctoral dissertations started to read: *Ein Tractat von denen Gelehrten, die von Gott mit vielen Kindern gesegnet worden* [*On Scholars Blessed with Many Children*] or *De eruditis studiorum intemperie mortem sibi accelerantibus* [*On Scholars who Hastened their Deaths by Too Much Study*]. Clark enumerates further,

> There are dissertations on academics who were precocious, or who were aged, or who were blind. There is a work on academics who perished by water, and one on those who died on their own birthdays. One studies academics who lived to be more than seventy years old. Another treats of academics who were incarcerated. There is one on those with good memories, one on those with bad morals, and one on academics of bad manners. There are dissertations on academics who were bastards, on those who were slovenly, on those who were timid, on those who were idlers ... [Others treat of] academics who could not speak properly, or could not see right.[99]

As Clark is at pains to emphasize, the two phenomena – the becoming-disembodied of the scholar and the 'strange fad' for dissertations on scholars' bodies – are 'roughly coincident': the dissertations 'treated the materiality of academics and academia, just as they were becoming most dematerialised.'[100]

Moreover, these two phenomena are also intertwined with a third: the outbreak of violent misogyny in German universities during the early eighteenth century, articulated most clearly in the very title of the most famous of those odd dissertations on the corporeal specificities of scholars: the 1705

---

[96] Ibid., p. 104.
[97] Ibid., p. 420.
[98] Ibid., p. 203.
[99] Ibid., p. 214.
[100] Ibid., pp. 214–17.

Dissertatio historico-moralis de malis eruditorum uxoribis, oder von den bösen Weibern der Gelehrten. On the Wicked Wives of Scholars gained its notoriety from inclusion in Lessing's early play, *The Young Scholar*, where the misogyny of the academy is dramatized in the cloistered space of the scholar, Damis', study – a space from which women are repeatedly excluded: 'How often has [Damis] said that so holy a place as a study must not be profaned by such unsanctified creatures as you? That the god of learning ... can't endure a woman.'[101] Indeed, Damis' sole interest in women is as a means of attaining fame through inclusion in a new edition of *De malis eruditorum uxoribis*, a plan which heightens his misogyny to fever-pitch: 'By what does one show that one is a human being? By reason. By what does one show that one has reason? When one knows how to value properly learning and the learned. A woman can never do this, and therefore she has no reason, and therefore is not a human being.'[102]

*

In the cloistered university, the abjected body can come to obsess disembodied research. Such a double-relation to the body is implicit in Howie's critique of the Cartesian imaginary at work in academic self-understanding: the male mind disembodies itself in order to gaze back at its own body from a spectral position.[103] This uncanny position of the scholar researching her own body from without is repeatedly commented upon in the medical portions of *The Magic Mountain*: early on, Hans hears 'the beating of his own heart ... quite outside of himself' and such a 'spooky' experience is heightened at the sight of an x-ray.[104] And yet the ascetic mode of life in the sanatorium is not just an ideal venue for cultivating practices of disembodied perception of one's body; just as with time, an assortment of various attitudes towards the body are toyed with. There is the recklessness towards the body shown by the dying youths;[105] Naphta's revival of Plotinean shame for the body;[106] Settembrini's contention that bodily suffering is 'to be systematically eliminated by means of a lexicon';[107] the 'Christian repentance before suffering' shown by Hans in his occasional ministrations

---

[101] Lessing, *The Young Scholar*, II.iii, p. 54.
[102] Ibid., II.xi–xii, pp. 70–1.
[103] Howie, 'Feminist Histories', p. 6. See also Bourdieu, *Homo Academicus*, pp. 32, 56.
[104] Mann, *The Magic Mountain*, pp. 88, 218.
[105] Ibid., p. 162.
[106] Ibid., p. 394.
[107] Ibid., p. 293.

to the sick;[108] Pepperkorn's 'mysticism of the body'[109] that undermines all theoretical positions in the name of life (much in the same way as Mannian irony does in general); and the spiritual freedom Frau Chauchat attains through bodily illness.[110]

Indeed, unsurprisingly considering the setting, the relation between body and disease is foregrounded throughout the novel, lingering precisely on those 'abnormal' bodies on which the dissertations described by Clarke above also focused. Once more, the novel proliferates various attitudes towards disease and death, and Hans encounters each of them in turn in a dialectical process that reads like a phenomenology of spirit of being-towards-death. There is the disquiet felt by the invalid at her body 'going its own gait without any reference to the soul' – the *rebellio carnis*, as Naphta names it;[111] and the frustration of being 'prevented by our physical, our animal nature from being of service to reason'.[112] Most of all, there is a series of disputes concerning the significance of death – whether it possesses meaning, whether it ennobles, whether it can lead to higher states of reflection – that pepper the novel, such as 'the great disputation on sickness and health' in '*Operationes Spiritualis*'.[113] This disputation is immediately subject to authorial critique, for it opens with a description of its very material conditions:

> One and all slightly feverish, at once nervously stimulated and physically lethargic from walking and talking in the severe frost ... all, without exception, so utterly absorbed that they stopped several times by the way, in a disorderly, gesticulating knot, blocking the path of the passers-by.[114]

This is another example of Mann's practice of irony: the intellectual postures of the characters are entertained, only to be relativized by the 'objective reality' underlying them. The various intellectual experiments in representing bodies are conditioned unknowingly by bodies; Mann draws attention to the embodied conditions underlying these disembodied discussions.

*

---

[108] Ibid., pp. 449, 317–18.
[109] Mann, *Letters*, p. 127. See Mann, *The Magic Mountain*, pp. 591, 602.
[110] Mann, *The Magic Mountain*, pp. 554, 595.
[111] Ibid., pp. 70, 559.
[112] Ibid., p. 243.
[113] Ibid., p. 448.
[114] Ibid., p. 448.

One corollary to this is a thorough-going ambivalence in regard to being-towards-death. Very early in the novel, Hans realizes that 'in one aspect death was a holy, a pensive, a spiritual state, possessed of a certain mournful beauty. In another it was quite different. It was precisely the opposite, it was very physical, it was material ... almost improper.'[115] Later, Hans observes a 'dignity' in death (it is a 'very solemn and majestic power'), only to then acknowledge it as 'a disreputable and impudent thing that makes one blush in shame'.[116] Such a dialectic of attitudes to death and illness seems ineluctable – the very fact that Naphta and Settembrini dispute for the most part on this exact topic suggests that it can only give rise to unresolvable arguments from within the walls of the institution. It is almost as if the precise form of the *antinomy* were being enacted: a multitude of contradictory opinions all generated from a false premise; but in this case the premise is less a proposition than the disembodied perspective of those debating.

André Gide's *The Immoralist* confirms this logic. This time it is explicitly a former scholar who becomes aware of the inadequacies of cloistered thinking in the encounter with disease and health – and once more it is the experience of tuberculosis that provokes him. Gide's protagonist too convalesces from the illness in the Alps, and his journey down the mountains exactly reverses Hans' ascent, in that: 'I felt I was leaving abstraction for life.'[117] 'An increase, a recrudescence of life' means that Michel rejects his former self, 'a sickly, studious being', as well as his former academic colleagues ('Most of them, I thought, did not really live – contented themselves with appearing to live, and were on the verge of considering life as a vexatious hindrance to writing').[118] He becomes contemptuous of abstraction as precisely that which never confronts life or death:

> As for the few philosophers ... whether mathematicians or neo-Kantians, they
> kept as far away as possible from the disturbing reality and had no more concern
> for it than the algebraist has for the existence of the quantities he measures.[119]

In its place, Michel develops a pseudo-Nietzschean taste for health, 'a taste for a more spacious, breezier life, one that was less hemmed in'.[120] However, such

---

[115] Ibid., p. 27.
[116] Ibid., p. 341.
[117] André Gide, *The Immoralist*, trans. Dorothy Bussy, London: Penguin, 1960, p. 139. I am indebted to Grace Whistler and her current research on rhetoric and morality in twentieth-century French literature for this reading of *The Immoralist*.
[118] Ibid., pp. 52, 88.
[119] Ibid., p. 88.
[120] Ibid., p. 89.

a dogged pursuit of vigour is cruel, and he ultimately loses his wife to the very same illness out of which she nursed him. Again, the point is roughly that neither cloistered abstraction nor the attempt to liberate oneself from it by pseudo-Nietzschean affirmation really does justice to life or death: Michel's two modes of existence again form an antinomy.

It is here we return to Howie – and perhaps we can glimpse in the logic rehearsed above some of the motivation for the transition from her early critique of the academy to her New Thinking on Living with Dying project, for there is no subject-matter more suited to showing up academic inadequacies and incapacities than illness and death. From within the university, all that is possible is the very same antinomic proliferation of claim and counter-claim that Howie reports in her 'How to Think about Death' lecture (transcribed in Chapter 6 of the present volume): death is meaningful or death is absurd; death individualizes or death relates us to others more closely; there is hope or there is despair. It is little wonder, then, that Howie concludes the lecture with a pessimistic account of the inability of academics, particularly philosophers, to provide consolation; nor is it any wonder that she was so intent on incorporating voices from outside the university into the project. What I am suggesting is that the New Thinking on Living with Dying network was a performance of Howie's own concept of critique (or the Mannian notion of irony, for that matter): the pretensions of academic discourse are questioned by means of a description of the context-specific ambiguity of such discourse. And, what is more, this performance of critique emerges directly out of Howie's early work on the 'cloistered ideal', for there is no aspect of this ideal that requires more scrutiny than its disembodied approach to bodies, in sickness as well as health.

Coda: The imaginary conditions of philosophy

Academic philosophizing rests on initial acts of abstraction, whether they consist in phenomenological epochē, logical symbolization or hermeneutic reinterpretation – or, to use examples from the preceding, whether they consist in a refusal of the market in the name of scholarly time, a form of institutional teaching that neglects historical conditions, or even an ascent up the Alps. Nevertheless, such abstractions hide themselves, for to abstract is precisely to avert one's gaze from conditions of production – in this case, philosophy's founding abstractions themselves. Philosophizing precludes examination of the very practices that make it possible. This is one of the reasons that critique is so important for philosophy: it uncovers not only the local, material conditions of thinking but the strategies by which such conditions are covered over as well. Only through such critique can these founding acts of abstraction be recognized, let alone described.

And yet such critique cannot be purely philosophical, because philosophy is that which forecloses investigation into its own conditions. Howie seems to be aware of this; hence she is so insistent on the need to supplement theory with empirical social science. She speaks of 'a commitment to social scientific research' as 'a commitment required by feminists',[121] and similarly praises Firestone for 'nudg[ing] feminist method back toward social science'.[122] This social scientific supplement makes possible scrutiny of philosophy's conditions of possibility – that is, philosophy, for Howie, can only become a fully transcendental enterprise by means of the social sciences. The conditions thereby described are *real*: the historical, material and embodied practices that concretely give rise to the abstractions that produce philosophies.

My method in this chapter has been slightly different. I have tried to follow Howie in subjecting academic practices to critique and using her findings to explore the types of spaces, times and bodies that condition the production of philosophy. However, rather than unearthing the real conditions of philosophizing with the help of the social sciences, I have attempted to identify its *ideal* – or to use a less ambiguous term, *imaginary* – conditions with the help of literature. Literature – just like the social sciences – shines a light on the activity of philosophizing, and articulates those very initiatory practices of abstraction that philosophy disregards; it too provides accounts of the spaces, times and bodies out of which thinking emerges. Such accounts are not real, of course; they are imaginative inventions. However, it is my contention that they supplement Howie's findings and deserve to be taken seriously as an external discourse that puts philosophy into context. Thus I want to appropriate something like Le Doeuff's argument in *The Philosophical Imaginary*: she opposes the view that 'the images that appear in theoretical texts are ... extrinsic to the theoretical work',[123] whereas I am suggesting that it is not just in 'theoretical texts' that such theoretical work is done by images. Literature rehearses the founding acts of philosophy in its imaginative reconstructions. Literary representations of thinking, just like philosophical imagery, are not 'dross coming from

[121] Howie, 'Becoming-Woman', p. 97.
[122] Gillian Howie, 'Sexing the State of Nature: Firestone's Materialist Manifesto', in Mandy Merck and Stella Sandford (eds), *Further Adventures of The Dialectic of Sex*, New York: Palgrave, 2010, p. 230.
[123] Le Doeuff, *Philosophical Imaginary*, p. 2.

elsewhere',[124] but part of critique. It is to be hoped that this essay has (if only very partially and in a different way than she intended) fulfilled Le Doeuff's hope for 'a reading which absorbs imagery entirely into the system's theoretical problems'.[125]

There is irony here of course: in a search for the ideal conditions of academic philosophizing, I have looked to Howie and Mann who both insist, in the name of a kind of irony, on the contextualization of everything ideal in terms of its real conditions. And the real conditions of this essay? The contemporary university in all its ambiguity.

References

Anderson, Pamela Sue, 'A Story of Love and Death: Exploring Space for the Philosophical Imaginary', *Literature and Theology: New Interdisciplinary Spaces*, ed. H. Walton, Aldershot: Ashgate, 2011, pp. 167–86.

Anderson, Pamela Sue, 'Michele Le Doeuff's "Primal Scene": Prohibition and Confidence in the Education of a Woman', *Text Matters* 1 (2011): 11–26.

Bourdieu, Pierre, *Homo Academicus*, trans. Peter Collier, Oxford: Polity, 1988.

Browne, Victoria, *Feminism, Time and Nonlinear History*, Basingstoke: Palgrave, 2015.

Browne, Victoria, 'Scholarly Time and Feminist Time: Gillian Howie on Education and Intellectual Inheritance', *On the Feminist Philosophy of Gillian Howie: Materialism and Mortality*, ed. Victoria Browne and Daniel Whistler, London: Bloomsbury, 2016, pp. 81–101.

Clark, William, *Academic Charisma and the Origins of the Research University*, Chicago, IL: University of Chicago Press, 2006.

Gaita, Raimond, 'Callicles' Challenge', *Critical Quarterly* 47.1 (2005): 40–52.

Gide, André, *The Immoralist*, trans. Dorothy Bussy, London: Penguin, 1960.

Harding, Sonia, *The Science Question in Feminism*, Milton Keynes: Open University, 1986.

Howie, Gillian, 'A Reflection of Quality: Instrumental Reason, Quality Audits and the Knowledge Economy', *Critical Quarterly* 44.4 (2002): 140–7.

Howie, Gillian, 'From Process to Product: Quality Audits and Instrumental Reason', *Contemporary Issues in Education*, ed. D. Preston, New York: Rodopi, 2004, pp. 19–36.

---

[124] Ibid., p. 7.

[125] Ibid., p. 18. My reading of Le Doeuff and of the problematic of the imaginary in general is indebted to Pamela Sue Anderson's development of Le Doeuff's ideas in, for example, 'Michèle Le Doeuff's "Primal Scene": Prohibition and Confidence in the Education of a Woman', *Text Matters* 1 (2011); 'A Story of Love and Death: Exploring Space for the Philosophical Imaginary', in H. Walton (ed.), *Literature and Theology: New Interdisciplinary Spaces*, Aldershot: Ashgate, 2011.

Howie, Gillian, 'Universities in the UK: Drowning by Numbers', *Critical Quarterly* 47.1–2 (2005): 1–10.

Howie, Gillian, 'Becoming-Woman: A Flight into Abstraction', *Deleuze Studies* 2 (2008): 83–106.

Howie, Gillian, 'Teaching Philosophy in Context: Or Knowledge Does Not Keep Any Better Than Fish', *Teaching Philosophy*, ed. Andrea Kenkmann, London: Continuum, 2009, pp. 1–22.

Howie, Gillian, *Between Feminism and Materialism: A Question of Method*, Basingstoke: Palgrave, 2010.

Howie, Gillian, 'Feminist Histories: Conflicts, Coalitions and the Maternal Order', *Studies in the Maternal* 2.1 (2010): 1–12.

Howie, Gillian, 'Sexing the State of Nature: Firestone's Materialist Manifesto', *Further Adventures of The Dialectic of Sex*, ed. Mandy Merck and Stella Sandford, New York: Palgrave, 2010, 215–35.

Howie, Gillian and Ashley Tauchert, 'Institutional Discrimination and the "Cloistered" Academic Ideal', *Gender, Teaching and Research in Higher Education: Challenges for the 21st Century*, ed. Gillian Howie and Ashley Tauchert, Aldershot: Ashgate, 2002, pp. 59–72.

Howie, Gillian and Ashley Tauchert, 'Introduction', *Gender, Teaching and Research in Higher Education: Challenges for the 21st Century*, ed. Gillian Howie and Ashley Tauchert, Aldershot: Ashgate, 2002, pp. 1–6.

Kerr, Clark, *The Uses of the University* (5th edn), Cambridge, MA: Harvard University Press, 2001.

Le Doeuff, Michèle, *The Philosophical Imaginary*, trans. Colin Gordon, London: Continuum, 2004.

Le Doeuff, Michèle, *Hipparchia's Choice: An Essay Concerning Women, Philosophy, etc* (2nd edn), trans. Trista Selous, New York: Columbia University Press, 2007.

Lessing, G. E., *The Young Scholar*, in *The Dramatic Works of G. E. Lessing*, Vol. 2, ed. and trans. Ernest Bell, London: Bell and Sons, 1878, pp. 24–107.

Lukács, Georg, *Essays on Thomas Mann*, trans. Stanley Mitchell, London: Merlin, 1995.

Mann, Thomas, *The Letters, 1889–1955*, ed. and trans. Richard and Clara Winston, London: Penguin, 1975.

Mann, Thomas, *Reflections of a Nonpolitical Man*, trans. Walter D. Morris, New York: Ungar, 1983.

Mann, Thomas, *The Magic Mountain*, trans. H. T. Lowe-Porter, London: Vintage, 1999.

Newman, J. H., *The Idea of a University*, http://www.newmanreader.org/works/idea/ [accessed 30 January 2016].

Newman, J. H., *The Rise and Progress of Universities*, http://newmanreader.org/works/historical/volume3/universities/index.html (accessed 30 January 2016).

Nietzsche, Friedrich, *Ecce Homo*, in *Basic Writings*, ed. and trans. by Walter Kaufmann, New York: Random House, 2001, pp. 655–802.

Okely, Judith, 'Gendered Lessons in Ivory Towers', *Identity and Networks: Fashioning Gender across Cultures*, ed. D. F. Bryceson et al., Oxford: Berg, 2007, pp. 228–47.

Purwar, Nirmal, *Space Invaders: Race, Gender and Bodies Out of Place*, Oxford: Berg, 2004.

Rothblatt, Sheldon, *The Modern University and its Discontents: The Fate of Newman's Legacies in Britain and America*, Cambridge: Cambridge University Press, 1997.

Ruin, Hans, 'Philosophy, Freedom and the Task of the University: Reflections on Humboldt's Legacy', *The Humboldtian Tradition: Origins and Legacies*, ed. Peter Josephson et al., Leiden: Brill, 2014, pp. 164–77.

Shakespeare, William, *Love's Labours Lost*, in *The Oxford Shakespeare*, ed. Stanley Wells et al., Oxford: Clarendon Press, 1986.

Whistler, Daniel, 'Howie's *Between Feminism and Materialism* and the Critical History of Religions', *Sophia* 53.1 (2014): 183–92.

Part 2

Living with Dying

How to Think about Death: Living with Dying

Gillian Howie

Transcript of public lecture delivered at the University of Liverpool, 21 March 2012.[1]

I made the initial error of not really checking what the purpose of the Engage seminar series was about, and then yesterday I realized it was to do with methods. Well I'm not really going to talk very much about methods, because, in philosophy, our philosophical method is pretty much our philosophical content. So it's not often that we step back and reflect on what it is that we're doing when we're doing philosophy. In fact there are tested definitions of what it is to do philosophy ... and there are also distinctions between analytic philosophy and continental philosophy, which are distinctions that were pretty much drawn from self-defined analytic philosophers, who wanted to distinguish themselves from what they called the mumbo-jumbo of Heidegger. So there was a sense that logic and language philosophy, [that] of Russell and Moore, was analytic philosophy, and Sartre, Heidegger, that sort of thing, was continental philosophy, and there were, if not different methods, certainly different approaches. And it has subsequently been said, that you can't define philosophy in terms of continental and analytic, because, of course, analytic philosophers come from the continent, people like Wittgenstein, Frege. So there's something else that's distinguishing them, and it could be said that analytic philosophers

---

[1] The lecture was given as part of the Engage@Liverpool training programme for PhD students from the Humanities and Social Sciences at the University of Liverpool. It is available to watch at https://www.youtube.com/watch?v=czaaTDr09bc [accessed 31 May 2016]. The original slides used by Howie in her presentation are currently available online (http://slideplayer.com/slide/4435559/ [accessed 31 May 2016]), and more details about her talk are also available (https://www.liverpool. ac.uk/engage/archive-events/core,events/core,events,archive/2011-2012/living-with-dying/ [accessed 31 May 2016]). The text was transcribed by Victoria Browne and Daniel Whistler and all the notes and citations in what follows are the editors' interpolations.

see what they're doing much more as scientists do, that they're contributing to problems, each of them is contributing to a problem which they hope will move the debate forward; whereas continental philosophers have big brushes and they paint with these elaborate strokes about the meaning of life and what it is to be in the world, without really paying that much attention to the detail of the problem. I think it's probably about time that we reassemble philosophy across different fault-lines, so we reassemble it in terms of what we're interested in, and what interests me now is the phenomenon, the psychology, the phenomenology of living with dying. Which means reassembling our philosophy in terms of addressing that problem, so it doesn't matter whether it's analytic philosophy or continental or ancient philosophy it has something to contribute to [the phenomenology of living with dying] as a way of understanding it. That's what interests me.

That said, of course I started with certain intuitions. An intuition is just something that puzzles you, provokes a question, provokes a problem, and the intuition was that if you have a poor prognosis, if you have the prognosis of a life-limiting illness, it really comes as a surprise. No matter what you think, no matter how much you know that you're going to die, when it's upfront and close it's very personal and quite different. So it interested me that it was a surprise. And the surprise indicated the uniqueness of my death. So this notion of a surprise: that it's surprising that we die, no matter the fact that we all know that we do, that it reveals something about the uniqueness – that it's really my death not yours, and nobody else's – seemed to me to lead often to what you might call an existential crisis. Now it sounds horribly adolescent and all sixteen-year-olds and seventeen-year-olds go through this – what's the meaning of life? – and in a sense, what I will claim is that the questions that arise at a certain point of poor prognosis are the same questions and problems we live with all the time, but we don't confront in a personal way. And when we do confront them, and it's up close and personal, actually we don't have the tools to deal with them. And people who have a poor prognosis of life-limiting illness report suffering depression and anxiety and dislocation and an evacuation of meaning. And that's what I want to explore.

So first I start with some intuitions, which were these: that it comes as a real surprise, that some time you think that everybody else will die but it just won't happen to you. There's a phenomenology attached, which is this sort of existential crisis which I want to explore. As a philosopher, you start by clearing the ground, and saying what you're not going to talk about, and you define your terms. I'm going to look at two competing claims: one is that death gives meaning to life and one is that life-limiting illness can evacuate meaning, that it's an existential crisis of meaning and purpose.

Now I'm going to return to the notion of what we do as philosophers, and touch on the idea of an ancient notion of philosophy as *therapeia*, which is of living well, and whether you can live well right up to death. Because my intuition was that if you have a life-limiting illness, it tends to interfere with the living that you can do up to the point of dying. So a quote here from Epicurus, which is just reminding us of what philosophy as therapy might look like: 'Empty are the words of that philosopher who offers no therapy for human suffering. For just as there is no use in medical expertise if it doesn't give therapy for bodily disease, so too there is no use in philosophy if it does not expel the suffering of the soul.'[2] So the research question, I guess this is the methodology bit, is how can we live right up to death, when you have a life-limiting illness. And then I'm going to map those thoughts onto a new AHRC [Arts and Humanities Research Council] research network we have, which has been thinking about living with dying, and I'll talk a bit about the activities of that network.

There are a few things that we can say about death. There are probably very few universals left that are uncontested and uncontestable, but this is true: it is transcultural and transhistorical that you cannot avoid it. And that of course takes us to what we mean by the term death, and I think that it does work as an irreversible breakdown of an organism. As a definition it's sketchy, but it at least provides some underpinning. There is a cessation of awareness, there's an inability to continue functioning, it's the end of sentience, end of movement. All carbon-based life forms that are alive will die, and everything that has died was once alive. Now we talk of the death of cars, of batteries, of ideas, we talk of the death of democracy, of feminism, modernity, the death of the author, and, for the sake of this paper, I'm going to accept the distinction between carbon-based/ non-carbon-based life forms. That means that this group: democracy, feminism, modernity, the author, are only said to die in a metaphorical or figurative sense. What I do know is that when I talk about my death, I refer to the end of my projects, activities, relationships and commitments; I know that my death curtails my projects and all that I once thought possible. I also know that because death signals the end of this cognitive subject, there will be no me to mourn the loss. And, for this reason, Epicurus may be right to claim that we should face death with indifference, because it means nothing to us. It's also true that the terms

---

[2] Epicurus, 'Letter to Menoecus', in *The Hellenistic Philosophers*, Vol. 1, trans. and ed. by A. Long and D. Sedley, Cambridge: Cambridge University Press, 1987, p. 155.

death and life are not exhaustive. It could be said not only that dying occupies the intermediate position between being dead and being alive, but also that, to some extent, everything alive is in the process of dying and everything dying is still alive. And this porous quality between living and dying is on occasion evident in ways that we talk about suffering, so a philosopher such as Kierkegaard will often talk about suffering in terms of dying. Now there's a distinction to be made between death and demise, where one signifies ... legal, social, political matters, and one the existential moment of it. It's slightly a false distinction because, of course, you only die in a situation. So you can't really take that existential moment out. But for analytic interest, that's what I'm going to try to do.

So I'm not going to talk about the different meanings that death has across cultures. I'm not going to talk about the different status that being dead has legally across cultures and across history. I'm not going to talk about why organisms die and not organs, nor am I going to talk about ... it's great being a philosopher, you can just clear the ground by saying all these things are not quite relevant to what we're discussing ... I'm not going to talk about the relationship between brain death and technical death: I know this occupies people and it's significantly important, but this just isn't what I'm interested in today. Nor am I going to talk about transhumanism which is a fascinating new strain of argument, that transhumanists are about avoiding this very existential question – it's about putting yourself in a fridge until you can be revived again because we can overcome the limits of mortality ... It's transhuman because we're defined in terms of our death: to overcome the limits of our mortality is to go beyond being human. That's the sort of transhuman enterprise, and I'm not going to talk about that. Nor am I going to talk about the ontological status of the dead (i.e. what status do the dead have) and those who are not yet alive (do they occupy the same ontological status?). Nor am I going to talk about the afterlife, because those who believe in an afterlife, I think, are really merely passing through; their notion of death is quite different from the type of cessation that I'm talking about. And so that's a different argument. Nor am I going to talk about the horrors that we inflict on people and how immune we can become to the death of others. I'm not going to talk about the banality of evil.

What does that leave? Really quite a lot. Right, there's a sort of Philosophy 101 syllogism: Plato is a man; all men are mortal; Plato is mortal. But the truth of this syllogism is something that, the personal truth of it, is something that we skit around, and we don't, many of us don't, apprehend in [it] anything more than cognitive sense. However, there's a stream of philosophy, philosophies of finitude, where philosophers argue that the meaning of being human is the fact that we die, that we are mortal. Since Plato, it's commonplace to assume that the meaning of death illuminates the meaning of life. And, for Plato, doing philosophy in the right way is not just about answering questions about dying, but it is in itself getting used to facing death calmly, indeed practising death, in which case there would be no fear. So philosophy as a practice would be about preparing us for something that's inevitable, so that we could face it without fear. Pierre Hadot reminds us that in most schools of ancient philosophy, philosophy is essentially meditation on death, and an attentive concentration on the present in order to live it in full consciousness. The thought there, which is quite common to Buddhist philosophies I think ... is the thought of impermanence – that by reminding ourselves of our mortality we attend to the present in a much more refined and open way. For others, neo-Platonists mainly, because there is no pure knowledge in the company of the body, wisdom is only possible when we are dead.

In different ways, Heidegger, Levinas, Derrida – that's your continental bit – all agree that death gives meaning to life. Heidegger would have us believe that the uniqueness of our existence is revealed to us through the fact we must die, that we must die alone, and no one else can die for us. Death as my peculiar possibility wrenches me from the 'they', and with a newfound perspective on what matters, I can take a stand in authenticity. This is what he calls the non-relationality of death. In anticipating death I take responsibility for myself, my own person, and my relations with others are severed. In moments of despair we cannot conceal our underlying anxiety with a seeming meaninglessness, banality and emptiness, devoting one's life to merely doing what is in one's culture. So for [Heidegger], that we will die is enough to wake us up to what he calls this banality, the mediocrity, the 'they'. It lifts us from it, so in a sense it matters differently; it's freeing, then. Anxiety in the face of death liberates us from possibilities that count for nothing, and lets us free for those that do count for something. We are distinguished, he says, from other animals by the fact that we experience ourselves as mortal. This means of course we can't face death neutrally, because it is *our* own innermost possibility. So we have a strand of philosophy, then, that claims that there is something very ... important, about facing up to death, because it reminds us of our mortality and that we are, individually, responsible for our lives.

Now, in response to Heidegger's non-relationality view of death, [Adriana] Cavarero[3] suggests that we need to think – now here's a bit of a conundrum –

---

[3] See Adriano Cavarero, *In Spite of Plato*, trans. S. Anderlini-D'Onofrio and A. O'Healy, Cambridge: Polity, 1995, Ch. 4 and *Relating Narratives*, trans. P. A. Kottmann, London: Routledge, 2000.

we need to rethink death along the lines of natality, thinking death in terms of birth. Which seems a conundrum, but what she wants to highlight is that dying is itself relational, that you are already in relations, and it is severing human relationships that matters. She then invites us to reconceive death as bodily dissolution and reintegration into cosmic life. This impersonal approach to death, one also attempted I think by 'new materialists' such as Deleuze, is at odds with her own view that birth has ontological significance because it's the appearance of a unique being. So I don't see how she can really rethink death along the lines of natality, when by thinking natality and birth she's thinking not only relationships, but also the appearance of a unique being; whereas when she's talking about death, it's a dissolution of that unique being into cosmic life. Alison Stone also tries to think death in terms of relations, so the significance of somebody's death, to the extent we anticipate it, is that they mourn for relationships that they will lose.[4] Yet the idea of my death happening to me as a web of relations, I think, is counter-intuitive because there is a radical asymmetry: I might mourn losing relationships with others, but actually I'm the one that's going to die. So you can't make it simply about a process of mourning and of loss, because it's my death, it's my life, and yes, I might mourn these relations, but nonetheless there is something peculiar to me, so there's an asymmetry there. And so I don't think it's enough to draw on a psychoanalytic account that would mean your death is just a psychic death of part of me, where each death just moves into another.

Right, so, all of these are approaches to the notion that death gives meaning to life, that try to, in a sense, give life to that syllogism. We have the notion that mortality, thinking about mortality, thinking about death as finitude, brings an attentiveness to the present, that it reveals a uniqueness, finitude, the personal nature of death. The third point is that, as we die, we construct our past so it forms a coherent narrative, and that's the meaning that we attribute to life and to death, so, as we die, we can look back and say, well, that was what I was doing – and it gives it a narrative. And then finally we have the thought that death gives meaning to life because it calls attention to relationships, the relationships that we're embedded in and that we may or may not lose.

Now the counterclaim is that far from giving meaning to life, dying evacuates meaning from life, and this interests me. 'The meaning of life,' says Terry Eagleton, 'is a subject fit for either the crazed or the comic.'[5] The idea

---

[4]   Alison Stone, 'Natality and Mortality: Rethinking Death with Cavarero', *Continental Philosophy Review* 43 (2010). See further Stone's contribution to this volume.

[5]   Terry Eagleton, *The Meaning of Life*, Oxford: Oxford University Press, 2008, p. ix.

that anyone can stand up and talk about the meaning of life, even if they haven't seen *Monty Python*, has to just be absurd on some fundamental level. There is something absurd, he says, about its overarching pretentiousness. Indeed, you could ask whether the question, 'what is the meaning of life?', is a meaningful question: is there any answer that you could think of, that you could give, that would be satisfactory? It's not like asking what the capital of the UK is.

All of that said, and I recognize the absurdity of talking about the meaning of life and living with dying, meaningfulness does seem to be related to purpose: a meaningful life is a life with purpose. If that's the case, then what do we mean by purpose? Well, for the sake of simplicity, we can say that there are broadly these two senses and meanings to purpose ... If you ask what is the purpose of a gadget, you are asking really about its function: what role does it play, what does it do, what's its function? Or you could attribute it to persons and behaviour: you say something like, what is the purpose of putting the light on? Again, for the sake of simplicity, you could say the first sense maps onto the notion of the premodern, so you have the sense of a divine plan, a telos, a soul. Life is meaningful to the extent it fits in with a broader purpose, a broader plan; your purpose is to fit in with that broader plan. And the second definition maps onto what we might call the modern. So, with the enlightenment (I dislike talking about the enlightenment as if it were a thing that occurred in a certain place, at a certain time, but give me that!) or for the modern, we might say that meaning is related to our projects: what you throw into the world is meaningful, so what you decide to do, how you decide to live gives meaning to the world – and that's related to intentions, values and objectives. For the modern, for the enlightened person, the premodern way of looking at things is misconceived, because to say your purpose is that you fit into another plan is similar to saying that a chicken has a purpose because it will end up as *coq au vin*. For the moderns, the premoderns were looking at people as though they were merely functions or instruments in a broader picture. And we're all very enlightened now ... since the death of God we're all thoroughly enlightened, and so we're all quite familiar with the notion that meaning relates to purpose, which relates to our projects and intentions. The question is whether scientific enlightenment leads to disenchantment of the world, or does it provide us with the tools to realize our projects. So, for the post-Kantians you could argue that without the divine plan, without a telos, we're all just abandoned, thrown into the world of individual projects, where meaning and purpose come back to you. For the critical theorists amongst us, there is an uneasy relationship

– but necessary nonetheless – between this and the disenchantment of the world: that our ethics, our moral judgments seem to be themselves without foundation.

So in the quotidian, in the everyday, in the pragmatic – what Thomas Nagel described as 'the creaturely'[6] – meaning and purpose relate to our projects. A project is a series of events and actions made meaningful by an underlying purpose. So objects in the world have meaning not just because language is a public matter, but because objects contribute something to our activity. An example deployed by Sartre is that of a mountain: is it to be climbed or painted? If my intention is to climb it, I perceive its height and the character of its landscape, the distance to the summit. All quite different things from the case where I intend to paint cloud movement across its peak in watercolour. Of course, the mountain is there – in Sartre's words, the craggy mountainside as a measurable 'coefficient of adversity'[7] – but what it means, how much it matters, relates to my project to paint or climb it. Even my relationships to people gain their textures through my projects, so the conversation I might have with somebody at a school gate matters due to the fact we have a mutual interest in how events might develop with the rugby coach or football coach, whether we'll complain about a certain teacher or not; easy-going banter with a friend matters because of a shared past, a negotiated present and an orientation towards the future; my activity at work means what it does with reference, sadly, to the institution's strategic plan for future development and investment. I am not Prime Minister, I am not a Nobel Prize winner in the sense of not-yet-being Prime Minister, not-yet-being Nobel Prize winner; but just as the repetitive toil of Sisyphus indicates the endless pointlessness and meaninglessness of activity, we can ask of our projects, is each one only and merely a repetition of the last? For Thomas Nagel, herein we can see the collision of our two viewpoints we discussed earlier: the meaningfulness of our everyday purposive activity and the meaninglessness when viewed through a broader lens. If meaningfulness resides in what matters and what interests me, then we are provoked into infinite regress – the infinite regress of justification: why does X matter? Because Y matters. Why does Y matter? And so on. The problem – and here we can hear the echo of the cosmological argument – is that reasons within life are incomplete, all internal reasons are incomplete, but absurdity is the situation which includes a discrepancy between what we aspire to and reality. We aspire

---

[6] See Thomas Nagel, *The View from Nowhere*, Oxford: Oxford University Press, 1986, *passim*.
[7] Jean-Paul Sartre, *Being and Nothingness*, trans. Hazel E. Barnes, London: Routledge, 2003, pp. 509–11.

to purposefulness, yet the reasons we can give for each activity are only ever incomplete. Absurdity, says Nagel, is 'a collision within ourselves'.[8]

In these very modern times, meaningfulness of our everyday activity is just based on our projects, on our plans: it takes account of the past, it is a negotiation with the present and a relationship to the future and the horizon of activity. Yet, we step back from that and we say: does it really matter about the strategic plan? You don't have to step back very far before you can answer that! But then you step back a bit further: why do I go to work? Does it really matter that I pay the bills on this and that? And the 'what matters' question just becomes more and more difficult to answer, until you reach the recognition that our everyday needs do not have and cannot have the purposefulness that we ourselves aspire to.

If our absurdity may occasionally disturb us, causing moments of existential anxiety – what else is mid-life crisis? – then how much more pressing, more critical when the meaningfulness of everyday activity is interrupted. When a patient receives a prognosis, then the future itself is disturbed and the problem of meaningfulness in time emerges. When projects are truncated, the present – the folds of the past and the future – seems exhausted and evacuated of meaning. My thought here isn't just that 'it's really frightening to think about dying!' – yes, of course it is! ... but actually a life-limiting illness does something else as well: what it does is take your future away, and by taking your future away it makes it very difficult to live the present, because our present is a negotiation of the present towards the future. If you don't have that future, how do you live the present, as thoroughly modern beings in an enlightened world in which there is no divine plan? This temporal fracture incites the question, 'was that it?' – Peter Greenaway's *Belly of an Architect* rumbling on, ravenously tempting[9] ... At the very moment that the patient experiences the greatest turbulence, the problem of everyday meaningfulness can arise and seem too toxic to bear. Those who still envisage the future as their own do not experience this temporal fracture or the existential exhaustion that follows. This death is my death, and the life in question is mine. It has an irrefutable first-person quality ... and here I think is the argument against postmodernism ... In any situation these things might compel us to change direction, to alter our conditions, but in this state the only appropriate response seems to be hopelessness. Without a future, with

---

[8]   Thomas Nagel, 'The Absurd', *The Journal of Philosophy* 68 (1971): 722.
[9]   Howie here refers to Peter Greenaway's 1987 film, *The Belly of an Architect*, a film which revolves around questions of dying ('Death? Who's talking about death?') as well as meaning ('You mean that's really all?').

only a degraded past, the present is a very poor place indeed. It has been said that to describe a personal situation that is without hope is to slam the door in the face of God. But what then? Does it need to be engulfed by hopelessness to be without hope?

So what I'm saying is that Heidegger was right up to a point: humans are the only animals that confront their own situation as a question, a quandary, a source of anxiety, a ground of hope, a burden, a gift … one that is absurd, and that until the visceral truth of aloneness and ownership of death is grasped, the rest, I contend, does remain merely abstract, a banal question too easily put. But, against Heidegger, I suggest that dying doesn't enable authentic existence; rather, it clogs the mind with terror and evacuates meaning from the world, from my world. Fear, anguished depression and a retrospective 'was that it?' can ruin the mind as it is lived up until death. The belly of an architect shudders in involuntary spasms. For some, it may be the case that they experience a sense of unity in their practical identity, this narrative arc: as I'm dying, I go, 'It all makes sense now! This is what I was about.' But, for most, death is just that which makes the narrative fragment into endless modal alternatives: what if I'd done that when I was sixteen? What if I'd stayed with them? What if I'd left them and gone over there? What if I'd moved to India? Endless modal alternatives of how things could have been different.

Lots of people have started thinking about hope, hopefulness and hopelessness, and there is an interesting correlation between work that is being done in psychology at the moment dealing with parents and children with cancer, and the medics, around the terminology of hope, because people are looking for hope. But what does it mean to be hopeful? There is a notion of hope which in both secular and non-secular versions is the idea of open-ended hope. This is an idea of hope as a creative process, a sense of journey, becoming or transformation. It is not a false hope; it is not the hope that someone will discover a miracle drug; it is not the hope of life-everlasting that the transhumans have. And philosophical reflection can disabuse us of such false hopes. So philosophy can help to iron out the kinks in reasons for believing certain things might be the case, and philosophy can help demonstrate the unreasonableness of other beliefs. But hope resides in the transformation of relationships with other human beings and with the non-human world in such a way that we can focus on their interaction and intrinsic worth. The practice of living well right up to death might require the cultivation of a specific habit of mind, that of hope. Open-ended hope is hope that doesn't hope for something; it is not object-related.

It all looks a bit twee and it is in a way, but there is a strand within existentialism, and it's also apparent in some phenomenologies, such as Luce Irigaray's (if she cared to be called a phenomenologist), that cultivating nature enables a certain attention not only to non-human objects, the non-human world, but also to ourselves. But this is also evidence-based, because parks were first designed due to the belief that they will bring about health advantages and that there were healing effects to greenery in stressful environments, such as hospitals and nursing homes. Studies show that, in hospital, those with a view recover faster, require fewer pain killers and suffer fewer post-operative complications. Employees with a view of nature report fewer illnesses, headaches and stress. Experiences of green spaces maybe allow our two senses, our two perspectives to co-exist. Often gardens are distinguished from artworks or nature more generally; however, I wonder if this co-mingling in parks enables our two perspectives to co-exist and it is this that helps us live with our own absurdity. So this is what Victor Frankl is suggesting where he's reporting the story of a friend who is dying, and his friend says, 'This tree is the only friend I have in my loneliness ... It [the tree] said to me, "I am here – I am here – I am life, eternal life".'[10]

Now, this sense of the eternal in the present is what Luce Irigaray calls a 'sensible transcendental', that in our everyday experience there can be moments of the transcendental that I have initially identified as these two senses of purpose. So we have the purpose of our everyday meaningful activity related to projects, purpose of the divine, the telos, divine plan. We've abandoned the divine plan, those of us who no longer believe in a monotheistic god, we're left only with the everyday purpose; yet maybe at certain points, such as life-limiting illness before prognosis, you're forced into that moment of absurdity, of thinking of your everyday in terms of the eternal. What can help us there ... unless you want to turn to a theistic paradigm which many do and which does help ... another option is to cultivate nature, which itself is transformative, creative and hopeful, even if your future is truncated, even if you don't have very long to live.

There is also the thought of cultivating communication. Kierkegaard might be right that some experiences just cannot be said, you cannot put into propositional form the experience of really confronting your own mortality. Well, how do we engage with it then? How do we talk to each other at those times? Kierkegaard has this thought of indirect communication, that the unsayable requires indirect speech – and I'll come back to that.

[10] Victor Frankl, *Man's Search for Meaning*, London: Rider, 2004, p. 62.

So, sort of concluding: philosophy shouldn't be the practice of death, but that of life, of living well right up to death. The question is whether the experience of particular philosophical practices can induce a habit of mind or a certain way of living to which others might aspire, even if only for a 'this moment', a habit of mind that allows us to live right up to death with hope. The strand of philosophy which is philosophy as *therapeia* is articulated by the pragmatist William James who said that this meant realizing that theoretical reason, pure reason alone, cannot provide answers to the questions that are most troubling. Philosophy can do the conceptual, causal work, but the reconsideration of living up to death, I think, also means coming across the limits of philosophy, and the limits of philosophy end at the point we start talking about cultivating nature and cultivating communication, because these are different practices. Philosophy may be able to, as I say, point out where our hopefulness is hope for an object that can't be realized; what it can't do is this practice which is about cultivating a state of mind of hopefulness even in the face of a shortened future.

So that takes me to the research network[11] [...] The research network is bringing together academics and practitioners interested in the psychology and phenomenology of living with dying. Because of clinical advances, people are having to face this existential crisis that I've been talking about for years: people can have a poor prognosis and still be alive four, five, six years later. Living from moment to moment with this existential crisis, this level of absurdity pointed out by Thomas Nagel, that's impossible: it's impossible to sustain it, and to sustain it well. So clinical practitioners are turning their attention to this extended life. There are structured pathways of care for people with terminal illness, but for people who are going to die in five years' time, clinical practitioners just try to keep them alive, that's what they're concerned with. But for those who are being kept alive, it is an ongoing negotiation of this existential crisis where they have no future, and so their normal projects seem meaningless.

So, we have three research workshops; our network brings together clinical practitioners, including psychology here (Peter Salmon who works on a cancer research group and John Ellershaw who is the director of the Marie Curie Palliative Care Unit) and theologians and philosophers and anyone else who is interested. And we have three research workshops identified. The first is *Thinking about Dying* which is just thinking through some of these issues around time, the future, meaningfulness, existential crisis ... Which takes on to the second

---

[11] Full details of Howie's research network, *New Thinking on Living with Dying*, are available at https:// newthinkingaboutlivingwithdying.wordpress.com/ [accessed 31 May 2016].

research workshop which is *Mental Health and Living with Dying*, because it is a very anxious time, a very stressful time, and more than that – can there be anything more than that! … and this does map on to concerns that people working with the elderly have … as your body changes, as you go through intense treatment, what your body can do and what it looks like also changes. And this sense of loss that people live with itself contributes to the feeling of meaningless or worthlessness of life as they're living it. So the challenge is to allow your body to change without feeling that as a loss, where you're always aiming back for a past that you can't recover. So changing identities, changing bodies, living with anxiety, that sort of thing, is the concern of the second workshop. And the third research workshop is the clinical model of care: whether it does make sense to have a structured pathway of care for such a long time, and how clinicians might talk to the patients who are undergoing that trauma, the unsayable. And then we have three public events: the first is with the Disability and Deaf Arts Festival,[12] because I believe that it is critical disability theorists who have the most to teach us about how to live a changing body without living that as a loss with norms that you are continually trying to recover. So we are trying to bring disability theorists together with disability practitioners as well as patients. The second is reading as therapy – this is with the Reader Group[13] – that sometimes the unsayable can be expressed otherwise. My intuition is that reading won't do it, but music might, but we'll see, so we're running a workshop on this. And the third – this is with Ness Gardens and Sefton Allotment Groups[14] – putting into practice the idea of cultivating nature, without, for example, having to take on the responsibility for a garden at a point when you're tired and not very fit, but just the experience of tending, being attentive to, enables the patients themselves to care for themselves. There's something transformative in that relationship. So, there are the three public events and the three research workshops, all of which are mobilized by this one thought, really, from Paul Ricoeur, who had a posthumously published book, *Living up to Death*: 'the mobilization of the deepest resources to affirm this life; my life unto death'.[15] The research question is, I say it again: how can we live right up to death, even that period during life-limiting illness when we know we only have a few years to live?

Thank you.

---

[12] For more details on DaDa Fest, see http://www.dadafest.co.uk/ [accessed 31 May 2016].
[13] For more details on The Reader, see http://www.thereader.org.uk/ [accessed 31 May 2016].
[14] See, respectively, http://www.nessgardens.org.uk/ [accessed 31 May 2016] and http://www.seftongreengym.co.uk/ [accessed 31 May 2016].
[15] Paul Ricoeur, *Living up to Death*, trans. David Pellauer, Chicago, IL: University of Chicago Press, 2009, p. 14.

References

Cavarero, Adriano, *In Spite of Plato*, trans. S. Anderlini-D'Onofrio and A. O'Healy, Cambridge: Polity, 1995.

Cavarero, Adriano, *Relating Narratives*, trans. P. A. Kottmann, London: Routledge, 2000.

Eagleton, Terry, *The Meaning of Life*, Oxford: Oxford University Press, 2008.

Epicurus, 'Letter to Menoecus', in *The Hellenistic Philosophers*, Vol. 1, ed. and trans. A. Long and D. Sedley, Cambridge: Cambridge University Press, 1987, 154–9.

Frankl, Victor, *Man's Search for Meaning*, London: Rider, 2004.

Nagel, Thomas, 'The Absurd', *The Journal of Philosophy* 68 (1971): 716–27.

Nagel, Thomas. *The View from Nowhere*, Oxford: Oxford University Press, 1986.

Ricoeur, Paul, *Living up to Death*, trans. David Pellauer, Chicago, IL: University of Chicago Press, 2009.

Sartre, Jean-Paul, *Being and Nothingness*, trans. Hazel E. Barnes, London: Routledge, 2003.

Stone, Alison, 'Natality and Mortality: Rethinking Death with Cavarero', *Continental Philosophy Review* 43 (2010): 353–72.

7

Gillian Howie's Situated Philosophy: Theorizing Living and Dying 'In Situation'

Christine Battersby

Introduction

In her posthumously published essay, 'Alienation and Therapy in Existentialism', Gillian Howie considers the claim that 'Philosophers, as strangers to the everyday and aspiring to be free from the demands of the particular and the quotidian, seem completely the wrong people to ask about fear, loss, pain and suffering.'[1] The article offers a robust defence against any such view, turning to Jean-Paul Sartre to position existentialist psychoanalysis in a tradition that treats philosophy not merely as 'an intellectual discipline concerned with concepts, theories, ideas, reason and argument', but as a mode of therapy: 'philosophical practice can help to cure mental or spiritual disorder and restore psychological health.'[2] As such, Howie positions Sartre, and also herself, in a counter-tradition which includes Indian and ancient Greek philosophical traditions, as well as Wittgensteinian and nineteenth- and twentieth-century pragmatist philosophers.[3] According to this counter-tradition, therapy is not simply a bi-product

---

[1] Gillian Howie, 'Alienation and Therapy in Existentialism: A Dual Model of Recognition', *Ethical Theory and Moral Practice* 17 (2014): 56. http://link.springer.com/article/10.1007/s10677-013-9466-8/fulltext.htm [accessed 4 October 2015]. The article was published online 2 October 2013, with the proofs corrected by Simon Hailwood (University of Liverpool) in September 2013. The article was changed by Howie extensively between early summer 2012 and the time of her death (27 March 2013), especially in relation to the theme of philosophy as therapy, and was thus clearly something that she worked on in the final months of her life. I am profoundly grateful to Simon Hailwood for information about the genesis of the article, as well as for allowing me to see a draft of the article from Summer 2012, as well as the (very different) paper which Howie presented in Münster (December 2010) at a workshop on the social and political aspects of 'New Thinking on Alienation'.

[2] Howie, 'Alienation and Therapy in Existentialism', p. 56. I have added in the missing comma after 'ideas'.

[3] Ibid., p. 56.

of philosophical practice, but 'its singular purpose and achievement'.[4] Thus, Howie concludes the article by avowing that 'Existentialist psychotherapy is aligned to the ancient tradition of philosophical therapy': it 'aims to reveal beliefs that have not been established and habitual behaviours that are harmful'.[5]

This essay was worked on by Howie during 2012–13, with the strong conclusion on the possibility of philosophy acting as a therapeutic cure added sometime between early summer 2012 and the time of her death from cancer in March 2013. Interestingly, and poignantly, it presents a more optimistic view of the capacity of philosophy to 'cure' inadequately grounded beliefs and mental habits than we find in the public lecture 'How to Think about Death: Living with Dying' (March 2012).[6] I will come back to the 'Alienation and Therapy in Existentialism' article towards the end of this essay. I will, however, concentrate for the most part on comparing the position that Howie argues for in the public lecture of 2012 with that of her 2010 monograph, *Between Feminism and Materialism: A Question of Method*.[7] I will focus, in particular, on the way in which Howie deploys – and elaborates on – the notion of life as 'situation'. This is a theme that is present in both the living-with-dying lecture and also in the book *Between Feminism and Materialism*; but there are also important differences between the two texts. As we will see, the lecture is strikingly original in terms of the way in which Howie develops the notion of 'situation', especially in relation to the question of living-towards-death. However, as the 'Alienation and Therapy in Existentialism' article makes clear, Howie's own position was still evolving in 2012 – perhaps, in part, due to her involvement with the *New Thinking on Living with Dying* interdisciplinary network of academics and practitioners which was set up in 2012, based at the University of Liverpool, and for which Howie acted as Principal Investigator.

Before looking at Howie's own account of living – and also dying – 'in situation', I need first to explain how the term features in two philosophical texts which Howie both refers to and also criticizes: Martin Heidegger's *Being and Time* (*Sein und Zeit*, first published 1927) and Jean-Paul Sartre's *Being and Nothingness* (*L'Être et le néant*, first published 1943). Both are foundational texts of existential phenomenology and, in this tradition, 'situation' is used in a quasi-technical way, being linked to the framework within which, against which, or

---

⁴ Ibid., p. 56.
⁵ Ibid., p. 68.
⁶ Gillian Howie, 'How to Think about Death: Living with Dying', transcribed as Ch. 6 of the present volume.
⁷ Gillian Howie, *Between Feminism and Materialism: A Question of Method*, New York: Palgrave Macmillan, 2010.

through which the freedom of the agent is exercised. So much existentialist phenomenologists agree on; but there are also clear differences in the way that 'situation' is treated by the individual phenomenologists.

Heidegger on situation and authenticity

I will start with Heidegger who uses two different German terms (*Situation* and *Lage*) – both translated into English as 'situation' – to emphasize the fact that human consciousness (*Dasein*) always involves an interpretative dimension and also choice, either in relation to an everyday mode of being-in-the-world or to a more authentic mode of being that involves care, resoluteness and being-towards-death. In their translation of Heidegger's *Being and Time*, the German term *Situation* is generally translated by Macquarrie and Robinson with a capital 'S'. By contrast, *Lage*, which is 'situation' in a more everyday sense (perhaps better translated as 'circumstances'), is given a small 's'.[8] I will not follow this convention, but I will nevertheless try to explain why Heidegger seeks to keep the two concepts distinct.

For Heidegger, *Situation*, in its more technical sense, is bound up with the uniqueness of the individual human existent or *Dasein*, and especially with the fact that *Dasein* finds itself born into a world and into an environmental locatedness that it does not itself choose. *Dasein* cannot help but be, but it can shape the kind of self that it will become; and it does this by resolutely facing up to the need to choose from amongst the range of possibilities that lie before it. It is through this 'resoluteness, or the repeated choosing of who I am' that *Dasein* 'acquires insight into its situation and discovers the possibilities of its unique selfhood'.[9] It is by resolutely choosing – and not simply drifting along – that the uniqueness of the individual human is shaped. As Schalow and Denker put it, for Heidegger, 'situation' in the technical sense 'is always a concrete situation of action that is disclosed in a concrete understanding'.[10]

'*Dasein*' – Heidegger's preferred term for the experience of being that is common to humans – does, in German, break down into two components: '*da*'

---

[8] Martin Heidegger, *Being and Time*, trans. John Macquarrie and Edward Robinson, Oxford: Blackwell, 1962, p. 346 n. 1 [H. 299 n. 1]. The reference in brackets is to the marginal notations which refer to the pagination of the later German editions of Martin Heidegger, *Sein und Zeit* (8th edn), Tübingen: Max Niemeyer Verlag, 1957.

[9] Frank Schalow and Alfred Denker, *Historical Dictionary of Heidegger's Philosophy* (2nd edn), Lanham, MD: Scarecrow Press, 2010, p. 16.

[10] Ibid., p. 16.

(meaning 'there' or 'here') which is an adverbial pronoun that locates an entity in a particular region of space; and *'sein'* (which means 'to be' or 'to exist'). *Dasein* is always 'in situation', and this situatedness always brings with it the need to interpret the world and resolutely choose from amongst the possible pathways ahead. For Heidegger, authenticity is linked not directly with choosing oneself, but rather with the resolute choice to choose what one will become.[11] There are multiple temptations that lead humans to block out, or simply not see, their situational positioning, and the choices that are required if one's potential as an individual is to develop and emerge. For those other (non-authentic) humans – whom Heidegger terms *'the they'* [*das Man*] – '*the Situation is essentially something that has been closed off.* The "they" knows only the "*general situation*" [*Lage*], loses itself in those "*opportunities*" that are closest to it, and pays Dasein's way by a reckoning up of "accidents" which it fails to recognize, deems its own achievement, and passes off as such.'[12] The German term for 'the *they*' is *das Man*, literally 'the one': a generalized term that denotes any arbitrarily selected human and, as such, no particular human with his or her specific character or dispositions. *Das Man* is someone abstractly considered, not a person whose authentic character has emerged through resolutely taking on responsibility for the emergent self. It is possible that each human existent or *Dasein* might remain forever amorphous, and Heidegger insists that it is only by establishing a different relation to time that we can escape the shallowness of the 'everyday', and that of losing oneself in accidental 'opportunities' and 'idle talk' which allow this characterless 'someone' to persist.[13]

Importantly, for Heidegger in *Being and Time,* this changed relation to time comes through mood, and through the feeling of dread/anxiety (*Angst*), which comes from facing the fact of *my* own death, and living one's life in the mode of being towards death.[14] Thus, for Heidegger, death – and, more specifically, 'my own death' – is not simply a given, but is one of the structures of the 'herme-neutical Situation' through which consciousness frames the world, and finds meaning in it.[15] Unlike animals which, Heidegger supposes, are unable to grasp the notion that they will someday cease to exist, human beings can anticipate death and do so in the mode of living that Heidegger calls 'being-toward-death'

---

[11] See Béatrice Han-Pile, 'Freedom and the "Choice to Choose Oneself"', in *Being and Time'*, in Mark A. Wrathall (ed.), *The Cambridge Companion to Heidegger*, Cambridge: Cambridge University Press, 2013, pp. 291–319.

[12] Heidegger, *Being and Time*, pp. 346–7 [H. 300].

[13] Ibid., pp. 346–7 [H. 300], 218–9 [H. 174–5], 368 [H. 321–2].

[14] Ibid., pp. 294–304 [H. 250–60].

[15] Ibid., pp. 279ff. [H 235ff.].

[*Sein zum Tode*].[16] This mode of anticipation is not simply the recognition of the inevitability of death, and neither is it simply the thought that my life will come to an end some day – even less is it simply to expect or await death in a despairing or passive fashion. Instead, this mode of anticipation [*Vorlaufen*] and being always 'ahead-of-itself' is integral to *Dasein* insofar as it develops the potentialities that lie within it. Furthermore, it is through projecting itself towards a horizon of future possibilities that *Dasein* is able to authentically address its concrete situation in the here-and-now. As McLean puts it, for Heidegger, 'death is not so much a future event which terminates [*Dasein's*] existence as it is a future inevitability *that brings Da-sein's present life into focus*'.[17] For Heidegger, it is consciousness of *my own* impending death that deepens the significance of the present, as *Dasein* chooses to maximize its potential in the specific spatial and environmental situation within which it finds itself located.

Situation in Sartre, Beauvoir and Merleau-Ponty

Sartre is influenced by Heidegger; but his *Being and Nothingness* does not privilege 'being towards death' as a mode of authentic living in the same way as Heidegger does in *Being and Time*. Instead, for Sartre, authenticity comes from avoiding bad faith. The latter is a form of self-deception which most commonly occurs when consciousness refuses to recognize the radical freedom that Sartre regards as integral to human nature. Although Sartre registers that bad faith can also result from disregarding the limits within which freedom is exercised, he also – famously – insists that 'man is condemned to be free'.[18] Sartre does not make a distinction between two types of situation in the manner of Heidegger, but he does nevertheless emphasize that the radical freedom to choose oneself that is common to all is always and only exercised over and against 'the situation' in which the agent finds herself or himself. For Sartre, 'the situation' is also not straightforwardly 'out there', but instead emerges in relation to the projects that the individual agent has. In particular, 'the situation' emerges as the embodied

---

[16] B. H. McLean, *Biblical Interpretation and Philosophical Hermeneutics*, Cambridge: Cambridge University Press, 2012, pp. 124–5.
[17] Ibid., p. 125.
[18] Jean-Paul Sartre, *Existentialism and Humanism*, trans. Philip Mairet, London: Eyre Methuen, 1977, p. 34. The phrasing in *Being and Nothingness* is slightly different: 'To be free is to be condemned to be free.' See Jean-Paul Sartre, *Being and Nothingness: An Essay on Phenomenological Ontology*, trans. Hazel E. Barnes, London: Methuen, 1957, p. 129.

consciousness ('being-for itself') reads meaning and significances onto the world in the light of his or her desires, hopes and goals.

Sartre insists that man is condemned to be free, but he is certainly not claiming that man is autonomous and self-determining. Instead there are brute 'givens' which define man's situation and which cannot be avoided. Freedom is only exercised within the limits of these constraints. In fact, freedom is only ever to be understood against a background 'situation' which has to be negated by the for-itself as it registers a lack or an absence in the world that it has been born into, and then seeks to compensate for the missing element. Hence, Sartre's claim that the given 'does not cause freedom'; nor is the given 'the reason of freedom', since it is only human consciousness that can find reasons for acting.[19] Instead, the given is 'the plenitude of being which freedom colors with insufficiency and with *négatité* by illuminating it with the light of an end which does not exist'.[20]

As an example of acting 'in situation', Sartre gives the example of a crag that I am wanting to climb. The crag appears to me as 'not scalable' in relation to my goal of climbing up a particular mountain or cliff. This goal is, however, just a 'secondary project' in terms of a deeper level goal that I have: such as, an interest in rock climbing or a need to get to a particular destination. This more generalized objective is, moreover, also merely a sub-project of the 'initial project which is my being-in-the-world'.[21] Sartre goes on to argue that if my primary project for being-in-the-world is caught up with rock climbing, the rock will reveal a different face to me than it will reveal to somebody with a different primary project, for example somebody caught up with an aesthetic appreciation of landscapes (photographing them, painting them and the like). How the world appears to me will depend on my primary project, and it is this primary project that transforms the 'givens' into a 'situation' that not only opens up opportunities for the agent, but that also, simultaneously, functions as an 'obstacle' or 'resistance' to the agent's desired goals or aims. As such, Sartre asserts that 'the situation' emerges at the conjunction of brute fact ('the givens') and freedom: it is, he says, a 'product' of 'the contingency of the in-itself and of freedom'.[22]

For Sartre, then, freedom enters into the world only in relation to a 'given' that requires negation. It is only because I have wants, goals, desires and

---

[19] Ibid., pp. 486–7.
[20] Ibid., p. 487. Hazel Barnes chooses not to translate the term '*négatité*' which Sartre uses for modes of judgement that include negativity in the sense of registering an absence, or an awareness that something that can be destroyed or changed (ibid., p. 632).
[21] Ibid., p. 488.
[22] Ibid., p. 488.

needs that features of the 'given' appear to my consciousness as being in need of change and, in so appearing, become part of the situation that motivates my action. 'Situation and motivation are really one', Sartre asserts.[23] What is revealed to the embodied consciousness that is being-for-itself is 'an obstacle' to my projects, and that obstacle in its turn reveals 'its coefficient of adversity across freely invented and freely acquired techniques'.[24] The phrasing here is revealing, since Sartre uses the adverb 'freely' in relation to the techniques and capacities that the embodied for-itself can draw on, even claiming at one point that 'in one sense it is *I* who choose my body as weak by making it face the difficulties which I cause to be born (mountain climbing, cycling, sport)'.[25] Although Sartre immediately goes on to stress the 'paradox' of freedom – that freedom only exists '*in a situation*' and that there is only 'a situation' through freedom – he nevertheless plays down the role of the bodily, social and cultural incapacities in terms of the way in which one's primary project emerges.

There are five structural elements of 'the situation' that are common to all human agents, according to Sartre.[26] These are 'my place' (the fact that each of us was born at a particular place, and born of particular parents); 'my past' (the temporal precedents out of which any new choice must emerge); 'my environment' (the instrumental things that surround me and which may be used, or which may hinder my actions); 'my fellowman' (Sartre includes here my nationality and the language I speak, as well as the way in which I need to confront meanings and labels that are generated by others and that limit, or enable, my choices); and, finally, 'my death' (which Sartre argues, against Heidegger, is always absurd, in that it always eludes the meanings one tries to impose on living).[27]

I'll come back to Sartre's view of death as the fifth structural element of the situation later, as I consider Howie's argument in her 'How to Think about Death' lecture. But what we also need to register here are three things: first, that Sartre plays down the role of the social, cultural and purely bodily in his account of 'the situation'; second, that Sartre maintains that agency always requires a reading of 'the situation', and involves a process of *negating* the givens that make up the situation; and, third, that for Sartre man is always radically free insofar

---

[23] Ibid., p. 487.

[24] Ibid., p. 488.

[25] Ibid., p. 489.

[26] Ibid., Part 4, Ch. 1, Sec II: 'Freedom and Facticity: The Situation', pp. 481–553.

[27] Part 4, Ch. 1, Sec II is subdivided into 'A. My Place' (pp. 489–96), 'B. My Past' (pp. 496–504), 'C. My Environment' (pp. 504–9), 'D. My Fellowman' (pp. 509–31), 'E. My Death' (pp. 531–53). For the claim that death is always absurd see p. 533. Much of subsection E is taken up with the argument against Heidegger.

as he is conscious and capable of seeing 'a situation' that he or she would like to change. Even in prison, the Sartrean being-for-itself could be said to be free insofar as consciousness remains aware of its imprisonment and is capable of drawing up plans for escape.

For Simone de Beauvoir, by contrast, some situations are so constraining that choice is effectively blocked off. In a 1982 interview with Alice Schwarzer, Beauvoir claimed that she had persuaded Sartre to modify his position, and that the published version of *Being and Nothingness* contains a more nuanced view of freedom:

> In an early draft of *Being and Nothingness*, [Sartre] spoke of freedom as if it were quasi-total for the entire world. Or, at least, as if it were open to all to exercise their freedom. I, on the contrary, insisted that there are situations in which freedom cannot be exercised, or in which it is mystifying to talk about freedom. He agreed with that. And, in the end, placed much more weight on the situation in which the human being finds himself.[28]

Beauvoir does, however, overstate the case, and traces of the totalizing view of freedom are still evident in *Being and Nothingness*. She has, in effect, credited Sartre with including in that text what seems to me one of the most original theses of her own *The Ethics of Ambiguity*, which was published in 1947. This clearly modifies Sartre's own starting point, making a distinction between freedom and revolt. The prisoner might dream of freedom; but freedom is not equated simply with the imagining of escape, instead 'the prison is repudiated as such when the prisoner escapes'.[29]

Beauvoir also includes embodiment within the 'givens' that constrain freedom, in a way that Sartre's model misses out. Indeed, Part I, Chapter 1 of *The Second Sex* has, in French, the title '*Les Données de la biologie*' ('The Givens of Biology'), signalling clearly both one of its main differences from – and also its relation to – *Being and Nothingness*.[30] Thus, biology was significantly absent from the five structural elements of the situation that Sartre picks out, and is hardly mentioned at all anywhere in *Being and Nothingness*. In addition, modes

---

[28] Alice Schwarzer (ed.), *Simone de Beauvoir Aujourd'hui: Six Entretiens*, Mayenne: *Mercure de France*, 1984, p.114. (The translation is my own.)

[29] Simone de Beauvoir, *The Ethics of Ambiguity*, trans. Bernard Frechtman, Secaucus, NJ: Citadel Press, n.d., p. 31.

[30] The philosophical grounding of Beauvoir's position is made less clear in English translations of the French text which renders this section either as 'The Data of Biology' or, in the most recent translation, the even less appropriate 'Biological Data'. What this phraseology misses out is Beauvoir's view – analogous to that of Sartre – that 'givens' are not determining, but aspects of the 'situation' that invite negation. See Simone de Beauvoir, *The Second Sex*, trans. Constance Borde and Sheila Malovany-Chevallier, New York: Vintage, 2011, pp. 21–48.

of lived embodiment were analysed by Sartre not in the section on 'Freedom and Facticity: The Situation', but under the heading 'Being-for-Others'.[31]

Maurice Merleau-Ponty makes a similar move to Beauvoir, in that he insists that one's bodily comportment and motility are integral to 'the situation' through which freedom is exercised. He writes, for example, that,

> Whether or not we have decided to climb them, these mountains appear high to me, because they exceed my body's power to take them in its stride, and ... I cannot so contrive it that they are small for me. Underlying myself as a thinking subject, ... there is, therefore, as it were a natural self which does not budge from its terrestrial situation and which constantly adumbrates absolute evaluations. [32]

This is a very different analysis from that of Sartre, for whom the height of the crag and its scalability were entirely dependent on the goals and projects that the individual for-itself possessed. Merleau-Ponty's position also differs from that of Sartre and Beauvoir in that he posits a shared human nature in ways that Beauvoir and Sartre would both deny. Partly as a consequence, he makes freedom not a matter of *negating* 'the situation', but a way of being 'intermingled' with the situation so that new opportunities arise. For Merleau-Ponty, freedom doesn't surge up out of nothing, since certain preferences have become sedimented through habit.[33] If men find themselves in a shared, earthly environment, then there will be shared habits – and a kind of shared universality and 'naturalness'.

Situation in Howie's *Between Feminism and Materialism*

In her 'How to Think about Death' lecture, Gillian Howie engages explicitly with Heidegger and Sartre on the question of living-towards-death, and develops her own distinctive account of the roles of mood, authenticity and anxiety, as well as of the way in which we should respond to despair. As we will see, Howie remains closer to Sartre than to other phenomenological theorists, although she does draw some insights from both Heidegger and Beauvoir (which means that at some points she does seem close to Merleau-Ponty). She also draws directly

---

[31] See Sartre, *Being and Nothingness*, pp. 481–553 for 'The Situation', and pp. 303–59 for embodiment.
[32] Maurice Merleau-Ponty, *Phenomenology of Perception*, trans. Colin Smith, London: Routledge and Kegan Paul, 1986, p. 440.
[33] Ibid., p. 441.

on her own experience, as well as from the testimonies of others who are living with poor diagnoses and life-limiting illnesses. I will come back to the living-with-dying lecture later, but first I would like to explore the way in which the term 'situation' functions in Howie's *Between Feminism and Materialism*.

Once one focuses on this issue, it becomes clear how central this concept is to the argument of Howie's 2010 monograph: with the word 'situation' being used over ninety times in the main text, and other related terms – 'situations', 'situated', 'situational', 'situatedness' and so on – adding around forty extra examples. Of course, not all of these instances are philosophically interesting; but most do fit with the way in which this vocabulary is employed in the phenomenological tradition. Howie herself places most emphasis on Sartre's *Being and Nothingness*. Heidegger's *Being and Time* is discussed, but not Heidegger's more technical usage of the term '*Situation*'. For reasons said to be due, at least in part, to 'personal preference', Merleau-Ponty features only very briefly – and primarily in the context of Howie's, also rather condensed, discussion of Beauvoir.[34]

I will start by making several general observations about the ways in which the language of situatedness functions in *Between Feminism and Materialism*, before moving on to explore how the Sartrean 'given' of death is treated in that text. First, like Sartre, Beauvoir and Heidegger, Howie maintains that 'the situation' only ever emerges in relation to human consciousness: it is never simply 'out there' in a naively materialist kind of way. Second, it is Sartre's account of 'the situation' and of lived embodiment and the for-itself that Howie finds the most productive for her project of developing a materialist and feminist framework capable of 'breathing life' back into 'feminist activism', both inside and outside the academy.[35] However, Howie modifies the Sartrean framework in some quite radical ways. In particular, she emphasizes, much more than Sartre, that the for-itself is always embodied and is located in a framework of historical, cultural and social constraints. These 'givens' can all be negated, but they are also pressing in a more materialist sense than Sartre's own analysis would suggest.

Third, Howie places the notion of situation at the hub of her understanding of what it is to be a woman: a move that places her closer to Beauvoir than to Sartre. Thus, Howie asserts: 'A woman is someone with a female body lived as her situation, demonstrating relevant resemblances to other members of the same kind.'[36] Nowhere does Sartre link 'situation' with sexual difference,

---

[34] Howie, *Between Feminism and Materialism*, p. 161.
[35] Ibid., p. 205.
[36] Ibid., p. 173.

or indeed with lived embodiment, in this direct kind of way. Howie favours abandonment of the sex/gender vocabulary, and advocates instead bringing back the terms 'women' and 'men' into philosophical, feminist and materialist discourse, whilst simultaneously emphasizing that it cannot be assumed that 'women form a coherent group with identical experiences and interests, regardless of geographic, class, ethnic, racial, or religious locations'.[37] Being a woman is to occupy 'a situation' in relation to choice, agency, significance and freedom; it is not simply a state of being.

Fourth, the notion of natural kinds that Howie draws on in her discussion of 'woman' is one that is based on concealed differences, disguised by the language of identity. She claims that 'sex, or the biological body, is one component of the cluster "woman"'.[38] In developing this position, Howie combines insights taken from Theodor Adorno with a broadly Sartrean understanding of what is involved in living 'in situation', claiming that 'A constellation of concepts is the appropriate analytic device to unpick and express the intersecting features of my situation-as-lived, of my identity. My identity is a dialectical relationship of non-identity, deterioration, and noncoincidence; expressible – if at all – through speculative dialectical logic'.[39] Because Howie reads both Sartre and Adorno as recognizing concealed differences sheltering beneath a language and conceptual scheme that privileges sameness, she finds resources within Sartre's philosophy – as also within that of Adorno – for effecting social change. The fact that the situation is not simply what is given, but an interpretation of the given in terms of one's values and projects, is part of what makes the notion of 'situation' key for political (and also philosophical) activism: the 'dynamic interaction between various factors operating within a situation' itself becomes a means of changing that situation.[40] Howie emphasizes that phenomenology avoids deterministic portrayals of subjectivity and of agency; but (like Adorno) she is critical of the 'thin story of mental contents and activity' that is offered by phenomenologists: 'the philosophical subject remains curiously untouched by their situation and, pertinently, by their capacity to exercise power as it is

---

[37] Ibid., p. 182. Toril Moi's *What is a Woman? And Other Essays*, Oxford: Oxford University Press, 1999, is used to ground this move. Others trace this insight back to Beauvoir, but I think Howie is wise to limit the discussion to Moi who extrapolates on Beauvoir's position as she argues against the gender/sex dichotomy as it is used in feminist theory. As Moi herself points out, Beauvoir herself does not use the gender/sex dichotomy (ibid., pp. 72ff.). Indeed, since the sex/gender distinction does not operate in the same way in the French language, there is something odd about trying to align Beauvoir's position with those of later twentieth-century Anglophone feminists.

[38] Howie, *Between Feminism and Materialism*, p. 173.

[39] Ibid., p. 175.

[40] Ibid., p. 119.

revealed through the object-complex. By talking about decision-making, rather than power-discourse, we can tie power firmly back to responsibility', Howie asserts.[41]

Death and illness in Howie's *Between Feminism and Materialism*

With this background behind us, we can now turn to look at the way in which the question of death features in *Between Feminism and Materialism*. And the most surprising thing to notice is the absence of any extended discussion of this issue. Howie twice registers that 'death' is included by Sartre as one of the five structural features of 'the situation' in *Being and Nothingness*, but whereas Howie comments in some detail on the way in which freedom negates the four other aspects of the situation, she is silent on the way in which 'my death' comes into play.[42] Instead, Howie deflects Sartre's account of death into a (rather troubling) account of illness and, in particular, of a tumour that can be – metaphorically, and literally – cut away.

> That I have a tumor is a biological fact, but there are no ensuing grounds from this for concluding anything about the meaning and value I will attribute to it. Indeed, the tumor will be revealed in light of my projects, and my future will be revealed in my attitude to the tumor. Strictly speaking, a situation is 'the contingency of freedom in the plenum of being in the world.' A thing never appears as brute in-itself, 'the hill' or 'the tumor,' but is revealed in light of an end that illuminates it, 'the hill as scaleable' or 'the tumor as removable.' Situation and motivation are the same thing.[43]

The problem of phrasing the question in this broadly Sartrean way is that, for Sartre, whether the crag was perceived to be scalable or not scalable was primarily determined by the goals and projects of the individual spectator who confronts it with particular ends and interests in view. Sartre is not like Merleau-Ponty who claims that there are certain 'natural' features of the human body which limit what can and cannot be achieved. Unfortunately, however, whether or not a tumour is or is not removable does not depend on perception in a similar, individualized kind of way.

[41] Ibid., p. 186.
[42] Ibid., pp. 164, 175.
[43] Ibid., p. 164.

In fact, it is Howie, rather than Sartre, who has exacerbated the problem of voluntarism by conjoining the claim that 'Situation and motivation are the same thing' with the insistence that having certain bodily characteristics – such as being categorized as female or being regarded as ill – is to be equated with living 'in situation'. Sartre himself made no such move, but instead explores the various modes of embodiment – including human experiences of illness and disease – in *Being and Nothingness* under the heading of 'Being-for-Others'.[44] It is here that we find Sartre claiming, first, that it is only by coming to register the body of a fellow human (an 'Other') that I learn how to perceive my own body as an object; second, that the primary encounter with that 'Other' is not as a body (but rather via his or her gaze); and, third, that the primacy of the consciousness of the Other means that perception of all human bodies (including my own body) is radically different from that of our perception of things.[45] Key to Sartre's analysis in this section is the distinction which he draws between the way in which my body appears to me as I am caught up with the pursuit of my underlying goals and projects in a pre-reflective way (what Sartre calls 'the body as being-for-itself'), and the way in which I subsequently become conscious of my body and pay attention to it. It is this second mode of self-consciousness which, Sartre argues, can only come about through internalizing the gaze and the perspective of a fellow human being (*L'Autrui*). This means that Sartre does not himself equate having awareness of one's own embodiment with living 'in situation'. Instead, he regards the modes of bodily awareness as having distinct and peculiar features which mediate the ways in which the agent negotiates the five structural 'givens' of 'place', 'past', 'environment', 'fellowman' and 'death'.

Sartre uses the terms 'body-for-itself' and the 'body-for-others' in order to capture the distinction between the two modes of living one's embodiment, arguing that the human body is never straightforwardly a thinglike entity (a body-in-itself), although in certain modes of our relations with others we try to neutralize the threat from the potential gaze of the Other either by seeking to render the body of the Other simply as thinglike, or by seeking to render ourselves thinglike and (temporarily) abasing one's own freedom to that of the Other.[46] Howie does explore bodily alienation, but not the complex modes of power-play and self-humiliation that Sartre focuses on in his accounts of love,

---

[44] Sartre, *Being and Nothingness*, Part 3, 'Being-for Others', Ch. 2, 'The Body', pp. 303–59.

[45] Ibid., pp. 358, 339, 345.

[46] Ibid., pp. 351–7. Sartre's primary account of treating the other as an object is in the section on 'Indifference, Desire, Hate, Sadism' (pp. 379ff.), with masochism as one of the main examples of the attempt to render one's body thinglike in relation to the for-itself of the other (pp. 364ff.).

desire, sadism and masochism. She does, however, emphasize the Sartrean distinction between 'the body as being-for-itself' – which Howie herself calls 'the lived body' – and the more second-hand way in which we come to know our own body as an object of awareness and of knowledge. Applying this insight to subjective experiences of disease and of illness, as Sartre also does, Howie explains:

> Sartre takes care to distinguish the lived body from the lived body as mediated by the Other. For instance, I live pain and its recurrences and patterns. I watch which foods to eat, I predict days when I will have no cramps and be able to walk without pain. However, once diagnosed, I come to know the illness that has taken hold of my body. I take the Other's point of view when living this 'disease' as an aggravated colon. To think of my body as composed of a heart, glands, ducts, and blood cells is already to frame it through the eyes of another person. ... When I have a pain or need an operation, I frame that pain in terms of tumors, blood cells, and lungs. I take an objective perspective on the pain-experience. Reflection turns pain into an illness.[47]

Adopting a personal tone, and developing an example that does not seem to be taken from Sartre (who looks to stomach and liver complaints for his examples), Howie goes on to state that there is a tension in the experience of pain and the reflective knowledge of having cancer.[48] Being diagnosed with cancer turns the pre-reflective consciousness of 'pain' and the habits of dealing with it into the reflective knowledge of being 'ill'. However, knowing that one is 'ill' remains 'somehow distinct from the body. It has its own form and comes and goes. It is as a psychic body that the battle is won or lost, where the tumor regresses or metastasises.'[49] This last claim shows that Howie's attempt to add the body-as-situation into the Sartrean analysis of embodiment has led her to overstate the degree of freedom that is involved in the experience of illness and also of disease. In Between Feminism and Materialism, Howie blurs the parameters of freedom as she explores the boundaries between living the body-as-situation (in which the situation is not simply a given, and can therefore be negated) and living the body-as-defined by-others. The latter includes the body viewed as a biological organism and is thus, sadly, less amenable to change. I think that by the time she came to deliver the 'How to Think about Death' lecture, Howie had given up on the claim that it is only as a psychic body that

---

[47] Howie, Between Feminism and Materialism, p. 168.
[48] Compare Sartre, Being and Nothingness, pp. 355–7 with Howie, Between Feminism and Materialism, pp. 162, 168–9.
[49] Howie, Between Feminism and Materialism, pp. 168–9.

the battle over a life-limiting illness is won and lost. On the other hand, in this last lecture there is an emphasis on the importance of the psychic attitude towards death, and an attempt to engage with the practices of promoting 'hopefulness'.

Howie's 'How to Think about Death'

I now want to turn to the lecture of March 2012, since this addresses this weakness in the 2010 monograph, and seems to me both the strongest and also the most personal philosophy developed by Howie. In it, Howie deals head-on – and in a way that neither Heidegger and Sartre themselves do – with the experiential question of how to live well and fully up until death when one's 'situation' in the world includes a full prognosis or an awareness of a life-shortening illness. As I have just indicated, the lecture ends on the theme of hope, and it also starts with the notion of philosophy as a thera-peutic practice, including a practice of meditating on and coping with death. Between these two optimistic moments, the lecture does however take us through some very dark moments which deal with hopelessness, anxiety, depression and despair.

It is necessary to look quite closely at what Howie says to notice the use of the term 'situation' at various key moments of the argument. There are five occasions on which the word is used:

1. We are told that we 'only die *in a situation*'.[50]
2. Howie claims that '*absurdity is the situation* which includes a discrepancy between what we aspire to and reality'.[51]
3. It is said that '*in any situation*' there are things that 'might compel us to change direction, to alter our conditions', but in the case of being diagnosed with a life-limiting illness, the inability to change the present or the future means that 'the only response seems to be hopelessness'.[52]
4. Howie emphasizes that to receive such a prognosis is 'personal' in the sense that it deals with *my* own death and *my* own life: 'Without a future, with only a degraded past, the present is a very poor place indeed. It has been said that to describe *a personal situation* that is without hope is to slam

---

[50] Howie, 'How to Think about Death', p. 134. The addition of italics for emphasis is, of course, my own.
[51] Ibid., p. 138.
[52] Ibid., p. 139.

the door in the face of God. But what then? Does it need to be engulfed by hopelessness to be without hope?'[53]

5. Howie agrees with Heidegger to a certain extent. He was right to say that 'humans are the only animals that confront *their own situation* as a question, a quandary, a source of anxiety, a ground of hope, a burden, a gift'. Howie is quick to add, however, an anti-Heideggerian rider: that this 'gift' is 'absurd; and that until the abysmal truth of the aloneness and ownership of death is grasped, the rest, I contend, does remain merely abstract – a banal question too easily put.' [54]

In addition to these passages where the word 'situation' is explicitly used, analysis of her lecture as a whole shows how she is engaging in a direct way with Heidegger and Sartre on death as a situation. Basically, she accepts Heidegger's assertion that there is something about 'my death' that is profoundly significant, and that changes one's attitude to everyday reality (what Heidegger called 'the ontic') once it is properly grasped. On the other hand, she denies Heidegger's claim that there is something ennobling about such a realization. For Heidegger, Howie points out, it is the 'peculiar possibility' of the awareness of *my death* that 'wrenches me from the "they"', so that 'with a newfound perspective on what matters, I can take a stand in authenticity'.[55] But Howie strongly disagrees, pointing out that a poor prognosis denudes one's sense of a meaningful present, and certainly does not promote an enhanced mode of living which gives weight and significance to the present moment of time. Instead, Howie agrees with Sartre (whose framework for imagining death is used extensively, but who is not often mentioned by name) that death is *absurd*.

Like Sartre, Howie adopts a model of meaningfulness whereby meaning is provided not from outside by some divine *telos* and also not by fulfilling some social function. Instead, meaning is read onto the world in terms of one's future projects: goals, intentions and desires that emerge out of one's past and in relation to the communities of fellow-human beings in the here-and-now. However, a full prognosis of a life-limiting illness closes off long-term projects, and introduces a temporal fracture between the present and the future, and

---

[53] Ibid., pp. 139–40. The quotation, 'When you say a situation or a person is hopeless, you are slamming the door in the face of God', is widely quoted on the internet and also circulated on Twitter. The most commonly cited source is the American Methodist minister Charles L. Allen (1913–2005), who attributes it to an unnamed 'great Scottish preacher'. See Charles L. Allen, *All Things are Possible through Prayer* (1958), Grand Rapids, MI: Revell, 2003, p. 51.

[54] Howie, 'How to Think about Death', p. 140. I have changed the punctuation here, to make more sense of what is said.

[55] Ibid., p. 135.

hence also between the present and the past, and between myself and those with whom I stand in relationship. Thus, Howie agrees with Sartre that 'my death' is not what gives meaning to life by providing a kind of narrative closure; instead a full diagnosis – something that Sartre does *not* talk about – evacuates all meaning from life, and is likely to produce despair, depression, terror and anxiety. The awareness of death 'clogs the mind', Howie says – adopting a very Sartrean formulation – and is thus very far from the kind of mood of steadfastness and resoluteness in the face of death that Heidegger privileges.[56]

In Sartre, this language of 'clogging' is generally linked to a body that has been temporarily stripped of its sense of itself as a tool for consciousness, and is instead 'invaded by facticity'. In this 'clogged' state – often induced by sexual desire – consciousness 'slides toward' a state of passivity, feeling itself 'overwhelmed' by a power that 'paralyzes' the mind, rendering 'consciousness opaque to itself', and also preventing it from being able to '"think of something else"'.[57] A similar language of bodily passivity is used by Sartre as he describes the 'obscene' body which seems flabby, graceless, clumsy or simply recalcitrant in the way in which it moves through space and responds to commands. In such moments, the body of the Other – which was 'originally a body in situation' – is (temporarily) 'stripped' of its intentionality, 'to make it exist as pure flesh'.[58] Clearly dissatisfied with the notion that one might find oneself trapped in this state of 'clogged consciousness' in which the 'I' feels itself trapped by a recalcitrant body, Howie looks to various feminist philosophers – especially Adriana Cavarero and Alison Stone – to see if their emphasis on natality and relationality can provide an antidote to despair or a way of evading the condition of Sartrean absurdity after being diagnosed with a life-limiting illness.[59] But she concludes that the answer does not lie there. Instead, at the end of her lecture she points to a further reversal of the Heideggerian perspective.

Conclusion

Whereas Heidegger, famously, privileges free-floating anxiety (*Angst*) – a generalized state of dread in which there is no object *in particular*, that is the object of

---

[56] Ibid., p. 140. Sartre argues against death as involving a narrative closure in *Being and Nothingness*, pp. 539, 545–8.
[57] Ibid., p. 388.
[58] Ibid., p. 389, and for the obscene see pp. 400–2.
[59] Howie, 'How to Think about Death', pp. 135–6.

the fear – Howie privileges instead free-floating *hopefulness* as an antidote to the *object-directed* dread ('my death') that wells up inside one at the announcement of the prognosis.[60] In fact, much of the latter part of the lecture is taken up with the question of how hope can be possible even where a complete prognosis has been offered, and there is nothing specific to hope for. And here Howie is, once again, engaged in a silent argument with Heidegger who claimed that, since hope is always directed towards some future good, 'its character as a mood lies primarily in hoping as *hoping for something for oneself*.'[61] For Howie, by contrast,

> hope resides in the transformation of relationships with other human beings and with the non-human world in such a way that we can focus on their inter-action and intrinsic worth. The practice of living well right up to death might require the cultivation of a specific habit of mind, that of hope. Open-ended hope is hope that doesn't hope for something; it is not object-related.[62]

Howie is, in other words, ascribing an exactly similar function to free-floating hope that Heidegger attributes to anxiety: it is *hope*, she insists, that allows the terminally ill subject to give weight and value to the here-and-now. For Howie it is *hope* in the face of death that makes *Dasein* authentic, not Heideggerian *Angst*.

Controversially, however, Howie also argues towards the end of 'How to Think about Death' that philosophy is unable to help with the cultivation of hopefulness, and that we need to look elsewhere – at the cultivation of nature, of gardens, at the creation and enjoyment of artworks – as we learn to develop the habits of hope, and embark on a journey which is itself transformative. Thus Howie claims that although philosophy may be useful in the analysis of hopefulness in a kind of theoretical way, 'what it can't do is this practice which is about cultivating a state of mind of hopefulness even in the face of a shortened future'.[63] But it seems to me that here Howie was wrong, and what her last work shows is that engaging in philosophy can itself be a part of the transformative journey and therapeutic practice. This is why I have been so pleased to find Howie's posthumously published article, 'Alienation and Therapy in Existentialism', which suggests that, in the months after the public lecture was delivered in March 2012, Howie herself came to revise the overly pessimistic view of philosophy that emerges by its close.

---

[60] Heidegger, *Being and Time*, pp. 393–6 [H. 342–5]; Howie 'How to Think about Death', p. 140.
[61] Heidegger, *Being and Time*, pp. 395–6 [H. 345].
[62] Howie, 'How to Think about Death', p. 140.
[63] Ibid., p. 142.

Read together, these two pieces offer an important new starting point for thinking about strategies for dealing with prognostic despair, showing how objectless hope needs to be cultivated as a 'habit' of mind that can transform the everyday – with philosophy *one* of the many therapeutic practices (along with gardening, art, the cultivation of friendships and the like) which are capable of effecting a changed relation to what both Sartre and Heidegger call our 'being-in-the-world'. I find Howie's analysis and response moving, and also profound in the way it seeks to push phenomenological analysis further, towards an understanding of objectless hope in the face of one's own anticipated death. The philosophy of living-towards-dying that emerges in these last works is original, is rich in potentialities, and is worth pursuing and developing further. What is important about Howie's final lecture is not *just* its poignancy. Nor does its significance lie in providing a kind of narrative closure to Howie's life as a philosopher – especially since Howie herself was strongly opposed to viewing death in any such way. Instead, we need to take its arguments seriously, and consider how valid is her analysis of prognostic despair and also the final 'leap' into the new absurdities of hope.[64]

References

Allen, Charles L., *All Things are Possible through Prayer*, Grand Rapids, MI: Revell, 2003.

Beauvoir, Simone de, *The Ethics of Ambiguity*, trans. Bernard Frechtman, Secaucus, NJ: Citadel Press, n.d.

Beauvoir, Simone de, *The Second Sex*, trans. Constance Borde and Sheila Malovany-Chevallier, New York: Vintage, 2011.

Han-Pile, Béatrice, 'Freedom and the "Choice to Choose Oneself" *Being and Time*', *The Cambridge Companion to Heidegger*, ed. Mark A. Wrathall, Cambridge: Cambridge University Press, 2013, pp. 291–319.

Heidegger, Martin, *Sein und Zeit* (1927) (8th edn), Tübingen: Max Niemeyer Verlag, 1957.

---

[64] Howie does not herself use the term 'leap'; but she does mention Søren Kierkegaard (1813–55) on three occasions in the 2012 lecture (pp. 131, 141), and he is the philosopher who first provided an extended analysis of objectless anxiety or dread (*Angst*), and who also argued for the possibility of moving beyond anxiety via a 'leap' into the absurd. For Kierkegaard, the absurd was bound up with an embrace of the paradoxes of faith. That clearly is not Howie's – much more secular – perspective; but it seems to me that Kierkegaard was very much on Howie's mind throughout the lecture. In fact, Kierkegaard's emphasis on 'indirect communication' is a topic to which Howie says that she will return later on in the lecture; and she does this in an (appropriately) indirect way as she deals with the role of therapy in handling the 'unsayable' at the very end of her talk (pp. 141, 143).

Heidegger, Martin, *Being and Time*, trans. John Macquarrie and Edward Robinson, Oxford: Blackwell, 1962.

Howie, Gillian, *Between Feminism and Materialism: A Question of Method*, New York: Palgrave Macmillan, 2010.

Howie, Gillian, 'Alienation and Therapy in Existentialism: A Dual Model of Recognition', *Ethical Theory and Moral Practice* 17 (2014): 55–69. http://link. springer.com/article/10.1007/s10677-013-9466-8/fulltext.html [accessed 4 October 2015].

Howie, Gillian, 'How to Think about Death: Living with Dying' *On the Feminist Philosophy of Gillian Howie: Materialism and Mortality*, ed. Victoria Browne and Daniel Whistler, London: Bloomsbury, 2016, pp. 131–44.

McLean, B. H., *Biblical Interpretation and Philosophical Hermeneutics*, Cambridge: Cambridge University Press, 2012.

Merleau-Ponty, Maurice, *Phenomenology of Perception*, trans. Colin Smith, London: Routledge and Kegan Paul, 1986.

Moi, Toril, *What is a Woman? And Other Essays*, Oxford: Oxford University Press, 1999.

Sartre, Jean-Paul, *Being and Nothingness: An Essay on Phenomenological Ontology*, trans. Hazel E. Barnes, London: Methuen, 1957.

Sartre, Jean-Paul, *Existentialism and Humanism*, trans. Philip Mairet, London: Eyre Methuen, 1977.

Schalow, Frank and Alfred Denker, *Historical Dictionary of Heidegger's Philosophy* (2nd edn), Lanham, MD: Scarecrow Press, 2010.

Schwarzer, Alice (ed.), *Simone de Beauvoir Aujourd'hui: Six Entretiens*, Mayenne: Mercure de France, 1984.

8

The Relationality of Death

Alison Stone

In this chapter I respond to some points made by Gillian Howie in her enormously rich talk 'How to Think about Death: Living with Dying'.[1] Howie remarks near the start that although we all know that we will die – as per the syllogism 'all human beings are mortal; X is a human being; X is mortal' – we rarely confront our mortality personally or take on the full existential import of the realization that *I* will die – that the general truth of mortality pertains to me personally. Howie observes, though, that various philosophers have developed approaches to death in its personal meaning for us. On their various views our mortality gives meaning to our lives, and by confronting the prospect of my death I can better appreciate this meaning and live more meaningfully, more fully and well, as a result. This is the argument made by Heidegger, for whom my realization that I am finite and that my death will be mine alone opens up for me the possibility of existing authentically. A second, distinct but related, position, also canvassed by Howie, is that death retrospectively gives narrative shape to my life. Here the thought is that for my life to be valuable and satisfying it must have meaning; this requires that my life have a narrative shape, hence a beginning, middle and end; therefore my death is necessary to my life having narrative shape, meaning, and value. Finally, the third position mentioned by Howie is the 'relational' approach to death that I began to develop in an article called 'Natality and Mortality: Rethinking Death with Cavarero'.[2]

Contrary to these approaches, Howie herself goes on to suggest that for someone with a terminal illness who learns that they have only a relatively short time left to live, the imminent prospect of their death threatens to strip their existence of meaning. Without any future other than the most immediate,

---

[1] Transcribed in Ch. 6 of the present volume.

[2] Alison Stone, 'Natality and Mortality: Rethinking Death with Cavarero', in *Continental Philosophy Review* 43 (2010): 353–72.

their projects are thrown into crisis and with it the meaning that they find in life through those projects. Whilst Howie insightfully explores several possible responses to this predicament, her diagnosis of the predicament remains informed by Heidegger, since in his view human existence is fundamentally structured around possibilities projected forwards into the future: 'Dasein [i.e. the human existent] *is* already its "not-yet", and is its "not-yet" constantly as long as it is'.[3] To be sure, Howie's focus is on the way that a prognosis of imminent death disrupts life's meaning, whereas Heidegger – as she positions him – analyses how my relation to my own death-to-come is constitutive of the very structure of my existence and thus its meaning. Yet it is on the basis, broadly, of Heidegger's analysis of that constitutive relation, and the role in it of possibility and futurity, that Howie explores how death can throw our projects and under-takings into crisis. Thus, of the three approaches to death's meaning that Howie sketches, it is Heidegger's with which she most aligns herself.

One of Howie's reasons for doing so, she indicates, is that she finds the 'relational' view of death that I proposed counter-intuitive, in particular because it denies the radical asymmetry (from each person's perspective) between their own death-to-come and those of others. To explain this I need to reprise the key features of my view. I suggested that death is a relational phenomenon in two main ways, both flowing from the relationality of the self. My point of departure was the feminist insight, articulated by Adriana Cavarero amongst others, that as beings who are born we are fundamentally constituted by and of our relationships with others, initially those who give us care in our infancies and childhoods, with our subsequent relationships radiating out from those initial bonds of physical and emotional dependency. Consequently I suggested, first, that each individual's death is bound up with the deaths of the others with whom they have had or maintained close relationships – so that if someone with whom I have been closely related dies, then part of me dies. Reciprocally, when I die, parts of the others with whom I have been intimately related will die too. These deaths will be *ours* – shared.

That last claim might seem to be true merely metaphorically: after all, after my mother died, my father literally lived on for a couple of years. Even so, it can be literally true that every death is shared insofar as each person is constituted of a web of relationships unfolding over time. For one of those relationships to end through the death of the other person involved in it is therefore for a part

---

[3] Martin Heidegger, *Being and Time*, trans. J. Macquarrie and E. Robinson, Oxford: Blackwell, 1962, p. 289.

of me to die too, to cease to exist. Only *part* of me, though, and one reason for that is that each of us inhabits other relationships in addition to any particular one that has ended. In that respect, then, my father lived on after my mother's death; nevertheless a fundamental thread that had made his life the life it was had ended. That led me to identify a second way that death is relational: when someone dies, what ends is a particular coalescence of relationships, those relationships – externally existing and as they have been internalized to form personality structures – that have been constitutive of that individual. So death is relational not only in that when I die parts of related others will die as well; also, *in* my dying a unique configuration of relationships will end.

I appreciate that this view might be found counter-intuitive on several grounds. It implies that death is a matter of degree – for instance, that someone who outlives nearly all her contemporaries counts as having largely died before the final event of her death comes. Wouldn't we normally think, rather, that this multiply bereaved person remains alive but with the quality of her life sadly reduced? Moreover, my relational view also implies that someone could recover from having largely died by forming new relationships, so growing into new life. We might think that all this overlooks the fact that a person's death is their absolute end, so that no losses that the person incurs in life can be of the same order as his or her death. Yet different people of course have very different intuitions regarding death (as on everything). Some are intuitive Epicureans, untroubled by the prospect of their death because they spontaneously subscribe to his advice: 'Death, … the most dreadful of evils … is nothing to us, since while we exist, death is not present, and whenever death is present, we do not exist.'[4] For others, though – John Donne perhaps – a relational view of death comes more intuitively: 'If a clod be washed away by the sea, Europe is the less … [and] any man's death diminishes me, because I am involved in mankind, and therefore never send to know for whom the bell tolls: it tolls for thee.'[5]

Howie contends, though, that one intuition in particular is violated by the relational view, that of the radical asymmetry between my death and those of others. Their deaths are events within my life, however harrowing and terrible, whereas my death will be no event in my life but the end of any possibility of

---

[4] Epicurus, *The Essential Epicurus*, trans. Eugene O'Connor, Amherst, NY: Prometheus Books, 1993, p. 63.

[5] John Donne, *Devotions upon Emergent Occasions* and *Death's Duel*, New York: Vintage, 1999, p. 103. Those who intuitively believe in an after-life won't have the particular intuitions or fears explored in this essay. They may well have different fears – of hell, for example – depending on how they envision life after death. My concern, like Howie's, is to consider how we relate to death insofar as we either assume that there is no after-life or fear that there may not be – both default positions in a secular age.

events happening to me. Reciprocally for others, my death will be an event within their lives – the same asymmetry obtains from everyone's first-person perspective. For Howie, Heidegger does more justice to this intuition. He is adamant that when others die I do *not* in any way die with them[6] and conversely that my own death necessarily confronts me and me only: 'When it [i.e. Dasein] stands before itself in this way, all its relations [*Bezüge*] to any other Dasein have been undone' [*gelöst* – dissolved].[7] Therefore, Heidegger says, my death is my ownmost [*eigenste*] and *non*-relational [**unbezügliche**] possibility.[8] No-one else can undergo my death for me – even when one person 'dies for' another, say by throwing herself between a child and a fast-moving car, she thereby comes to *her* death, not that of the child whose life she has saved.

I want to examine further this intuition to which Howie refers, which I will re-formulate as the awareness that when I die the whole world will end, for me – the world not *qua* totality of facts but in a phenomenological, first-personal sense. To be plausible, a relational view of death needs to accommodate this intuition. However, *contra* Howie, I believe that the relational view can do so, because the world whose end I anticipate and fear is a *shared* world. Its being shared is constitutive of its character through-and-through, and it is by virtue of its being shared that I am attached to it and do not want it to end.

Howie's intuition concerns the radical asymmetry between my death and those of others. Is this the same intuition that I have when I become vividly aware that when I die, I won't be there any more, not *ever*, and I feel gripped and sickened with terror? Perhaps what I am aware of then is that I will never experience anything again, or never be conscious of anything again. The inadequacy of those last formulations is that what I fear is not the loss of some private, inner realm but my no longer ever being *there*, *in* the world around me. This latter formulation too is imperfect, though: it is not primarily that I fear the reality of the world continuing without me – as I know it will; rather what I find fearful is that from my perspective there will no longer *be* any world at all. Of course the latter sentence, too, sounds odd: I will be dead, so I won't have a perspective at all any more. But the disappearance of that perspective is the necessary correlate of the disappearance of the world onto which that perspective looks. Necessarily, along with there ceasing to be a world that is there for me, I will be no longer be there in it.[9]

---

6   Heidegger, *Being and Time*, p. 282.
7   Ibid., p. 294.
8   Ibid.
9   We might think that I am not expressing Howie's intuition differently but voicing a different

To make more sense of these locutions we need to distinguish two senses of *world*: (1) the world as the totality of facts, considered from a third-person viewpoint, which will outlast any and every individual just as it has long pre-existed them; and (2) the world as a phenomenon that is indissolubly there *for* someone who is 'in' it, not primarily in a bare spatial manner but as a subject making sense of, experiencing, and inhabiting that world. This is the world in the phenomenological sense, as necessarily the correlate of *Dasein*, the meaning-making human subject. More specifically, in Merleau-Ponty's elaboration in *The Phenomenology of Perception*, the world is the whole that inexhaustibly transcends all the particular things, others, and situations that I perceive.[10] Yet this transcendence of the world vis-à-vis my perception itself appears *within* my perception, in that particular things always present themselves as going beyond what I perceive of them. Beings present themselves as having depths, and probing these depths reveals further depths, which opens an ever-receding horizon of further depths: the world. The world in this sense is a phenomenon, but an ambiguous one, for it appears to me only as that which extends beyond and encompasses all the finite things that appear and ever could appear to me.

Admittedly, the view that world and subject are correlates has been criticized by Quentin Meillassoux[11] for failing to recognize that the world is actually the subject's prior condition, and so has priority. The subject is, indeed, a bodily subject, and its body is a material object within the world. The body-subject is a site at which materiality turns around or folds back on itself to comprise a sensing body that can apprehend the same material world of which it is woven. This fold or opening onto the world will close up when that subject dies, like a wound healing up as if it had never existed, but, like the healed body, the world as the material realm of objects and processes will continue. The material world that is the subject's prior condition, though, is the world in sense (1), but it is the world in sense (2) that is involved in my advance relation to my own death. So we may accept that the world in the phenomenological sense is only one sense or aspect of the world, which also has a material subsistence; but it is that phenomenological sense of the world that is at stake in reflection on one's death.

---

intuition. I doubt we can definitively resolve this either way, first because intuitions only become fully determinate in being expressed and articulated, and second because my mortality is at the edge of what I can think at all, thus necessarily tending to exceed any particular linguistic and conceptual formulations.

[10] Maurice Merleau-Ponty, *The Phenomenology of Perception*, trans. C. Smith (reprint edition), London: Routledge, 2002, pp. 18ff.

[11] Quentin Meillassoux, *After Finitude*, trans. R. Brassier, London: Continuum, 2008.

It is the world in this first-personal sense that will disappear finally, irrecoverably, when I die. Simultaneously, I will lose any memory that that world ever was: it will be as if this world, in all its wonders and terrors, had never been at all. I take it that it is this predicament that Howie characterizes in terms of 'radical asymmetry', in that, for me, others' deaths – quite unlike my own – are events *in* the world, not the loss *of* the world. However, we can extricate the intuition from Howie's characterization and reformulate it in an alternative way that dovetails with my relational view. To do so it is helpful to remember how Heidegger grasps the same radical asymmetry in terms of death being *non*-relational. His analysis provides a foil against which a relational reformulation can be sketched, whilst other ideas of Heidegger's can positively help us to develop that view. I will bracket here the many interpretive complexities around Heidegger's claims; my reconstruction will be broad-brush.

For Heidegger, one reflection of the asymmetry between my death and those of others is that anxiety, not fear, is the appropriate response to my awareness of my inevitable death. Fear is appropriate to finite objects that pose me a threat – precipitous drops off mountain paths, wild animals. My death can be no such object, though, because the disappearance of the world that is the condition of possibility of any objects appearing to me at all is necessarily of a different order to any appearances or disappearances of these objects. In other words, my death is of the order of the ontological and not the ontic, Being and not entities.

To convey the singular character of my death Heidegger describes it as a possibility for me (a *Seinsmöglichkeit*) – but a very peculiar one. Ordinarily the projects and activities in which I engage are my 'possibilities' in at least two senses. First, I undertake these activities with a view to goals that I am concerned to realize in the future, so that what I am doing shades into the future (that is not yet actual). Second, because these activities are not fully present or actual, in principle I could always stop doing them, continue doing them, or begin to do them differently. However, for the most part we 'fall' into the realm of *das Man* and misunderstand our possibilities, our open and undecided futures, as being fixed by the pre-existing norms and categories shared in the public world around us. In doing so we unquestioningly accept these norms, treating them as if they were unchangeable and assuming that they prescribe the same unchangeability to the activities on which I have embarked.[12] My death, however, is a certainty – I will undoubtedly die at some point – and (abstracting

---

[12] Charlotte Knowles, 'Falling and Fleeing: A Heideggerean Analysis of Complicity', presented at *Becoming Oneself: The Problem of Gendered Complicity* (Birkbeck College, 23 June 2015), pp. 7–8.

from complications of suicide) my death is not a possible project within my life, but will spell the absolute end of my undertaking any projects; in this latter sense my death is an *im*possibility.

Yet Heidegger calls my death 'the possibility of the absolute impossibility of Dasein' [*die Möglichkeit der schlechthinnigen Daseinsunmöglichkeit*].[13] I *can* after all assume the project of being-towards-my-death. The fact that my death will inescapably come, and as the complete cessation of my possibility-structured existence, presents a possibility for me. This arises only because of my awareness of my mortality – which we all necessarily have, although by and large we evade that awareness, escaping into the reassuring stabilities of *das Man*. It is always possible, though, for me to become openly and consciously aware of my mortality, albeit that this requires a continual struggle against the impulse to relapse back into *das Man*. But to the extent that I grasp that my death will be my own, my death being of a different order to the deaths of others that are episodes within my world, I gain a distinctive possibility. That my existence alone will end when I die – this existence that I have been leading from my birth, navigating through the specific circumstances in which I have been thrown – reveals it as the one existence that has been mine to lead, for which I alone have been and remain responsible. It falls to me alone to decide how to respond to these circumstances in which I am uniquely placed. Grasping all this provokes anxiety, hence the temptation to 'fall' – but also the possibility of choosing to exist authentically, not in a one-off decision but as an ongoing process of committing and re-committing oneself against the temptation of falling. The possibility that death opens up to me, then, is that of existing authentically.

However, other threads in *Being and Time* can point us in a more relational direction: specifically the recognition that 'the world of *Dasein* is a with-world [*Mitwelt*]'.[14] By implication, to the extent that – straining at the very limits of what I can conceive – I anticipate the end of 'my' world, I am anticipating the end of the world in which I am *with* the others with whom I have close relationships. I may not consciously realize this, but if each subject's world is always a with-world, then the ending towards which my fear is directed is, nonetheless, the ending of a with-world – a world that I share and inhabit with others, not accidentally but essentially and pervasively.

When discussing being-with-others in *Being and Time*, Heidegger makes some important claims which point towards the picture of death I want to

---

[13] Heidegger, *Being and Time*, p. 294.
[14] Ibid., p. 155.

develop. He has already proposed that we most basically relate to the world not as subjects over against a realm of objects but in everyday practical involvement with equipment embedded in networks of purpose and meaning. He then maintains that other individuals are not merely added onto this but, in fact, that the presence of others is the precondition of my being able to maintain these practical, meaningful relations in the first place.

> The Others who are thus 'encountered' in a ready-to-hand, environmental context of equipment, are not somehow added on ... to some Thing which is ... just present-at-hand; such 'Things' are encountered from out of the world in which they are ready-to-hand for Others ...[15]

Thus the world of my involvements is only there for me through its being there for the others with whom I share it. As a meaningful world, it only has the meanings it does through the multiply intersecting involvements of these others. My world is shared not accidentally but necessarily and constitutively.

Less helpfully, however, Heidegger tends to treat the with-world as public, anonymous, and centred on work. Regarding anonymity, he takes it that the others with whom I share the world are generally given for me as the unnoticed framework of reference for my own projects, and as people that I assume to be like me, the same as me. In the first instance, though, each of us is born into relations of dependence upon those who care for our material and emotional needs, usually our parents, and often our mothers above all. These intimate relations of dependency precede our entrance into the public sphere (although the public sphere structures these relations in many ways). We come to internalize the fabric of these intimate relations so that they comprise our personality structures – for example, traditionally the imagined-cum-experienced relation of the little boy to his father as law-giver and law-enforcer became internalized to form the relation of the ego to the demanding and punitive mental agencies of superego and ego-ideal.[16] Even before the formation of an organized personality structure, externally unfolding as well as internalized relations arguably constitute the developing self (what Freud calls the ego, *das Ich*, in incipient guise). So Daniel Stern maintains;[17] in his view the infant first acquires a sense of its self as it models its incipient actions, reactions, and perceptions on its care-giver, so that the self is from the outset a sense of self-*with*-that-other.

---

[15] Heidegger, *Being and Time*, p. 154.
[16] Sigmund Freud, *The Origins of Religion: Totem and Taboo, Moses and Monotheism and Other Works*, ed. A. Dickson, Harmondsworth: Penguin, 1985.
[17] Daniel Stern, *The Interpersonal World of the Infant: A View from Psychoanalysis and Developmental Psychology*, New York: Basic Books, 1985.

Alongside internalized relationships external relationships continue to unfold, with the internal and external ones shaping one another. Internalized relationships form the template for new external relationships – as when we fall in love with people who resemble our parents – and these new relationships impact upon the evolving internal web in turn. Thus my with-world is first and foremost shared with those with whom I am intimately related and on whom I depend emotionally – first my early care-givers, then an expanding circle of others in addition to or instead of those care-givers but always, more or less directly, cast in their model. I would also suggest, *pace* Heidegger, that in these early relations we come to make sense of the bodily differences between different individuals, including their differences *qua* female and male. Thus others are initially there for me not as an anonymous homogeneity but as a heterogeneous group of very specific individuals, my interactions with whom are highly affectively charged.

My internal and external relationships with others feed right through the fabric of my experience. No-one encounters a milieu of bare facts other than through deprivation; rather, we primarily encounter things and people through the prism of our existing relationships, which give meaning, richness, and colour to a world that would otherwise be affectively dead. The accumulated presence of the others who matter to me imbues the world around me with meaning. More than this, these others are also co-present in the world with me. Sometimes we experience things directly alongside one another, as when my daughter and I watch a film together and share in the emotional ups and downs of the narrative. Sometimes we do things separately but in the awareness that we have often done them together or could do so now. When further apart, say when I am visiting a city abroad, I want to tell my daughter about it and I hold to the awareness that she, too, has had experiences of visiting new places, with me and apart from me. These are just some of the myriad ways in which related individuals share the world, both when directly together and when more physically distant. The sharing nevertheless remains, and plausibly it is because it is so all-pervasive that this sharing often goes unnoticed, and that it may not be recognized that being shared is a structural feature of the world. In fact, to perceive the world is to perceive it with others and to perceive it *as* perceived with others, even without remarking on the fact. Reciprocally, to relate to others is to relate to them *as* inhabitants of a shared world.

My suggestion, then, is that our relationships are constitutive of the first-personal worlds in which we each live. Let me broach this through a brief excursus into Simone de Beauvoir's 1946 novel *All Men are Mortal*.[18] The novel is in part a thought-experiment conducted in novel form, revolving around the character Raymond Fosca, who centuries ago drank an elixir that gave him immortality. Initially we encounter Fosca through the actress Regina, who is tormented by the thought that her own death will erase her presence from the world as if she had never lived. For his part, Fosca is as if dead to the world; he doesn't eat, barely moves, neither sleeps nor speaks, and seems to struggle even to see people or hear their utterances. Regina is drawn to the challenge of capturing his attention and then, learning from Fosca that he is immortal, comes to desire his love so that her memory at least can be preserved eternally. Fosca, though, tries strenuously to persuade Regina that immortality is 'a terrible curse', partly by telling her his life-story since his birth in 1279.

Now, in part, Beauvoir has it that Fosca's existence is meaningless – before it becomes temporarily re-animated through his infatuation with Regina – because he cannot engage in any projects; having endless time ahead in which he can do everything, he sees no point now in doing anything. But ultimately, as Fosca says, this pointlessness arises because he cannot form relationships with others: 'you'd [soon] lose interest in everything', he tells his friend Carlier, 'because you'd be alone in the world';[19] his destiny is to endure the 'bitter taste of solitude and eternity'.[20] Forming genuine bonds with others is impossible for Fosca because he knows that they will die, as he has already experienced many times before: when Regina says to him 'we'll do great things together' his face darkens and he says 'A lot of people have told me that'.[21] He has already lost sons, wives, grandchildren, and many others – with whom, moreover, all his relationships had already failed, blighted by the awareness that Fosca does not share the mortal condition of these others. Fosca now embraces the relationship with Regina as an illusion in which he can temporarily immerse himself – yet which very quickly crumbles away.

Beauvoir's central point, then, is that without meaningful relationships Fosca's endless life shrivels to emptiness and his world to a domain of bare facts: he is 'alive and yet lifeless', he says, he is no-one.[22] He has ceased even to inhabit

---

[18] Another way to expand on this suggestion would be in dialogue with Lisa Guenther's analyses in *Solitary Confinement: Social Death and its Afterlives*, Minneapolis, MN: University of Minnesota Press, 2013. See below.

[19] Simone de Beauvoir, *All Men are Mortal*, trans. E. Cameron, London: Virago, 1995, p. 253.

[20] Ibid., p. 271.

[21] Ibid., p. 52.

[22] Ibid., p. 29.

the same kind of world in which ordinary mortals live[23] – his is a 'post-human' condition (his former wife Beatrice exclaims at one point that he is of another species), but an undesirable one. His condition is undesirable, though, because he is the only immortal; Beauvoir leaves open the possibility that his world would become meaningful again if other human beings were immortal too. Thus Beauvoir's literary thought-experiment illuminates the fact that the world has value and significance for me only insofar as I share it with others; absent my relationships with those others and the world becomes empty. Moreover, it is not that the world remains the same but has had certain finite objects taken out of it. The lived character of the world has been transformed, in fact depleted, radically emptied out of significance: only if Regina can bring Fosca back to life, he says, will 'the world return to its original shape'. If I fear my death because, for me, the whole world will end when I die, it is the world as a *with*-world that I wish to continue, and one shared with the particular others for whom I care. So insofar as I want 'my' world to continue – i.e. I want not to die – equally I want the others to live on with whom this world is co-maintained. Conversely, to live on Fosca-like after they have all died is a prospect scarcely less terrifying than that of 'my own' death.[24]

Much more could be said about Beauvoir's complex and multi-layered novel, but here I have simply used it to give support to my proposal that the world is relational through-and-through.[25] In this sense, my death when anticipated from my first-person perspective remains relational: this death will mark the end of the *shared* world, not of a world that is simply 'mine'. To rephrase one

---

[23] Ibid., p. 37.

[24] It might be objected that Beauvoir's thought-experiment tells against the relational view, because after all Fosca survives the deaths of those he loves. Doesn't that show that their deaths leave Fosca untouched in his own life? I'm not convinced; we could alternatively say that Fosca *has* largely died, hence the emptiness of his world, although if he can form new attachments – as he does to Regina – he can regain a degree of life.

[25] The way that Beauvoir imagines Fosca's plight bears comparison with the predicament of prisoners subjected to solitary confinement, as Guenther analyses it. She shows that solitary confinement radically reduces and deranges the capacities of prisoners to perceive and make sense of what is around them; such prisoners often move through hallucinations and acute anxiety to a state of blank deadness and dullness. Guenther concludes: 'Without the concrete experience of other embodied egos oriented toward common objects in a shared world, my own experience of the boundaries of those perceptual objects begins to waver' (*Solitary Confinement*, p. 35). Sharing the world with others is necessary not only for my having a concrete sense of who I am in that world but also for my being able to perceive and inhabit that world at all – the world is constitutively shared, and if it is not shared, it loses much of the significance and the contours that make it what it is. Further, Guenther describes prisoners subjected to solitary confinement as undergoing social death. On some accounts social death is a civil and political status, the paradoxical one of lacking such status, of being without rights, citizenship, or access to social membership. Yet, from the perspective that death is relational, reciprocally the kind of deprivation of social relationships that prisoners suffer in solitary confinement actually does inflict on them a level of death – ontologically speaking as well as socio-politically.

of my earlier claims, world and *inter*subjectivity – not single individual subjectivity – are correlates, and the world presents itself as one onto which multiple
embodied subjects are open, principally those particular subjects with whom
each of us is intertwined. Without their co-presence – if I were essentially
alone in the world like Fosca – this world would shrink to be something more
like a bare mass of objects; its essential contours and not merely its contingent
contents would change. To be sure it may feel to me, when I am gripped by a
terror of my death, that I dread the simple loss of my consciousness or experiences, something that will befall me alone. Nonetheless, what is dreaded on
closer inspection is the loss of a communal world that only exists *as* shared and
that is pervaded through-and-through by its status as shared – shared not with
humanity in the abstract but with the particular, irreplaceable others who have
been crucial for me.

That the world whose ending I anticipate is essentially shared tells against
radical asymmetry. On an asymmetric view the deaths of others occur in my
world. But, as we have seen, those others are not straightforwardly 'in' my world
in the first place, because they play a continual role in bringing that world into
being. I may turn and consider them as if they were objects, but primarily they
are present in my existence as those for whom there is the world that I also
inhabit. If I temporarily regard these others as objects, I so regard them against
the background of a shared world that actually is only available to me through
their prior intersubjectivity. Likewise, then, the deaths of these others are not
unequivocally events in a world that is solely 'mine'. Rather those deaths alter
and sometimes transform the shape and structure of that world *qua* shared,
and their loss imparts to the world, as I (amongst others) continue to carry
it forward, a more-or-less temporary diminution, depletion, or constriction.
When someone I love dies the world loses something, it is lessened – not such
that there is a finite pocket of absence within it (although that may be so, as
when I pass the office, now uncannily empty, of a recently died colleague), but
so that a whole strand of the world's meaning has leeched out of it. So, just as my
death will be the complete end of the world (for me), already the deaths of the
others who are closely related to me diminish this world. As such these deaths
already constitute a partial version of what my death will be more finally.

This bears on our capacity to anticipate the prospect of our own deaths, a
puzzling capacity if my own death is absolutely beyond the limits of my existence.[26] On the other hand, if when related others die I already undergo part of

---

[26] This is one of Derrida's critical points *vis-à-vis* Heidegger in *Aporias*: since my death is absolutely

what will happen when I die, then I do foretaste my own death here. This does not bring my death-to-come wholly within my compass, though, for the loss of others is already at the limits of my experience – just as was the relationship that has been lost, as it unfolded ambiguously between myself and the other, on the threshold of and not simply 'in' my world. That death is relational, then, can explain not only our capacity to anticipate our death but also our ability to do so only imperfectly.

We can unfold a few more implications of these thoughts by retracing the broad outlines of Heidegger's unfolding of the consequences of death's (supposed) non-relationality, and re-thinking them in light of death's relationality. Confronting the prospect of my death will not individuate but 'relationalize' me, revealing to me the ultimate value or the fundamental impact upon me of the relationships with which I have been living. Yet perhaps this very 'relationalization' shows that Heidegger's analysis of finitude still holds. Perhaps I grasp that when I die *my* relationships will end – *these* unique relationships in which I have been situated – which I alone can decide to carry forwards, break off, or conduct differently, more attentively perhaps or with new determination to change them.

In this light, though, we notice something amiss with the statement that I *alone* can act with respect to these relationships. Relationships unfold between at least two parties, each contributing in principle as much as the other, even through inaction or negativity. My actions and attitudes alone cannot exhaustively shape how a relationship will go, and I cannot control the degree and manner to which others are responsive to me. Despite my efforts a relationship may decline and recede, foster and take root, or take an unsuspected course. To be aware of the importance of my relationships for me is to be aware of how profoundly I am shaped by these phenomena that I cannot control, that are *not* mine alone, and for which I do not and cannot have sole responsibility.

To be sure, I can resolve afresh to try to steer a certain relationship in a particular direction. Nonetheless, my 'relationalization' in the face of my death makes another family of attitudes appropriate as well, ones directed not towards my future possibilities but instead towards the past and present actualities of our relationships. When a relationship is rewarding, enriching and valuable,

---

beyond the limit – there's no path (*a-poros*) to it, no step (*pas*) up to it (Jacques Derrida, *Aporias*, trans. T. Dutoit,Stanford, CA: Stanford University Press, 1993, pp. 8–9) – I can't anticipate my death, hence can't exist authentically towards it. My conclusion is the converse of Derrida's: because our deaths are entwined so that my death is after all not absolutely beyond my life, I can – albeit ambiguously, inadequately – anticipate my death.

a fitting response is to treasure and cherish it and feel gratitude that it exists, gratitude that is directed at least partly towards the other party. Affects of this kind are oriented towards what is already *given to* me, not towards that which *I can* possibly do. If a capacity on my part is called forth here it is the capacity to receive or welcome what is given. But perhaps a Heideggerian ethic of responsibility is still in place here: it is *my* responsibility to cultivate dispositions of gratitude for and graceful reception of what I share with others, their unique set of bequests to me. There is something to this – yet to concentrate exclusively on *cultivating* these dispositions is to focus solely on the activity of the self in a way calculated to hinder the formation of these very dispositions, insofar as they are dispositions to receive and not to do. The perplexing thing about receptivity is that it itself has to be received, to a considerable extent at least.

Setting this further perplexity aside for now, I hope that we can see that because death is relational in the way I have sketched it follows, not that Heidegger's ethic of authenticity is totally out of place, but that it needs supplementation by an ethic of gratitude and receptivity for the relational histories in which we already find ourselves.[27] Gratitude is not the only receptive attitude I might have. For example, when loved ones die, sorrow and regret may well be in place too – sorrow that the course of those relationships is now fixed, that the misunderstandings and failings that occurred within them cannot now be undone or overcome. I might nonetheless feel gratitude for what we shared, or resentment that the failings unavoidably set in. Gratitude is indicative rather than exhaustive of the character of an ethical attitude of receptivity – its orientation towards givens rather than possible actions.

Gratitude for relationships might seem unconnected with mortality, but my point is that the apprehension of the latter heightens the former. Insofar as I am aware of my death as a personal prospect facing me, I am thereby aware that my relationships will end and that I have them to enjoy only for a finite time, along with the world as it is disclosed in their light. Being only temporary, a relationship is the more to be cherished (impossible as it is to maintain this attitude at all times).

---

[27] Gratitude fits, at least, in the measure that these relationships are fulfilling. However, in our initial relationships we attach to our care-givers *and* to the norms and power relations that they transmit to us, which we take on so that our care-givers will recognize and love us (Judith Butler, *The Psychic Life of Power: Essays in Subjection*, Stanford, CA: Stanford University Press, 1997). But many of our inherited norms and power relations are oppressive, binary gender norms for instance. In such conditions our relationships will rarely be wholly fulfilling – yet, to complicate matters further, the nature of our earliest attachments means that we often come to derive fulfilment precisely *from* our own constriction and self-limitation – e.g. in conforming to gender norms even when they restrict our powers and skills.

I have responded to Howie by expanding my earlier conception of relational mortality, in which I focused on how my death is entwined with those of others. In that essay I neglected a third aspect of this entwining: its connection with the world as it discloses itself to our interconnected selves. It was because I omitted that aspect that my earlier account could not take account of the intuition of Howie's which I have re-expressed here as the apprehension that when I die the whole world will, from my perspective, disappear (rather than it being simply that I will disappear from the world, as is third-personally the case). Nonetheless, we should take into account that the world is essentially shared and that I am attached to it *as* shared. We can then see that when I fear the disappearance of 'my' whole world when I die, what I fear is still – under another of its aspects – the loss of the intimate relationships to which I am deeply attached.

References

Beauvoir, Simone de, *All Men are Mortal*, trans. E. Cameron, London: Virago, 1995.

Butler, Judith, *The Psychic Life of Power: Essays in Subjection*, Stanford, CA: Stanford University Press, 1997.

Derrida, Jacques, *Aporias*, trans. T. Dutoit, Stanford: Stanford University Press, 1993.

Donne, John, *Devotions upon Emergent Occasions* and *Death's Duel*, New York: Vintage, 1999.

Epicurus, *The Essential Epicurus*, trans. Eugene O'Connor, Amherst, NY: Prometheus Books, 1993.

Freud, Sigmund, *The Origins of Religion: Totem and Taboo, Moses and Monotheism and Other Works*, ed. A. Dickson, Harmondsworth: Penguin, 1985.

Guenther, Lisa, *Solitary Confinement: Social Death and its Afterlives*, Minneapolis, MN: University of Minnesota Press, 2013.

Heidegger, Martin, *Being and Time*, trans. J. Macquarrie and E. Robinson, Oxford: Blackwell, 1962.

Howie, Gillian, 'How to Think about Death: Living with Dying', *On the Feminist Philosophy of Gillian Howie: Materialism and Mortality*, Victoria Browne and Daniel Whistler (eds), London: Bloomsbury, 2016, pp. 131–44.

Knowles, Charlotte, 'Falling and Fleeing: A Heideggerean Analysis of Complicity', presented at *Becoming Oneself: The Problem of Gendered Complicity*, Birkbeck College, 23 June 2015.

Meillassoux, Quentin, *After Finitude*, trans. R. Brassier, London: Continuum, 2008.

Merleau-Ponty, Maurice, *The Phenomenology of Perception*, trans. C. Smith (reprint edition), London: Routledge, 2002.

Stern, Daniel, *The Interpersonal World of the Infant: A View from Psychoanalysis and Developmental Psychology*, New York: Basic Books, 1985.

Stone, Alison, 'Natality and Mortality: Rethinking Death with Cavarero', *Continental Philosophy Review* 43 (2010): 353–72.

9

Reflections on Living up to Death

Morny Joy

In the conclusion of an address, 'How to Think about Death: Living with Dying,' that Gillian Howie presented in March 2012, she refers almost wistfully to Paul Ricoeur's book, *Living up to Death*.[1] She states that the planned three research workshops of the upcoming Research Network project, New Thinking on Living with Dying, were inspired by Ricoeur's announcement of making the last years of his life an affirmation of life in this world – animating the deepest resources of his being so as to realize such a disposition. Howie had not mentioned Ricoeur's work earlier in this presentation, so its importance came as something of a surprise. Yet, in retrospect, Ricoeur's vital aspiration seemed to pervade her text as a possible incentive to be examined, even potentially accepted, in contrast to many other approaches that she dismissed.

During this address, Howie also eloquently reveals her own philosophical leanings, and the questions she hopes to pursue. First, however, she deliberates about the efficacy of philosophy to provide sufficient sustenance for questions that she thinks are most relevant. Identifying herself as a thoroughly modern being 'in an enlightened world in which there is no divine plan',[2] she has no time for facile consolations. Howie intends to investigate the 'porous quality' of the intermediate state between life and death, and in what way one can take responsibility for one's life. Yet this cannot be separated from the devastating existential fact that: 'I am the one that's going to die'.[3] Such a realization, as far as Howie is concerned, does not facilitate authentic existence, as Heidegger would attest. Instead, for Howie, 'it clogs the mind with terror and evacuates

---

[1] Paul Ricoeur, *Living up to Death*, trans. David Pellauer, Chicago, IL: University of Chicago Press, 2009.

[2] Gillian Howie, 'How to Think about Death: Living with Dying', Ch. 6 of the present volume, p. 139.

[3] Ibid., p. 136.

meaning from the world, from my world'.[4] While she considers that philosophy can supply conceptual and causal explanations, she deems it incapable of furnishing adequate responses to the utterly harrowing situation of impending death.

Howie is quite explicit, even blunt at times, about the options she does not intend to explore. She is not particularly inclined to examine in depth the work of Heidegger, Levinas, Derrida and Deleuze on this issue. She is also not appreciative of Adriana Cavarero's suggestion of viewing death as a reintegration into a mode of cosmic existence. She deems this impersonal stance towards death to be at odds with Cavarero's earlier emphasis on birth, natality and the integrity of each person's existence. What engages Howie, when philosophy reaches its limit, is the ability to discern certain activities that, from a practical perspective, can nurture ways of living that generate hope. But, in this context, formal philosophical analysis is left behind. It is hope, featuring in a number of guises, to which Howie will give careful consideration. She has also become aware that fostering hope may involve cultivating specific habits of mind that are attuned to one's present existence. But this orientation of hope needs to be a non-attached version, i.e. one that no longer seeks the satisfaction of attainment. It is on this matter of non-attachment that the pertinence of Ricoeur's own position in *Living up to Death* becomes apparent. Perhaps, then, it is time to undertake an exploration of Ricoeur's reflections on this topic so as to determine if, indeed, his work could have been of help to Howie in her own quest.

It is not so much in the book itself, *Living up to Death*, that Ricoeur actually provides the most insightful comments on this disposition. They can be found more readily in certain commentaries made during interviews, especially one where he responds to François Azouvi and Marc de Launay, in their edited book *Critique and Conviction*. There, he observed, 'My own experience of the end of life is nourished by this deepest wish to make the act of dying an act of life.'[5] Such a statement was made approximately ten years before his death, long before the posthumously published *Living up to Death*, which reflects the final ten years of his life. Yet, to understand in some depth the manner by which Ricoeur arrived at this position, I think that it is necessary to delve even further back into his past. A further indication as to the specifics of this pivotal time is disclosed in another late interview – this time with Sorin Antohi. Here Ricoeur reflects:

---

[4] Ibid., p. 140.
[5] Paul Ricoeur, *Critique and Conviction*, ed. F. Azouvi and M. de Launay, trans. K. Blamey, New York: Columbia University Press, 1998, p. 156.

For there is, after all, and since the beginning of my work sixty years ago, the idea of mortality which traverses everything through and through. At this time, I was welcoming this ... I would not say joyously, but I had concluded my book with the idea of assenting to finitude. I was an avid reader of Rilke, and I ended with this verse: *Hier sein ist herrlich*: 'being here is sumptuous, wonderful, magical.' Now, in my old age, with the proximity of death, I repeat again: *Hier sein ist herrlich.*[6]

Such a remarkable reminiscence requires in turn a retrospective journey to situate the actual circumstances and the very book that, sixty years ago, influenced Ricoeur to make such a significant pronouncement. It introduced certain themes that, I believe, have remained the mainstay of his work. Ricoeur admits that the book he is referring to above is *Fallible Man* (first published 1960). This book succeeded *Freedom and Nature: The Voluntary and the Involuntary* (first published 1950). Together, these two books constitute the two initial volumes of a projected three-volume investigation that would explore the vagaries of the human condition, which he named *Philosophy of the Will*. This three-volume opus would comprise what he terms respectively an eidetics, an empirics and a poetics of the human will.[7] He described 'fallibility' as a primordial mode of weakness that constituted the locus of possibility, though never the inevitability, for the appearance of what he termed, at that time, 'evil'.[8] In *Fallible Man*, Ricoeur undertook an extensive study of the notion of human fallibility or fragility in relation to human willing. As he remarks, this study can involve two principal lines of investigation: 'It may be asked, indeed, in what feature of its primordial constitution this possibility of failing resides more particularly. On the other hand, one may ask about the nature of this possibility itself.'[9] In their respective French publications, *The Voluntary and the Involuntary*, which was a phenomenological study of the human will (the eidetics), had preceded *Fallible Man* (the empirics) by ten years. The two works were distinct, yet they shared similar interests (even if from different perspectives) about the travails

---

[6] Sorin Antohi, 'Memory, History, Forgiveness: A Dialogue between Paul Ricoeur and Sorin Antohi', *Janus Head* 8.1 (2005): 20.

[7] The eidetics would be a phenomenological study in the manner of Husserl: *Freedom and Nature: The Voluntary and the Involuntary* (trans. E. V. Kohák, Evanston, IL: Northwestern Press, 1960 [1950]). The empirics would be the study of *Fallible Man* (trans. C. A. Kelble, Chicago, IL: Henry Regnery, 1967 [1960]), while the final unpublished volume, on the poetics, was slated to deal with the transformative aspects of the will in relation to regeneration. Ricoeur modelled his work on Karl Jaspers' earlier trilogy.

[8] In his early works, Ricoeur used the term 'evil' as coextensive with 'sin'. In his later works, however, he preferred to use the term 'suffering' as a word that indicated the virtual endemic human situation where human beings inflicted unmerited harm on one another.

[9] Paul Ricoeur, *The Symbolism of Evil*, trans. E. Buchanan, Boston, MA: Beacon Press, 1967, p. 146.

of human existence. In the above-mentioned Antohi interview, Ricoeur graphically describes how he endeavoured to do justice to the 'bound yet free' human will and its potentialities, despite its fragility. It is in this connection that Ricoeur will disclose his own deeply felt commitment to life itself and his own attempts to affirm the wonderment of human existence.

This dedication is most obvious in the concluding section of *The Voluntary and the Involuntary*, Chapter 3, which is named 'The Way of Consent'. In this chapter, Ricoeur challenges the traditional distinction between mind and body, which he describes as 'the virulent form of dualism of freedom and necessity'.[10] From this perspective, precedence is often given to 'the realm of necessity', where birth, the aging body and the spectre of death are aligned with necessity. Ricoeur attempts in this section to counter the dominance of the way of nature or necessity. To help alleviate this situation, Ricoeur expands on his explorations in the earlier sections of the book which were more concerned with what he terms 'the reciprocity of the voluntary and involuntary'.[11] He posits this constructive interaction as a way of countering such an unacceptable dualism. As he declares:

> The involuntary has no meaning of its own. Only the relation of the voluntary and the involuntary is intelligible ... Far from the voluntary being derivable from the involuntary, it is, on the contrary, the understanding of the voluntary that comes first in man. I understand myself in the first place as he who says 'I will'. The involuntary refers to the will as that which gives it its motives and capacities, its foundations, and even its limits.[12]

Such an approach allows Ricoeur to initiate his descriptions always with a focus on the voluntary. He then refines his description by adding particular qualifications to account for the interruptions of the involuntary. This helps to make the description initially intelligible. Next, the involuntary aspects are themselves carefully examined in accordance with what Ricoeur views as their 'partial intelligibility'. Finally, there is a synthesis of both, which Ricoeur posits as effecting a complete understanding of the manner in which the voluntary and involuntary can function interdependently.[13]

Although Ricoeur is employing a Husserlian phenomenology as his basic method, there are nonetheless moments where he is already expressing doubts

---

[10] Paul Ricoeur, *Freedom and Nature: The Voluntary and the Involuntary*, trans. E. V. Kohák, Evanston, IL: Northwestern Press, 1966, p. 444.

[11] Ibid., p. 4.

[12] Ibid., p. 5.

[13] Ricoeur does not subscribe to the Hegelian variety of synthesis with the ideal merging of both components. For him the dialectic is a process of constant interchange with no desired or inevitable merger.

about the make-up of the Husserlian Cogito which he will later dismiss when he turns toward hermeneutics.[14] As a result, while he is reluctant to concede everything to the involuntary or necessity, Ricoeur is equally concerned about what he terms 'a triumphant consciousness'. As he explains, 'In all the instances when idealism posits an equation of the self-consciousness of the Cogito and the absolute transparence of consciousness, it rejects the ring of shadows which surrounds the focus of consciousness'.[15] This insight prompts Ricoeur to undertake a portrait of the complex and intricately interrelated dynamics that he discerns existing between the voluntary and the involuntary, between freedom and nature.

There is another intriguing element that Ricoeur will add to this already potent mixture. This is the event of birth. He begins by acknowledging that this is not a topic that many philosophers have been concerned with – the preoccupation with death being a far more prominent subject of deliberation. It is quite exceptional that Ricoeur decided to focus on the phenomenon of birth at such an early stage in his career in the late 1940s. Birth, however, also belongs to the domain of necessity. In signalling a beginning, it is 'a relation hidden from my consciousness'[16] that can never be accessed by memory.[17] Ricoeur states: 'My birth is the beginning of my life: in it I was placed, once and for all, into the world, and placed in being before I was able to posit anything voluntarily'.[18] As a result, although birth is qualified by necessity, it marks an initial moment of the vital journey to consciousness. 'I have always begun to live when I say "I am"'.[19] This consent to a life that was not of his own choosing indicates, from Ricoeur's perspective, an affirmation of life in this world. It is a definitive act that has transformative implications. He attests that this consent signifies an affirmation: 'Yes to my character, whose constriction I can change into depth … Yes to the unconscious, which remains the indefinite possibility of motivating my freedom. Yes to my life, which I have not chosen but is the condition which makes all choice possible'.[20]

This affirmation of life was reiterated more recently when, in an interview with Azouvi and de Launay, Ricoeur revisited the impetus that had informed these remarks which were made initially in the concluding pages of *The*

---

[14] This aspect of Ricoeur's work will be treated later in the chapter.
[15] Ibid., p. 464.
[16] Ibid., p. 434.
[17] Ibid., p. 442.
[18] Ibid., p. 433.
[19] Ibid., p. 441.
[20] Ibid., p. 479.

Voluntary and Involuntary: 'I had not wanted to be crushed by the problem of death: I wanted in this way to give its rightful place to the theme of birth.'[21] In this same set of interviews, Ricoeur also enlarged on these observations, making a deliberate connection with his more recently expressed ideas about the disposition of 'living up to death'. He declared: 'I, therefore, project not an after-death but a death that would be an ultimate affirmation of life. ... What is important is to be living up until the moment of death.'[22] Such an attestation pervades much of Ricoeur's *oeuvre*. Nevertheless, he remained extremely responsive to the signs of finitude and the seemingly endemic vulnerabilities, especially that of suffering, that are symptomatic of human existence.

Again, in Chapter 3 of the final section in *The Voluntary and Involuntary*, Ricoeur investigates other related dimensions of human finitude. He examines the sorrows of finitude,[23] especially the bad finite or the sorrow of formlessness,[24] and the sorrow of contingence.[25] In these analyses, Ricoeur vividly depicts experiences of negativity, e.g. illness, aging and portents of death, all of which reinforce the threat of 'brute existence'. These experiences are constant reminders of the challenge mortality poses and the danger of acquiescing to necessity as a dominant force. He then searches to find ways in which consent to life can offer alternative perspectives. In so doing, Ricoeur does not resort to easy platitudes. He does not mince words: 'WHY SAY YES? Does not consenting, mean giving up, and laying down arms? Is it not surrender, in every sense of the word – whether surrender to an opinion, to an order, or finally to a necessity?'[26]

In giving his own response to this challenge, Ricoeur strives to assert that acquiescence does not necessarily imply surrender. 'How can we justify the *yes* of consent without passing a value judgment on the totality of the universe, that is, without evaluating its ultimate suitability for freedom? When I say, this is my place, I adopt it, I do not yield, I acquiesce.'[27] Nevertheless, such an adamant confirmation automatically entails the introduction of a substantive worldview that can sustain this extremely positive interpretation. Such a development in turn introduces intimations of what Ricoeur calls 'transcendence'.[28] But this is no *deus ex machina* of a metaphysical variety. While he is well aware that the consent to one's situation in a worldview that moves beyond the

---

[21] Ricoeur, *Critique and Conviction*, pp. 93–4.
[22] Ibid., p. 156.
[23] Ricoeur, *The Voluntary and the Involuntary*, pp. 447–8.
[24] Ibid., pp. 448–50.
[25] Ibid., pp. 450–6.
[26] Ibid., p. 466.
[27] Ibid., p. 467.
[28] Ibid.

limits of phenomenology is a risky wager, Ricoeur is not yet ready to supply a metaphysical rescue mission. While Ricoeur concedes that for some, such as Jaspers, an engagement at the limits of philosophy implies 'a leap from existence to transcendence',[29] he prefers to initially survey other alternative positions as potential solutions. This is not an evasive strategy that rejects transcendence but a careful review that evaluates two transcendent options other than Christianity. These are Stoicism and Orphism.

In assessing these two possible transcendent worldviews, Ricoeur treads carefully, acknowledging the rich insights they both bring to diagnosing the human condition and to presenting possible therapeutic remedies. Yet despite their respective recommendations, he finds both Stoicism and Orphism wanting. Consent to one's own particular existence is, in both cases, compromised. Ricoeur worries that in Stoicism the existing mode of consent appears to be destructive because it endorses detachment, a withdrawal from an engaged existence. In explaining this, he observes: 'Stoic consent would appear as a kind of detachment and scorn through which the soul retires into its own circularity.'[30] As such, while there is respect for the worldview or whole, the status of one's subjectivity, especially in the crucial interaction between a subject and an overarching worldview, is not at all evident. If subjectivity is regarded as simply a part of this whole, then: 'I myself am only one being *among* beings.'[31] Consequently, there does not seem to be a distinct subjective agent who is able to consent. In addition to this shortcoming, it would also appear, as a result of the attitude of detachment, that the subjective dimension has become objectified. Consequently, Ricoeur fears that the body itself is thereby objectified and reduced to a virtual corpse, which is utterly 'devoid of carnal density.'[32] What ultimately emerges from these basic Stoic principles for Ricoeur is a form of approbation of the whole at the expense of its part(s). Ricoeur protests: 'To discover the Whole as a cipher of Transcendence is no longer to choose, no longer to act; it is not even to consent. It is to admire and contemplate … Contemplation, wonder, contribute to a *detour* from consent.'[33] For true consent to occur, according to Ricoeur, any willed affirmation of existence involves a dialectic between consent and necessity that is not simply an impersonal assent

---

[29] Ibid., p. 468.
[30] Ibid., p. 470.
[31] Ibid., p. 472.
[32] Ibid., p. 471.
[33] Ibid., p. 472; my amended translation. The term 'cipher of Transcendence' is a reference to the work of Jaspers, and his description of limit experiences, which lead more to poetic, rather than literal or conceptual renderings. Jaspers had a strong influence on Ricoeur's early work.

but an active, embodied decision, always realized in a specific context. Stoicism, on Ricoeur's account, evades this personal mode of consent.

In his rebuttal of Orphism, Ricoeur disapproves of its tendency toward mysticism, to its unqualified celebration of transcendence. This honouring of the wonders of creation obscures what Ricoeur regards as a deceptive temptation. This is the invitation to become ensnared in a grand metamorphosis, where Orphism becomes identified with the natural world. For Ricoeur, however, wonder at the created world alone is not sufficient. Such an extravagance leads to the denial of consent. Thus, Ricoeur asserts: 'In a sense admiration is not complete if consent is not attained: if I do not accept myself.'[34] What is required for consent is that a subject needs to accept their own character with its faults and inevitable limitations. In so willing, 'I *make* myself be. I am my own *capacity for being*.'[35] Again, willing and acting are central components of Ricoeur's own position of affirmation of this world.

Yet Ricoeur is not quite ready in *The Voluntary and Involuntary* to propose any specific form of transcendence as exemplary. Even though his work is testing the boundaries of phenomenology and he has forecast a move in the direction of transcendence by way of poetics,[36] he is reluctant to make a decisive pronouncement. This attitude is symptomatic of a noticeable hesitancy on Ricoeur's part to take a confessional stance. This will, in time, become even more evident.[37] In his work thus far, Ricoeur has invoked the term 'poetics' in its widest frame of reference, encompassing religion. However, Ricoeur's previously forecast third volume of a trilogy on the will, which was to focus on a poetics of human will, would never be composed. It appears that during the writing of *The Voluntary and Involuntary* Ricoeur's priorities had undergone a change. He was no longer committed to producing an affirmative volume about 'a poetic of the experience of creation and recreation pointing toward a second innocence'.[38] In explaining this decision in his 'Intellectual Autobiography', Ricoeur admitted why he was not ready to enter into theological territory.

---

[34] Ibid., p. 477.
[35] Ibid., p. 55.
[36] Poetics has different resonances in Ricoeur's work. It refers to a metaphoric and symbolic approach to depictions of reality. As such, it can have both literary and religious references.
[37] Ricoeur will refer to his mode of methodological agnosticism in a number of places: one of the most notable of these is in his 'Intellectual Autobiography'. Here he states: 'I cannot say as a philosopher where the voice of conscience comes from – that ultimate expression of otherness that haunts selfhood. Does it come from a person who is other whom I can still *envisage*, from my ancestors, from a dead or living God, but one absent from my life as the past is from reconstructed history, or even from some empty space?' (Paul Ricoeur, 'Intellectual Autobiography', in *The Philosophy of Paul Ricoeur*, ed. Lewis Edwin Hahn, Peru, IL: Open Court, 1995, p. 53).
[38] Ricoeur, 'Intellectual Autobiography', p. 13.

Ricoeur declares: '[A]s for the poetics of Transcendence, this was never written, if by this title one expects something like a philosophy of religion, for lack of a theological philosophy. My primary concern, which has never wavered, not to mix the *genres* together has instead drawn me closer to the notion of a philosophy without any absolute.'[39] Instead, he undertook one of his famed detours with his following work, *The Symbolism of Evil*.[40] A journey into philosophical hermeneutics would begin. This venture indicates a definite shift in Ricoeur's approach, as hermeneutics refutes any assertion of unassailable knowledge. Ricoeur clarifies his position: 'This [hermeneutics] puts into question a presupposition that was evident in both Husserl and Descartes, namely the uniqueness, the transparence, the apodicity of the Cogito.'[41] No longer will Ricoeur subscribe to a mode of transcendental eidetic reflection, but he will henceforth refer to his approach as that of hermeneutic phenomenology – a qualified form of knowledge mediated through an interpretative process of understanding and explanation.

There is, nevertheless, another crucial dimension that appears in Ricoeur's work at this time – although it is not thematically developed – that of hope. This 'category of hope', which he adapts from Kant, will come to play a central role in Ricoeur's future work. It is an integral element in a development that marks Ricoeur's turn away from theology to another orientation that, under the tutelage of Kant, he names philosophical anthropology. It is a fascinating exercise to try and account for this initial appearance of hope in Ricoeur's work. One plausible explanation is Ricoeur's reluctance to take an explicit theological route. Given this decisive choice, which signals an absence of certainty about divine existence and intervention, hope could perhaps provide a measure of reassurance. But a question automatically arises: hope in what? Perhaps it offers a sense of solace that the process of consent had not been an empty gesture. But at this stage in the development of his ideas, Ricoeur appears unwilling to

---

[39] Ibid., pp. 13–14. Ricoeur gives a rationale for the lack of a poetics volume: 'I would not, however, say that nothing was accomplished of what I then termed poetics. *The Symbolism of Evil, The Rule of Metaphor, Time and Narrative* do aspire in several ways to the title of poetics, less in the sense of a meditation on primordial creation than in that of an investigation on the multiple modalities of what I will later call an ordered creation, illustrated not only by the great myths on the origin of evil, but also by poetic metaphors and narrative plots. In this sense the idea of ordered creation still belongs to a philosophical anthropology in which the relation to biblical faith and theology is held in abeyance. For this reason, were not the final words of *The Voluntary and Involuntary* 'willing is not creating'? And was this statement not a premonition of the subsequent abandonment of this grand project?' (ibid.)

[40] Ricoeur is renowned for his various detours from the straight and narrow philosophical path. He variously engaged at stages of his work with structuralism, narrative theory, history, and ethics.

[41] Ricoeur, *Conviction and Critique*, p. 16.

supply direct answers, let alone a defence of this move. One must wait for later philosophical explanations. Instead, for the time being, Ricoeur prefers to wax lyrical about hope. 'Hope is not the triumph of dualism but the sustenance on the way of conciliation. It does not detach itself, but becomes involved. It is the mysterious soul of the vital pact which I can close with my body and my universe. It is the pledge of reaffirmation.'[42]

These are not words of clarification, but of evocation. It would appear that they reflect Ricoeur's personal experience in his struggles to negotiate the process of consent in his own life, as he began to move beyond the certitudes of his Calvinist upbringing. They also express his repudiation of Stoicism, Orphism, as well as purely rationalist justifications. 'We clearly reject the pretensions of an overly zealous apologetics which would pretend to derive God from nature or from subjectivity by a simple rational implication.'[43] What this process does signify is a transformation where Ricoeur personally acknowledges that there has been a profound deepening of reflection as he interiorized the process of consent. This is because by consenting to his limitations, both patience and receptivity have also been cultivated.[44]

In the 1950s and 1960s Ricoeur's work underwent a remarkable re-orientation – both qualifying and even reconstituting his former attitudes and approaches. It would take him some time to process and incorporate these extensive revisions into a philosophical position. But what has become apparent is that Ricoeur no longer assumes that he occupies a position of authorial control. Nor does he deem that proofs and truths dictate the terms of unequivocal conviction. These alterations also herald a conspicuous change in Ricoeur's definition of the 'self' who is engaged in negotiating these adaptations. He observes: 'By Self I mean a non-egotistic, non-narcissistic, non-imperialistic mode of subjectivity.'[45] This self-effacing stance will guide Ricoeur in his future involvements with people, texts and commitments. All of these movements reflect a mode of abnegation, of a refusal to dominate and control.

Ricoeur undertakes to give a philosophical account of this most significant change of direction in both his life and work in a 1970 article, 'Hope and the Structure of Philosophical Systems'. He admits that he is interested in the intelligibility of hope (*intellectus spei*) insofar as it differs from the more traditional

---

[42] Ricoeur, *The Voluntary and the Involuntary*, p. 480.
[43] Ibid., p. 468.
[44] Ibid., p. 479.
[45] Paul Ricoeur, 'Philosophical Hermeneutics and Theological Hermeneutics', *Studies in Religion/ Sciences Religieuses* 5.1 (1975): 30.

theological notion of the intelligibility of faith (*intellectus fidei*). Faith, from this latter perspective, is most often associated with a metaphysical system in quest of a certain knowledge of God. The intention of hope is ordered toward an endeavour that is more open-ended in its expectations. Ricoeur states that: 'Hope is not a theme that comes after other themes, an idea which closes the system, but an impulse which opens the system, which breaks the closure of the system; it is a way of reopening what was unduly closed.'[46] Given this insight, hope, from a philosophical perspective, can open a superabundance of possibilities.[47] To fully appreciate the dynamics of hope, Ricoeur's most pressing concern is to explore the impact of Kant's three Critiques, but most importantly that of the *Critique Pure Reason*. This is because it is the dialectic of this first Critique that is held responsible for 'the destruction of absolute knowledge',[48] thus establishing not only the grounds for a philosophical anthropology, but also for the introduction of hope. Ricoeur summarizes his project:

> Between hope and absolute knowledge we have to choose. We cannot have both.
> Either one or the other, but not both together. It is the function of the Dialectic
> of Pure Reason to destroy the absolute object, to which absolute knowledge
> could be equated: the metaphysical subject; a non-contradictory concept of free
> causality; and above all a philosophical concept of God, let us say the god of the
> philosophers.[49]

Ricoeur is not a proponent of the union of Athens and Jerusalem, much preferring Kant's distinction between *denken* and *erkennen*, as well as the doctrine of transcendental illusion that refutes the idea of a complete conformity between the idea of a supreme reality and its necessary empirical existence. This rebuttal, however, will then permit Ricoeur to propose the role of hope as it mitigates the abandonment of absolute reason:

> Such is the first step of a philosophy of hope: it consists in an act of renunciation
> by which pure speculative reason gives up its claim to fulfill the thought of the
> unconditional along the line of knowledge of empirical objects; this repudiation
> by reason of its absolute claim is the last word of theoretical reason.[50]

Ricoeur's encounter with Kantian philosophical limits, especially as defined in *Religion within the Limits of Reason Alone*, enabled him to fashion hope in

---

[46] Paul Ricoeur, 'Hope and the Structure of Philosophical Systems', *American Catholic Philosophical Association. Proceedings for the Year 1970* 44 (1970): 64.
[47] Ibid., p. 69.
[48] Ibid., p. 64.
[49] Ibid., pp. 64–5.
[50] Ibid., p. 65.

a remarkable manner. Ricoeur's appeal to hope informs his philosophy with a singular status that results from the renunciation of any form of domination at the same time as allowing for an invocation of hope. In distancing himself from traditional metaphysics, he has provided an alternative orientation where, although one can never profess ultimate assurance, there is an anticipation that trust in alternate frameworks of being and determining will prevail. In this way, he set his own course with a distinctive mode of philosophizing that honours the integrity of his fellow human beings, while not completely dismissing intimations of an otherness. Yet this otherness escapes all attempts at closure:

> The final accent placed on the category of hope certainly marks my distance in relation to security and to guarantees that an ontology of being in itself would provide for thinking. I am far removed indeed from this type of metaphysics. But my major concern has never been to know if and how I could survive deconstruction of 'metaphysics' itself; it has been instead to do metaphysics in another manner, precisely of a hermeneutic philosophy.[51]

What needs to be kept in mind in tracing Ricoeur's itinerary as he develops his singular way of doing philosophy is that he has identified himself as 'not a theologian, but a philosopher'[52] who has a strong reliance on Kant. But not all of his work is in debt to Kant. This is evident in his later works such as *Oneself as Another; Memory, History, and Forgetting; The Course of Recognition*.[53] Yet there remains one final movement to examine in Ricoeur's philosophical journey. In the last ten years of his life he recorded fragments, some short, others of a profound nature, that were posthumously published under the title of *Living up to Death*. Yet, as I noted near the beginning of this chapter, many of his thoughts about 'living up to death' were recorded in interviews. In Azouvi and de Launay's interview he is especially frank. This is most obvious when he turns his attention to what living up to death demands. Here Ricoeur discovered that a final form of abnegation was required.

As his actual death approached, Ricoeur took upon himself a final form of detachment – not from life or even from the prospect of death, but from the expectation of immortality, or personal survival after death. This was not the same detachment that he had criticized in the Stoics, which was that of

---

[51] Paul Ricoeur, 'Reply to G. B. Madision', in *The Philosophy of Paul Ricoeur*, ed. Lewis Edwin Hahn, Peru, IL: Open Court, 1995, pp. 9–5.

[52] Ricoeur, 'Hope and the Structure of Philosophical Systems', p. 57.

[53] Paul Ricoeur, *Memory, History, Forgetting*, trans. Kathleen Blamey and David Pellauer, Chicago, IL: University of Chicago Press, 2004 [2000]; Paul Ricoeur, *The Course of Recognition*, trans. David Pellauer, Cambridge, MA: Harvard University Press, 2005 [2004].

indifference, but was instead an active decision. As he described his disposition: 'What is important is to be living until the moment of death, pushing
detachment as far as the mourning for the concern for an afterlife.'[54] As to
his inspiration for this avowal, he acknowledges the work of the medieval
Flemish mystic, Meister Eckhart, and his notion of *Gelassenheit*, or letting be/
detachment. Ricoeur describes his application of this term: 'It seems more
and more obvious to me that this culture of "detachment" – to borrow the
magnificent title from Meister Eckhart's writings and to enlist myself along with
him in the tradition of Flemish mysticism – implies bracketing the concern
with personal resurrection.'[55] But this rigorous demand, as Ricoeur realized
it, was closely linked with Freud's work of mourning. For Ricoeur, following
Freud, mourning is a process that involves a relinquishment of those emotional
attachments and other involvements that have been held especially dear. The
separation from such valued objects can feel as if one has lost a part of oneself.
This exacting combination was indeed crucial to the habit of mind that Ricoeur
cultivated as a way of preparing for death.[56]

Ricoeur will nonetheless assert that this is not a morbid process. He affirms
that 'joy is still possible, when everything has been given up.'[57] There is, of course,
suffering, which Ricoeur views as a price that must be paid.[58] Nevertheless,
he warns such suffering must never be solicited but needs to be borne with
equanimity.[59] But his own last days of life were not necessarily untroubled.
Catherine Goldenstein recalls this period in the Postface to *Living up to Death*:

> This was a difficult period for him: to the humiliation of finding himself so
> weak, dependent, 'suffering' and not 'acting' … I retain the memory of his
> painful struggle with himself, despondency, sometimes fear, and despite all our
> efforts, especially at night, the sense of solitude of someone on the way out, but
> always repeating beyond such torments his will to 'honour life' until death.[60]

Ricoeur struggled with all the strength he could summon to maintain his
affirmation of life. His death is a testament of fidelity to this desire. For this
achievement, he must be esteemed for providing an exemplar of what living up
until death can demand. It has been a lengthy process in following Ricoeur's
footsteps during his philosophical explorations, specifically those that are

---

[54] Ricoeur, *Conviction and Critique*, p. 156.
[55] Ibid.
[56] See Ricoeur, *Memory, History, Forgetting*, pp. 69–80 for further treatment of this topic.
[57] Ricoeur, *Conviction and Critique*, p. 157.
[58] Ibid., p. 156.
[59] Ibid.
[60] Goldenstein in Ricoeur, *Living up to Death*, pp. 95–6.

significant for the framing of his life-affirmation and a refusal to be governed by necessity. His consent to existence was based on a rejection of all that attempted to control, monopolize or otherwise try to dictate the terms of reference.

At the beginning of this chapter, I asked whether Ricoeur, and his disposition of living up to death, could have helped Howie. Her own tendency seemed ordered towards whether a certain habit of mind could help to nurture hope. Yet she also specified that such hope needed to be of a non-attached variety. It is apparent that Howie would not have had the time required to follow Ricoeur's own philosophical development in detail. But would his conclusions have helped provide either a measure of solace, or even a provocative challenge? It is impossible to draw any firm conclusions. Yet it may well be that Ricoeur's journey with his consent to life, with its appeal to hope, would have provided her with substantial matter for consideration. His detachment from any consolations such as the promise of life after death might not necessarily have given her pause – as she had no such aspirations to begin with. But his radical detachment may have impressed her. Ricoeur, nonetheless, has a way of persuading many people to follow in his philosophical footsteps – as a man of integrity and compassion, his work continues to stimulate intense exchange about the vicissitudes of life and the insoluble dilemmas they continually pose.

References

Antohi, Sorin, 'Memory, History, Forgiveness: A Dialogue between Paul Ricoeur and Sorin Antohi', *Janus Head* 8.1 (2005): 14–25.

Howie, Gillian, 'How to Think about Death: Living with Dying', *On the Feminist Philosophy of Gillian Howie: Materialism and Mortality*, ed. Victoria Browne and Daniel Whistler, London: Bloomsbury, 2016, pp. 132–44.

Ricoeur, Paul, *Fallible Man*, trans. C. A. Kelbley, Chicago, IL: Henry Regnery, 1965 [1960].

Ricoeur, Paul, *Freedom and Nature: The Voluntary and the Involuntary*, trans. E. V. Kohák, Evanston, IL: Northwestern Press, 1966 [1950].

Ricoeur, Paul, *The Symbolism of Evil*, trans. E. Buchanan, Boston, MA: Beacon Press, 1967 [1960].

Ricoeur, Paul, 'Hope and the Structure of Philosophical Systems', *American Catholic Philosophical Association. Proceedings for the Year 1970* 44 (1970).

Ricoeur, Paul, 'Philosophical Hermeneutics and Theological Hermeneutics', *Studies in Religion/Sciences Religieuses* 5.1 (1975): 14–33.

Ricoeur, Paul, *Oneself as Another*, trans. Kathleen Blamey, Chicago, IL: University of Chicago Press, 1992 [1990].

Ricoeur, Paul, 'Intellectual Autobiography', *The Philosophy of Paul Ricoeur*, ed. Lewis Edwin Hahn, Peru, IL: Open Court, 1995, pp. 3–73.

Ricoeur, Paul, 'Reply to G. B. Madison', *The Philosophy of Paul Ricoeur*, ed. Lewis Edwin Hahn, Peru, IL: Open Court, 1995, pp. 94–5.

Ricoeur, Paul, *Critique and Conviction*, ed. F. Azouvi and M. de Launay, trans. K. Blamey, New York: Columbia University Press, 1998 [1995].

Ricoeur, Paul, *Memory, History, Forgetting*, trans. Kathleen Blamey and David Pellauer, Chicago, IL: University of Chicago Press, 2004 [2000].

Ricoeur, Paul, *The Course of Recognition*, trans. David Pellauer, Cambridge, MA: Harvard University Press, 2005 [2004].

Ricoeur, Paul, *Living up to Death*, trans. David Pellauer, Chicago, IL: University of Chicago Press, 2009 [2007].

10

Learning to Die, Finally

Claire Colebrook

The title of this chapter is taken from Jacques Derrida's last interview: *Learning to Live, Finally.* Here, as elsewhere, Derrida refers to the gift of death, which opens my world to that of the other, because death is singular.[1] In a typically hyperbolic manner, Derrida argues that when the other dies, *the whole world dies*: something untranslatable is lost permanently. *If* humans live their lives with a sense of how that life might be viewed as a whole (and this is certainly a big 'if,' for we might want to question such a sense of living well in an epoch of hyper-consumption with no thought for a future), then it is also the case that whatever memorial is left behind – from memories of other persons to archival material – cannot be controlled by the one who dies. Others will read my texts, recall experiences, quote me and mourn me, but the being who lived can never be brought to present. Confronted, then, with the death of 'an' other – any other – we are brought up against that which can never be saved, archived, maintained or preserved. For Derrida, death is an opening to a radical outside, beyond my world, my sense, my context. If we start to think of the death of our species, and the fact that no matter how much monumental material we leave *what we have lived must be lost forever*, would we change how we lived? What happens when the species faces death, and becomes aware of its having delimited and individuating experiences in time that will at once leave a trace or memorial while also being absent from any capacity to give an account of what is left behind?

If one were to live forever, all possible lives would eventually be experienced, and if this were to occur there would be nothing to individuate 'a' life. Given that we do not live forever, our lives are always singular, but this raises a problem: can we say that because I only have this life here and now that I

---

[1] Jacques Derrida, *Learning to Live, Finally: The Last Interview*, trans. Pascal-Anne Brault and Michael Naas, New York: Melville House, 2011, p. 29.

must live with a sense of the singularity and responsibility of my existence, with every choice I make carrying the burden of all the choices I do not make, and all the responsibilities I fail to honour? Being oriented towards one's death would require a constant sense of one's life as one's own, and therefore as having a certain meaning. My life would be defined by the choices, projects and encounters that make it this life and no other; it is death that gives life meaning, because death forces one to form one's life with a sense of its end (both in terms of its finishing point and its goal). There is, however, another way of thinking about the relation between meaning and the end of life, and that is to say that it is only by not confronting death that a life has meaning. I have projects, goals, relationships and a sense of my life as a whole that can all be rendered senseless in the face of death. Oddly, both these senses – of death as that which imposes and that which destroys meaning – are evidenced in Gilles Deleuze's discussion of 'a' life. Discussing a Charles Dickens character who is poised between living and dying, Deleuze writes that what comes to the fore is the absolute singularity of 'a' life. Poised between living and dying, the meaning of the self in terms of the *individual* is vanquished, and yet it is precisely when all general predicates fall away that one experiences *individuation* (which is neither iterable nor graspable in any terms other than the 'thisness' of 'a' life). Deleuze therefore suggests two modes of meaning in relation to death: a narrative, general meaning of the person oriented towards living their life as a recognizable and memorable whole, *and* the utter singularity of individuation that is lost when 'a' life ceases:

> What is immanence? A life ... No one has described what *a* life is better than Charles Dickens, if we take the indefinite article as an index of the transcendental. A disreputable man, a rogue, held in contempt by everyone, is found as he lies dying. Suddenly, those taking care of him manifest an eagerness, respect, even love, for his slightest sign of life. Everybody bustles about to save him, to the point where, in his deepest coma, this wicked man himself senses something soft and sweet penetrating him. But to the degree that he comes back to life, his saviors turn colder, and he becomes once again mean and crude. Between his life and his death, there is a moment that is only that of *a* life playing with death. The life of the individual gives way to an impersonal and yet singular life that releases a pure event freed from the accidents of internal and external life, that is, from the subjectivity and objectivity of what happens ...[2]

---

[2] Gilles Deleuze, *Pure Immanence: Essays on A Life*, trans. Anne Boyman, New York: Zone Books, 2001, pp. 28–9.

A similar 'conundrum' (to adopt Gillian Howie's term) is expressed in Mark Doty's 'A Display of Mackerel', where the singular individual is what is lost in death; the self of social meaning and recognition, by contrast, is repeatable. Unlike Deleuze, Doty suggests that the singular life that dies is *perhaps* best set aside in favour of a self who finds some harmony, unity and ongoing life in the world:

> Suppose we could iridesce,
> like these, and lose ourselves
> entirely in the universe
> of shimmer – would you want
> to be yourself only,
> unduplicatable, doomed
> to be lost?[3]

In this chapter I want to explore the two seemingly divergent modes of the relation between meaning and death, *and* explore the ways in which the prognosis of the death sentence intensifies this seemingly arcane theorization in such a way that the force of the conundrum cannot be dissipated. Death is both that which defines, delimits and borders a life, allowing life to be lived as *this* life; death is also that which seems to reduce the definition and meaning of one's life to nothing. The end of one's life is at once that which gives form and closure, and that which destroys all form and sense.

*

It was Peter Brooks in *Reading for the Plot* who originally tied the arc of narrative to the death drive.[4] Drawing on Freud's death drive, where the organism wants to die, but 'die in its own way', Brooks describes the motor of narrative plots. The disturbance that initiates any narrative – some loss or incompletion – generates a desire for an end, but this end must be a well-formed end, an end that brings the beginning or promise of the narrative to some sense of fulfilment. We might say that the novel (and narrative more generally) gives us the notion of a natural death. A being begins in incompleteness, but lives with an openness to becoming, and gradually flourishes towards a fulfilment of its capacities or what it has the potentiality to be. There is something about what life *means* that is tied to a proper end, or an end of one's own. If there were no death, life would have no meaning: if I could live forever, then all possibilities would eventually

³   Mary Doty, 'A Display of Mackerel', in *Atlantis*, New York: Harper Perennial, 1995, p. 15.
⁴   Peter Brooks, *Reading for the Plot: Design and Intention in Narrative*, New York: A. A. Knopf, 1984.

be lived through. Nothing would be uniquely mine; nothing would carry the burden of an individuating decision, and eventually everything that could come to pass would come to pass.

This is one way to read Friedrich Nietzsche's concept of eternal return: rather than being defined by the distinct choices that make one's life one's own, one would live each moment *as if* it were for all time. One would experience time as if all things would come into being. Such a life would be light, liberated from the individuation of being responsible for all that one does not do. Nietzsche asks us to imagine living the life we have now, over and over again: if anything were even slightly different it would not be the life that it is, and would be another life entirely.[5] For Nietzsche, it is not the case that I have a life that I must then render meaningful by way of the formative decisions I make; rather, I become who I am by acting *as if* what befell me were something I would affirm eternally. Such a life is not bounded by the ending or death that imposes its finitude upon decisions. Such a life is liberated from meaning; it is this life and no other, and nothing is to be gained from mourning or lamenting that it might have been otherwise. And, as the extension of this Nietzschean line of thought by Gilles Deleuze makes clear, one might ultimately arrive at an ethics of 'becoming-imperceptible': *not* defining myself by who I am (by way of all the decisions and predicates through which I form my life), but liberating myself from the point of view that generates my world, ultimately becoming-with all of existence, *sub specie aeternitatis*. Not only would I never have to decide just who I want to be, or how I want to live my life, there would be nothing to distinguish the narrative arc of my life – lived in this here and now – from any other life.

One might contrast two traditions in modern philosophy: a Kantian emphasis on a subject who becomes who he is by giving a law to himself, and who does so precisely because life itself is *indifferent* and offers no foundation or meaning; and a post-Nietzschean undoing of the self by granting powers of difference to a life or milieu that goes well beyond the self, and well beyond the meaning and sense we give to the world.[6] These two traditions are at odds with each other, and yet both assume the relation between meaning and life as the ultimate problem. For modern-day Kantians it is the meaning and definition I bestow upon my life that generates ethics, normativity, value and personhood; if I were to behave in any manner whatsoever at any time, then I would not be the unique individual that I have determined myself to be. Crucial to the sense

---

[5] See Alexander Nehamas, 'The Eternal Recurrence', *The Philosophical Review* 89.3 (1980).
[6] Catherine Malabou, 'The Eternal Return and the Phantom of Difference', trans. Arne De Boever, *Parrhesia* 10 (2010).

of one's life as a whole is not only a coherent and narrative understanding, but a comportment towards death. I do not live merely to survive at all costs, but to live well – and to live with a sense of the worthiness of things beyond my own existence. It is only with a life lived towards a death that is *one's own* that a life would have meaning, with meaning – in turn – having less to do with language and communication, and more with decisive individuation. Death and meaning are intertwined inextricably; death is what delimits and defines a life. By contrast, as I have already suggested, there is a counter-tradition that affirms impersonality, overcoming the distinction that renders one's life into a meaningful whole, and becoming one with a life that is neither one's own, nor human. If one tradition stresses meaning and narrative, or a sense of being-towards-death that grants one's life distinction, another embraces a figural death, or a death before death: to live as if one were not attached to one's own point of view, as if one's life and decisions ultimately were not one's own but simply aspects of an impersonal and unbounded whole. Such a philosophical divide is more than just an academic quibble, and cuts to the very heart of how one ought to comport oneself to one's life.

Martin Heidegger insisted that being-towards-death and recognizing that one must decide just what possibilities one would, and would not, pursue constituted an authentic grasp of one's existence, whereas simply living as if 'everybody dies someday' was inauthentic, a failure to take up one's 'ownmost' potentiality. It is not as though one has a self and world, and then chooses how to live; one lives, one is thrown into this world and no other, and from that original being-in-the-world one is authentically and unavoidably confronted with the necessary finitude of existence. At its most extreme, the pressure of such a being-towards-death would come to the fore in the event of a diagnosis or prognosis: what sort of narrative could one bestow upon a life that had its imagined narrative arc interrupted? One might then be at odds with one's own life.[7] By contrast, a counter-Heideggerian tradition (sometimes even indebted to different aspects of Heidegger) stresses an overcoming of one's sense of ownness. I have already mentioned Deleuze and the task of 'becoming-imperceptible' but there are also contemporary versions of Buddhism (and other traditions of 'mindfulness') that seek to annihilate the attachments to one's own life, living as if one were already an aspect of a whole well beyond one's own life and time. In this respect one has abandoned the meaning and sense of one's own life (the

---

[7] See Alexander García Düttmann, *At Odds with AIDS: Thinking and Talking about a Virus*, trans. Peter Gilgen and Conrad Scott-Curtis, Palo Alto, CA: Stanford University Press, 1996.

meaning of a novelistic or narrative life), but has perhaps found meaning of a different genre. Rather than living as if one were an individual oriented towards being remembered well, and being able to grasp all one's decisions *as if* one were a law-generating member of the kingdom of ends, this other sense of meaning would be epic, with every life making up a whole of multiple points of view, sub-genres and (perhaps like early epics) open to additions and mutations with the passage of time.

Perhaps, then, one should not simply read this tension as a division of academic traditions that are divided over just what is more meaningful: the individual bounded by death, or the grander life beyond the individual's death. These scholarly divisions touch upon just how we comport ourselves to life. It may well be (as I will argue here) that one does not simply choose to live one's life like a character in a novel, *or* – to quote Deleuze and Guattari – in a 'becoming-molecular' that is no longer bounded by chronology or identity but embraces the eternal return of difference. Death is both highly individuating, and utterly destructive of all sense. Death is both that which allows life to become 'a' life, and that which annihilates fleeting and ephemeral distinctions. Death *is* difference – that which sets us apart and alone from a broader milieu of life – and indifference, destructive of ownness and personhood. This is why it is somewhat heavy-handed to divide philosophy between those who stress the meaning and individuation of being-towards-death, and those who affirm the grander sense of life beyond individual existence. The two are intertwined and perhaps unavoidable. It is individual death and finitude that marks out life as one's own, while a sense of life beyond one's death liberates one from the burden of ownness.

Meaning in general is achieved by differentiation, marking or noting something *as something* in such a way that it is recognizable beyond its own singular existence. Karen Barad[8] has made a claim for the relation between meaning and materiality right down to the quantum level of existence; there is no such thing as 'matter' devoid of all relation, time, becoming and individu-ation. To exist is to exist in some way that is utterly singular. This also means that all existence, in the singularity of its 'thisness', must die; even more importantly, death would be a question of thresholds. 'I' am composed of a whole series of events, compositions and relations that come into being and cease to exist. Rather than say that the 'I' is what remains present beneath change, one might

---

[8] Karen Michelle Barad, *Meeting the Universe Halfway: Quantum Physics and the Entanglement of Matter and Meaning*, Durham, NH: Duke University Press, 2007.

say that the 'I' (or one's life) is this ongoing series of endings. How, then, is it that the ending of 'a' life – this highly singular composition of fleeting ends and becomings – comes to feel like such a violent cut into life? I would suggest that for all the seeming abstraction and attention to the inhuman in both Deleuze and Guattari's and Barad's work, one way to respond to the force of death is by way of a thought of matter (and by way of a seemingly subtle distinction between ways of thinking about thresholds of matter and life).

If matter were timeless stuff or a simple substrate then it would be outside relations and becoming, but this is not so. Matter is neither what goes through time, nor what changes through time; matter is a dynamic, multiple, constantly composing and decomposing encounter among forces. What something *is* emerges from what it encounters, and therefore all 'identity' is the outcome of a coming into being that is also necessarily a passage to non-being. For Barad, matters, even at an inhuman level, are always matters of concern – bound up with relations, forces and (one might even say) desire. It is therefore not anthropomorphic in any simple sense to think of death and meaning as intrinsic to all life. If one defines meaning as having a sense of one's life as a whole, or of thinking of life in terms of narrative, then this conception is quite specifically human (and possibly narrowly Eurocentric in its emphasis on personhood and a certain novelistic level of individuation). If, however, meaning is defined by the enactment of one potential rather than another, of contracting the range of possibilities to a relatively stable and habitual domain (a rhythm or refrain), then meaning *is* life, or the creation of an ongoing territory (a set of relations). This notion of a meaningfulness of matter right down to the quantum level has implications for how one might think of an ethics of facing death. If, as Barad asserts, there is no such thing as meaningless matter – blank neutral stuff devoid of all relation or dynamism – then there is no underlying substrate, nothing that simply 'is' without change, encounter or without 'world.' In some respects this is akin to Deleuze and Guattari's claim for a reversal of the notion that only humans are artful animals, with the rest of the world and life being dominated by habit. For them, 'music is not the privilege of human beings: the universe, the cosmos, is made of refrains; the question in music is that of a power of deterritorialization permeating nature, animals, the elements, and deserts as much as human beings'.

If death and meaning are inextricably intertwined, their relation is neither simple nor constant. It oscillates impossibly between death as that which makes my life unavoidably my own, and death as that which renders my individuation null and void in the face of existence as a grander whole. Perhaps this relation between death and meaning is even more odd today, and for several reasons. The human species is facing extinction, or – at least – has been given the prognosis and death sentence of confronting its own end. Even without contemplating its own end, the intensified rate of non-human species extinctions, and the 'end of the world' (as the end of the affluent Western world), might prompt the thought of how death, meaning and life come into relation when one is talking about the whole of life, human and non-human. It may be that the human species (and life) as a whole is becoming aware of impending death, and this may well have intensified a sense of what it means to be human (as evidenced in the more reflective strands of post-apocalyptic culture). The sense of the end of the human is now so widespread and unremarkable that it has become the default narrative frame for Hollywood blockbusters: from television series such as *True Blood* (2008–14), *The Walking Dead* (2010–15) and *Colony* (2016) that pit an increasingly threatened humanity against its others, to films that display a depleted and besieged humanity (*Elysium* [2013], *Oblivion* [2013] and *Mad Max: Fury Road* [2015]). It may also be that the part of humanity that took itself to be uniquely and blessedly human (European man, aware of himself as a member of the kingdom of ends) begins to sense his difference from many other ways of being human that are not burdened with the individuating weight of 'being-towards-death'. I have already mentioned the recognition of non-Western traditions and the realization that attachment to one's unique and singular individuality, and even one's species, might be a quite limited and partial tradition of thought. Even within the Western tradition, there have been ways of thinking about life *not* as oriented to one's ownmost potentiality that is delimited by one's singular death, but as properly oriented to a world that can be intuited if one transcends one's finite and personal point of view. In her book on Deleuze's Spinoza, Howie outlines Deleuze's Spinozist theory that adequate intuition or the 'third kind of knowledge' is a form of beatitude that achieves eternity by overcoming the finitude or causal and partial relations; to grasp an event as an expression of divine substance is to intuit being as such, to become one with the world. Howie is highly unsympathetic to Deleuze's sleight of hand that would pass directly from a certain type of knowledge to the achievement of eternal joy and blessedness. Significantly, she resists Deleuze's overcoming of the distance between the world that we know and the world as it is. [9] Grasping something fully as an expression of the one substance that is both the world and God is both an adequate fulfilment of knowledge, and the acquisition of an

---

[9]   Gillian Howie, *Deleuze and Spinoza: Aura of Expressionism*, New York: Palgrave, 2002, p. 170.

eternal and impersonal joy. One might then think of life *either* as that which is given meaning only through the finitude and ownness that compels one to form one's life into a significant whole, with death being that which individuates, *or* one might think of life in its human and individuated mode as that which needs to be transcended in order to intuit life as such. One finds meaning either in the arc of a life delimited by death, *or* one overcomes bounded life with meaning then being generated by a continuity or connectedness with a life beyond death. If Peter Brooks invoked Freud and the death drive to describe an organic meaning (and narrative life) where a being wants to die but 'die in its own way', one could cite another Freud for whom an 'oceanic feeling' of losing the limits of the self intimated a return to a paradisiacal plenitude.[10] Either meaning is given through ownness bounded by death (with meaning being organic, narrative, individual and temporally projected) *or* meaning is more like a sense 'of something far more deeply interfused',[11] released from chronological time, character, personhood and the specified world.

To think about meaning in relation to a life presupposes both a connect-edness beyond language and writing in their narrow sense, and – even when it is a striving beyond the self by imagining that which extends beyond my death – individuation. If, as Barad insists, it makes no sense to talk about matter without meaning, this is because even at the inhuman and pre-organic level *what something is* has to do with its encounters and relations. Something *is* something by way of the actualization of some potentials rather than others. If one wants to talk about 'a' meaningful life, where encounters and relations are attributed to a person who persists through time, then individuation requires that a life be bounded, or be *this* life. It is death that delimits and marks my life as *my life*; if I were to live forever or indefinitely, then I would go through all possibilities and be all people. But I have to live this life, and make these choices, always knowing that death will bring my projects to an end, but also make them mine. Any narrative is like every other narrative in having an end, but it is also always *this* narrative with *this* end. Genres tend to begin the same way; one establishes a narrative frame and expectations by way of opening with a plot that promises some degree of predictable trajectory, such as a crime committed, a desire unfulfilled, a threat, intrigue, loss or mystery. A text must establish a

---

10 Sigmund Freud, *Civilization and its Discontents*, trans. and ed. James Strachey, New York: Norton, 1961, p. 12.

11 William Wordsworth, 'Lines Written a Few Miles Above Tintern Abbey', in *William Wordsworth: The Major Works: Including The Prelude*, ed. Stephen Gill, Oxford: Oxford University Press, 1984, p. 134.

genre or mode in order to then become singular by way of its ending. Life is defined by its end – not necessarily its end in terms of function or goal, but its end in terms of always being *this* life with delimited possibilities. We want the story to end, but to do so in its own way; the story does not *stop* but provides a sense in which what happened in the beginning has some connection (tragic or felicitous) with what occurs finally.

In this respect, Brooks can be seen to extend a tradition of *life as narrative*, and life as blessed with a natural end, that goes back as far as Aristotle, who was already drawing on quoted wisdom when he stated that we should 'call no man happy until he is dead'. Happiness (or *eudaimonia*, well-spiritedness or living well) cannot be attributed to a contingent series of actions – such as how much was earned, or even how much pleasure was experienced. Rather, happiness has to do with a form of life, and with deciding how one ought to live precisely in terms of one's life as a created and readable whole.[12] Happiness or the life well-lived bears a relation to death precisely because it is death that will bring my projects to an end, and that will then also give my life some monumental quality: I will (or may) live on in the minds and memories of others, but will do so only if I have lived my life with some coherent and meaningful sense of life as a whole. My life and happiness bear a relation to death not only because death imposes an end and therefore possible wholeness to my life, but also because a life is – on this picture at least – ideally monumental. I become who I am not by living haphazardly and at the whim of every pleasure and inclination, but because decisions are made with some sense of how I would like to be remembered, viewed or honored. This is so even if that ideal of self-memorialization occurs before actual death; we may act with a sense of how we will be remembered, and we may even act well by disregarding how we are viewed in our own time, knowing that we are living well for a time and life not our own. Saints, heroes, martyrs and maybe even terrorists can scorn the life of the now, but they do so by dying for what would give their life sense and meaning in a future they will never live, but one in which they imagine that they might be viewed. If we do live with a sense of *this life*, then this is because death either individuates or allows for a thought of time to come in which my individuation will mean something.

So what would it mean for a species to start having such a sense of itself, of dying – *of being the species that it is by having this trajectory and no other*? And what might it be for a species to imagine itself, like 'a' life, as having this time

---

[12] Alasdair McIntyre, *After Virtue: A Study in Moral Theory*, London: Bloomsbury, 2013, p. 250.

and no other, and therefore that its end will be the loss of the world, leaving an inadequate inscription? We might want to reject the notion that life has worth only when lived as a being-towards-death, but before we do reject this idea, perhaps we should think about whether such a notion might illuminate how we think about human life, the life of the species.

In the remainder of this chapter, I want to draw upon Gillian Howie's 2012 seminar, 'How to Think about Death: Living with Dying'. To begin with, I want to intertwine two problems or (to quote Howie again) 'conundrums'. Rather than see two divided philosophical ethical traditions that would contest whether one finds meaning at the level of an individual life or by way of some broader life beyond one's own time, it would be better to reflect upon the overwhelming importance granted to the relation between life and meaning, even if – as Jacques Derrida insists – everything we do to memorialize the sense of our lives can never coincide with life itself. Or, to draw upon the work of Paul de Man: giving a face, wholeness or figuration to a life is necessarily also a defacement and disfiguration of the singularity of a life.[13]

The second conundrum is raised explicitly by Howie. When an individual is given a prognosis it may be that impending death generates the evacuation of meaning, *or* death might finally be experienced as that which bestows meaning. As I have already suggested, this requires us to give two accounts of meaning, and death. The first would be natural; our life unfolds through time towards death, and we all die, and it is only with the whole of one's life that we can have some sort of sense. When Aristotle quotes the saying of calling no man happy until he is dead, and Freud says that the organism wants to die but die in its own way, they draw upon a concept of natural meaning (a meaning in the time of life), with time unfolding in such a manner that there is the ongoing creation of form. By contrast, one can also be thrown towards a non-natural death, where death truncates that supposedly natural unfolding such that one lives out of time, or at odds with one's being-towards-death. The prognosis appears to be exceptional, out of time and destructive of the meaning we ought to have.

I want to argue that this seemingly non-natural death should be the way we think about all death, and nature. Indeed, it is by way of narrative and figuration (or a certain lure of organic wholeness) that one can think of death as a forming and meaning-bestowing power. Well before the concept of the Anthropocene took hold of a wide variety of academic disciplines, and well before anthropogenic climate change became a widely accepted notion, there

---

[13] Paul de Man, 'Autobiography as De-facement', *MLN* 94.5 (1979).

had been a great deal of work questioning whether what we experience as 'life' or 'nature' is not the most fabricated of entities. The notion of a harmonious, stable, bounded, landscape-like nature that is in accord with a moral vision of time is – as Kant argued – the consequence of reflective judgement: we act *as if* nature were created in line with our rational and virtuous vision of time and the future.[14] There is nothing natural about nature, and the meaning-bestowing death that gives form and sense to a life is a powerful (and possibly necessary) fiction. There would be, then, the death of nature (or a natural death) where death is imagined as the narrative closure that gives form; and then there would be the death of nature, where there is no nature. Today, we are confronting the death of all life, or even the death of life as we know it, and such a death feels violent, untimely and out of joint. We, 'we humans', seem not to accept the rise and fall of our own species' extinction as part of the ebb and flow of 'life'; we seem not to accept that what we have imagined as 'nature' will also, one day, die its 'natural' death. On the contrary, there is no shortage of cultural production that imagines the saving of the world (from fantasies about saving the planet in Hollywood cinema, to supposedly more elevated endeavours to avoid 'existential catastrophe' of the loss of intelligent life).[15] This avoidance of accepting that humanity, 'civilization' and 'nature' might come to an end 'naturally' suggests that the idea of a body that comes into being, lives its own time and 'dies in its own way' is perhaps something one can only project onto an other life, never one's own. Perhaps the prognosis exposes the fiction of 'dying in one's own way'. In the absence of a nature that would be somehow ours, and of a time that would be hours, how do we live and die?

In addition to the conundrum of death being both the bestowal of meaning and the evacuation of meaning, Howie also notes the oddity of the prognosis of death coming as a surprise. We know that 'everyone dies', and that we all die 'someday' and yet a prognosis seems to come as the most violent and shocking of events. Here, again, we might draw some connections to our present: perhaps the seriousness of climate change, ecological destruction and the Anthropocene have come as a shock, but this would be so *only* if we had somehow been living as if industrialism, techno-science, imperialism and colonialism could somehow occur and allow nature to remain as 'nature'. But I think it is becoming evident that this conception of time, nature and death is one we must confront

---

[14] Immanuel Kant, *Critique of Judgment*, trans. Werner S. Pluhar, Indianapolis, IN: Hackett, 1987, p. 236.

[15] Nick Bostrom, 'Existential Risks: Analyzing Human Extinction Scenarios and Related Hazards', *Journal of Evolution and Technology* 9.1 (2002).

as no longer sustainable. The species is coming to an end; or, at least, the 'man' of European memory and 'being-towards-death' has reached his limit. Nature is coming to an end, and it will be the case – with increasing science and technology – that we will all have a prognosis that precludes us from living with the glib half-knowledge that 'everyone dies'. We will have to learn to die.

In addition to the problem of meaning, and the surprise of the prognosis, Howie mentions the ways in which reflection upon nature or art may provide consolation, in the event of a prognosis that seems to cut life short. But she also makes an enigmatic remark about music, and I think this is worth pursuing when traditional forms of art such as landscapes and well-rounded narratives will be more and more at odds with our traumatized Earth. If, as Howie suggests, 'reading won't do it,' this may well be increasingly true in a world that cannot be rendered coherent, that cannot be an object of reason or reflective judgement. What sort of consolation can nature offer if nature is dying? What meaning can we project for the future if the future is dying, if we *can't* think of life in terms of memories, legacy, surviving, living on? What if this grand tradition of philosophical and cultural archiving, of defining oneself through a rich past and imagined future, were given a prognosis, a death sentence?

I think the questions and 'conundrums' posed by Howie's lecture require us to think about two conceptions of what individuates: meaning, or singularity. Following the deconstructive work of Derrida and others, we might begin by asking how something might live on after my life (a memory of me, a memoir, a figure, a video). Something can only live on if it is incarnated, given a body. For something to live and have a body means it is *this thing here* that will also decay. The more individuated, 'mine', or singular something is, the more fragile and exposed to death it is. (If Western culture is primarily inscriptive and archival and does *not* rely on orality and living memory, it has at once a greater indelibility – such that it has marked the earth at a geological scale – but also harbours the potential for a catastrophic prognosis. Everything that has gone by the name of 'man' may be erased.) If meaning is construed as the ongoing sameness and recognition of repeatable identity, or what can be preserved by way of inscription, then singularity is that which is defaced or disfigured by memorialization. No matter how well-formed and memorable our lives may be, death erases and cuts off that singular life – or 'a' life – that *is just its existing*, without essence and without sense. This is why there is always, despite the naturalness, expectedness and time of death, something of a surprise, an evacuation of meaning, and an event that escapes all reading.

If one experiences a prognosis, or a death that is at odds with 'being-towards-death', then one may do all one likes to give form, shape and meaning, but perhaps what needs to be confronted is a different sense of meaning (one that is 'musical' or one that is not that of reading, but the singularity of an evanescent tone). Such 'meaning' does not take the shape of shared, communicable, repeatable sense, but exposes a certain 'mineness' or singularity. What I value is what – when destroyed – leaves nothing. I am my attachment to singular and unrepeatable and unjustifiable objects – this is true at the level of the species and the individual. If, upon the death of a friend or a child, one were told that one could easily find another friend or adopt a smarter, prettier, more loving child, that would be no consolation at all. If, as 'humanity' is given a prognosis, we are told that it would have been better for such a species not to have been, or that another form of species would be better, we may feel no consolation at all. This is *not* because we are attached to the stories and meaning of 'humanity' – but rather because it is *this* singular and threatened 'we' that does not live up to the ideals of man as a kingdom of ends that we are already mourning. We can no longer have a sense of a life well-lived, or a life that will live on in memory. This is more and more true across registers: the 'life', 'humanity' and 'nature' that we are beginning to mourn was only possible because someone else's life was erased: it was European colonization (with slavery, industrialism, and the harnessing of human and non-human energy) that enabled what appeared to be a cyclic benevolent nature, and a noble 'being-towards-death'. With the collapse and exposure of that enterprise of violence and appropriation, depictions of a self-renewing earth ought to appear as the alibis that they have always been.

How might one give solace (or meaning) if death does evacuate meaning? In conclusion I would suggest that all death – of individuals, or eco-systems, of species – be seen as a death that is given by a violent prognosis. If there is no natural and meaningful time of death, then *all* loss would be irreparable and meaningless, and all meaning would require disfiguration and defacement of the singularity of life. It may be, as Barad has argued, that one needs to think of all matter in terms of meaning, but if this is so then meaning cannot be confined to narrative wholeness, sense, lived time, organicism and certainly not to memorialization.

I want to return one more time to Howie's 'conundrum' regarding death as an evacuation of meaning, even if death can also be the bestowal of meaning. It is certainly the case that meaning in a propositional, personal, human sense is erased by death, and yet death may also be what displays a certain 'thisness' or far more singular conception of individuation. From my narrative or personal point of view, life is experienced in terms of a before and after, with an ongoing progress and coming to fulfilment. But a certain conception of death destroys that locatedness and sense and exposes us to the singularity that is experienced as utter loss. Most of our practices of death are narrative, 'natural' and meaningful: life insurance, living wills, retirement savings, the tradition of the narrative life and the right time of death. But one might want to question how human life came to be figured in this organic, bounded, narrative and meaningful form. One might say that many humans and non-humans died in order to shore up a Western tradition that fetishized the meaning of nature, and security of a life lived as a narrative whole.

Death as prognosis comes as a surprise because it breaks with the idea of some natural trajectory coming to an end. Just as one might think about two notions of meaning (as coherent wholeness or as singularity), one might also suggest that there would be two deaths: the natural, general death of 'everyone dies', and the singular death that destroys the self of narrative form. This is what is happening at a species level; it may well be that all species come to an end 'someday', but we are increasingly living in a world where we have been delivered a prognosis. It is this sense of an untimely end that seems to challenge the extent to which nature would be solace. The species – and whatever is left of nature – has been given a prognosis.

Something happens to meaning, where what is left is not a story (not a nature of ongoing eternal existence), but something like a 'thisness'. This singularity or even remainder might prompt us to think of two senses of monument: the first would be like a war memorial, tombstone or obituary, where we mark out the sense of a life by referring to what this person or event meant in a broader historical whole. The second sense is not one of readable sense, and does not take the form of a 'who' or a 'we', but simply *that* something is no more. One day we will have been, and what will be left will be inscribed and singular; it will not have our sense or even a shared and communicable sense. I want to suggest this it is this sense of meaning or individuation that marks a life that really dies, that dies its own death.

The human species will die. 'We' will die. These two events are not quite the same. The first is a statement about life in general, and may be situated within a narrative about the general ebb and flow of nature whereby everything that comes into being will pass away; the second has to do with a new mode of being-towards-death that has generated a sense of 'the human' as a finite and end-oriented 'we'. It is because 'we' have been handed a prognosis (by the Anthropocene, by anthropogenic climate change) that 'we' are constituted as a global humanity with a sense of impending non-being. We can therefore extend Howie's three claims about meaning, the surprise of the prognosis, and the consolation of art to observe that the twenty-first century has been dominated by attempts to write a redemption narrative for humanity in the face of a prognosis. What has come to be known as post-apocalyptic fiction and cinema, from Cormac McCarthy's *The Road* to *The Walking Dead*, offers various modes of framing and rendering meaningful a species that is confronting its own extinction. If we think of nature non-anthropomorphically, then nature is not that which continues as the same in my absence; nature is not a Constable landscape that possesses its own harmony. A non-humanized nature would be no 'nature' at all. It would have no telos, no sense, no narrative and no proper end. Rather than indulge in post-apocalyptic narratives that imagine the species saving itself and its own future, it might be better to think of 'our' death as radically disruptive, discontinuous and the outcome of a surprising prognosis that evacuates all narrative meaning. Rather, then, than think of an ethics in which we continue to imagine a 'we' that suffers the wound of its own doing, and then redeems and saves itself and humanity to live longer, we might see the prognosis as an opportunity to think beyond a time of our own making. We should perhaps think of what the human species will have been, how we will have lived, and whether – if this history were to be repeated over and over again without any other future or possibility – whether we would say yes to that time, that humanity? And if we were not to say yes how might we live?

References

Barad, Karen Michelle, *Meeting the Universe Halfway: Quantum Physics and the Entanglement of Matter and Meaning*, Durham, NC: Duke University Press, 2007.

Bostrom, Nick, 'Existential Risks: Analyzing Human Extinction Scenarios and Related Hazards', *Journal of Evolution and Technology* 9.1 (2002).

Brooks, Peter, *Reading for the Plot: Design and Intention in Narrative*, New York: A. A. Knopf, 1984.

De Man, Paul, 'Autobiography as De-facement', *MLN* 94.5 (1979): 919–30.

Deleuze, Gilles, *Pure Immanence: Essays on A Life*, trans. Anne Boyman, New York: Zone Books, 2001.

Derrida, Jacques, *Learning to Live, Finally: The Last Interview*, trans. Pascal-Anne Brault and Michael Naas, New York: Melville House, 2011.

Doty, Mary, *Atlantis*, New York: Harper Perennial, 1995.

Freud, Sigmund, *Civilization and its Discontents*, trans. and ed. James Strachey, New York: Norton, 1961.

García Düttmann, Alexander, *At Odds with AIDS: Thinking and Talking about a Virus*, trans. Peter Gilgen and Conrad Scott-Curtis, Palo Alto, CA: Stanford University Press, 1996.

Howie, Gillian, *Deleuze and Spinoza: Aura of Expressionism*, New York: Palgrave, 2002.

Kant, Immanuel, *Critique of Judgment*, trans. Werner S. Pluhar, Indianapolis, IN: Hackett, 1987.

Malabou, Catherine, 'The Eternal Return and the Phantom of Difference', trans. Arne De Boever, *Parrhesia* 10 (2010): 21–9.

McIntyre, Alasdair, *After Virtue: A Study in Moral Theory*, London: Bloomsbury, 2013.

Nehamas, Alexander, 'The Eternal Recurrence', *The Philosophical Review* 89.3 (1980): 331–56.

Wordsworth, William, 'Lines Written a Few Miles Above Tintern Abbey', in *William Wordsworth: The Major Works: Including The Prelude*, ed. Stephen Gill, Oxford: Oxford University Press, 1984.

11

'What the Living Do': Poetry's Death and Dying

Deryn Rees-Jones

In his critical book *The Sense of an Ending*, first published in 1967, Frank Kermode memorably begins with the assertion that 'It is not expected of critics as it is of poets that they should help us to make sense of our lives; they are bound only to attempt the lesser feat of making sense of the ways in which we try to make sense of our lives.'[1] On the few but now retrospectively important occasions when I met for conversations with my colleague Gill Howie neither of us ever spoke directly about our experiences of death, or how to make sense of it: not she as a woman with breast cancer, not I as someone with a recent experience of living with, and nursing at home, someone with a terminal illness. I am not quite sure how that silence arose: perhaps it was to do with knowing something needed not to be spoken as well as a desire to reside in the not-knowing of the moment. What we did do, however, was to express an ambivalence about intellectualizing our own experiences – cue our laughter – had I not better think of something else to do with this precious time (she); was thinking about this a way of leaving the difficulties behind and working them through or a way of staying lost in them and the past (me)?

Nevertheless, there was also a strong joint sense that this difficult encounter – this 'living up to death' – was something worth staying with in our professional as well as our personal lives, even as we encountered death from very different perspectives. On each occasion that we did meet, Gill's urge to me – memorably – was that I should write a poem. I have perhaps up to now failed her, at least for the moment, in this request, as I might also fail her as a critic making sense of the way we make sense of our lives through poetry. It is in response, however,

[1] Frank Kermode, *The Sense of an Ending: Studies in the Theory of Fiction*, Oxford: Oxford University Press, 2000, p. 3.

to her instinct that poetry might have some sort of an answer to death, that it might make or take up a different kind of thought and a way of making sense of life in ways other than linear argumentation, in which the spirit of this essay resides.

*

My thoughts on death begin and circle around Kermode's landmark book, *The Sense of an Ending*, but also pick up implicitly on a kind of challenge from various philosophical quarters (Heidegger's reading of death as the 'possibility of impossibility' variously taken up or contested by Blanchot, Derrida, Bataille, Levinas) that we are unable to imagine our own death. Kermode describes this inability to 'really' imagine our own death as a kind of cheating:

> If you imagine yourself being shot, your body being rolled away in a barrow by soldiers, you are cheating yourself by substituting for your own body someone else's or perhaps an impersonal dummy. Your own death lies hidden from you.[2]

If death creates meaning, is constitutive of our own existence, its way of making meaning can also constitute a trap in its foregrounding of a self in relation to chronological time. Tom Lubbock, the art critic, memorably describes the diagnosis of his terminal brain cancer as placing him somewhere which runs counter to linear narrative:

> Either there is an ending, with death. Or there is an overcoming. And both are satisfactory conclusions. But prolongation, unclear survival, is also a familiar narrative form. There is the shaggy-dog story that I and my family live in ... The tale is spun out, with an ending wanting to be endlessly deferred.[3]

Such deferrals in some ways are the condition of life itself (especially if you take on a Beckettian worldview). In the case of a terminal diagnosis, however, they are forced into a state of acuteness, and framed within the dying or recovering dichotomy (which of course is a very real one) and provoke deep anxiety. In Siri Hustvedt's fictional meditation on the relationship between gender and art, *The Blazing World*, a life is constructed, via diary entries, letters, third-person accounts, to tell the story of Harriet Burden, an artist who only becomes successful by adopting the persona of young men who stand in for her and with whom she collaborates to create a series of successful 'fictional' artistic

---

[2]   Ibid., p. 161.
[3]   Tom Lubbock, *Until Further Notice, I Am Alive*, London: Granta, 2012, pp. 137–8.

personas and careers. Hustvedt's novel is not a novel about living with an illness. But it is an account of how we give meaning to a life which, by the terms of its place within a realist chronology, must come to an end. In the last sections of *The Blazing World*, narrating her own end-of-life experiences, Burden writes movingly of the tension between the experiences of the mind and the body, foregrounded as it dies:

> Every dying person is a cartoon version of the Cartesian dualist, a person made of two substances, *res cogitans* and *res extensa*. The thinking substance moves along on its own above the insurrectionist body formed of vile gross matter, a traitor to the spirit, to that airy cogito that keeps on thinking and talking. Descartes was far more subtle about mind-and-body interactions than many crude commentators admit, but he was right that thoughts don't seem to take up any room, not even in one's head. What are they? No one knows.[4]

What strikes me most in this passage is the relationship set up between the material body, its changes and deteriorations in illness, changes which register in terms of the way we perceive ourselves as well as others perceive us, on the one hand, and the foregrounding of the fact that thoughts (which might be said to be the place in which we exist) lack material form, on the other. As Burden's ending becomes inscribed in the text the narrative prose through which she translates herself fragments into something that seems to resemble, in its negotiation with silence and space, poetry on the page. The self disintegrates into a Whitmanesque, transcendent otherness:

> I am multitudes.
> This earth a spot, a grin, an atom.
> I am made of the dead.
> Even my thoughts are not my own any more.[5]

Burden (whose spirit has been embodied and indeed abandoned by a variety of other characters) speaks, but so also does novelist Hustvedt and the tension between the author's imagining and the character's representation of self provides an interesting dynamic even as we read and suspend our disbelief. We wait for the character's death in absolute certainty that it is being controlled by a living author creating her ending on the page. The capacity of the author to imagine becomes replaced also by the spaces between which enact failure of the self, push towards the body as a failure of the self, the self petering out and becoming less able to represent itself in language, as self dissolves.

[4] Siri Hustvedt, *The Blazing World*, London: Sceptre, 2014, p. 336.
[5] Ibid., p. 340.

For Barthes, all writing depends on the relationship between the voice, the page and the body when he writes of the 'disjuncture' which occurs when writing begins: 'the voice loses its origin, the author enters his death'.[6] Both Lubbock and Hustvedt open up author, fictional character and reader to ways of addressing, through narrativizing, the experience of death. Both are moving and important – Hustvedt's sustained fictional depiction of a woman living with a terminal illness is especially so – but both nevertheless function within the realist teleological model of life and death; even as they open up to dissolution and silence these very different accounts of dying exhibit a desire to move forwards towards a discernible end which is also the death of author or a character (it is interesting to note that a common device in books written about the end of a person's life is the framing preface or afterword by the surviving family member or spouse).[7]

For Kermode the only true representation of death is silence and my thoughts about the lyric and its relationship with death start then, with a preoccupation about whether and how the complexities of the lyric as a complex structure built around space and silences might be a useful model for thinking about the experience of death. In *Ends of the Lyric*, Timothy Bahti makes a convincing argument for the lyric's ability to end without what we would normally think of as closure, identifying the lyric's power to 'end with such stunning power and curious frequency in inverting their ends into nonends, and their readings into rebeginnings or not-yet-readings'.[8]

As such, the lyric is a way of thinking about and inhabiting the self in a way which eschews teleology or the linearity of realist chronology, the plot of which depends on a beginning, middle and an end; suggesting that it does this places the lyric as a kind of 'never-ending' but also transitory experience in language that simultaneously resists as well as enacts (rather than represents) death's very possibility. By being and not being in the moment, by escaping the fictions and structures of plot and favouring a different kind of dense and multiply-evocative patterning, the lyric offers a place for the self to reside which is both transitional, repeatable, modulating, there and not there, and, while rooted in a historical context, fluctuating in its historical engagements.

---

[6] 'Death of the Author' in *Image-Music-Text*, London: Fontana, 1993, pp. 142–8, 142.

[7] While Kermode suggests that literature exists precisely to make sense of this displacement between knowing we will die and being unable to imagine it – that we put a narrative in the place of the silence of death – he mistakenly conflates imagination as fantasy or day-dreaming with a different kind of imagining/creation of a self in language, throwing, as it were, the baby (dummy) out with the bath (death) water. This kind of substitution of the 'impersonal dummy' is not a dishonesty, rather it is a version of empathic thinking which allows for the creation of another kind of space between author and text; it brings the writer and the reader closer to a realist presentation of death in language.

[8] Timothy Bahti, *Ends of the Lyric: Direction and Consequence in Western Poetry*, Baltimore, NJ: Johns Hopkins University Press, 1996, p. 15.

I will also suggest that the lyric offers a way of thinking which encounters death through a formal encounter with empty space and silence. Such spaces and silences, as we will see, can be found in its echoes and reinventions of image, of other poems or words, in the absences and presences of repeated sounds, and its representation on the page as space (line breaks, stanza breaks, ends of pages, end of the poem). The spaces and silences which do not occur only at its end but which are what frames it place the silence of ending as a space that is integral to its existence. And while perhaps none of these claims for the lyric in themselves are particularly new or revelatory, my instinct is that, as a model for thinking about narrativizing self in the face of death, the process of both writing and being intimate with the lyric as a reader, encountering its intricate and embodied musical textures, offers a paradigm for living with and up to death which emphasizes hope (to pick up on a word used by Gill in her last lecture) rather than anxiety and despair in the face of the chronological boundaries and timelines.

*

Jorie Graham's work has constantly explored time, transcendence, and the relationship between body and spirit, experimenting with philosophical ideas in experimentation with poetic forms. In this sense 'San Sepolcro' could be seen as the philosophical blueprint to which she repeatedly returns and rewrites over the next thirty years of her career; we might see it as a touchstone to her developing aesthetic which affirms both the movement of the self as central to the act of imagining and writing, and her continuing interest in material existence and the presence of the body in lyrical thinking. I quote the poem in full.

San Sepolcro

In this blue light
   I can take you there,
snow having made me
   a world of bone
seen through to. This
   is my house,

my section of Etruscan
   wall, my neighbor's
lemontrees, and, just below
   the lower church,
the airplane factory.
   A rooster

crows all day from mist
    outside the walls.
There's milk on the air,
    ice on the oily
lemonskins. How clean
    the mind is,

holy grave. It is this girl
    by Piero
della Francesca, unbuttoning
    her blue dress,
her mantle of weather,
    to go into

labor. Come, we can go in.
    It is before
the birth of god. No one
    has risen yet
to the museums, to the assembly
    line – bodies

and wings – to the open air
    market. This is
what the living do: go in.
    It's a long way.
And the dress keeps opening
    from eternity

to privacy, quickening.
    Inside, at the heart,
is tragedy, the present moment
    forever stillborn,
but going in, each breath
    is a button

coming undone, something terribly
    nimble-fingered
finding all of the stops.[9]

---

[9] Jorie Graham, 'San Sepolcro', *The Dream of the Unified Field: Selected Poems*, Manchester: Carcanet, 1996. It is also worth pointing out, although I am unable to discuss it here, that Graham also includes in the 1983 volume, *Erosion*, in which 'San Sepolcro' was originally published, a poem titled 'The Sense of an Ending'.

San Sepolcro is in a small hilltop town on the borders between Umbria and Tuscany and the birthplace of Piero della Francesca, the painter of the fresco the Madonna Del Parto (finished around 1460) (or the Madonna in Labour, parturition) to which the poem implicitly refers. The fresco, which now resides in a museum, was painted in a church in Monterchi, near to San Sepolcro; according to stories, della Franscesca painted the fresco in seven days when he had returned home as his mother was dying.

As we have seen, the poem consists of eight stanzas, grouped into six lines each, apart from the last, which is three lines long. The six-line stanzas shaped by a variable pattern of longer and short indented lines sets up a dynamic between internal and external space, the private and the revealed, preoccupies Graham's poem's form which steps down as it continues to move towards the church from the hillside, and travels as it does through historical time. In evoking the Etruscan past Graham moves back in time through an archaeology of landscape, the Etruscan wall is the only remnant of the pre-Roman civilization which has replaced it. Yet the poem also takes us to an interior world, both geographically and spiritually, which is, the poem maintains, 'before the birth of god'. It is a pre-time. 'No one has risen yet', says the speaker of the poem, in a line which sits between the spiritual and the secular, rich with double meaning: there has been no literal awakening or spiritual forgiveness. But this is a time before both birth and death.

As the eye reads the poem on the page, that loss of three lines is already noted as a divergence in structural pattern – consciously or unconsciously – as our eye moves to encapsulate the poem's shape from the start to the end of the page. That movement in form from six to its half in the final three lines, as things both come undone in the instant of unbuttoning, and also 'stop', opens the poem up not simply to silence but also to beginnings through our impulse to regain the remaining three lines at its end which have been 'lost'. Likewise, the structurally embodied movement of thought back and forth in each stanza, between indentation and return to a left-hand margin, marks and reiterates a movement of forward thought as well as movement across stanzas. It is an encounter with loss which is also echoed in the movements in stresses between series of single-stressed lines, which are followed by iambics and then their inversions to create a constantly modulating pattern against which rub the formal repetition of the stanzaic patterning, punctuation and meanings of words which are pushed and pulled within this structure. Thus, for example, we see in the spaces and silences that occur in breaks across line-endings and stanzas, a negotiation with meaning and an embodiment of silence within the syntactical structures:

A rooster

crows all day from mist
    outside the walls.
There's milk on the air,
    ice on the oily
lemonskins. How clean
    the mind is,
  holy grave.

With the introduction of the rooster at the end of stanza one, we must bridge our perception of it as it stands alone on a line, across the space of the line break to a new negotiation of it, not as form, not as the way it looks, or how it exists as a word in language, but as the way it sounds as we meet it in the next stanza. The space between material existence and other ways of knowing the world outside the relationship of word to thing becomes accentuated in the reference to sound, to time, to the blurred vision or intellectual fog of crows, days, mists. The stress pattern of these lines likewise plays with iambic (unstressed stressed) expectations to further such experiences of renegotiation and knowing what we see and how we know it. Thus the unstressed syllable of rooster, 'er', breaks the rhythm as its sound enacts a musical gap between itself and the rooster's cry on the next line. The double stress on 'all day' which follows what looks like, because of the line break, another unattached single stress, heralds the iambic (unstressed stressed) of 'There's milk' and introduces the first anapest 'on the air' (unstressed, unstressed stressed) which in the subsequent line is immediately inverted to the (stressed unstressed unstressed) 'ice on the'. The effect of this when spoken aloud is of a kind of lurch forward, even a potential reversal of thinking as well as a stilling, especially when we see how those rhythmic starts and stops and inversions work alongside the commas (always weighting and slowing the end of a line), and the full stops positioned once to emphasize the physical stop of the walls at the end of the line, and mid way through lines after a distinct turn of thought from physical to discursive/ reflective comments, before reaching another ending emphasizing physical halt with the word 'grave'.

These rhythmic movements seem to arise from a series of free associations linked by colour and texture. Thought is embodied as rhythmic movement and associative thinking, and its disturbances that shift it away from an iambic pattern; world becomes thought as rhythm, and the way we tell that world thus becomes the way we inhabit/move through it in language, and the spaces between words, which allow us to make sense of words, reminding us (as rhyme reminds us) of what we have lost and what is present.[10]

I will return to the ending of the poem shortly, but it is worth pointing out here that the movement towards the poem's end is carefully staged, and enacted simultaneously through the form of the poem, as well as through the repetition of the word 'this' which occurs in various ways four times in the poem, undergoing, as the poem progresses, a transformation into sounds which echo it after the statement which sits at its centre: 'This is / what the living do: go in.' After this statement the memory of 'this', as it were, is taken over by the echoing sound pattern of 'it's', 'privacy', 'inside', 'is' 'present'; and, in the final juxtaposition of life and death as the poem 'ends'; with 'is', and 'stops', the final word of the poem.

In contrast to the particularity and immediacy evoked by the word 'this', locating things in the here and now, Graham's reference to the idea of 'going in', suggesting a permanent state of movement without arrival, appears in three different ways within the poem. At the end of stanza four, midway through the poem as we are asked to see the girl 'unbuttoning / her blue dress, / her mantle of weather / to go into / labor. Come, we can go in.' Going in becomes the act of moving from outside to the interior of the church, it becomes the act of going into labour, of creating another through looking and identifying, but also of becoming a self in the moment.

Alongside this geographical and historical 'movement' (being here, in the this, going in, looking back) Graham also provides, through her evocation of the rooster at the beginning of the poem, an intertextual layering to the poem which provokes a different kind of engagement with the past as well as with meaning in the present as we move in our consciousness between the poem we are reading and the knowledge, memory, intimation of the existence of another poem. Graham calls on Elizabeth Bishop's well-known poem 'Roosters' (published in her volume *North and South* in 1946), not simply in the invocation of the bird and the colour blue, but in a series of complex thematic and structural associations which work to echo, underpin and open up the poem's meanings. 'At four o'clock' begins Bishop's poem, firmly rooted in chronological time, 'In the gun-metal blue dark / We hear the first crow of the first cock.'[11] The reference also works on the level of looking and how we look when we remember the lines of Bishop's poem – when she talks about the pins on a map being 'an active displacement / in perspective' and the fact

[10] For a brilliant analysis of rhyme's relationship with time, see Denise Riley, *The Words of Selves: Identification, Solidarity, Irony*, Palo Alto, CA: Stanford University Press, 2000, p. 159.
[11] Elizabeth Bishop, *Complete Poems*, London: Chatto and Windus, 2004, pp. 35–9, 35.

that della Franscesca was not only the great practitioner of perspective, but its theorist. But in multiple other ways, Graham's poem is ghosted by Bishop's earlier poem to create a live if subsumed dialogue with theoretical issues, not least the Bishop whose lines argue that 'Old holy sculpture / could set it all together / in one small scene, past and future'; and especially at the end of the poem when Bishop writes how 'The sun climbs in, following "to see the end" / faithful as enemy, or friend.' Bishop's tight use of the three-line rhyming stanza in 'Roosters' creates a different kind of stoppage, as does the closure of rhyme at the end of her much longer poem.

Graham, in interview, has spoken about Bishop's work and how she has

> ... spent a good deal of my life thinking about that action in Elizabeth Bishop's revisionary descriptions. The issue of how far she is from the event, whether she is thinking *back* on the event or not, became very essential to me. Metaphysically.[12]

The complex echoes that Graham sets up with Bishop's poem concerning time and art are deepened further by a film (which seems to have perhaps inspired or brought together Graham's own memories of seeing the Madonna), by the Russian filmmaker Tarkovsky, *Nostalgia*, which she saw in 1982, the year before *Erosion* was published. The film features the della Franscesco fresco, out of context, as a backdrop to an image set horizontally against it, in which a gathering of women pray to a clothed image of the Madonna, dressed in flowers. For Graham, the encounter with the film was central to clarifying something in her aesthetic development which she has described in terms of an engagement with real time:

> The filmmaker, having made a traditional movie up to that point, in which representational time is different from actual time (days go by and only four minutes go by on screen), opens the camera and does not interrupt the shot again from the minute his character tries to cross that water. He tries three times. He goes halfway across. The candle is blown out by the fumes. He goes back and tries again. He slogs – the water is knee high – all the way back. You can imagine how slow this is on screen. A director will normally cut this and make it *look* as though it were continuous. Tarkovsky does not interrupt the reel. Finally, the third time, the character makes it – touches the far wall.[13]

---

[12] Jorie Graham, 'The Art of Poetry, No. 85: Interview with Thomas Gardner', *The Paris Review* 165 (Spring 2003). http://www.theparisreview.org/interviews/263/the-art-of-poetry-no-85-jorie-graham [accessed 1 June 2016].

[13] Ibid.

By drawing on Tarkovsky and Bishop, Graham layers and textures the poem in terms of a historical and artistic past, as well as in terms of an aesthetic tracking of perception through the idiom of poetry, painting and film. The narrator of the poem goes in to look at a picture; our way of knowing, that is, passes through two other media which are actively engaged in embodying movement rather than stasis at this point in time which dramatizes a life about to become.

Working across this kind of deep layering is the foregrounded way in which the poem evokes a moment of suspended time, 'before the birth of god', and the intricate way in which this is entwined with both the spiritual and the material, and the beginning of birth which perhaps ironically marks the end of the poem. Graham has later referred to her preoccupation as a poet with being

> an attempt to enact the time in which it takes to see the thing, the time in which that seen thing is living and constantly changing, the time it takes to "take" those actions down, the time in which my language is occurring, your reading is occurring, – to make of all that a piece. The mutability of the external meeting the mutability of the internal.[14]

Piero's still image of the Madonna opening her dress, which so anticipates movement, sees her flanked by two angels who are pulling back curtains to reveal her presence. The curtains that open on to the Madonna reveal within a textured pink ribbing which seems to allude to the inside of the female body. Thus, as we 'go in' in the poem, we step into the picture, a metaphorical internal body is opened up to us, alongside the Madonna whose internal body, and her labour, exists in the moment before this great unbuttoning.

Agency and authority of the self, and the invocation of the other, both through the birth of a child who is separated from the mother's body, and through the encounter with the image of the woman in the pictures, twist into a sense of a turning into the object self, and how that self has been made. In doing this, the imagery works in subtle contrast: we are asked to experience in quick succession the difference between the whiteness of 'snow' and 'bone', and to take on in some way snow's impermanence and bone's relative permanence as the two images become overlaid. The world and the body have become one, with that peculiar collocation of 'seen through to', which suggests not just the opacity of bone, through which we see the world, but 'seen through' in the metaphorical sense.

The end of 'San Sepolcro', that deliberately halved stanza length, presents the image of persona going into the church, into the picture, going into the

---

[14] Ibid.

experience of the image of the virgin unbuttoning her dress. The image of the buttons on the dress of the Madonna's opening dress gestures towards linear time (they have a beginning and an end at the top and bottom of the dress) and that length is segregated into buttons that measure each movement of opening. At the same time as we are going in to the church (moving towards death?), we are faced with the prospect of a future of something about to begin:

> each breath
> is a button
>
> coming undone, something terribly
> nimble-fingered
> finding all of the stops.

The stop is the end of the poem; it is reiterated by the full-stop at the end of the poem. But the stanza itself gestures in its pattern of six lines to an incompleteness that emphasizes the movement of the eye to the restored six lines of the poem's other stanzas and to the beginning of the poem. 'Undoing of all the stops' is a prerequisite for the revelation of birth, but as such it is also the beginning of an end.

I would like to return for one final time to Kermode and his suggestion in *The Sense of an Ending* that the representation of time in the sound of a clock as 'tick tock' and not 'tick tick' is a 'tiny model of all plots' – the acoustic model as he calls it of the 'genesis of tick and apocalypse of tock': 'The fact that we call the second of the two related sounds tock is evidence that we use fictions to enable the end to confer organization and form on the temporal structure.'[15] By contrast the triple stop we have at the end of Graham's poem (the word stops, the full stop, the end of the poem which opens us up to the space of the page) reiterates its ending, so too (as well as the stanza patterning) does the ambiguity of the word 'stops' open up another creative place in which we must acoustically reside. The 'stops' here make reference to the buttons that are being unbuttoned as well as the actual hesitations at the unbuttoning. But we must also hear a reference to music, the closing of a fingerhole to produce a note, the phonetic articulation of interruption of a flow of air, underpinned by the earlier use of the word 'breath'. Thus ultimately ending turns us away from words to music and the poem offers a way of being in life which does not disavow death but lives with and makes something of its presence. This encapsulation through action of such a complex idea is the central power of the poem as we see the

---

[15] Kermode, *The Sense of an Ending*, p. 45.

lyric's linguistic music which foregrounds an ambiguity of meaning, decon-structing the relationship between silence and space and the material nature of language that exists as voice or printed page. Graham writes, then, of birth and death both stilled and ongoing in her lines which note the 'present moment, forever stillborn, but going in'. But these moments have the potential for joy and the discovery of a new kind of being in the world; they offer what might be perceived as a new kind of time and a new kind of coherence.

*

It would be a crass thing indeed to suggest that poetry might make us, at the often difficult and physical and mentally painful end of our end of life, feel better. Poetry is not palliative care. A terminal diagnosis (which can sometimes be both as reliable and unreliable as any other prediction about life expec-tancy in terms of the precision it can give about life quality and life span) summons us to approach death in a way that confirms what we already knew about the fragility of our own existence. But it also offers a shockingly new and compressed framework in which we might imagine, recall and reinvent ourselves. The point where consciousness begins or ends, and the status of a living biological entity, is recorded as no longer being, is only a step in a series of transitions in which we transfer our own lives and their meaning into the realm of the other. Della Franscesca's response to maternal death was to paint an image of the about to become life of a child. The lyric, as exemplified by Graham's poem, offers a rich and layered way of conceiving the self in time. Its form and its model of closure does not have the potential to alter the reality of life and death, but it does have the potential to reinvent and deconstruct that reality, and to do it in a way which might allow us also to continually encounter the 'not-being' which creates meaning as well as the language which evokes or represents the being that is lost. Such a space is exemplified in 'San Sepulcro', a literal tomb (sepulchre) which is also simply also a town. The space which acts to structure the lyric's form, and its ontology which is built on tensions between seen spaces and voiced pauses (which are not always consistent) and the musical repetitions which sit around that silence, allow the self a compressed place of complex habitation which is always implicitly dependent on the existence of death, but which does not place death 'a step away'. The lyric offers a place not so much to make sense of ourselves, but in which to make ourselves, as poet and as reader. It is here, in an always active awareness of death as integral to life, where ends are always connected to beginnings; and it is here where we might engage in such transferences between negotiations of time, memory and imagination, and to do so with such affective charges, as we die as well as remember the dead. It is this place, and its time, which I would like to celebrate.

With thanks and also i.m. to MM for introducing me to, and for long conversations about, the Madonna Del Parto.

References

Bahti, Timothy, *Ends of the Lyric: Direction and Consequence in Western Poetry*, Baltimore, NJ: Johns Hopkins University Press, 1996.

Bishop, Elizabeth, *Complete Poems*, London: Chatto and Windus, 2004.

Graham, Jorie, *The Dream of the Unified Field: Selected Poems*, Manchester: Carcanet, 1996.

Graham, Jorie. 'The Art of Poetry, No. 85: Interview with Thomas Gardner', *The Paris Review* 165 (Spring 2003), http://www.theparisreview.org/interviews/263/the-art-of-poetry-no-85-jorie-graham [accessed 1 June 2016].

Hustvedt, Siri, *The Blazing World*, London: Sceptre, 2014.

Kermode, Frank, *The Sense of an Ending: Studies in the Theory of Fiction*, Oxford: Oxford University Press, 2000.

Lubbock, Tom, *Until Further Notice, I Am Alive*, London: Granta, 2012.

Riley, Denise, *The Words of Selves: Identification, Solidarity, Irony*, Palo Alto, CA: Stanford University Press, 2000.

12

Cancer Sucks: Photography and the Representation of Chronic Illness

Nedim Hassan

In her public lecture 'How to Think about Death: Living with Dying', Gillian Howie concluded her absorbing discussion by considering the limits of philosophy.[1] While she revealed how various philosophers have provided a significant examination of death from a range of perspectives, when exploring the question of whether philosophy can 'induce a habit of mind or a certain way of living to which others might aspire, even if only for a "this moment", a habit of mind that allows us to live right up to death with hope', Howie ultimately contended that philosophy is ill-equipped.[2] Consequently, she turned to other forms of practice and was interested in how phenomena such as gardening or tending to green spaces, reading and music may involve the cultivation of nature and communication that could foster states of hopefulness even in the face of a shortened future.[3]

This interest in practice was reflected in the events scheduled for the 'New Thinking on Living with Dying' research network, funded by the Arts and Humanities Research Council, that Howie spearheaded throughout 2012 and into 2013. Scheduled events featured practitioners such as artists and clinicians, as well as academics. Contributors to the events came from a range of fields such as disability studies, philosophy, English literature, comedy, poetry, visual arts and medicine. The first public event that the Research Network organized, *Changing Capacities: Changing Identities*, illustrated the way in which network members, and Howie in particular, welcomed opportunities to learn from creative practice.

This event, which was held at the University of Liverpool on 1 September 2012, was co-organized with DaDaFest (Disability and Deaf Arts Festival). Its aim was

---

[1] Gillian Howie, 'How to Think about Death: Living with Dying', Ch. 6 of the present volume, pp. 131–44.
[2] Ibid., p. 142.
[3] Ibid.

to provide a multidisciplinary examination of the notion of life-limiting illness as well as to explore the implications of the often profound changes to our sense of self and embodied experience that such illness may entail. Therefore, while the event featured scholarly presentations that utilized perspectives from fields such as philosophy, disability studies and sociology, it also hosted various exhibitions and performances. In line with the core themes of DaDaFest 2012, performances and the art works displayed often troubled established ways of thinking about life-limiting conditions and the notion of 'sick' or 'disabled' bodies.

This chapter focuses upon the way that one of the exhibitions at the *Changing Capacities* event facilitated reflection on peoples' experiences of cancer and raised broader questions about the representation of this life-limiting and sometimes terminal illness. The exhibition that will be examined is *Cancer Sucks*, a photographic exhibition that was put together by the late performer/model Tutu and the photographer Ashley Savage. Tutu had been diagnosed with breast cancer in 2009 and *Cancer Sucks* was a project that she and Savage conceived with the aim of documenting her experiences with the disease. The photographic project was shot in several locations including hospitals, studios, Tutu's home in London and during a stage performance. It continued right up until Tutu's death on 28 March 2012.

Exhibiting *Cancer Sucks*

At the *Changing Capacities* event we displayed images from the *Cancer Sucks* exhibition and, as the Research Network administrator at this time, I played a large part in organizing this display. A digital slideshow, rather than framed prints, was utilized due to the limitations of space at the venue. We also arranged for Ashley Savage to come to the conference event and field questions about it. The slideshow was in chronological order and one advantage of this was that it enabled us to show numerous images, not just the thirty that existed in framed prints at that point. As Savage indicated in an interview prior to the exhibition: 'In choosing the images for the slideshow, I just went with what I thought were the most iconic when taken from the hundreds we had done but there are others that could also have been included. They are in chronological order so as to show the treatment stages and some are happy, some are sad, they just are what they are. They represent Tutu in life and in death.'[4]

---

[4] Ashley Savage, '*Cancer Sucks*: *DaDaFest*. Interview by Nedim Hassan and Janet Price', 2012, http://www.dadafest.co.uk/cancer-sucks/ [accessed 1 June 2016].

The *Cancer Sucks* slideshow was presented to three separate groups at the *Changing Capacities* event. The show lasted for approximately ten minutes and was then followed by a question and answer session involving Ashley Savage. As the Chair for that session, I was struck by how moving the experience was. People sat in silence as the montage of digital images was projected onto a large screen. Some smiled at the more light-hearted and performance-based shots, others were in tears when faced with the distressing images of pain and suffering that Tutu endured during her illness. Some of those images were stark and featured graphic depictions of Tutu's treatment and its effects, but the audience (made up mainly of academics, members of DaDaFest and members of the general public) seemed captivated, rather than repelled.

Once the show had finished it was clear that it had prompted some in the audience to reflect upon their own experiences, as well as to explore issues in relation to cancer treatment and Tutu's personal circumstances. For example, one audience member made the following comment after seeing the *Cancer Sucks* exhibition: 'It's an incredibly emotive thing to see. I went through my dad dying in the same way but really living life to the full even towards the end and I wondered in terms of Tutu's spirit how you felt she coped with it? One of the problems around cancer and the language is to fight it, fight it and it puts horrid emphasis on it and if you end up dying, you have like failed then, lost the bottle, but that is rubbish.'[5]

Thus, the exhibition had facilitated a fascinating discussion and had fostered reflection upon powerful personal experiences. For the remainder of this chapter I will explore the value of this type of exhibition further. Using *Cancer Sucks* as a case study, I will discuss the potential that this type of photographic exhibition may have for conveying experiences associated with cancer and other chronic illnesses. This will be accomplished by first considering debates about photography as a medium for communication and second by focusing specifically upon issues regarding the photographic representation of people with chronic illness. Finally, having situated it in relation to the aforementioned issues and debates, I will then analyse the way that *Cancer Sucks* portrays Tutu and her experiences of cancer in more depth.

---

[5] Unpublished transcript from *Changing Capacities: Changing Identities* (University of Liverpool, September 2012).

Photography as a medium for conveying truth

Writing about the *Cancer Sucks* project Ashley Savage stated that Tutu was 'insistent that all of the fluffy, pink breast cancer imagery was not the way to go, she wanted to show the disease for what it was in her experience.'[6] Here Savage suggests that photography can be a powerful medium for conveying the truth about particular experiences such as those endured by the cancer sufferer. Before I examine the implications of this for the specific *Cancer Sucks* project, it is useful to consider this point on a more general basis.

As Jae Emerling points out, from at least the inception of modern photography in the nineteenth century, there has been debate about its ontological status. Some commentators such as the French poet Charles Baudelaire saw photography as the simple representation of the real – 'simple mimetic reproduction – a copy of some pre-existing original.'[7] Whereas others in this period such as the inventor, William Henry Fox Talbot, suggested that the new invention was an art form involving different creative applications – it was about *creating pictures*, not merely reproducing reality. This tension between photography's status as art and as documentary has persisted in more recent discourse. For instance, writing in 1977 Susan Sontag stated that: 'The history of photography could be recapitulated as the struggle between two different imperatives: beautification, which comes from the fine arts, and truth-telling.'[8] As I will elaborate later, given that it involved both graphic images of cancer treatment in medical settings and shots of Tutu in a more explicitly performative role (such as on stage), this tension between the imperatives of truth-telling and beautification is useful for a consideration of the *Cancer Sucks* exhibition.

Prior to examining *Cancer Sucks* in more depth, I want to maintain a focus on theoretical discussion that makes problematic the notion that photography is a medium that has the potential to convey truth. Two critical perspectives that are of relevance in this case are those of Roland Barthes and Marshall McLuhan. Both of these theorists examined photography in relation to objectification. In line with his interrogation of other mass media, McLuhan was especially interested in the broad social and personal consequences that were instigated by the onset of the medium of photography.[9] McLuhan argues that one of the distinctive aspects of the photograph is that, unlike television, it 'isolates

---

⁶   Savage, '*Cancer Sucks*'.
⁷   Jae Emerling, *Photography: History and Theory*, New York: Routledge, 2012, p. 21.
⁸   Susan Sontag, *On Photography*, London: Allen Lane, 1978, p. 86.
⁹   Marshall McLuhan, *Understanding Media: The Extensions of Man*, London: Abacus, 1973, p. 15.

single moments in time'.[10] For him the photograph is dislocated from time and space and perhaps because of this people are turned into 'things', they are easily objectified since the photograph has the potential to extend and multiply 'the [de-contextualized] human image to the proportions of mass-produced merchandise'.[11] Hence, McLuhan compares photography to a 'Brothel-without-Walls' because images, such as those of celebrities, 'can be bought and hugged and thumbed more easily than public prostitutes'.[12]

This concern about the ubiquity of photography is also echoed in the later work of Sontag. She argues that: 'Whatever the moral claims made on behalf of photography, its main effect is to convert the world into a department store or museum-without-walls in which every subject is depreciated into an article of consumption, promoted into an item for aesthetic appreciation'.[13] Both of these theorists, then, seem to be disturbed by photography as a form that reduces real people and events into isolated fragments and produces a form of 'photographic seeing' that is estranged from the more natural (and variegated) way that human beings perceive visual things.[14] Indeed, for McLuhan there is almost something sinister about photography because, even though he suggests that the photograph is reductive and 'a substitution of shadows for substance', it also has permanence that survives change: 'The avid desire of mankind to prostitute itself stands up against the chaos of revolution. The brothel remains firm and permanent amidst the most furious changes'.[15]

While he writes about photography in less negative terms, Barthes also finds objectification deeply troubling in *Camera Lucida*. Barthes is disturbed by issues of ownership and control that are triggered by photography's representation of the self. In the photographic image, the self never coincides with the representation because, as Barthes argues, 'it is the image which is heavy, motionless, stubborn (which is why society sustains it) and "myself" which is light, divided, dispersed; like a bottle-imp, "myself" doesn't hold still, giggling in my jar'.[16] Despite our best efforts, then, Barthes contends that photographs cannot adequately convey the self because this is a concept that is continually shifting and difficult to capture. When we do capture a person in an image, this is inevitably inadequate because it does not convey the self that we and

---

[10] Ibid., p. 201.
[11] Ibid., p. 201.
[12] Ibid., p. 202.
[13] Sontag, *On Photography*, p. 110.
[14] Ibid., p. 97.
[15] McLuhan, *Understanding Media*, p. 202.
[16] Roland Barthes, *Camera Lucida: Reflections on Photography*, New York: The Noonday Press, 1981, p. 12.

others experience in all its complexity. Yet, as both Barthes and McLuhan point out, this inadequacy has not prevented the proliferation of photography in societies and the increased circulation of images. Such issues are compounded for Barthes by the uses of photographs and the issues of ownership they bring. Barthes laments the loss of his own agency and subjectivity when photographs of him are used in ways beyond his control.[17]

Although they come from theorists who were somewhat critical of photography, these discourses concerning photography's potential to adequately convey an accurate sense of *self* and concerning who has *control* over one's image are, I would argue, pivotal to understanding the significance of an exhibition like *Cancer Sucks*. This is because, as I will clarify later, the exhibition had the potential to evoke both of these challenging issues regarding agency and the representation of the self (that of course extend beyond issues of photography) for its audience, and in some cases it prompted them to reflect upon such issues in more depth.

Issues of control and images of people with chronic illness

Barthes' anxiety over the loss of ownership and control of self that is the corollary of the capturing of the photographic image is particularly pertinent when considering photographs of people with chronic illness. As Arthur Frank points out in *The Wounded Storyteller*, the development of modern medicine involved a kind of *colonization* of the body of the ill person; it 'claimed the body of the patient as its territory'.[18] In the nineteenth century, this process of colonization was aided by technological advances in photography. Erin O'Connor asserts that the photograph was 'idealized as the representational medium that offered unmediated access to the truth of physical form'.[19] She goes on to demonstrate that the consequences of this were often damaging for individuals suffering with chronic conditions. For instance, when utilized as evidence in case reports of anorexia nervosa, photographs helped to justify the omission of an inquiry into the psychological elements that underpinned self-starvation.[20] Consequently, images constructed 'anorexia as a disease whose essence is

---

[17] Ibid., p. 15.
[18] Arthur, W. Frank, *The Wounded Storyteller: Body, Illness, and Ethics*, Chicago, IL: University of Chicago Press, 1995, p. 10.
[19] Erin O'Connor, 'Pictures of Health: Medical Photography and the Emergence of Anorexia Nervosa', *Journal of the History of Sexuality* 5.4 (1995): 546.
[20] Ibid., p. 549.

confined to the surface of the body' and practices such as force-feeding could be supported by references to images of 'healthy' body types.[21]

These measures were, therefore, implemented with very little regard for the patient's wishes or psychological state partly because of the photograph's presumed objectivity and status as a form that depicts truth. However, this colonizing of the body that became central to the practice of modern medicine has been challenged in a variety of ways. In more contemporary time periods, Arthur Frank has pointed out that ill people have begun to 'recognise that more is involved in their experiences than the medical story can tell'.[22] Thus, various people have strived to develop their own personal voices and to tell their stories of their experiences with illness. Likewise some people have sought to reclaim their body images from the colonization process that was aided by the apparent objectivity of medical photography.

The photographic work of the late Jo Spence has been recognized as highly important in this regard. After being diagnosed with breast cancer in 1982, Spence began using photography as a 'therapeutic tool'.[23] At the same time she began to critically evaluate the medical system she had entered when being diagnosed, and some of her photographic work was conceived as a challenge to the orthodoxies of this system, as well as a reflection on her experiences with the disease. Interestingly, Spence acknowledged the concerns about objectification raised by McLuhan but highlighted photography's positive potential. She wrote that: 'Photography transforms a living scene into a piece of two dimensional graphic art – a representation of the moment but drained of all life, sound and smell – an abstraction, a fragment of the moment but unlike our ephemeral memory it can be shared.'[24] A photograph's potential to be shared was, for Spence, highly powerful because it could function as an 'arena for discussion' and could act as a 'call to action'.[25] Therefore, Spence constructed some images that were designed to inspire the viewer to ask questions about conditions like cancer.

Similarly, during their analysis of the published diary of Sara Bro, a Dutch TV and radio presenter who was diagnosed with breast cancer and underwent surgery in 2001, Henriksen et al. highlight the photographic image's potential for disrupting conventional cancer narratives. They argue that Bro's visual narrative 'is most explicitly preoccupied with the performance of not fulfilling

---

[21] Ibid., p. 549.
[22] Frank, *The Wounded Storyteller*, p. 6.
[23] Terry Dennett, 'Jo Spence's Auto-therapeutic Survival Strategies', *Health* 15.3 (2011): 224.
[24] Spence cited in ibid., p. 235.
[25] Spence cited in ibid., p. 235.

the expectations of the role of a sick cancer patient'.[26] This performance is accomplished through an interesting use of montage that juxtaposes photographic images and textual commentary in a way that serves to disrupt narrative meaning relating to Sara Bro's cancer experiences. Henriksen et al. argue that the montage destabilizes meaning in order to evoke the 'chaos and uncertainty' of the cancer experience for the reader.[27]

Such creative work with photographic images as that exhibited by Spence and Bro illustrates that, despite the reservations of Barthes and McLuhan, photography is a medium that has the potential to enable people who are dealing with chronic illness to reclaim ownership of their bodies on their own terms. Furthermore, the work of Sara Bro, in particular, makes apparent that photographic images can be incorporated into projects that can convey a rich sense of the variegated embodied and affective experiences involved with a condition like cancer. Thus, rather than closing down meaning and objectifying the individuals involved, such work implies that in some circumstances photographs are a potent resource for the opening up of the exploration of different meanings related to illness.

Garland-Thomson asserts that photographic images of breast cancer survivors can become particularly powerful when they are publicly displayed because they may disrupt viewers' expectations regarding 'the ceaselessly circulated erotic breast', replacing it with a contradictory spectacle that borrows from both the pin-up genre but also the medical photograph.[28] As will be seen below, Tutu's poses during some of the *Cancer Sucks* images invoke those associated with the fashion pin-up, yet partly what serves to disrupt such images being subject to a conventional erotic gaze is their juxtaposition with medical settings and their consistent exposure of the scarred, post-mastectomy breast.

Cancer Sucks

Turning explicitly to the *Cancer Sucks* exhibition that was displayed at the *Changing Capacities* event, the discussion of the theoretical and creative work mentioned so far provides a useful context for analysis. As indicated at the

---

[26] Nina Henriksen, Tine Tjørnhøj-Thomsen and Helle Ploug Hansen, 'Illness, Everyday Life and Narrative Montage: The Visual Aesthetics of Cancer in Sara Bro's Diary', *Health* 15.3 (2011): 291.

[27] Ibid., p. 293.

[28] Rosemarie Garland-Thomson, *Staring: How We Look*, Oxford: Oxford University Press, 2009, pp. 157–8.

beginning of this chapter, one of the intentions behind the construction of the project was to utilize photography's potential as a medium of 'truth-telling'. We have now explored some of the potential difficulties with the concept of the photograph as representing 'truth' and conveying a sense of self. Yet despite these difficulties it was clear that *Cancer Sucks* was conceived as a series of images that would portray realities that had hitherto been marginalized in other dominant discourses. As Ashley Savage clarified during an interview:

> Tutu sought *to represent the reality that was hers*, without compromise. She wanted to show cancer for what it was, or could be, in some extreme cases. She wanted to explore the physical and psychological ravages and trauma she endured, and this to her, was far from pink and pretty. At the same time, we both realised that by doing so, we would alienate the majority of cancer charities and organisations as the imagery we were producing were far removed from the representations generally chosen. [Italics added][29]

Savage's choice of language is significant here because it indicates that both he and Tutu were keenly aware of the existing politics of representation that had been predominant in relation to breast cancer imagery. As her experiences with the illness progressed, it seemed that Tutu became more alienated from the proliferation of 'pink and pretty' imagery that was associated with the disease. She suggested in an interview with the *Guardian* newspaper that she could not relate to the 'pink, fluffy' imagery and that the *Cancer Sucks* project was her way of conveying her experiences of the disease.[30]

   This critical approach coheres with other perspectives (from activists, artists, writers and so on) that challenge the 'pinkification' of breast cancer. This term refers to the way that the colour pink has become a 'leitmotif in almost everything related to breast cancer, and has become a globalized brand for the sake of breast cancer initiatives'.[31] A troubling aspect of this 'pinkification' includes the way that campaigns and products have largely built on and reinforced stereotypes of traditional femininity.[32] In particular, imagery and text associated with breast cancer charity campaigns have often focused upon the loss of the breast that may be a consequence of cancer treatment. This potential loss has been

---

[29] Savage, 'Cancer Sucks'.
[30] Stephanie Theobald, 'Cancer's Not Pink', *Guardian*, 25 March 2012, http://www.theguardian.com/lifeandstyle/2012/mar/25/cancers-not-pink-women-rebelling [accessed 3 August 2015].
[31] Venke Frederike Johansen, Therese Marie Andrews, Haldis Haukanes and Ulla-Britt Lilleaas, 'Symbols and Meanings in Breast Cancer Awareness Campaigns', *NORA: Nordic Journal of Feminist and Gender Research* 21.2 (2013): 143.
[32] Ibid., p. 153.

related to the negative impact on appearance and the concomitant sense of a loss of attractiveness that may be felt. This focus can serve to construct the notion that breast cancer is a disease that 'is first and foremost about breasts' and that campaigns and treatment are concerned with protecting appearances and ideas of traditional femininity, rather than primarily about saving lives.[33]

Critiques of 'pinkification' have also pointed to the way that businesses have utilized the pink ribbon and related imagery as part of cause-related marketing.[34] Various scholars have argued that companies are primarily linking their products with the pink ribbon campaign in order to enhance their reputation and increase profits.[35]

The *Cancer Sucks* project was partly devised to challenge both the 'feminized' representation of breast cancer and the way in which businesses have exploited such representation for commercial gain. Indeed, Ashley Savage spoke at length about this issue in an interview:

> In challenging the 'pinkification' of breast cancer Tutu hoped to open up the possibility of a new dialogue which would address the real issues and emotions encountered by cancer sufferers, their families, their carers and the companies profiting from the disease. By feminising and glamorising breast cancer, corporations are more able to promote and profit from the disease without realistic representations or acknowledgement of its impact. She wanted no part of this.[36]

Taking this point into account, stark depictions of the wounds and the physical and emotional impacts of treatments seemed to become central to the *Cancer Sucks* project (see Figures 12.1 and 12.2 for examples). This is because they provided a counterbalance to the more glamorized (and stereotypically 'feminized') representations that have been prevalent in breast cancer imagery. Appreciated in this context, then, I would argue that photographs of Tutu in medical settings and during treatments such as radiotherapy in *Cancer Sucks*, while they do not feature the types of juxtaposition evident in Sara Bro's work, nonetheless have the potential to radically subvert the dominant discourses relating to gender and the representation of breast cancer mentioned above. They may accomplish this by providing compelling visual evidence that, as

---

[33] Ibid. See also Phaedra C. Pezzullo, 'Resisting "National Breast Cancer Awareness Month": The Rhetoric of Counterpublics and their Cultural Performances', *Quarterly Journal of Speech* 89.4 (2003): 346.

[34] Johansen et al., 'Symbols and Meanings in Breast Cancer Awareness Campaigns', p. 145.

[35] Ibid. See also Samantha King, *Pink Ribbons, Inc. Breast Cancer and the Politics of Philanthrophy*, Minneapolis, MN: University of Minnesota Press, 2006, p. 10.

[36] Savage, '*Cancer Sucks*'.

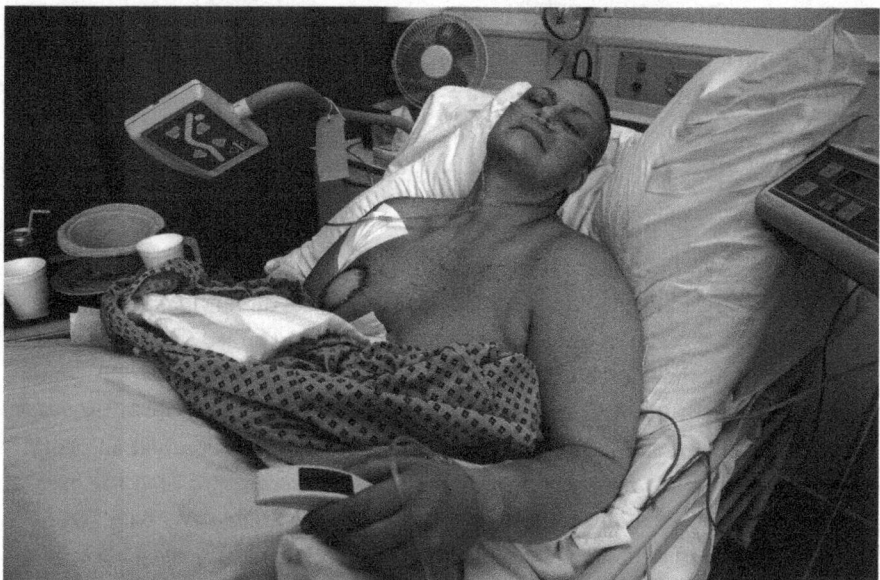

Figure 12.1 Mastectomy (credit: Ashley Savage)

Alan Radley might put it, suffering is borne by women during breast cancer.[37] In other words, the kinds of image laid bare in *Cancer Sucks* indicate that suffering is *embodied* during cancer, a reality that for Tutu and Ashley had all too often been marginalized in other public representations of the disease.

Making that aspect of cancer experience *visible*, therefore, seemed of paramount importance to the *Cancer Sucks* project. This is a powerful issue in its own right. For, as Alan Radley makes clear, issues of visibility are important for those suffering with a chronic illness or life-limiting health condition and can often lead to attempts to mask ailments to forestall the risk of stigmatization.[38] Yet here in this exhibition there is evidence of a remarkable desire on the part of Tutu to provide viewers with access to that which is often hidden away, as Ashley Savage put it during a response to a question at the *Changing Capacities* event: 'it's very graphic some of it, is it not? But that is how she wanted to do it.'[39]

Another consequence of the often graphic and stark portrayal of cancer during the *Cancer Sucks* exhibition was that it conveyed the difficulties involved with Tutu's cancer treatment process. After viewing the slideshow, certain

---

[37] Alan Radley, 'Portrayals of Suffering: On Looking Away, Looking at, and the Comprehension of Illness Experience', *Body & Society* 8.3, p. 16.
[38] Ibid., p. 17.
[39] Unpublished transcript from *Changing Capacities: Changing Identities* (University of Liverpool, September 2012).

audience members commented upon how it revealed the suffering that Tutu endured during the various clinical procedures and treatments she received. During the ensuing discussion with Ashley Savage, he indicated that some of these procedures were not necessarily carried out with Tutu's full informed consent. As Savage later commented during personal correspondence with the author:

> With regard to the treatment Tutu received and its efficacy, Tutu told me that when the surgeons explained that they would give her a tummy tuck and use the flesh they had removed to reconstruct her breast she assumed that was a tried and tested method. When things went wrong a week after the reconstruction and the flesh turned black requiring a complete removal of the entire breast, she investigated and discovered that this method of reconstruction had allegedly been outlawed in several countries due to its low success rate. Had she been informed or aware of this prior to surgery she said she would never have agreed to undergo reconstruction by this method or would at least have given it considerable thought and more research.[40]

Thus, although Savage stressed that 'in retrospect I am sure that the consultants believed they were acting in her best interests', he also suggested that Tutu's treatment process was bewildering for her at times and that it exacerbated the traumatic nature of the events that unfolded prior to her death.[41]

Moreover, because *Cancer Sucks* is a project that 'sought to show the process and type of treatment received and its impact both physically and emotionally', its exhibition fostered a broader reflection upon the agency of the cancer patient and of those who are approaching death.[42, 43] At the *Changing Capacities: Changing Identities* event, this reflection was made especially evident during some of the plenary discussions at the end of the event. For instance, when responding to a closing keynote paper from Margrit Shildrick one speaker said that: 'We had the story of Tutu as seen through the photographs and she apparently went to her death ... and was unaware what was happening; she clearly had little control and was given extremely limited information, understanding or ability to negotiate it because of the blocks put upon her by the medical

---

[40] Ashley Savage, 'Message from Ashley'. Unpublished message to Nedim Hassan, 5 August 2015, email.

[41] Ibid.

[42] Indeed, this emphasis on images of the clinical processes involved with cancer treatment, and not just images of the impact of such treatment, differentiates *Cancer Sucks* from other photographic projects instigated at this time, such as fashion photographer David Jay's work in The SCAR Project (see his 'The SCAR Project', *Social Semiotics* 22.1 [2012]: 39–46).

[43] Ashley Savage, 'Message from Ashley'.

Figure 12.2 Tutu after mastectomy with her partner Erica (credit: Ashley Savage)

staff with whom she came into contact.'[44] Although it exaggerates negative aspects of Tutu's treatment process discussed above, this interpretation of the photographic exhibition and subsequent question and answer session with Ashley Savage is interesting precisely because it highlights issues of power and control within medical settings. In contrast with O'Connor's aforementioned argument that nineteenth-century photographs of anorexia patients fulfilled a role as a kind of validator for medical discourse, it seems that the *Cancer Sucks* exhibition, replete with images of clinical cancer treatment and its impact, could facilitate critical debate about the ethics of medical discourse and practice.

Conversely, however, *Cancer Sucks* is an exhibition that does not solely position Tutu as a woman who was defined by her illness. Sharing some similarities with the work of Sara Bro mentioned above, the project provides a diverse range of images of Tutu that serve to disrupt the notion that she was merely fulfilling the role of a cancer victim. In an interview Ashley Savage stated that 'a lot of the images in the Cancer Sucks series have a beauty of their own, a beauty in "otherness", which we hoped would have impact on the viewer in a multi-dimensional way and in doing so challenge and subvert preconceptions.'[45] One

[44] Unpublished transcript from *Changing Capacities: Changing Identities*.
[45] Ashley Savage, *Cancer Sucks*.

Figure 12.3 Tutu crying outside the hospital (credit: Ashley Savage)

of the ways in which the series does this is by conveying Tutu as an individual with multiple personae. The numerous images depict her in different guises – vulnerable 'cancer patient' (see Figure 12.3); burlesque performer; a brave 'clown' in the face of illness; a lover and object of erotic desire; a daughter; a model and so on. Indeed, as I reflected upon the exhibition and watched the series of images once again during the preparation of this chapter it occurred to me that there was something distinctly unsatisfactory about such labels that I was trying to impose upon the multitude of images I was seeing. Not least because some of the images are open to multiple interpretations.

Furthermore, *Cancer Sucks* foregrounds Tutu's actions as performance. Sometimes, this is conveyed by displaying her in clear performance contexts such as on-stage at a night club or in the backstage area. Yet in other images conspicuous performances feature within quite sterile medical environments (see Figure 12.4). It is almost as if the suggestion in these images is that Tutu's persona cannot be restricted by the medical environment, even though this often has connotations of seriousness and can be actually incredibly daunting for some.

Performances like this highlight once again the embodied experience of the ill person. Indeed, they are a reminder that embodied expressions are significant

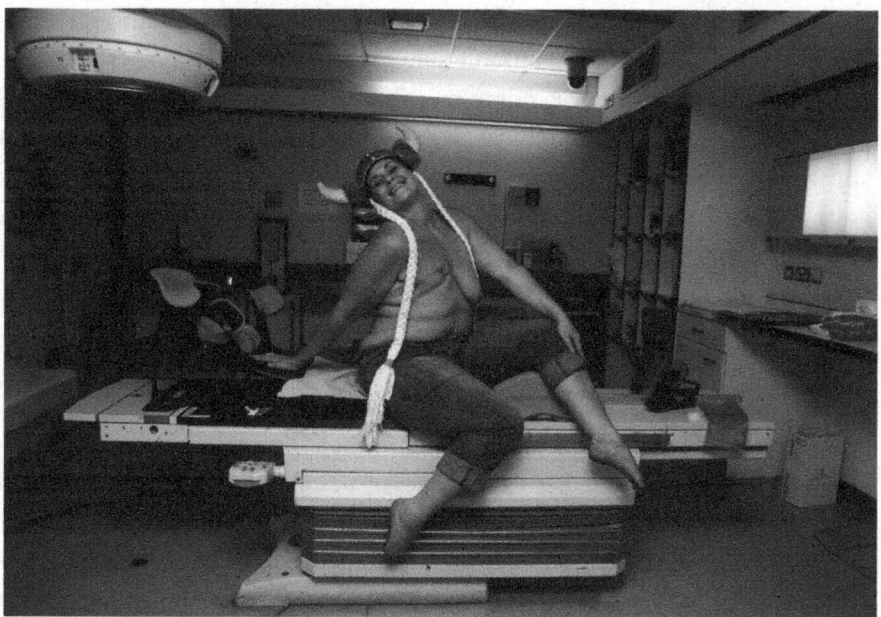

Figure 12.4 Tutu prior to radiotherapy (credit: Ashley Savage)

because, like music, they herald the 'possibility of becoming something new'.[46] Building on the phenomenology of Merleau-Ponty, the notion of 'becoming' is embraced by Shildrick as a way to understand and explore the 'inherent fluidity and lack of completion' of all bodies (not just those experiencing chronic illness).[47] In *Cancer Sucks* Tutu's performances may disrupt the 'perceived stability of normative expectations' associated with how the body with breast cancer is perceived to be within medical settings.[48] Not only is the body visible, not only does it betray marks of suffering and of the clinical process, but in many of these images the ill body is portrayed as ambivalent and in transition. It can be joyously dramatic amidst the machinery of biomedicine (Figure 12.4) and it can be the subject of sensuous erotic touch even in the aftermath of painful medical procedures (Figure 12.2). In short, Tutu's process of 'becoming' documented in such images foregrounds the 'shifts and flows' of her embodied

[46] David Aldridge, 'The Body, Its Politics, Posture and Poetics', *The Arts in Psychotherapy* 23.2 (1996): 108.

[47] Margrit Shildrick, *Dangerous Discourses of Disability, Subjectivity and Sexuality*. Basingstoke: Palgrave Macmillan, 2012, p. 25.

[48] Ibid., p. 5.

transformations but also lays bare that these are 'irregular and contingent transformations and reversals that unsettle subjectivity – and identity – itself'.[49]

Therefore, one of the overriding meanings that may be derived from this
bold exhibition once again returns us back to the notion of self-identity but
also to Howie's consideration of how people may live right up to death with
hope. Perhaps in this exhibition what we are faced with is the foregrounding
of Barthes' contention that the photographic image is too 'heavy' to contain a
person's sense of self as it is experienced by them and others. At the same time
the exhibition, despite the sometimes stark imagery, could convey the notion of
hope that Howie envisages 'as a creative process, a sense of journey, becoming
or transformation' that if cultivated may enable an individual to 'live well, right
up to death'.[50] The power of this exhibition, then, lies not only in its making
visible aspects of the embodied experiences of an individual with a chronic (and
sadly terminal) condition. It lies in its disruption of what the notion of 'the self'
during the process of clinical treatment means. By presenting us with Tutu's
multiple (often rich and colourful) identities, *Cancer Sucks* has the potential to
offer hope that, although experiences of treatment during chronic illnesses like
cancer can be traumatic, people can still display agency and creativity and need
not be defined by such experiences.

References

Aldridge, David, 'The Body, Its Politics, Posture and Poetics', *The Arts in Psychotherapy*
    23.2 (1996): 105–12.
Barthes, Roland, *Camera Lucida: Reflections on Photography*, New York: The Noonday
    Press, 1980.
Dennett, Terry, 'Jo Spence's Auto-therapeutic Survival Strategies', *Health* 15.3 (2011):
    223–39.
Emerling, Jae, *Photography: History and Theory*, New York: Routledge, 2012.
Frank, Arthur W., *The Wounded Storyteller: Body, Illness, and Ethics*, Chicago, IL:
    University of Chicago Press, 1995.
Garland-Thomson, Rosemarie, *Staring: How We Look*, Oxford: Oxford University
    Press, 2009.
Henriksen, Nina, Tine Tjørnhøj-Thomsen and Helle Plough Hansen, 'Illness, Everyday
    Life and Narrative Montage: The Visual Aesthetics of Cancer in Sara Bro's Diary',
    Health 15.3 (2011): 277–97.

---

[49] Ibid., p. 25.
[50] Howie, 'How to Think about Death', p. 140.

Howie, Gillian, 'How to Think about Death: Living with Dying', *On the Feminist Philosophy of Gillian Howie: Materialism and Mortality*, ed. Victoria Browne and Daniel Whistler, London: Bloomsbury, 2016, pp. 131–44.

Jay, David, 'The SCAR Project', *Social Semiotics* 22.1 (2012): 39–46.

Johansen, Venke Frederike, Therese Marie Andrews, Haldis Haukanes and Ulla-Britt Lilleaas, 'Symbols and Meanings in Breast Cancer Awareness Campaigns', *NORA: Nordic Journal of Feminist and Gender Research* 21.2 (2013): 140–55.

King, Samantha, *Pink Ribbons, Inc. Breast Cancer and the Politics of Philanthropy*, Minneapolis, MN: Minnesota University Press, 2006.

McLuhan, Marshall, *Understanding Media: The Extensions of Man*, London: Abacus, 1964.

O'Connor, Erin, 'Pictures of Health: Medical Photography and the Emergence of Anorexia Nervosa', *Journal of the History of Sexuality* 5.4 (1995): 535–72.

Pezzullo, Phaeddra C., 'Resisting "National Breast Cancer Awareness Month": The Rhetoric of Counterpublics and their Cultural Performances', *Quarterly Journal of Speech* 89.4 (2003): 345–65.

Radley, Alan, 'Portrayals of Suffering: On Looking Away, Looking at, and the Comprehension of Illness Experience', *Body & Society* 8.3 (2002): 1–23.

Savage, Ashley, '*Cancer Sucks: DaDaFest*. Interview by Nedim Hassan and Janet Price', http://www.dadafest.co.uk/cancer-sucks/ [accessed 1 June 2016].

Shildrick, Margrit, *Dangerous Discourses of Disability, Subjectivity and Sexuality*, Basingstoke: Palgrave Macmillan, 2012.

Theobald, Stephanie, 'Cancer's Not Pink', *Guardian*, 25 March 2012, http://www.theguardian.com/lifeandstyle/2012/mar/25/cancers-not-pink-women-rebelling [accessed 3 August 2015].

All photographs are used with kind permission of Ashley Savage. Photographs are copyright of Ashley Savage, http://www.savageskin.co.uk [accessed 1 June 2016].

13

Movie-making as Palliative Care

Amy Hardie

A terminal diagnosis used to mean you would die within months. Now it can mean you have several years to live. How do we negotiate those years, with an increasingly infirm body? It seems likely many of us will spend time in a hospice or palliative care environment, where our medical and pain needs will be supported and managed. In this chapter, I will consider what the artist can bring to the palliative care environment, where the ethos is problem-solving. Where do artists fit into the hierarchy of clinical proficiency? Patients in a hospice feel cared for, and their pain can be brought under control. Does this also reinforce the patient as vulnerable, and the staff as expert? And what does it mean, to be an expert in someone else's journey to death? Can a specific art form – the documentary – provide the tools for a subtle engagement with mortality? The chapter outlines an approach that was developed through the research network set up by Gillian Howie: 'New Thinking on Living with Dying', based in Liverpool. Referring to three documentary films, *The Edge of Dreaming*,[1] *Tuesdays*[2] and *Seven Songs for a Long Life*,[3] it traces the development of collaborative use of the tools of cinema to engage with end of life. Using documentary camera, sound and screenings, an interactive patient-centred approach was created which allowed a layered involvement with the decisions and values that give meaning to people's lives in their last months and years. The results, both as a creative body of work, and as independently evaluated impact, suggest that the urge to create, to make meaning and share pleasurable experience is deeply rooted and becomes even more urgent when one is close to death.

[1] Amy Hardie, *The Edge of Dreaming* [documentary film], 2010, http://www.edgeofdreaming.co.uk [accessed 2 June 2016].

[2] Amy Hardie, *Tuesdays* [short documentary film], 2011, http://www.amyhardie.com/tags/maggie_s_centre [accessed 2 June 2016].

[3] Amy Hardie, *Seven Songs for a Long Life* [feature documentary film], 2015, http://www.sevensongsfilm.com [accessed 2 June 2016].

Documentary making as research

Howie's questions addressed core issues of mortality: how does the sense of 'who I am' change with the bodily alterations caused by life-limiting illness? Are these changes we can accommodate within our current identity or do we need to become a different person? Her research questions are also my research questions, although I work in film and she was a conceptual philosopher. These questions have become more pressing after the last twenty years where new medical and scientific advances (such as stem cell transplants) have rapidly increased life expectancy. Yet, just as medical treatments have risen in efficacy, so has patient uncertainty. If you have a terminal diagnosis, your prognosis now may be several years. Or you may still die within months. How do we cope with this uncertainty? How does it change our sense of who we are? How should palliative care respond? Can the public have clarity around their end of life choices?

When Howie contacted me in February 2013, she had already been living with a cancer diagnosis for a number of years. She asked me to advise her on using a camera to reflect on the process she was going through. Her intention was to answer her research questions from inside the experience – embodied philosophy in extremis. We talked on the phone and made a plan. However, within weeks her respiratory system failed and she died in the Marie Curie Hospice in Liverpool on 26 March. It was a shock. She was vibrant, young and it seemed a colossal waste. Gillian's considerable philosophical talents were focused especially on one major research question: how can we live well right up to death? Her own experience allowed her to talk with authority on questions stemming from her diagnosis: What rescues us from the shock of a terminal diagnosis? How can we deal with the abrupt loss of a future? What is our present when it is no longer linked to a future for which we can make plans? How is the narrative of our life affected when we are told we are at the final page or final chapter? Does it hang together, or does the diagnosis fragment the narrative – do we imagine all the other 'what ifs' and find ourselves saying – so was this it? To what extent is purpose a pre-requisite for hope, and can we still find hope after we have been told we are going to die?

The three documentary films discussed in this chapter attempt to find ways of communicating and expressing suffering, hope and envisaging one's own death as particular to the individual. Each of them was shown as work in progress in the network set up by Howie and many of the themes and questions debated through these seminars are explored in the films. There are answers provided by individuals in the films and answers the audience will produce in their response to the screenings. These are not philosophical films, nor are they asking any of these questions directly. But as in the 'indirect speech' of Kierkegaard, answers are produced through the observation of real people, living those questions as they navigate their way through a terminal diagnosis. Each film has been widely screened, and each explores a different model of public engagement, but with a common theme: finding a way we can talk to each other about our human mortality.

Why make documentary films? Why respond to terminal disease with art, rather than medicine? Isak Dinesen pointed to the power of narrative when she wrote: 'All human sorrows can be borne if you put them into a story or tell a story about them.'[4] There is a rich seam of literature dealing with suffering and death, from Gilgamesh 5,000 years ago who sought, and lost, the plant that granted eternal life, to the daily blogs of people writing about their life with a terminal illness. And yet, these stories must often be slanted towards some sort of 'winning through', as the current culture in the UK and US is aspirational, making us highly motivated towards success. In a medical context, success means overcoming illness and regaining perfect health. It is difficult for doctors and patients and families to admit defeat, and to accept that they have not been able to beat the disease, even at the very end of a long life.

This emphasis on success makes it hard to see the value in loss or crisis. Yet poetry and stories have described the 'healing crises' for thousands of years. Think of any classic or any fairy story: Persephone's rape and her devastated mother; Lear driven mad by his children's betrayal; Hansel and Gretel abandoned in the woods. Paul Tillich summed it up when he wrote, 'Truth is deep and not shallow; suffering is depth and not height. ... The depth of suffering is the door, the only door, to the depth of truth.'[5] The truth is that none of us will defeat death. Modern medicine and decisions about lifestyle have extended our average life expectancy. But sometimes if you want to survive for those extra years, you have to accept crisis, and loss, and embrace a radical change of identity. This is not easy. It is something that each film explores, whether it is the loss of bodily appearance, loss of a vocation, loss of function, loss of time and energy so that the old pursuits are no longer possible. Disease can destroy our ability to carry out many of the activities that routinely bring us pleasure. Each film asks the question: are there ways to combat this loss, to find a way to live well in the last months or years?

---

[4] Isak Dinesen, *The Human Condition*, Durham, NC: Duke University Press, 1958, p. 175.
[5] Paul Tillich, *The Shaking of the Foundations*, New York: Wipf and Stock, 1948, p. 53.

The Edge of Dreaming

The questions above became the subject of my own documentary practice after an extremely personal engagement with dying. As a rather rational scholar, I did not normally pay very much attention to my dreams. However, I had a particularly vivid dream one night: I had dreamt that my horse was dying, and he asked me to film him. The dream was so unexpected and vivid it woke me up. I was so worried by the dream that I went out in the night to check on him, and found him lying dead. I filmed him, and started thinking about the event that is death. When I had a second and third dream that were equally vivid, I paid more attention to them. In these two dreams, I was told first that I would die that year, and then shown how I would die. When my lungs started failing, I began to investigate the power of the idea of death. This produced the first film, *The Edge of Dreaming.* I set out to document the year during which my death had been foretold with my customary tools: camera and microphone, curiosity and a willingness to go wherever the process of investigation and reflection led. As a documentary maker for twenty years I had discovered that the process of researching, filming, editing and screening a documentary yielded an understanding that was both intellectual and visceral, both intimate and philosophically satisfying. I explored the link between brain and body as my breathing became more difficult, and I was diagnosed with progressive fibrosis of the lungs. Although I had trained in ethnographic and observational film-making at the National Film School, I had never turned the camera on myself before. It felt odd to turn the skills of waiting, looking and observing, on to my own situation. I had become a 'character' in a documentary.

Michelle Citron talks about autobiographical film-making as 'something that gives voice to my unconscious, allowing me to have a dialogue between that which I know, and that which I don't even know that I know'.[6] I was aware that there was an inversion of the usual order of my director's intentions: instead of my sifting the film material to shape it into a story, the dreams were offering me a story that was shaping my experience and perhaps even my bodily self. I wondered if I could use the process of film-making as a way to create that dialogue with myself and with audiences. Film-making makes use of several tools that allow articulation and communication of process and change. These range from the written text and spoken word, whether used as interview in sync,

---

6   Michelle Citron, 'Fleeing from Documentary: Autobiographical Film/Video and the "Ethics of Responsibility"', in *Feminism and Documentary*, ed. Diane Waldman and Janet Walker, Minneapolis, MN: University of Minnesota Press, 1999, p. 281.

Figure 13.1 Still from *The Edge of Dreaming* (credit: Amy Hardie)

or as a voice over, through images, music and sound, to the tools of editing, some of which function subliminally. The interplay of these resources creates a time-based document that communicates on several levels. This has been beautifully articulated by scholars of cinema and psychoanalysis, Izod and Dovalis, in their timely book, *Cinema as Therapy: Grief and Transformational Film*:

> Cinema is pre-eminently the medium which engages people in a virtual dialogue with their own and their culture's unconscious, more deeply than is commonly taken for granted ... film theatres are designed to foster shared experience and become, as the auditorium lights go down, a temenos or sacred enclosure. They create the social and cultural conditions necessary to shared remembering of forgotten or misplaced memories. As a liminal space or container, the cinema functions as the centring source of such shared images. This helps intensify the emotional experiences that films can provoke and assists their digestion. As a medium of images (both visual and aural), cinema is able to bring us back to our own and the culture's psychological depths.[7]

Could the process of making art from my experience act as a way of talking?

---

[7] John Izod and Joanna Dovalis, *Cinema as Therapy: Grief and Transformational Film*, London: Routledge, 2015, p. 2.

Could I find hope, and meaning, through the creative process of filming and editing a documentary film, during this very difficult time?

My research areas followed my attempts to reverse my lung condition. After I was told that fibrosis is irreversible medically I pursued neuroscience and psychotherapy in the hope of understanding the link between brain and body. It was a shamanic journey (my first), recommended by a neuroscientist as a way of reproducing the brain chemistry of the dreaming brain, that reversed the lung disorder. My lungs gradually improved until I was discharged. This was shocking, and delightful, to me, all at once. To allow the audience to see what I experienced behind my closed eyelids during that shamanic trance, I worked with an animator to create the dream-like surreal images that transformed my health. Images taken from my home life were slowed down and drawn over with inks, and other images (such as a snake) created from filming a boa constrictor. Bones and stones, fire and archive images from previous films are cut as a montage to disorientate the recognizable day-to-day reality that has been the guiding aesthetic in the film up to this point. This aesthetic of the real, using the grammar of home movies, had been gradually concentrated and intensified as the film progressively asks the audience to become more aware of the unconscious forces that influence our actions. A focus on concrete details with unsettling sound design has previously invested the quotidian with extra significance – condensation running down the inside of a window, leaves falling and curling around a swaying child's swing, a driving lesson that is then seen as the shadow of the car with the same music, played this time backwards. When we enter the shamanic journey, it is the unconscious that must be visualized and experienced: it has surfaced to full consciousness. This journey marks a turning point in the film, both in terms of the story and subject matter, and this is reflected in the freedom with image and sound. After this climactic moment, the aesthetic in the film returns to the everyday home movie, but with the surreal trance imagery transposed into everyday life, as the birthday party is celebrated with an enormous fire-breathing snake, and the final image of footsteps emerges in the liminal space between land and sea.

One aspect of making art from my own encounter with mortality became increasingly important. This was the role of the community around me. It began when I held test screenings to see if my dream was communicating to others, and rapidly expanded as I explored the history of how dreams have been used in some cultures as an entry point to collective decision-making. Based on seventeenth-century accounts, Iroquois enacted dreams in community, and this has been described as the beginnings of Gestalt therapy. Tracy Marks explains: 'The dreamwork of the Iroquois was not only an early precursor of the dreamwork and analysis of Freud and Jung; it is very similar to the approach to dream interpretation used today by many psychologists trained in Freudian, Jungian and gestalt dream techniques.'[8] I hoped to engage the audience to make a shift in their attention throughout the film, beginning by asking them to use the problem-solving elements of their brain, and, as the film continued, realize that they would not be able to comprehend or solve 'the problem' with their rational selves. It then invites them to descend into their unconscious in order to allow change to sweep over them. I wondered if the aesthetics of the film, and the power of the story, could seduce the audience into accompanying my transformational journey. As Izod and Dovalis point out, cinema is perhaps uniquely capable of encouraging this:

> As a modern technological and imaginal space that has an extraordinary capacity to articulate the imagination, cinema creates a psychic borderline area – a field with both the means and space to entice the psyche into discovering new life. The familiar physical world dissolves, engendering sensitivity to the realm of the imagination. Spectators become immersed in the viewing, drawn further in by the archetypal images that films typically present.[9]

Cinema and the moving image have become a central storytelling medium of our time. Powerful images and sound compress time through editing: sequences that could not be shown during the last 60,000 years (except in our dreams) have, for the last 100 years, become ubiquitous on our television, computer and cinema screens. The rapidity of the change is breathtaking, and it is likely that cinema will continue to develop as the pre-eminent 'storytelling' of our age. However, in one aspect, cinematic storytelling has lost power. It is not live. Its stories are no longer created by an individual in front of an audience. Cinema consists in pixilations projected by light, and when the end credits roll the audience is left alone. The storyteller has left the room. There is no longer a person or a cinematic reality to engage with. The powerful discussions during these early test screenings had made me appreciate the potential for co-creating meaning by involving community in the process of making. I wanted to find a way to retain the live quality of interaction between storyteller and audience inside a cinema context. This grew in importance as I travelled with the film from festival to festival, and

---

8 Tracy Marks, 'The Iroquois Dream Experience and Spirituality', 1998, http://www.webwinds.com/yupanqui/iroquoisdreams.htm [accessed 2 June 2016].
9 Izod and Dovalis, *Cinema as Therapy*, p. 80.

saw that the audience wanted to explore questions of their own dreams, meaning and mortality, but were politely ushered out of the cinema before the next show.

I experimented with a small workshop that allowed participants to work with each other, to find a way of talking that used the experience of the film as a launching pad for their own exploration of the research questions: how do we find meaning, hope and purpose if we have experienced the existential crisis produced by our own inevitable death? Cinema scholar and psychoanalyst John Beebe argues that a core quality of cinema is its potential to answer such questions: 'There are films which induce an unexpected new consciousness in many who view them … in addition to wanting to be entertained, the mass audience is in constant pursuit, as if on a religious quest, of the transformative film.'[10]

This sense of film as potentially transformative informed the development of the screenings to include interactive workshops. These were designed to follow the layered structure of the film, in that they approached the themes of mortality from different angles and using different tools. My aim was that each of the participants would find their own answers as they integrated the experiences of each workshop exercise. The exercises were drawn from neuroscience, from a traditional Scottish death-rite, and from Jungian psychology, mirroring the investigative background of the film. The workshops had a strong impact on the participants, with more and larger workshops requested internationally. Eight countries hosted workshops, each having a distinctively different demographic, from hospital staff in Barcelona to young film-makers in Reykjavík, Iceland, but the workshop model remained identical and participants showed a remarkable cohesion of response. In the UK, one participant described the relationship of the workshop to the film in terms of audience engagement:

> Because of the spaciousness in the film, the poetry in the images, I found myself more and more drawn into the film. There was space for me. In an odd way I was perhaps even more aware than usual that I was watching a screen. The screen was playing out something about me. I was drawn into a participatory role, actively witnessing and engaging with themes and issues that are both universal and deeply mine. Not only was there a film that had a big effect just by watching it, but by having a talk and two hour workshop the next day, I was able to ground my engagement. I had a very profound experience in the workshop. Two days on, I am still in the midst of transformation. Some of the answers I and others in the audience found and expressed in an open forum made this experience a completely different paradigm of cinema.[11]

---

[10] John Beebe, 'Jungian Illumination of Film', in *Psychoanalytic Review* 83.4 (August 1996): 582.
[11] Kathy White, email communication with author, September 2010.

Tuesdays

The audience after a documentary, particularly when they have watched it in a cinema setting, is powerfully engaged with the subject matter of the film. Developing this awareness in public discussion and then taking it further, so that individuals could explore the insights they had produced through the screening, seemed to me an essential, if under-utilized, part of what cinema has to offer. I was inspired by the above description of 'a completely different paradigm of cinema' to further investigate the iterative process of film-making as a way of engaging more deeply with the characters in the film, and with the audiences for the film. Through the Maggie's Centres[12] in London, I was able to make a film, *Tuesdays*, with a ground-breaking therapeutic group led by Lesley Howells, who met weekly on Tuesdays after a secondary cancer diagnosis. I filmed for a year in Dundee, using this time to develop tools of co-creativity and the camera as reflective mirror.

For this film I developed an approach that uses the camera as a metaphorical mirror. Using interview techniques (mainly reflective listening, but also asking questions designed to help each person articulate their widest perspective on their situation), I spent hours filming people talking and then edited this down to a few minutes of key points. One woman had been attending the group for almost two years, and had outlived her disease prognosis by at least a year. We watched the edited interview in private. This was emotional for her, as she felt intensely seen and heard. She also saw herself, and liked what she saw. This creative mirroring was further developed when the woman agreed to show the short piece to the group. They found it very emotional, and responded to her by telling her they had never known how wise she was, and how thoughtfully she was preparing to leave her partner. The participants in the film all talked of the importance of retaining hope, and independently showed that hope required an individual journey of self-assessment – rather along the lines of the questions Atul Gawande has recommended each doctor ask their patient:

> Well-being is about the reasons one wishes to be alive. Those reasons matter not just at the end of life, or when debility comes, but all along the way. Whenever serious sickness or injury strikes and your body or mind breaks down, the vital questions are the same: What is your understanding of the situation and its

---

[12] There are currently seventeen Maggie's Centres built next to major National Health Service (NHS) cancer hospitals in the UK and abroad. Each is beautiful, and staffed with healthcare experts providing free practical, emotional and social support to people with cancer, their family and friends.

Figure 13.2 Still from *Tuesdays* (credit: Amy Hardie)

potential outcomes? What are your fears and what are your hopes? What are the trade-offs you are willing to make and not willing to make? And what is the course of action that best serves this understanding?[13]

This focus on individual values and choices is a pre-requisite to envisioning, as Howie put it, 'this death as their own'. The camera had become a remarkably pleasurable way of achieving this. Individual filming sessions in participants' homes were interwoven with filming during their group support sessions. When we showed the final short film in the cinema to an audience, including all the women's healthcare professionals, the result was both very emotionally satisfying for the participants, and also allowed the healthcare professionals involved with them to get to know them as people. Indeed, one woman's doctor said this was the first time he had got to know her as a person in several years of treatment. There is, though, an ironic codicil to this process of iterative mirroring. When the film was released on DVD and used in ways without the women's presence, they remarked on the loss of control involved at this stage. The participants' images and words continue an independent existence in other people's minds. As we discussed at the time, this could be seen as a rehearsal for a process of letting go that for some people is part of accepting death.

---

[13] Atul Gawande, *Being Mortal*, London: Wellcome, 2015, p. 259.

Seven Songs for a Long Life

The final film to be discussed in this chapter is *Seven Songs for a Long Life*. I became film-maker in residence in 2011 at one of the largest hospices in Scotland, and aimed to further develop co-creativity within the film-making process in a larger environment, the day care unit at Strathcarron Hospice. I began by working with families where one parent had been diagnosed with a terminal illness, usually secondary cancer, and was coming into the hospice one day a week to the day care ward, where their medications would be monitored. While there, they would also be able to speak to doctors, nurses, occupational, physio and complementary therapists, and have relaxation classes, hair-dressing, manicures, make-up, home-baking and a three-course lunch. To find a 'way of talking' with the hospice day care patients, I began by teaching film-making skills within the family group. This allowed families to create archives of their intimate family life, and also created a new channel of communication. This was often wordless, but perhaps the intense observation through the camera was even more powerful, as child filmed parent, child filmed sibling, parents filmed each other and their children. We projected these short films on living-room walls, and watched the recognition between family members of how much they meant to each other. It was a productive environment to work in and Dr Erna Haraldsdottir, head of education at Strathcarron, and Dr Marilyn Kendal from Edinburgh University's Department of Public Health set up on-going interviews to evaluate the impact of the filming on patients, families and staff. The following quotes are drawn from their interviews. They provide an interesting sounding of how it was for the patients and staff during the process of filming. Through open-ended questions, they were encouraged to talk about their reactions to the camera. Patients explained how they enjoyed the opportunity to participate in an activity shared with their families: 'We had such fun learning different shots and doing the cameras ... The thing I enjoyed the most about the morning we spent with Amy was my children working together ... they were all excited ... It was great for us all to be doing something.' It quickly became apparent that a focus on creating memories for later was uppermost on parents' minds. Patients wanted to leave a legacy. I knew from my own experience during *The Edge of Dreaming* that I had found comfort in consciously creating a film legacy of everyday family routine for my children – so that they could, if necessary, show it to their children and remember the texture and sounds and glances, jokes and cuddles of growing up: 'My family ... they really liked it. I think secretly they know that they can still have Mum on it when I'm not here so it'll be good.' A nurse watching the

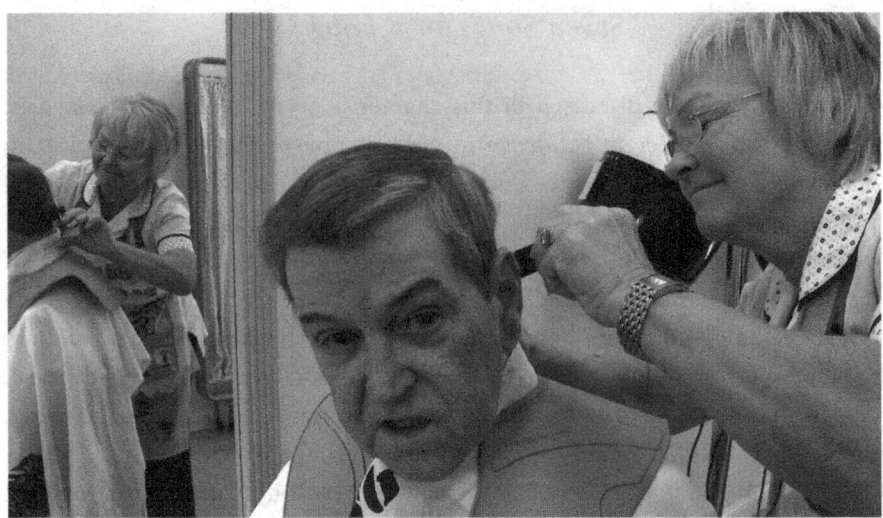

Figure 13.3 Still from *Seven Songs for a Long Life* (credit: Amy Hardie)

process noted: 'It's a marvellous, marvellous comforter for the relative to have because, you know, they've got it for always … it's very concise and they're able to think about what they want to say and it also enables them to say things that they've probably never even said in the rest of their life. … It's just so important that they do get a chance to say goodbye and tell the people that they're leaving how much they'll miss them and how much they've been loved.'

As time passed, patients became more and more interested in the process of film-making itself. We followed a practical and interactive process: we would talk, bounce ideas around, I would film, screen the rushes back, we would edit, I would screen the edited short, we would use that a springboard for further open-ended discussion and camera experimentation. This process allowed patients and staff a great deal of creative control over the direction of the filming process, and had results that surprised us all. The patients had begun to access the camera's potential as a tool for self-exploration at this very tender, very uncertain time of life. It began as a process of acceptance: 'when I saw myself, the camera doesn't lie and I went "Oh, that's me", you know so I'm not saying I got a shock but I didn't really see myself like that until I saw it on the film. Do you know what I mean? And I think in a way I thought it was quite good because I thought, well, it's like an acceptance. Do you know what I mean? You've just got to accept it.'

Very quickly, the patients took the opportunity to create small movies that delighted audiences – other hospice patients, staff and families. When we

Figure 13.4 Still from *Seven Songs for a Long Life* (credit: Amy Hardie)

screened the small films, the results were emotionally intense for the partici-pants and the hospice audiences – delight in the pleasure of the films and the bittersweet sadness of seeing patients who had died since filming. More and more DVDs were requested and sent off to far-flung family members. Much of the pleasure of the short films was produced by the patients' singing. It emerged that one of the nurses, Mandy Malcomson, was a passionate singer, and related to her patients through music whenever possible. Although the first patient who sang to the camera did it to avoid talking, the results were so eloquent that other patients also began to sing. Over time the way the patients used the songs changed. In the beginning, songs were used as a distraction from illness, from the experience of being a patient. The performances were a way of proving to themselves and those around them that they were more than 'patients'; that they were still people with dreams and desires. They used the songs to distract themselves and the hospice audience from the possibility of death. After their first songs, each patient began to use the camera to talk about the subjects that mattered most to them – and eventually each approached the subject of their own death. As Marjory Mackay, Clinical Director of Strathcarron Hospice, notes of the patients:

> They possess certain knowledge – that a particular illness with which they have been labelled and whose assault they have felt deeply, will shape and shorten their life and will most likely expedite their death. Their hopes and dreams and all that we ordinarily take for granted about 'our tomorrows' have been dashed. They have come face to face with the reality of their own mortality.[14]

Their stories as they began to express them were varied and extraordinary – as perhaps all life stories are, when we can take the time to get to know them. The young man with Multiple Sclerosis, Iain, is a former speedway racer. His story is about whether he can adapt to daily pain and accept the shocking changes to his body. The man who opens the film with a Sinatra song, Tosh, never does adapt to or acknowledge his cancer, and that works well for him: he honed a strategy of resolute denial and diversion as a way of living in the moment. Some stories were entirely unpredictable: Julie was a young single mother who has always loved dancing, but been too shy to dance in public. Iain was the youngest ever DJ signed to a major record label, who used to get a crowd of 3,000 on their feet at Tiffanies in Leeds. When they met at the hospice, Iain chose music for her, and as Julie started to dance again, she gained the confidence to get the whole ward dancing. In the last year of filming the patients began to use song to reflect on their fears and hopes around end of life. A former leading singer in amateur opera, Dorene, gave up singing when the cancer spread to her bones. Encouraged by nurse Mandy, she found the courage to sing again during a physiotherapy session. Her voice is powerful, perfectly tuned. She goes on to sing some of the most beautiful moments of the film.

The patients utilized the inherent creativity of an art form as flexible as film to develop their self-expression. Their renewal of a sense of their self as a person able to create and contribute pleasure and value became the most important element in our collaborative process: 'It works both ways ... It's not just a one way thing this, we appreciate getting help but we also like to help people as well. Even though we're not well, we can always do something for other people, you know, so it's a two-way thing so I think it's terrific.' By the end of the three-year filming period the patients had fully embraced the shared creative endeavour of making a documentary film. The intensity with which this was grasped is

---

[14] Quoted in Amy Hardie, 'Movie Making as Palliative Care', http://centreformedicalhumanities. org/11003-2/ [accessed 22 November 2015].

an indication of one of the dangers of being a patient in palliative care: the increasing reliance on other people, being constantly seen as in need of care, as a recipient, rather than a contributor. In the final third of the film, the patients have chosen songs to express their surrender to, or continued battle with, death. The duet between the nurse Mandy and Nikki of 'Everybody Hurts' is an astonishing and vibrantly emotional expression of Nikki's survival after days of pain. As Marjory Mackay from Strathcarron observes:

> By drawing us into their world of living while dying, they teach us what is possible if we embrace the tension of living in the knowledge that we are dying. There is no room for procrastination! But there is space for hope, for making the most of every opportunity, for cherishing everything that we have and focusing on the things that matter most. They show us their determination to face the reality of losses, even when they seem layered one on top of the other. They teach us not to like loss but to live with and through it – and in spite of it retain dignity and strength and love for life. The irony is that if we acknowledge that our days are numbered – even if we don't know the actual number – it changes what we do and how we see everyone, everything, today and in the future.[15]

The transformative power of film

The film *Seven Songs for a Long Life* was selected by the UK Palliative Leadership Collaborative as an opportunity to encourage the general public to engage with their own future plans and death. Over 70 hospices paired with cinemas throughout the UK to screen the film followed by a contextualizing discussion. Screenings have been held from Brighton to Inverness, London to rural Wales, and audiences have included healthcare workers, artists, people with a life-limiting condition, carers, school-children, nursing and medical students, and the general public. The critical response from media was generous, if sometimes a little bemused. *Total Film*, while awarding the film four stars, asks: 'How can a documentary about terminally ill patients waiting out an uncertain timeframe for their impending demise ever be a joyous and positive film? In this case, director Amy Hardie emphasises the sense of community among six patients, a nurse and a fundraiser as they meet the harrowing prospect of death with good humour and a shared love of music.'[16] Felperin in the *Guardian* notes the power

---

[15] Quoted in Hardie, 'Movie Making as Palliative Care'.
[16] Matt Looker, 'Review of *Seven Songs for a Long Life*', *Total Film*, 2015, http://www.gamesradar.com/movies-to-watch-2-october-2015/ [accessed 2 June 2016].

of documentary: 'Hardie has a particularly good eye for the evocative, quiet moments';[17] and in its film awards for 2015, Vulturehound ranked *Seven Songs for a Long Life* as one of its top five films of 2015.[18]

Independent evaluation of its impact on the cinema audience was carried out by the Scottish Collaboration for Public Health Research and Policy (SCPHRP). The public were asked to fill out a questionnaire after the screening, and there was room for comments. The film was screened on BBC in the UK in 2015, and is scheduled to screen on PBS in the US and YLE in Finland in 2016. The Scottish Documentary Institute ran a productive campaign to get the film out to audiences. Relevant websites and Facebook pages have attracted a dialogue about mortality, with thoughtful and often heartfelt postings. Excerpts of the film have focused debates on the use of film in palliative care. The film has reached a surprisingly large audience – almost double the average BBC2 Scotland share of 5.4 per cent on its transmission (9 per cent, with 60,000 more viewers then watching on iPlayer within four weeks) – and increased rapidly, tripling its viewers and Facebook comments within the first four weeks. This increase must be through word of mouth and social media, as there was no advertising budget. This is confirmed by the high number of tweets about the screenings: 110,000 impressions and 316 mentions in October.

The questionnaires showed a high response to the power of film as a trans-formative experience, both in the quantitative analysis of the questionnaires, and in the qualitative narrative of comments and workshop feedback.[19] These are encouraging results: many writers have noted the human distress caused by our natural avoidance of the topic of death, and deep reluctance to think about or discuss our own, or our loved ones' end of life plans. Why was the film working so well in terms of lowering anxiety around end of life care? Some of the answers are suggested by the individual comments and discussions in the

---

[17] Leslie Felperin, 'Review of *Seven Songs for a Long Life*', *Guardian*, 1 October 2015, http://www.theguardian.com/film/2015/oct/01/seven-songs-long-life-review-honesty-documentary-hospice-dying [accessed 2 June 2016].

[18] Ben Rogers, 'Vulture Hound Film Awards 2015', http://vulturehound.co.uk/2015/12/best-films-of-the-year-5-seven-songs-for-a-life/ [accessed 2 June 2016].

[19] The questionnaire results were as follows:
After watching the film: 95 per cent of the audience agreed or strongly agreed that given the subject matter, they enjoyed this film more than they expected; 85 per cent of the audience agreed or strongly agreed that they felt more confident to talk and listen to others about their end of life plans; 60 per cent of the audience agreed or strongly agreed that they felt more confident to think about and share their own end of life plans; 90 per cent of the audience agreed or strongly agreed that they would recommend this film as a way of helping others approach the subject of a terminal diagnosis; 85 per cent of the audience agreed or strongly agreed that they felt less anxious about the prospect of what would happen if they eventually needed hospice care; 95 per cent of the audience agreed or strongly agreed that hospice care can be part of life.

questionnaires, workshops and discussions after film screenings. Some focused on how the experience of watching the film had changed their mental state, calming anxiety around end of life: 'A wonderful medium through which the mystery and fear of hospice admission and care can be alleviated'; 'A moving and beautiful film. We are very lucky to have this opportunity to think about our mortality.' Further comments point up that reflecting on their experience is a cause for taking action: 'My elderly parents died last year – both in hospital. This film made me think how different things might have been for them in a hospice'; 'Unfortunately many hospitals and hospices do not have the resources to provide such strong support'; 'End of life discussing needs to be highlighted, awareness revised, thank you for leading the way'; 'Diagnosed 4 years ago with breast cancer myself and at the moment all seems to be okay, but I'm very aware that could change and found the film very helpful for me.' Other comments spoke to the difficulty of talking about this area, the privilege of being allowed access to how different people cope with a terminal diagnosis, and expressed the desire that the conversations should take place as widely as possible: 'Beautiful film – a real privilege to be able to share the journey of some wonderful people'; 'I hope more people see this film and share the joy, the laughter, and tears.'

Other comments described how the film spoke to one of the aims Howie had identified: the desire to live well to the very end: 'I wept a lot but felt the music and special people in the film left me uplifted and hopeful for a great end of life journey – for myself and others I love'; 'Very moving but also very positive, life is indeed for the living – right up to the last moment.' Others focused on the creativity shown in the film, and its power to bring hope and meaning: 'The power of music shines through and the joy of participation was obvious'; 'Singing is pure medicine for the soul'; 'The music and humour carried the film, as indeed this is what also gives the characters their strength.' The complexity of communication that gives film its power was referred to, along with the seemingly contradictory emotions that the film produced. The complex layering of a documentary, which is time-based communication, utilizing image and real sound, sound-effects and music, text and voice-over, allows the audience to be engaged on several levels, sometimes simultaneously, sometimes concurrently: 'I liked the way it lifted off from real. It did what a documentary is meant to do'; 'Film about death that brings me to life … this is the first documentary film which makes me cry and be happy at the same time.'

One of the key conceptual shifts that Howie had articulated as part of the solution to the 'existential terror' that a terminal diagnosis can bring was 'the ability to envisage the future as my own – this death is my death'. This became a key focus for discussion between audience and the panels of film-maker and characters after the screenings. The energy, both fear and hope, that became evident in these discussions on this topic suggested this as the area for deepening public engagement. In close collaboration with the Education Department of Strathcarron Hospice we designed interactive sessions where four main characters in the film – Julie, Iain, Dorene and nurse Mandy – would lead viewers though a guided series of questions to establish what they could do to envisage the future as their own, and live well right up to the end. We also designed an education pack for use in schools, nursing and medical training, and for patients and carers. Workshops to run after the film allowed audiences to interact with each other in pairs and small and large groups. These workshops were designed for the general public, and very gently led them through questions that would allow them to reflect, possibly for the first time, on the values by which they had lived their lives, and how they could take those values as a blue-print to 'envisage this death as their own', as Howie had put it. People's answers often surprised them. One respondent discovered as he went through the questions that imagining his life after a cancer diagnosis, paradoxically, brought a feeling of expansion, rather than the expected narrowing of life to a full stop: 'There would still be hugs and dancing and singing. I'd still hang out at the allotment, but invite other people to help with the heavy work. I'd do more of doing nothing. I'd have more time ... I'd have more time!'[20] This unexpected transformation from fear to a new perspective, during a period of reflection after the film has finished playing, suggests that the aims of transformational cinema may well be best met if we expand the cinema experience. Offering audiences a structured time after the film allows them to deepen their engagement with their own process by using the film as a sort of accelerated dialogue with themselves, making the energy generated by each individual's film response available to them as they confront their own mortality.

References

Beebe, John, 'Jungian Illumination of Film', *Psychoanalytic Review* 83.4 (August 1996): 579–87.

Butler, Larry, email communication with author, 2015.

Citron, Michelle, 'Fleeing from Documentary: Autobiographical Film/Video and the

---

[20] Larry Butler, email communication with author, September 2015.

"Ethics of Responsibility"', *Feminism and Documentary*, ed. Diane Waldman and Janet Walker, Minneapolis, MN: University of Minnesota Press, 1999, pp. 271–86.

Dinesen, Isak, *The Human Condition*, Durham, NC: Duke University Press, 1958.

Felperin, Leslie, 'Review of *Seven Songs for a Long Life*', *Guardian*, 1 October 2015, http://www.theguardian.com/film/2015/oct/01/seven-songs-long-life-review-honesty-documentary-hospice-dying [accessed 2 June 2016].

Gawande, Atul, *Being Mortal*, London: Wellcome, 2015.

Hardie, Amy, 'Movie Making as Palliative Care', http://centreformedicalhumanities. org/11003-2/ [accessed 22 November 2015].

Hardie, Amy, *The Edge of Dreaming* [documentary film], 2010. http://www. edgeofdreaming.co.uk [accessed 2 June 2016].

Hardie, Amy, *Tuesdays* [short documentary film], 2011, http://www.amyhardie.com/ tags/maggie_s_centre [accessed 2 June 2016].

Hardie, Amy, *Seven Songs for a Long Life* [feature documentary film], 2015, http://www. sevensongsfilm.com [accessed 2 June 2016].

Izod, John, and Joanna Dovalis, *Cinema as Therapy: Grief and Transformational Film*, London: Routledge, 2015.

Looker, Matt, 'Review of *Seven Songs for a Long Life*', *Total Film*, 2015, http://www. gamesradar.com/movies-to-watch-2-october-2015/ [accessed 2 June 2016].

Marks, Tracy, *The Iroquois Dream Experience and Spirituality*, 1998, http://www. webwinds.com/yupanqui/iroquoisdreams.htm [accessed 2 June 2016].

Rogers, Ben, 'Vulture Hound Film Awards 2015', http://vulturehound.co.uk/2015/12/ best-films-of-the-year-5-seven-songs-for-a-life/ [accessed 2 June 2016].

Tillich, Paul, *The Shaking of the Foundations*, New York: Wipf and Stock, 1948.

White, Kathy, email communication with author, 2010.

14

Experience and Performance whilst Living with Disability and Dying: Disability Art as a Pathway to Flourishing

Janet Price and Ruth Gould

In 2012, a public event entitled 'Changing Capacities: Changing Identities' was co-organized by the New Thinking on Living with Dying research network led by Gillian Howie and DadaFest (Deaf and Disability Arts Festival), as part of the latter's 2012 festival, themed 'Transactions'. DaDaFest is an innovative disability-led arts organization, based in Liverpool and working more widely across north-west England, nationally and globally. It is committed to widening the presence of disabled actors and performers within the public view, to the involvement and training of disabled people as creators and producers of art, and to broadening the opportunities for disabled people to view and participate in the arts as a source of creative pleasure.[1] It achieves this in part through delivering a biennial festival, along with other arts events which promote high-quality disability and deaf arts, as well as art that comes from the cultural perspective of those living with disability or long-term illness. The work DaDaFest produces is often edgy, challenging disability stereotypes, questioning thinking about the normative body (the 'body beautiful'), and undermining stigma and prejudice about the appearance of disabled people, about ways in which they live their lives. As Laura Ferguson, an artist with scoliosis who has worked for many years to develop new ways of seeing her and others' bodies, writes:

> I realize that the idea of deformity having its own beauty, without the need of fixing or altering, is a radical one. But I believe in an alternative vision of aesthetics in medicine, one that gives more value to process, to empathetic connection, than to fixing or curing. Art is a good place to look for an

---

[1] See further, http://www.dadafest.co.uk [accessed 6 February 2016].

alternative aesthetic: a place where the less-than-perfect body can be shown to have its own kind of beauty, grace, sensuality, originality.[2]

The 'Changing Capacities: Changing Identities' event offered a chance to address questions affecting those living with disability and with life-limiting, non-curable conditions, and created a space to explore 'thoroughly contemporary, yet at the same time ancient, questions about the implications of "living with dying"'.[3] One of Howie's key ideas was that critical disability theory – and the edgy, challenging disability arts that are linked to its ideas – 'may have the most to teach us about how to live a changing body without living that as a loss with norms that you are continually trying to recover'.[4] Accordingly, the aims of the event, in bringing together ideas from within philosophy, disability theory and critical-disability art, were to question prejudice and stigma about death, illness and disability; bring theories of critical disability to bear upon the medical field of prolonging life, death and dying; address the potential of disability art and other creative initiatives to radically challenge the experience of disability, chronic illness and death; and examine how combining critical disability art and theory can bring about new thinking on living with dying.

The power of art

Life with terminal cancer is an ongoing series of embodied shifts – in cellular constitution, health experience, medical response and personal choice – that may, in fact, go on for a number of years. Terminal does not mean immediate. And, alongside dealing with bodily change and its consequences, as Howie discussed, one has to engage with the existential crisis, the fear of dying, the sensation of being without purpose or meaning as the future disappears. One has to work out how to live the present when the future has been taken away. How does one 'cultivate a habit of mind that allows (one) to live right up to death, with hope'?[5] It is at this point, the point of hope, that Howie felt philosophy's limits are exposed. And, although she had worked through many diverse philosophical traditions, she recognized that something other was possible,

---

[2] Laura Ferguson, 'Toward a New Aesthetic of the Body', Literature, Arts and Medicine blog, 21 October 2007, http://medhum.med.nyu.edu/blog/?m=200710 [accessed 27 January 2016].

[3] As set out on the New Thinking on Living with Dying blog, https://newthinkingaboutlivingwithdying. wordpress.com [accessed 6 February 2016].

[4] Gillian Howie, 'How to Think about Death: Living with Dying', transcribed as Ch. 6 of the present volume, p. 143.

[5] Ibid.

something that was offered by reading, music, the arts, cultivating nature, gardening, walking and access to a green world, thus challenging the use of the intellect alone and combining it rather with a more direct engagement with the phenomenology of the body, the senses stimulated by sight, touch, sound, taste, smell – the intensities of feeling that can be generated, the sensibilities opened through engaging with different environments and experiences. Courtney Davis offers a very profound detailed description of how she used her urge to paint as a route towards maintaining and enhancing hope, wellbeing, a positive psychosocial subjectivity:

> I felt the need to respond to my illness in some creative way (maybe turning illness into something creative is a way of taking control?), but I really could not find the words. It felt as if there were no words to adequately express what I had been through or what I'd experienced in the hospital. Words seemed too intellectual, too distant and too controlled to express something that felt raw, profound, and frightening. My illness was all about my body, and painting seemed to be all about the body too: the smell of the paint and the feel of the paint and the brush on the canvas, the movement of my hand and arm, the lack of an internal editor (since I really had no idea if I was doing the painting 'right' or not), the emotional impact of the colors and shapes, and the lack of the need to 'intellectualize' the process. During this illness, I felt in a very profound way the metaphorical inadequacy or incompleteness of my vocabulary. There is a level of vulnerability that can't be intuited from the bedside but can only be experienced.[6]

DaDaFest's 2012 festival 'Transactions' was the latest in a series of trans-entitled festivals, that take 'trans' as indicative of a shift, change or connection. Indeed, this first year would be the start of an eight-year journey to explore variations on the prefix 'trans', which explores our constant state of change. Through this focus DaDaFest intended to highlight the ways in which disability and art together work across/trans, creating new conceptions and possibilities. Conversations about 'Transactions' with Howie brought a new angle to our thinking as we discussed what this meant in the face of not only disability but also of life-limiting conditions. The transactions initiated at this point in our lives may be some of the most crucial we undertake. And those facing death are faced with what may feel like a loss – certainly a change – in the identity they have held and in their capacities for thought and action. Knowledge of our own impending

---

[6] Cortney Davis, 'When the Nurse Becomes a Patient: A Story in Words and Images', Literature, Arts and Medicine blog, 2 June 2015, http://medhum.med.nyu.edu/blog/?p=9073 [accessed 27 January 2016].

death may lead us to an accounting of what will be gained and what lost, to take stock of the impact of forthcoming grief, loss, pain and distress on the debit side. We think of the complexity of negotiations we may have to undertake: with health staff, friends and family, benefits advisors – as to how we will manage, who we will see, how much we will do, what we will eat, when and how take our medication. This commonly experienced and broad range of incursions into a previously independent life can rapidly push individuals away from feeling in control, recognized as someone who has agency and personal preferences. With the onset of disability and particularly with a diagnosis of life-limiting illness, those around that individual can abruptly lose a sense of them as someone who can manage their own life, who has the capacity to make decisions. Life can come to be managed by and through others rather than being self-directed.

It is at such points that the potential for living life with hope becomes so crucial. And it was the potential for critical disability theory and art to enhance this option that underpinned the 'Changing Capacities: Changing Identities' event. What made this event different to many university seminars was that alongside the academic papers – by Carol Thomas, Ria Cheyne and Margrit Shildrick – were very different styles of presentations. Together we identified the work of photographers and video artists to be displayed – Amy Hardie, Tutu and Ashley Savage, and the Waterfront Project who, in addressing loss and dying, created sculpture and other artwork that could form a small temporary exhibit, all of which provided stimuli for attendees to view and debate. Finally were two comedians, David Roche who challenged the audience with laughter around disability and dying, and Liz Bentley who was able 'to brilliantly satirise the frustrating experiences many face when dealing with healthcare professionals and environments'.[7] The work was as serious as that of any academic in its drive to understand and find ways that people can, without regret, approach living with dying.

The day-long event spoke directly not only to the aims of New Thinking on Living with Dying but also to DaDaFest ideals in challenging disability prejudice and enhancing the potential of disability art. Such work has major resonance for disabled people, can impact profoundly upon their lives. As Ruth Gould put it at the time, 'I have a passion for disability and deaf art as we work to capture unique cultural perspectives and the nuances created by the distinctness of the lived experience of disability. And it has changed my life too.'[8] Throughout

[7] As described on the New Thinking on Living with Dying blog, https://newthinkingaboutlivingwith dying.wordpress.com/public-events/ [accessed 27 January 2016].
[8] Ruth Gould, private communication, 2016.

the event, we were offered the opportunity to address how such art might also engage with the issues faced by those living with dying. But DaDaFest has clear political aims that extend beyond its individual impact. For the 2014 Festival it established a manifesto that stated its overall intentions. These have clear resonances with the thinking behind 'Changing Capacities: Changing Identities': to not only deliver change on an individual level but also to broaden social thinking about the treatment of people facing a slow or prolonged death.

> The power of the arts to influence social change is inestimable. Through them we learn to see life differently, we learn empathy with others, we learn how to connect, appreciate and give. The arts are our context to promote social change, to highlight inequality and move us to appreciate our place in the world. The fact that we link our work so closely to the need for change does not in any way detract from our dedication to high quality disability and deaf arts – it strengthens it.[9]

Disability arts would not have been possible without disability politics coming along first. It is what makes a 'disability artist' different from an artist with a disability.[10] As disabled people began to organize themselves in the 1980s, they saw the multiple evidence, in films, TV, theatre and other cultural representation, that an individual with an impairment was predominantly marked by deviance, by evil or negativity.[11] The expansion in identity politics around the social model of disability drew on a distinction between impairment (alterations in one's physical body, appearance or emotional state) and disability (the social and cultural responses to embodied difference of stigma, prejudice and discrimination which precipitate access limitations and a lack of appropriate services).[12] It was against these negative responses to impairment that activists organized themselves. The theory, not that disabled people are socially deviant but that society casts them as such, was developed initially with the view that disability was not about the body, a move that was intended to expose the social nature of this othering. In contrast to this rejection of the body that took place within the early days of the UK disability movement, within America there was recognition of the importance of theorizing embodiment from a political and

---

[9] DaDaFest, *DaDaFest International 2014: Art of the Lived Experiment* Festival Brochure, Liverpool: DaDaFest, 2014.
[10] Alan Sutherland, 'Disability Arts, Disability Politics', in A. Pointon with C. Davies (eds), *Framed: Interrogating Disability in the Media*, London: British Film Institute, 1997, p. 159.
[11] David Hevey, *The Creatures Time Forgot: Photography and Disability Imagery*, London: Routledge, 1992.
[12] UPIAS, *Fundamental Principles of Disability*, London: Union of the Physically Impaired against Segregation, 1976.

cultural disability perspective. And for DaDaFest's work, this theory has been vital as the idea of corporeal and embodied subjectivity is central to developing thinking about both disability and performance.

Lennard Davis maintains that a normal body is a theoretical premise from which all bodies, by definition, must fall short.[13] If there is, in fact, no normal body then embodiment exhibits myriad deviations from the supposed ideal body – what Rosemarie Garland-Thomson terms the 'normate' individual. She argues that the normate is the failed subject position of the cultural self, the figure outlined by the array of deviant others whose marked bodies shore up the normate boundaries.[14] But further, extending the above argument about bodies, David Mitchell and Sharon Snyder argue that 'the prostheticized body is the rule, not the exception'.[15] Although differences exist to varying degrees they are erased through 'prosthetic intervention', through building an illusion that accomplishes an erasure of difference, a false recognition of the embodied individual as same and whole. It is not that we are all alike but rather our complex and multiple differences are managed and simplified through recognized categories. And where the move to erasure cannot take place, where the difference from normal is too extreme, the hope is that the individual can at least be returned to what society holds to be a degree of acceptable difference, one that does not disturb.

We see, as people approach the end of their lives or as they grapple with changing bodies, that much is offered by social and medical staff to apparently alleviate their physical discomfort and their sense of difference as they think through cancer or lose hair through the impact of drugs. Living with cancer, they occupy a liminal space, not fully well, not always ill, the difficulties of dying denied and redressed in palliative care talk. But these interventions may simply offer the appearance of 'a fix', something to which Tutu alluded in her photographs of living with breast cancer, *Cancer Sucks*.[16] She and Ashley Savage strove to refute the 'pinkification' of breast cancer and show some of the joy, the elation, the hysteria and the horror that accompanies living through it by photographing without restraint the differing moments and moods she experienced. In doing so they have created photographs that stimulate laughter, sorrow, disgust and delight, images that demand recognition of Tutu as a distinct individual, clearly

[13] Lennard Davis, *Enforcing Normalcy: Disability, Deafness and the Body*, New York: Verso, 1995.
[14] R. Garland-Thomson, *Freakery: Cultural Spectacles of the Extraordinary Body*, New York: New York University Press, 1996, p. 8.
[15] David T. Mitchell and Sharon L. Snyder, *Narrative Prosthesis: Disability and the Dependencies of Discourse*, Ann Arbor, MI: University of Michigan Press, 2000, p. 7.
[16] See further Ashley Savage, *Cancer Sucks*, http://www.savageskin.co.uk [accessed 6 February 2016].

separated from what threatens to become the bland generalizability of breast cancer survivors' 'pinkness'. We see very clearly the progressive display of Tutu's living – and dying – experience, her changing capacity and visible changes in her identity, including an identity as performer to which she takes recourse even at some of what appear to be the most difficult moments.

In Amy Hardie's documentaries of individuals attending hospices, one of her main achievements is to remove them from the generality of an illusory sameness as people diagnosed with 'approaching death', to offer instead detailed and intimate images of their individuality: the still-young-looking woman sitting, relaxed, on the grass with earth on her hands, repotting plants, surrounded by sounds of nature; the old man with a trilby on his head, swinging his cane as he sings his way down the institutional corridor and back out to his life away from medical intervention and their insistence on his upcoming death, a death of which he wanted no part. He refused to fill out a Disability Living Allowance Form that is intended to offer financial support in the last six months of life, denying that he was dying. And later in the video we see him flirting, singing and laughing with friends and family, the very picture of life. Hardie says of these videos,

> All of my work is about encouraging and making more vibrant, more real and more meaningful, individual discourses and then perhaps, not always, but very often, turning them into narratives that mean something to the person and then, that will also mean something to the audience who never knew that person but who, because of the way I turned it into a narrative, will then find they can relate to that, and it says something about them.[17]

Hardie's, Tutu's, and Savage's work thus demonstrates how – against the veils of misunderstanding and misrepresentation that situate disabled or ill bodies within acceptable norms whilst concealing much of their lived experience – some of those who exhibited in the 'Changing Capacities: Changing Identities' event rebel. They demand instead recognition of the individual within their work.

Difference and the loss of normality

Many of those who are managing the process of living with cancer as well as

[17] Transcribed comment from *Changing Capacities, Changing Identities* (Transcript Three), Liverpool, 1 September 2012.

many disabled people (particularly those newly disabled) seek to recapture their body as it was before their diagnosis, returning to a moment prior to illness. Recruiting physical therapy, prosthetics and surgery amongst other biomedical interventions, the goal of rehabilitation is to follow the path of returning the body to as close to a normal state as possible. However, if the truth is that the body was originally not normal, then it can clearly never be 'normal' again. Once disability or illness has disrupted one mode of functioning for the body (what may have been deemed normative), that body can only ever mimic a normative state, reiterating and mirroring as closely as possible what is deemed to be the 'natural' body, that mythical and non-existent state. Some, following breast cancer surgery, choose the path of prosthetic reconstruction, others such as the model Matuschka choose to live one-breasted. In the 1990s she produced high-end fashion magazine-style photographs of herself that opened a debate about the visibility and privacy of those with breast cancer.[18] Around much cancer management is a silence, and cancer treatment is normalized – with the hair loss that accompanies chemotherapy covered over with wigs, and breast reconstruction presented as a chance to return to the sexualized 'normality' of pre-cancer days.[19] Reconstruction hopes and fears have also been exacerbated by the scandal surrounding the PiP implant.[20]

Within disability circles there is much debate about not only the value and politics of rehabilitation, but also about how, within the social model, there had been a denial of the changes bodies undergo through disability, aging and illness. The early failure of the social model to incorporate any understanding of pain, fatigue, distress and other aspects of emotion or affect was a major and early criticism by feminist disability scholars. But it had broad implications for all disabled people in that the model establishes a defiantly masculinist take on impairment/disability through its denial that embodied experience (including at the psychosocial level) plays a role in living with a non-normative corporeality. When there is a refusal to accept and adapt to the processes of bodily change, and to the fatigue, pain and discomfort that can be an insistent part of these, their apparent 'failure of utility' reflects in the inevitable failure of disabled and dying people to match normative standards of embodiment. The drive to

---

[18] R. Garland-Thomson, *Staring: How We Look*, Oxford: Oxford University Press, 2009.

[19] Indeed, it is not only women who worry about the appearance of their breasts, sagging and drooping with age or growing in size, but men too. Gynaecomastia – enlarged breasts, 'man boobs' – is one of the commonest sources of concern with their appearance amongst men. And trans-people face major concerns if they are having top surgery.

[20] See L. Davies, 'Breast Implant Scandal: 3,500 Private Clinic Patients Referred to NHS', *Guardian*, 24 February 2012, http://www.theguardian.com/world/2012/feb/24/breast-implant-scandal-patients-nhs [accessed 3 February 2016].

ensure that all individuals mirror the ideal body as closely as possible, whatever the cost to them in terms of pain or discomfort, can create depression, despair and loss of hope. Feminist work has played a major part in the application of theory to the impaired (medical) body, understanding it not simply as a natural biological given but rather as a phenomenological experience, undergoing a continuous process of becoming. Claire Cunningham is a disabled dancer who has discovered, through her disability, new ways of becoming:

> I'm interested in the potential of my own physicality. I've rejected the idea of trying to make my body look as if it's not disabled. I don't want to be compared – I think there's a danger when disabled people are compared to nondisabled people. I'm also interested in the lived experience of disability – what skills disability brings. If you live in the body that has greater fragility, it changes your attitude to physical space. It brings greater awareness. I can use this in my work.[21]

Despite the ubiquity of disability, the notion of it as performance, both in theory as well as lived experience, has been slow to emerge within disability studies. Disabled people are used to being the object of others' staring, of attention paid by unknown by-passers. And those living with dying may have to accustom themselves to unexpected stares as they thin and prematurely age. Whilst Butler has theorized performativity as reiterative acts performed to establish identity or subjectivity, disabled people, through the attention that many attract, are frequently conscious, rather than subconscious, performers of their daily lives, using comedy, theatre and art to challenge stigma. David Roche, the Canadian comedian and author, insists that, when he first encounters audiences, for 'the first three minutes that people [are free to] stare at me, there is an outcome. They are just interested, they don't hate me, and that is a great skill to be able to know that.'[22]

Like Roche, Garland-Thomson argues that staring has work to do. It functions to reduce the visual novelty of impairment, induce a sense of familiarity, enable starers to see the starees as distinct individuals, part of the wide tapestry of human variation, and thus to be no longer strange but rather a fellow human. She says, 'recognition then, relies on a combination of identification and differentiation. The trajectory of recognition is this: I recognise you by seeing your similarity and your difference to me, and then I make your strangeness

[21] Martin Bewick, 'Dance without Limits', *Lifestyle* 43 (May 2015).
[22] Transcribed comment from *Changing Capacities, Changing Identities* (Transcript Two), Liverpool, 1 September 2012.

familiar. In other words I see you as you are.'[23] If recognition truly worked in this way, then the prejudice against others would dissipate. However, it is not an 'all at once' process but works iteratively, with stigma continuing to play a powerful role in how disabled people are viewed. And it is in finding ways of living with a changing body, whether of disability or dying, that creativity and performing can play a role.

Facing living with dying

Back in 2002, when DaDaFest was known as North-West Disability Arts Forum, we were key partners in a publication designed to capture the work and thoughts from disabled people who were living with life-limiting conditions. We called this 'Shelf Life'. It brought together artists from across the UK – writers, poets, photographers and visual artists – all with a view on what it meant to die young. In a foreword to the publication, Nabil Shaban states,

> Death has been my walking companion for as long as I can remember ... I have felt its seething, whispering resentment all my life. Always a chancer, looking for cracks in my armour. But what it cannot handle is my smile. When you are a disabled person who expects to die at any given moment, what is death but a close encounter with an old friend.[24]

And thus, Nabil faces down death, not with the belief in life never-ending but by negotiating his way through day-to-day life towards death with hope, defiance, the valuing of friendship – and with a smile!

It could be thought of as an urban myth, but there is a notion that many disabled people have a more positive capacity to face up to their mortality than non-disabled people. Certainly, close encounters with death can change you and lead you to live life as much as possible to the full. Yet to know what middle age can be when you are twenty-five or younger certainly affects how one engages with the world, not only in terms of expectations and aspirations but also in how one copes with a body that is failing. The arts created from such places arguably offer so much richness in addressing head-on the fear of dying, especially of death at what we would normally perceive as the wrong time. The arts created from a disability perspective allow work to be shaped from the lived experience of disability – the social, personal and political viewpoints that may encourage

---

[23] Garland-Thomson, *Staring*, p. 158.
[24] Nabil Shaban, 'Foreword', *Shelf Life*, National Disability Arts Forum, 2002.

us to make work from the emotive places of pain, isolation, discrimination, fear, through to the exhilaration of joining in with those who are like-minded, laughing at society's stereotypes and celebrating our own lives, be they long or short, filled with mixtures of pain, sorrow, joys or making merry. The artists we continue to engage with through DaDaFest often have insight into issues that challenge and move the viewer into new understandings and appreciation of the most fundamental of human experiences. This is especially potent when the artist reflects our mortality and the fact that none of us get out of here alive. To quote Nabil again:

> I am so in love with death, that in my home, on the bookshelf, are certain artefacts associated with mortality; momento mori items such as skulls [human and animal], dead seahorses and scorpions. This iconic Shelf Death holds up a mirror to my own constantly anticipated shortended Shelf Life.[25]

Howie had written previously about the ways in which living with dying, with cancer in particular, was always spoken of as a fight, a battle that has to be won, to be faced with bravery. We all know, however, that many find the demands to be 'terrifically brave all the time', an enormous pressure.[26] And the reality is that, whether we fight or not, all of us die if not sooner then later. The necessity, rather, is to find peace and dignity in the process of dying. As Ranjana Srivastava, a palliative care physician, writes:

> This recognition allows patients to halt toxic treatment, opt for effective palliation and articulate their goals for the end of life. It permits their oncologist to open up new conversations that don't include the latest million-dollar blockbuster therapy with a bleak survival curve but to mention the therapeutic benefit of teaming up with hospice workers to write letters, preserve photos and record memories. I would say that this candid admission from a patient is the difference between bemoaning death as a medical failure and viewing life as a welcome gift.[27]

Howie had developed a sophisticated critique of this language of fighting and war. One of the things this language conceals, in fact denies, is the constant anxiety and denial engendered in individuals living with the changing body that presages death. The prospect of losing bodily control, a loss that is not just

---

[25] Ibid.

[26] Transcribed comment from *Changing Capacities, Changing Identities* (Transcript One), Liverpool, 1 September 2012.

[27] R. Srivastava, 'Oliver Sacks, Who Has Taught Us So Much, Now Teaches Us the Art of Dying', *Guardian*, 25 July 2015, http://www.theguardian.com/commentisfree/2015/jul/25/oliver-sacks-who-has-taught-us-so-much-now-teaches-us-the-art-of-dying [accessed 6 February 2016].

of a single battle but of a whole life, creates conflicting and generally negative emotions. Accordingly, she was searching for 'ways of living with changing bodies, changing capacities without always feeling that anxiety or loss or regret because if you feel you are losing something all the time you can't live in the moment … [you can't] find ways of living in a body that changes, without regret'.[28] Yet, as Howie addressed her own changing body, facing the prospect of imminent death, it is imperative that we are not tempted to believe that the rest of us have stable bodies, fixed identities, undisturbed by the demands of time, place or other people playing upon our bodies. And as we see the anxiety and regret of others it is tempting to reach for today's fix-all solutions: exercise; meditation; mindfulness. They are touted as ways of managing pain and distress – and may prove really helpful to some. But to others a stiff gin, a box set and warm settee may prove as valuable in generating moments of hope.

Fighting or flourishing: A changing body

The Disability Movement has long held a concept of the variability and change that occur within living bodies. They tease those regarded as non-disabled with the concept of TAB – Temporarily Able Bodies – the notion that no one exists within a stable and permanently able body. And, as Shildrick argues, it is important that our thinking moves beyond any easy oppositional notions; rather, 'it has been used to argue for a certain commonality, a breaking down of the binary of disabled/non-disabled that contests the hierarchy of value that has been so injurious to those with disabilities'.[29] But the necessity is further to extend this concept of variability and change to those who are already disabled, to incorporate notions of intersectionality and, in more direct recognition of our phenomenological embodiment, the intercorporeality expressed through our relationships with others. As critical disability theorizing moves beyond ideas of unified corporeality, new work has placed 'far less stress on closure and completion' and authors are seen as part of an active, open and embodied interwoven process of becoming, along with the embodied others whom they describe.[30] In the words of Deleuze and Guattari:

[28] Transcribed comment from *Changing Capacities, Changing Identities* (Transcript One), Liverpool, 1 September 2012.
[29] Margrit Shildrick, 'living on; not getting better', *feminist review* 111.1 (2015): 13.
[30] Margrit Shildrick, '"Why Should Our Bodies End at the Skin?": Embodiment, Boundaries, and Somatechnics', *Hypatia* 30.1 (2015): 21.

We know nothing about a body until we know what it can do, in other words, what its affects are, how they can or cannot enter into composition with other affects, with the affects of another body, either to destroy that body or to be destroyed by it, either to exchange actions and passions with it or to join with it in composing a more powerful body.[31]

The potentials and possibility within bodies together are undecideable in advance, open to future potential. Our hybrid and variable bodies are jointly seen as extending beyond their obvious boundaries, not ending at the skin but rather reaching through and around others, developing new agency and intentions. And, amongst disabled and non-normative bodies, their coming together produces unexpected results, exploited within disability art to develop challenging, novel, sometimes beautiful, sometimes raw and visceral performances. We are all of us undergoing constant bodily change. Although often the variations caused by aging or illness are seen as wholly negative events, Shildrick argues that an alternative, possibly a vital approach, is to focus rather on the continual process of change, on understanding not simply what has been lost in terms of particular skills or capacities. She thus urges on us a continual awareness of 'how one can present oneself as embodied differently', of how 'we are all becoming different forms of ourselves as we go through life' including in the period leading to up to death. Janet Price writes,

Living with multiple sclerosis, with its relapses and remissions, I have had to live through three to four major changes in capacity, changes which precipitated identity changes. Although not leading to dying in the short term, there is a small death in each relapse. With each loss, I have grieved. But it has not been all about loss. I gained new foci in my life, discovered new skills and learned new ways of being as I engaged with a shifting world from my evolving embodiment.[32]

The discrete events of life that structure shifts in our capacities and identities are necessitated by the intrinsic and necessary risk and uncertainty of our quotidian lives. Living with a changing sense of the body – through surgery, the impact of anaesthetic and painkillers, or through chemotherapy – alters the experience of how one moves, feels, thinks, expresses oneself. The attempt to hold onto sensation, what one feels and knows during a period when the body, the mind are potentially losing connection with the world demands that one

[31] Gilles Deleuze and Félix Guattari, *A Thousand Plateaus: Capitalism and Schizo-phrenia*, trans. Brian Massumi, Minneapolis, MN: University of Minnesota Press, 1987, p. 257.

[32] Janet Price, private communication, 2016.

be open to and adapt to whatever comes. And in human terms, what counts is the individual and joint recognition of our capacities for joy and suffering, for celebration and endurance. This moves us beyond moments of shame, prejudice and blame, beyond the potent negative stereotypes within attitudes towards disability and illness towards a positive focus on human flourishing. To illustrate:

> ... Of the most striking things about [Oliver] Sacks' pieces is that they are so little occupied with his medical situation, and place much more emphasis on his human one. A few sentences here and there about his various treatments lead him to his most pressing concern: how to find meaning, connection, and some fun in his last months (a trip to visit lemurs, for instance). 'Weak, short of breath, my once-firm muscles melted away by cancer, I find my thoughts, increasingly, not on the supernatural or spiritual, but on what is meant by living a good and worthwhile life – achieving a sense of peace within oneself,' he wrote in 'Sabbath,' his final essay.[33]

Disability thought, particularly post-conventional feminist disability thinking, has much to offer our ways of understanding embodied change and shifting perception. Yet we can engage with such ideas and feelings not solely through academic analysis. Differing forms of art, particularly art that is conceived and constituted by disabled people and those living with dying, provides us with differing routes to perceive these shifts, to feel their impact, to take time to soak up others' experience of the breaks and movement, the losses and gains, that we experience through our embodiment. Engagement with art offers a creative experience, one capable of addressing the ever-shifting phenomenological experience of uncertainty within one's body, a body constantly changing in its sensations, experiences, expressions due to the embodied impacts of disability or the slow inevitable approach of death. And individuals can gain much through art that helps to address the fears, insecurities, hopes and anxieties that such changes can precipitate.

Disability art has been particularly skilled at sharing these times of change, the dissolution of apparently secure fleshly foundations. Performers at DaDaFest 2012 – such as: Brian Lobel in *BALL and Other Funny Stories about Cancer*; Liz Bentley in *AAA Rating* with her ukulele, Casio keyboard and details of how she organized her mother's funeral in 24 hours; and Evelyn Glennie, world-famous percussionist, who demonstrated to a hall full of people how her art

---

[33] S. Seltzer, 'Oliver Sacks' Final Essays Demystified Dying', in *Flavorwire*, 31 August 2015, http://flavorwire.com/535586/oliver-sacks-final-essays-demystified-dying [accessed 27 January 2016].

relies on her using her whole body as a sounding board[34] – have all found ways of moving beyond simple verbal description of bodily breakdown, repair and loss. Through mechanical cartoons, the mapping of movement both locally and through more distant time and space, and visual and sensory approaches to sharing the experience of change, they invite others to reach out and become part of a broader corporeal experience together.

> An unexpected, quirky and provocative performance about illness and the changing body over time, Lobel's work challenges the stories of cancer survivors and cancer martyrs that have come before – infusing the 'cancer story' with an urgency and humour which is sometimes inappropriate, often salacious and always, above all else, honest and open. You'll laugh, you'll cry, you'll want to perform a self-exam.[35]

Similarly, performers have demonstrated the breakdown in usually secure intellectual structures such as patterns of speech and language, or of thought processes. Jess Thoms, who has Tourettes, performs a powerful, funny and deeply provocative piece called *Backstage in Biscuitland*, centred on the repetitive appearance of hedgehogs, biscuits and inventive swearing, and some dangerous and unscripted leaps and falls, thus sharing the unexpected and unpredictable structures of her world. She says, 'It's not about mocking or commiserating – it's about reclaiming the most frequently misunderstood syndrome on the planet and … Changing the World One Tic a Time.'[36] Although not directly about dying, these diverse examples of disability art capture some of the events that are a part of that process for some, as body, intellect, emotions and senses become disconnected and re-ordered in the jerky, indeterminate dissolution of the self on the road to embodied becoming, whether into living or dying.

Conclusion: Potentials in dying and the power of disability art

Through an injection of some of the more current concepts of queering and cripping, critical disability ideas circulate as challenges to stable identities and work across intersections of gender/sexuality, dis/ability and race/culture/ethnicity to the 'trans' in all of us. The recognition that we perform our

---

[34] DaDaFest, *DaDaFest 2012: The Festival of Disability and Deaf Arts*, Festival Brochure, Liverpool: DaDaFest, 2012.

[35] Ibid.

[36] On Jess Thoms, see further, http://www.Touretteshero.com [accessed 3 June 2016].

gender and dis/ability raises questions for the art we create and engage with. And, as the examples above suggest, we have multiple options as we weave our way through the shifting identities and bodies to find sources of political and personal direction and strength. On an individual level, simple acts of creation, of pleasure in the moment, of taking control of small instants of new possibility, offer individuals a differing perception of the world through which they move, in which they continue to be active, creating, building, perceiving, as they live an ongoing process of becoming. Under change, their embodied sense of self and their relationships with the world and those around them makes present their shifting intercorporeality as they progress together, often in leaps and lurches, sometimes as a seemingly out of control process – whether from cancer or disability, its treatment or rehabilitation, the pain control, the fitting of prostheses. But within this rolling process are moments of stillness, times when the pain is controlled, the nausea stilled, the body settles. And we have the potential to use all of this to create or perform, to engage with such creations, to pull together all the resistance generated to the conflicting strands of bodily disgust and denial, of aesthetic rejection, of exploitation and attack. Can this open society up to change, such that our ways of being, our supposedly disruptive bodies and minds, are not out of place, not an unwelcome disruption to all that insist on a society of order and coherence, but are seen instead as something to be welcomed, valued and recognized as enriching the world we share, as offering routes to follow, maps that lead both to new and exciting possibilities, and to peaceful places of gentle flourishing for those living and living with dying?

In acknowledgement of all that Gill Howie shared with us and enabled us to learn, of the ways in which she enriched our living and her wisdom will support our dying.

References

Bewick, Martin, 'Dance without Limits', *Lifestyle* 43 (May 2015).

Changing Capacities, Changing Identities, (Transcripts 1–3), Liverpool, 1 September 2012.

DaDaFest, *DaDaFest 2012: The Festival of Disability and Deaf Arts*, Festival Brochure, Liverpool: DaDaFest, 2012.

DaDaFest, *DaDaFest International 2014: Art of the Lived Experiment*, Festival Brochure, Liverpool: DaDaFest, 2014.

DaDaFest, *DaDaFest Manifesto*, Liverpool: DaDaFest, 2014.

Davies, L., 'Breast Implant Scandal: 3,500 Private Clinic Patients Referred to NHS', *Guardian*, 24 February 2012, http://www.theguardian.com/world/2012/feb/24/breast-implant-scandal-patients-nhs [accessed 3 February 2016].

Davis, Cortney, 'When the Nurse Becomes a Patient: A Story in Words and Images', *Literature, Arts and Medicine Blog*, 2 June 2015, http://medhum.med.nyu.edu/blog/?p=9073 [accessed 27 January 2016].

Davis, Lennard, *Enforcing Normalcy: Disability, Deafness and the Body*, New York: Verso, 1995.

Deleuze, Gilles and Guattari, Félix, *A Thousand Plateaus: Capitalism and Schizophrenia*, trans. Brian Massumi, Minneapolis, MN: University of Minnesota Press, 1987.

Ferguson, Laura, 'Toward a New Aesthetic of the Body', Literature, Arts and Medicine blog, 21 October 2007, http://medhum.med.nyu.edu/blog/?m=200710 [accessed 27 January 2016].

Garland-Thomson, Rosemarie, *Freakery: Cultural Spectacles of the Extraordinary Body*, New York: New York University Press, 1996.

Garland-Thomson, Rosemarie, *Staring: How We Look*, Oxford: Oxford University Press, 2009.

Hevey, David, *The Creatures Time Forgot: Photography and Disability Imagery*, London: Routledge, 1992.

Howie, Gillian, 'How to Think about Death: Living with Dying', *On the Feminist Philosophy of Gillian Howie: Materialism and Mortality*, ed. Victoria Browne and Daniel Whistler, London: Bloomsbury, 2016, pp. 131–44.

Mitchell, David T. and Snyder, Sharon L., *Narrative Prosthesis: Disability and the Dependencies of Discourse*, Ann Arbor, MI: University of Michigan Press, 2000.

Seltzer, S., 'Oliver Sacks' Final Essays Demystified Dying', *Flavorwire*, 31 August 2015, http://flavorwire.com/535586/oliver-sacks-final-essays-demystified-dying [accessed 27 January 2016].

Shaban, Nabil, 'Foreword', *Shelf Life*, National Disability Arts Forum, 2002.

Shildrick, Margrit, 'living on; not getting better', *feminist review* 111.1 (2015): 10–24.

Shildrick, Margrit, '"Why Should Our Bodies End at the Skin?": Embodiment, Boundaries, and Somatechnics', *Hypatia* 30.1 (2015): 13–29.

Srivastava, R., 'Oliver Sacks, Who Has Taught Us So Much, Now Teaches Us the Art of Dying', *Guardian*, 25 July 2015, http://www.theguardian.com/commentisfree/2015/jul/25/oliver-sacks-who-has-taught-us-so-much-now-teaches-us-the-art-of-dying [accessed 26 January 2016].

Sutherland, Alan, 'Disability Arts, Disability Politics', *Framed: Interrogating Disability in the Media*, ed. A. Pointon with C. Davies, London: British Film Institute, 1997.

UPIAS, *Fundamental Principles of Disability*, London: Union of the Physically Impaired against Segregation, 1976.

Index of Names

Adorno, Theodor W. 7, 8–9, 22–3, 25–8, 60, 61–2, 64–71, 74–8, 82–4, 95, 155

Beauvoir, Simone de 152–3, 154, 173–4
Benjamin, Walter 22, 66
Butler, Judith 22, 33–4, 35, 178

Caverero, Adriana 135–6, 161, 165–6, 182

DaDa Fest 14–15, 142–3, 229–30, 231, 267–84
Deleuze, Gilles 1, 6–7, 59–61, 64, 65–7, 72, 75–6, 116–17, 136, 182, 198, 202–5, 278–9
Derrida, Jacques 135, 176–7, 182, 197, 207, 209, 216
Descartes, René 6, 29, 86, 109, 217

Eagleton, Terry 11, 136–7
Engels, Friedrich 71, 73
Epicurus 11, 133–4, 167

Foucault, Michel 5, 54, 60, 61, 76
Freud, Sigmund 5, 71–2, 172, 199, 205

Graham, Jorie 15, 217–27
Greenaway, Peter 139, 140

Hegel, G. W. F. 72, 81
Heidegger, Martin 12, 13, 60, 64–5, 74–6, 131, 135–6, 140, 146–9, 151, 153–4, 159, 163, 165–6, 168, 170–3, 176–7, 182, 201–2, 216
Horkheimer, Max 8, 22, 25, 82–3
Howie, Gillian
  activism 2, 4
  Between Feminism and Materialism 1, 2, 4–6, 8, 16–17, 21, 24–33, 43, 47–52, 61–3, 97–9, 146, 153–9
  concept of critique 1–2, 21–5, 32–3, 107, 116–18, 123–4

context principle 1–2, 28, 117–18
criticisms of Deleuze 1, 6–7, 59–79, 116–17
Deleuze and Spinoza: Aura of Expressionism 6–7, 59, 61–2, 65–6, 204
on dialectical materialism 4, 26–8, 29–33, 68–71
on hope 13, 99–100, 140–2, 157, 161–3, 193–4, 268
'How to Think about Death' lecture 12–13, 99, 123, 131–44, 146, 151, 153, 158–63, 165–8, 181–2, 194, 207–9, 212, 229, 263–4, 277–8
Living with Dying project 1, 2, 11–13, 14–16, 123, 133, 142–3, 146, 181, 215–16, 229–30, 247–9, 267–8, 270–3
on postmodernism 3, 43, 87–8
on sex/gender 31–3, 39–40, 48–50
on *therapeia* 11–12, 132–3, 140–2, 143, 145–6, 162–3
on third-wave feminism 3–6, 23–4, 26, 31–3, 43–57
on universities 1, 9–11, 90–1, 96–100, 103–11, 116–18
Humboldt, Wilhelm von 107, 118
Husserl, Edmund 66, 184–5

Irigaray, Luce 8–9, 59–61, 70, 71–8, 91–4, 141

Kant, Immanuel 66, 78, 81, 189, 191–2, 200–1, 208
Kermode, Frank 215–16, 218
Kierkegaard, Søren 134, 141, 163, 249

Lacan, Jacques 61, 71, 72, 77, 92–3
Le Doeuff, Michèle 104–5, 124–5
Lessing, G. E. 103, 119–20
Levinas, Emmanuel 135, 182, 216
Lukács, Georg 69, 115–16

Mann, Thomas 111–16, 117–18, 120–4
Marx, Karl 4–5, 23, 27, 29–31, 45, 47, 50,
    55, 60, 61, 68–9, 71, 73–4, 89, 96
Merleau-Ponty, Maurice 153, 154, 156,
    169, 243
Moi, Toril 24, 34–5, 155

Nagel, Thomas 138, 139, 142
Newman, John Henry 107–8, 118
Nietzsche, Friedrich 5, 59, 66, 67, 69–70,
    75, 104, 200

Ricoeur, Paul 13–14, 143, 181–95

Sartre, Jean-Paul 7, 131, 138, 145–6,
    149–53, 154–6, 156–9, 160–1
Savage, Ashley 15, 229–45, 270, 272–3
Shildrick, Margrit 240, 243, 270, 278–9
Spinoza, Benedict 6, 59, 60, 64, 66, 75–6, 204
Stone, Alison 13, 23, 76–7, 136, 161,
    165–80

Tauchert, Ashley 85–7, 98, 104–11
Tutu 15, 229–45, 270, 272–3

Wittgenstein, Ludwig 11, 131, 145
Woolf, Virginia 62–3, 67–8, 72, 98